MURDER IN SAMARKAND

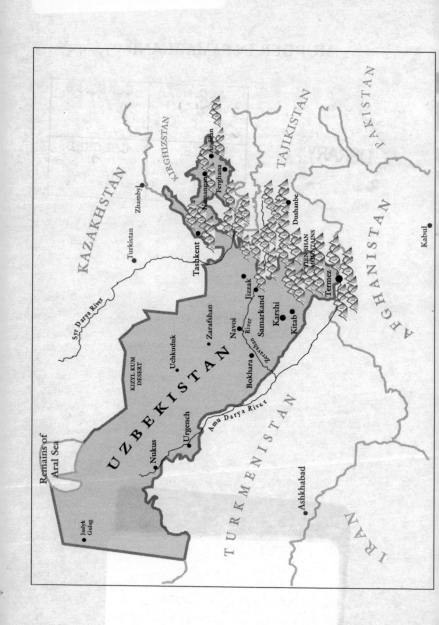

MURDER IN SAMARKAND

A British Ambassador's Controversial
Defiance of Tyranny in the War on Terror

CRAIG MURRAY

MAINSTREAM PUBLISHING

EDINBURGH AND LONDON

This edition published, 2007

First published in Great Britain in 2006 by
MAINSTREAM PUBLISHING COMPANY
(EDINBURGH) LTD
7 Albany Street
Edinburgh EH1 3UG

ISBN 9781845962210

A catalogue record for this book is available
from the British Library

Typeset in NewBaskerville

Printed and bound in Great Britain by
Cox & Wyman Ltd, Reading

For Bryan Harris, a friend in need.

We travel not for trafficking alone:
By hotter winds our fiery hearts are fanned:
For lust of knowing what should not be known,
We make the Golden Journey to Samarkand.

James Elroy Flecker
1884–1915

dup - faxed prev

Kenneth L. Lay
Chairman and
Chief Executive Officer

Enron Corp.
P. O. Box 1188
Houston, TX 77251-1188
(713) 853-6773
Fax (713) 853-5313

April 3, 1997

Via Fax: 512/463-1849

The Honorable George W. Bush
Governor of the State of Texas
PO Box 12428
Austin, Texas

Dear ~~Governor~~ *George* Bush:

    You will be meeting with Ambassador Sadyq Safaev, Uzbekistan's Ambassador to the United States on April 8th. Ambassador Safaev has been Foreign Minister and the senior advisor to President Karimov before assuming his nation's most significant foreign responsibility.

    Enron has established an office in Tashkent and we are negotiating a $2 billion joint venture with Neftegas of Uzbekistan, and Gazprom of Russia to develop Uzbekistan's natural gas and transport it to markets in Europe, Kazakhstan, and Turkey. This project can bring significant economic opportunities to Texas, as well as Uzbekistan. The political benefits to the United States and to Uzbekistan are important to that entire region.

    Ambassador Safaev is one of the most effective of the Washington Corps of Ambassadors, a man who has the attention of his president, and a person who works daily to bring our countries together. For all these reasons, I am delighted that the two of you are meeting.

    I know you and Ambassador Safaev will have a productive meeting which will result in a friendship between Texas and Uzbekistan.

Sincerely,

Ken

bush-3.doc

Natural gas. Electricity. Endless possibilities.

CONTENTS

Preface

This is the story of my Mission to Tashkent in the years 2002 to 2004. To the best of my knowledge and ability this is a true story, though it is told largely from memory.

But most importantly it is the truth as I perceived it. Our backgrounds, experience, emotional states, the acuity of our senses and the depth of our understanding all affect our perception. Different people can thus experience the same events and have a different take on what happened. I am not saying that mine is uniquely correct. This is what seemed to me to be happening, and how it felt to be me, experiencing it.

I also wanted to debunk the notion that I am a heroic figure. I am not. Standards of morality vary, but many would judge that in my private life I behaved pretty badly. In the small hours of the night, I tend to agree. What I think I did right was to refuse to go along with some absolutely dreadful things the West was at best overlooking, probably condoning and arguably encouraging in the name of the War on Terror.

When I was at school, I recall we used to debate how we would have reacted had we been German in the 1940s and ordered to go along with some of the horrors of the Nazi regime. I don't think in my wildest dreams I imagined I might ever actually face that kind of dilemma. But my brilliant career, resulting in my appointment as Ambassador at the age of 43, ended with me writing in an official telegram to Jack Straw, British Foreign Secretary: 'I will not attempt to hide my contempt for such casuistry, nor my shame that I work in an organisation where colleagues would resort to it to justify torture.'

Something happened on 11 September 2001 that caused the West to lose its moral bearings in a way that led government machines, and those who worked in them, to move a significant way down the path of contempt for individuals. The Nazis went much further down that path, but it is undeniably the same one. To me, the astonishing thing was that my colleagues, ordinary decent people, followed unquestioningly. In the whole Foreign and Commonwealth Office (FCO), I know only of Elizabeth Wilmshurst, Carne Ross and a clerk in the Eastern Department, whose name even I have forgotten, who refused and resigned. The scary thing is the eagerness of the authoritarian forces in government, especially MI5 and MI6, to grasp this opportunity to try to land a lethal blow on Western liberalism. I have a feeling that liberalism will yet prove too strong for them. If we lose liberalism, al-Qaeda has won.

It will surprise readers in many countries that the British government has the power to censor books by former civil servants and even to ban them completely. In the current shift towards authoritarianism, Jack Straw has announced to Parliament that the government intends to tighten these rules still further to make such suppression even easier. There has been no proposal for the public burning of books yet, but give it time. In an effort to prevent the complications of a ban, I have succumbed to censorship and made a number of changes and omissions. Where this has happened, I note the fact in the footnotes.

I have reported many conversations as direct speech. I have an excellent memory for dialogue, but I am not claiming that every single word is precisely correct. I am, however, confident that the tone and meaning are 100 per cent correct. The direct speech may be regarded as a stylistic device to drive the narrative forward.

I may have got the odd date wrong but not, I believe, any of significance. A few names have been changed to protect the guilty, several to protect the innocent and a very few because I could not remember the real ones. I have changed the names of quite a few Uzbeks to protect them from retaliation by the regime. Serious and trustworthy journalists or researchers who need the real names should contact me.

I had wanted to publish a large number of documents to

corroborate my story, but the government has informed me, and indeed informed Parliament, that they will take legal action should I do so. As that could result in the book being blocked, I have reluctantly removed the documents, even though I had obtained the formal release of a number of these. It is, however, little realised that the British government claims the power to prevent the publication of documents even when they have been released under the Data Protection Act (DPA) or Freedom of Information Act (FoIA). It claims that it still retains copyright over any document produced by the government, so even if something is obtained legitimately under the DPA or FoIA, it still cannot be published without the government's consent.

Plainly, the government is trying to claw back the very limited gains in Freedom of Information in the UK. I have therefore posted the documents to the web, where they can be viewed for free. You can find them at:

http://www.craigmurray.co.uk/documents/docs.html
http://www.blairwatch.co.uk/murray/docs.html
http://dahrjamailiraq.com/murray/index.php.

The latter especially should be safe from technical or legal attack, but in the event of any attack on these sites, I hope they will spring up elsewhere and be found with a little creative googling.

I have not used any established system of rendering Russian or Uzbek names, opting for a personal choice of what is readable.

Several conversations that originally took place in Russian are given in English.

C.M.

Abbreviations

BAT	British American Tobacco
CEELI	Central and Eastern European Legal Initiative
CIA	Central Intelligence Agency
CTPD	Counter Terrorism Policy Department
DFID	Department for International Development
DSA	Diplomatic Service Association
EBRD	European Bank for Reconstruction and Development
ECGD	Export Credit Guarantee Department
EU	European Union
FAC	Foreign Affairs Committee
FCO	Foreign and Commonwealth Office
FDA	First Division Association
GCHQ	Government Communications Headquarters
HRPD	Human Rights Policy Department
HRW	Human Rights Watch
HuT	Hizb-ut-Tehrir
ICG	International Crisis Group
IMF	International Monetary Fund
IMU	Islamic Movement of Uzbekistan
JTAC	Joint Terrorism Analysis Centre
LE	Locally engaged embassy staff
MCS	Management Consultancy Services
MFA	Ministry of Foreign Affairs
MOD	Ministry of Defence

NGO	Non-Governmental Organisation
NSA	National Security Agency
ODIHR	Office for Democratic Institutions and Human Rights
OSCE	Organisation for Security and Cooperation in Europe
OSI	Open Society Institute
PAC	Permitted Arts Committee
PUS	Permanent Under Secretary
QBP	Queen's Birthday Party
UN	United Nations
UND	United Nations Department
UNDP	United Nations Development Programme
WMD	Weapons of Mass Destruction

CHAPTER 1

Awakening

Chris looked pretty amazed.

'OK, let's go,' didn't seem to be the standard reaction from a British ambassador to the news that a dissident trial was about to start. The Land-Rover drew up to the embassy door and out I went, still feeling pretty uncomfortable at people calling me 'Sir', opening doors and stopping their normal chatter as I passed.

We turned up outside the court, where a small wicket entrance led through an unprepossessing muddy wall into a dirty courtyard containing several squat white buildings. Like much Soviet construction, it looked unfinished and barely functional. To enter the courtyard, we had to give passport details to two policemen sitting at a table outside the gate. They took an age to write everything down with a chewed-up pencil in an old ledger. I was to find that the concealment of terrible viciousness behind a homely exterior was a recurring theme in Uzbekistan.

About a hundred people were hanging about the courtyard waiting for different trials to begin. I was introduced to a variety of scruffy-looking individuals who represented a range of human rights organisations. Puzzlingly, the seven or eight I met seemed to belong to the same number of groups, and most of them would not talk to one another.

One short but distinguished-looking man with a shock of white hair and big black specs was so full of self-importance that he wouldn't talk to anyone at all. Chris, bustling around doing the introductions, pointed to him and said, 'Mikhail Ardzinov – he says it is for you to call on him.' I was puzzled, as the question of who called on who involved taking about eight paces across the courtyard. Chris explained that Ardzinov was feeling very important, as his group was the only one that was registered and thus legal. The others were all illegal. Peculiarly, Ardzinov's registered group was called the 'Independent Human Rights Organisation of Uzbekistan'. None of this meant much to me at the time, and I certainly hadn't been an ambassador long enough to feel my pride compromised by taking eight paces, so I went over and shook the man's hand. I received a long cool stare for my effort.

But even at first meeting, I could not help but be impressed by some of these people. One gentleman had been a schoolteacher until he was thrown out of his job for refusing to teach the President's books uncritically. He now spent time at trials of dissidents, normally the less-reported ones in obscure places. He documented them painstakingly by hand and sent details to international organisations. I asked how he lived, and he said largely on the kindness of others. Judging by his clothes, gaunt face and sparse frame, that kindness was a limited commodity. I asked if he was not in danger of arrest. He said he had 'only' spent a total of four months in custody in the past three years. An unhealthy flush burned in his cheeks, and his eyes alternated between a normal genial twinkle and flashes of real anger. They were unforgettable, yet they are not the eyes I saw that day which haunt me still.

Nor are Dilobar's. Lovely as she is, I am afraid I cannot recall her eyes. But during the conversation, mine had been drifting to her graceful figure in blue as she stood under an old corrugated iron canopy to my left, tall and striking amid a group of older local women in their flowered dresses, velvet jackets and hijabs – a Muslim scarf that in Uzbekistan is colourful and covers the hair but none of the face. Her fine black hair flowed long and free down her back. Her light-blue cotton dress was full, reaching right to the neck, wrists and sleeves, though close fitting around her slim waist.

Chris brought her over and introduced her as Dilobar Khuderbegainova. Something was hammering insistently at my dulled senses. What was wrong – Khuderbegainova – oh! This was the sister of the victim of this show trial. Yes, her eyes were filling with tears. Her brother was going to be executed, and I was trying to make out her legs through her dress. I was filled with self-loathing.

Speaking with great dignity, she said that her brother was a good man and the whole family would remember me for coming. I thanked her and held out my hand. Another mistake. Muslim women don't shake hands with strange men. For a moment she was taken aback, but then she held out her hand and clenched mine firmly, and a smile almost troubled her lips. I wanted to say 'Don't worry' and promise to help, but realistically what could I do – and if I could do nothing, why was I there?

Chris was looking at me curiously.

'Bit hot,' I said, before going to sit down under the tree. My momentary self-hatred turned to real anger against a system that promotes torture and execution, as well as against fellow diplomats for their complacent acquiescence.

We waited two hours in the heat for the trial to start. It was 44 degrees centigrade in the shade that day, and we didn't have much of that in the courtyard. Finally, there was a sudden bustle of activity, and we entered through a door that led straight onto stairs down to a basement. The atmosphere changed completely. The short staircase was lined with perhaps a dozen paramilitaries – Ministry of Interior forces – in grey camouflage, carrying machine guns. There was so little space left to pass that a tense scrum developed. I was only about three steps down when one of the paramilitaries, for no reason I could discern, pulled me back by the arm. I snapped. Wheeling round, I grabbed him by the throat and pushed him back against the wall (admittedly it was only about three inches and he was a very small militiaman). I raged uselessly in English, 'Don't you touch me, do you hear? Do not touch me.'

Silence fell, and everyone looked aghast. I don't think the militia knew who I was, but I was obviously foreign and therefore probably not shootable. These people pushed others about all their lives, and no one ever pushed back. My little militiaman gave a nervous laugh, and chatter just started up again. We carried on down to the courtroom as though nothing had happened.

The atmosphere in the courtyard had been apprehensive but resigned. Now the tension was palpable. The six prisoners were already in the 'dock'. This was a large cage, constructed roughly out of what looked like concrete reinforcing rods welded together; the door was fastened with two enormous padlocks. Fourteen heavily armed militiamen stood shoulder to shoulder around the cage. The six accused squatted inside on what looked like two low school benches, with not quite enough room for the three men on each.

Loved ones tried to push between the guards to say a few words of encouragement. The accused barely turned their heads, though some managed wan smiles. All were very gaunt and clean-shaven with shorn hair. Five looked middle aged and, from the ripples of skin, as though they had once been better fleshed. Their hair was whitening. The sixth, Khuderbegainov, looked like a teenager (he was 22). He coughed periodically and, in contrast to the languor of the others, cast his eyes around quickly and furtively. He looked very skinny indeed, which accentuated features I would judge were already sharp.

Of the six, three had already been in jail for some two years. The charges were multiple, but different permutations of the six were accused of a number of different offences. For example, three were charged with the armed robbery of a jeweller, four with the murder of two policemen. All were charged with attempting to overthrow the government and undermine the constitution.

This was one of a series of trials of Muslim activists in Uzbekistan. I knew some of the statistics already – Human Rights Watch (HRW) alleged that there were some 7,000 political or religious prisoners. I had heard allegations of torture but not in detail. In three weeks of Foreign Office and other UK government briefings prior to taking up my post, there had been scarcely a mention of human rights and none of torture. The briefing I had been given put the emphasis first on FCO internal management procedure, second on Uzbekistan's supportive role in the War on Terror and third on Central Asia's economic and commercial potential in hydrocarbons, gold, cotton and agro-industry. I could have written a paper on hydrocarbon pipeline options for Central Asia, but nothing had prepared me for the reality of the War on Terror as I was about to encounter it.

In the courtyard, I had met a very helpful young man from HRW called Ole, who was going to let me share his Uzbek interpreter in the court. He filled me in on some of the facts. I later checked these out. Two of the defendants charged with murder had actually been in jail at the time of the killings, serving sentences for 'religious extremism', and over a dozen other people had already been convicted of these murders. There was no suggestion that all those charged were involved in a conspiracy, or even knew one another, or that the murders had been carried out by a mob. The simple Uzbek government tactic was to use a genuine crime (and two policemen had indeed been murdered) to convict lots of opposition people whom the regime happened to want put away or, better still, executed. And they would, of course, not be listed as political prisoners but common murderers, rapists or whatever. In that year – 2002 – some 220 prisoners were officially executed in Uzbekistan, in addition to those murdered in police or security-service custody, in prison or who simply 'disappeared'.

The courtroom was chokingly hot. I felt beads of sweat running down my body, inside my shirt, tickling and dribbling down. The judge looked like the first goon out of central casting: swarthy and thick set, floppy hair swept back, dressed in black trousers and a white shirt that strained at his belly. He started out with a diatribe at the prisoners for wasting the court's time.

The jeweller who had suffered the armed robbery said that three of the men, wearing balaclavas, had tied him up and held him while robbing him of an improbably large sum of money. They had shot at him with pistols but missed. A defence lawyer was asking him why no bullets or bullet holes had been found in the room. The jeweller supposed rather weakly that the bullets had gone out of the window. As he was allegedly tied up on the floor at the time, the defendants must have been very bad shots indeed. The defence lawyer was making hay with this.

The judge had been making a show of not listening whenever the defence spoke, whittling at his fingernails with his knife or chatting with the rapporteur, who similarly stopped writing whenever the defence said anything. But somehow it must have penetrated the judge's thick skin that this prosecution witness was not going down well. He interrupted the defence lawyer with a sharp rebuke and then instructed the defendants to stand while he harangued them.

He said that they represented evil in society. They were thieves and murderers who sought to undermine Uzbekistan's independence and democracy. Their list of crimes was long, and it would be better if they admitted their guilt. He concluded that he was astonished that they had found the time to commit so many crimes when they had to stop to pray five times a day. He evidently considered this a hilarious sally and guffawed loudly, as did the prosecutor, rapporteur and various other cronies. But I swear I noticed a few narrowed eyes among the militiamen. Later, he again amused himself hugely by interrupting a defendant who was giving evidence about a conversation.

'I don't suppose anyone could hear you through your long Muslim beard,' snapped the judge. 'I see the prison service removed it for you!' He slapped his ham of a thigh as he delivered the remark. He was a real monster. On several occasions, he told the defence to shut up and stop wasting time. As he was the judge, and there was no jury, I suppose he had a point.

Eventually, the jeweller was asked to identify which three of the six defendants had robbed him. He peered uncertainly at the benches – plainly he had no idea. Pressed by the defence, he managed to identify – and the odds against this must be very high – entirely the wrong three out of six. This made the judge very angry.

'You are mistaken, you old fool!' he bellowed.

The judge then read out the names of the three who were charged with this particular crime and asked them to stand.

'Are these the men?' he asked the terrified jeweller, who stammered his assent.

'Let the record show they were positively identified by the victim,' said the judge.

This was pure farce, but I had to pull myself back to the terrible reality behind this bizarre charade. These six nervous men were facing execution by firing squad, their brains blown out, spines smashed, hearts exploded by high-velocity bullets. The family would not be informed of the execution, so for months they would not know if their loved one was dead, believing him perhaps dead while he still languished, or perhaps alive when he was well rotted. This was a deliberately refined cruelty, as was the practice – inherited from the Soviets – that when the family was finally informed of the death, they would be charged for the bullets that killed their relative.

It was at this minute I was caught by those eyes I will never forget – they were Khuderbegainov's. He had spotted me in the crowd, a Westerner in a three-piece suit, out of place and time. Who was I? Maybe this strange apparition brought some kind of hope. Maybe the West would do something. *Maybe he wasn't going to die after all.* The drowning man had caught a fleeting glimpse of straw on the surface. His eyes bored into mine: small, dark, intense, filled with a desperate hope. He was urging me, with every mute fibre of his being, to do something. And there was hope in those eyes. I looked back. I don't do telepathy, but I stared at him, trying to say, 'I will try, in God's name, I will try,' with my own eyes. He smiled and nodded, a confidence shared, and then looked away again.

Once more I thought, 'What am I doing here? What right have I to give false hope – is that not just one more cruelty?' But then came an iron resolve – I would help; I would dedicate every fibre of my being to stopping this horror in Uzbekistan. I would not spend three years on the golf course and cocktail circuit. I would not go along with political lies or leave the truth unspoken. The next bit of the trial set that resolve, like catalyst added to epoxy resin.

An old man was assisted to the witness stand. He had a little white beard, sparse white hair and wore a black lacquered skullcap and a dull-brown quilted gown. He was shaking with fright. One of the accused was his nephew. The old man's statement was read out to him, in which he confirmed that his nephew was a terrorist who stole money to send to Osama bin Laden and had travelled to Afghanistan to meet the al-Qaeda leader.

'Is this your testimony?' asked the prosecutor.

'But it's not true,' replied the old man. 'They tortured me to say it.'

The judge said that accusations of torture had been dismissed earlier in the case. They could not be reintroduced.

'But they tortured me!' said the old man. 'They tortured my grandson before my eyes. They beat his testicles and put electrodes on his body. They put a mask on him to stop him breathing. They raped him with a bottle. Then they brought my granddaughter and said they would rape her. All the time they said, "Osama bin Laden, Osama bin Laden". We are poor farmers from Andijan. We are good Muslims, but what do we know of Osama bin Laden?'

His quavering voice had got stronger, but at this he physically collapsed and had to be helped out. The judge then stated that the prisoners' connection with Osama bin Laden was not in doubt. They had confessed to it.

I had seen enough and left. Those three hours in court had a profound effect on me. If these were our allies in the War on Terror, we were not on the clear moral ground which Blair and Bush claimed so boastfully.

I sent a telegram back to London, explaining in detail what I had seen at the trial. Shortly thereafter, sentence of death was passed on Khuderbegainov and long sentences given to his 'accomplices'. The Human Rights Policy Department (HRPD) in the FCO agreed we should take up the case, and the wheels clunked into motion for the long process of agreeing an EU démarche, or formal protest.

In the meantime, Dilobar and her father came to call in my office.

I welcomed them, accepted their thanks for attending the trial and said that I had been shocked by what I saw. I asked the father what they could tell me by way of background to the trial.

What followed was my first encounter with a phenomenon that was to bedevil me for the next two years: the inability of Uzbeks in human rights cases to tell their story in a plain and concise manner. This is well recognised by those working in the field. Various reasons are given: sheer terror of saying anything against the government, the effect of social shaming, and cultural propensity to roundabout story-telling. But the phenomenon is very real and very frustrating.

The Khuderbegainovs are a well-established Tashkent family, previously in favour with the regime. The father was the former head of a Tashkent state radio station. He told me the story of his arrest for questioning. They came for him while he was attending a family wedding. He was in tears as he recounted this and seemed unable to get past his despair at being arrested in such a humiliatingly public fashion and perhaps his astonishment that a wedding should be violated.

Now, weddings hold an important position in most cultures, but Uzbek society takes this to extremes, with a family not infrequently spending three years' income on a daughter's wedding. There is no doubt, therefore, that it is extremely bad form to desecrate one, but the poor man spent 30 minutes telling me nothing but that he had been arrested at a wedding. With his son sentenced to death, this was hardly the most important point. I felt greatly for his anguish, but if we were to be able to do anything, we needed more practical information.

I therefore asked Dilobar to continue the story. I learnt from her that her brother had been educated at one of the Saudi-funded Arabic schools that opened in Tashkent in the 1990s. Then, on a single day in February 1999, three large bombs exploded in Tashkent, killing scores of civilians. The government immediately blamed this on the Islamic Movement of Uzbekistan (IMU), even though they had no history of bombings and investigation showed the devices used in the well-coordinated explosions to have been sophisticated. The government also accused the main democratic opposition party, Erk, of involvement in the bombings and outlawed it. The Erk leader and opposition presidential candidate, the poet Mohammed Salih, was already in exile in Germany but was sentenced to fifteen and a half years' imprisonment in his absence.[1]

Most analysts now believe that these bombs were planted either by the Karimov regime or by warring factions within that regime. By blaming Islamic extremists for the bombs, the government was able to step up its efforts to fight back the post-Soviet religious revival. To this end, they closed the religious schools, including the one Khuderbegainov was attending, and many of their pupils and teachers were rounded up and dispatched to the gulags after confessing under torture to having been part of an Islamist plot.

Khuderbegainov's well-connected family received a tip-off about his impending arrest, so he ran away to Tajikistan, where he made contact with rebel groups. From there he was sent to Afghanistan to fight with the IMU alongside the Taliban, but he didn't like what he saw and ran away from there, too.

For a year, he scratched a living as a bazaar trader before eventually being arrested crossing the Tajik–Uzbek border. He was then imprisoned for some months in Uzbekistan and severely tortured, which had caused permanent liver damage. Under torture, he had confessed to the range of crimes featured in the trial. The family had not known he had been captured until the trial began. It was during the son's incarceration that the father had himself been imprisoned. His brutal interrogation had ostensibly focused on the whereabouts of his son, who in fact was already in custody at the time.

I judged that Dilobar believed this story herself. I wondered whether this was the whole truth about Khuderbegainov's involvement with the IMU and the Taliban, but, even if it wasn't, he plainly had not received a fair trial on the charges for which he had been sentenced to death. I thanked the impressively composed and articulate Dilobar and her father, and promised to do what I could. We had already decided to move for an EU démarche, but I was racking my brains for further action that might forestall the execution and so decided to contact the UN. Their Human Rights Committee can issue stays of execution, which in theory a state is obliged to respect. In practice, Uzbekistan has conducted executions in defiance of such UN notices in other cases.

* * *

The next day, Chris came into my office and tossed a brown envelope onto my desk. 'You may not want to look at these – they're pretty horrible,' he said.

I was beginning to understand enough about the country to have an inkling of what might be in the envelope, and I waited until Galina had left the room after bringing my cappuccino and biscuits before opening it. The envelope contained a number of photos of a naked corpse. It was a heavy middle-aged man. His face was bruised and bloodied, and his whole torso and limbs were swollen and a livid purple. He was such a mess that it took a little while for me to work out what I was looking at. I said a short prayer, rather to my own surprise, then went back through to Chris's office.

'Where did we get these?'

'His mother. That's Mr Avazov. He was a prisoner in Jaslyk gulag, right up in the desert. He was a member of HuT [Hizb-ut-Tehrir, the party of Islamic liberation] and that's where they take the hardline dissidents. Anyway, his body gets delivered back to his mum in a sealed metal casket. She's ordered not to open it and to bury it the next day. A local militsiya is left to guard it. The militsiya man falls asleep and Mum sneaks down, gets the casket open, body onto the kitchen table, and gets out the Kodak.'

'Without waking up the militsiya man?'

'He was probably pissed.'

'Look, Chris, I don't know what happened to this poor bugger, but I think we should go big on this one. I really want to get serious with this regime, and this could be the case we need. But we have to be certain of our ground.'

Chris mused, 'The photos are pretty good. I am sure Alistair in HRPD in London said that they could get pathology reports done if they had good enough photos.'

'Great. Try it.'

My appearance at the Khuderbegainov trial had caused quite a stir. Ambassadors in Tashkent just did not attend dissident trials. It brought Matilda Bogner, Australian head of the local office of HRW, to the embassy to see me.

'They tell me that you're not like a normal ambassador,' she opened.

'I certainly hope not,' I replied. 'I am struggling to work out what this embassy actually does all day.'

'Not a lot,' she said. 'Chris is pretty good, but I think he is pretty well frustrated.'

She filled me in on the human rights situation, and it was grim. No opposition parties, no free media, no freedom of assembly, no freedom of religion, no freedom of movement. Not only did they still require exit visas for those who wanted to leave the country, you needed an internal visa, or *propiska*, in your passport just to leave the town where you lived. Matilda reckoned there were, at an absolute minimum, 7,000 people imprisoned for their religious or political beliefs. She filled me in on the cases of Elena Urlaeva and Larissa Vdovna, who had recently been committed to a lunatic asylum for demonstrating outside the parliament. Both were now strapped to their beds and receiving drug treatment that amounted to a chemical lobotomy.

I thanked Matilda and said I hoped we would be able to work closely together. I then asked her about the attitude of other embassies. She said the US were in denial. They viewed President Karimov as an essential partner in the War on Terror and had convinced themselves that he was a democrat. Of the other embassies, in her opinion only the Swiss really gave a stuff about human rights. Unfortunately, the countries that genuinely care about human rights – the Scandinavians, Dutch, Irish, Canadians and Australians – didn't have embassies in Uzbekistan.

A fortnight later, Chris received from London the report on the photos of the corpse of Mr Avazov. The pathology department of the University of Glasgow had prepared a brief but detailed report of their findings. The victim had died of immersion in boiling liquid. It was immersion rather than splashing because there was a clear tidemark around the upper torso and upper arms, with 100 per cent scalding underneath. Before he was boiled to death, his fingernails had been ripped out and he had been severely beaten around the face. Reading the dispassionate language of the pathology report, I was struck with a cold horror.

CHAPTER 2

Instructions

I had been selected over a year previously for the position of Her Majesty's Ambassador Extraordinary and Plenipotentiary to the Republic of Uzbekistan. After receiving this news, I still had a further six months to work as British Deputy High Commissioner in Accra, Ghana. Following that, I had six months in London urgently trying to learn Russian. I then had the chance to spend six weeks as a student in St Petersburg, putting a gloss on those new language skills.

When I returned from St Petersburg in June 2002, Fiona and the children were waiting for me at Heathrow Airport. My son Jamie was fourteen, my daughter Emily, eight. Jamie was at Glenalmond, a Scottish public school. It was only mid-June, but he was already on holiday. It is a general rule that the more expensive the school, the fewer weeks you get for your money. Emily was at the local state primary school in Gravesend, where we lived. Fiona now drove us home around the M25 in our old Renault 21 estate.

There was a lot to do before setting out for Tashkent. Back from St Petersburg, I returned immediately to attending the Diplomatic Service Language Centre in the Old Admiralty Building on the Mall. There, we worked very hard to get me through the Russian language functional level examination. Normally, you would take this after eleven months of study, but I had only six. The exam was tough, but I passed.

Fiona and I had to attend a week-long course on how to be an ambassador, which might have been of great help if you had not already been in the Diplomatic Service for 20 years. I also had to attend a series of individual briefings with government departments and others with an interest in Uzbekistan.

The most important contact I would have was with the Eastern Department of the FCO. This department would be my direct line management, responsible for my instructions but also for my budget and management issues. As the geographical department, they had the direct responsibility for the embassy, although much of my reporting on a day-to-day basis would be aimed at FCO functional departments, such as the Counter Terrorism Policy Department (CTPD), United Nations Department (UND) or HRPD. That is not to mention the other Whitehall ministries such as the Department for International Development (DFID) or the Ministry of Defence (MOD) to which we also reported. But the Eastern Department was the starting place.

It had a strange atmosphere. You may be surprised to hear that the FCO was generally not a stuffy place to work. It contains a lot of bright sparky people, many of them young. Creativity was encouraged, and there was a kind of intellectual democracy that belies the strict official hierarchy. But the Eastern Department wasn't like this. Physically, it is spaced out around a set of commodious rooms at the corner of the FCO side of Downing Street, overlooking Number 10. The atmosphere in the department seemed to be unpleasant – heavy, pompous and serious. A pall of misery appeared to have settled. I don't think I ever saw people there joke and smile together. I reckoned there was something wrong, but I wasn't going to be working in the department – indeed I was going to be several thousand miles away – so I wasn't too worried by my initial impression.

The Head of Department, Simon Butt, would be my line manager. He saw me briefly in his splendid office overlooking St James's Park. I got no sense of warmth from him, and he said pretty quickly that he had largely delegated Uzbekistan to his deputy, Dominic Schroeder.

Dominic looks like an actor made up to play the Mikado. He is very tall, with a big belly and a round bald pate. He greeted me much more warmly and talked chiefly about managerial issues. The embassy was expanding in the light of the new importance attached to Uzbekistan post 9/11. In particular, a defence section had been added, headed by an army colonel. This meant that the office accommodation was no longer sufficient.

The ambassadors had lived in a flat on the first floor of the embassy, but the offices were now being expanded to take over the whole building. They therefore needed to find a new Residence. This had not been easy due to the lack of large houses in Tashkent, and though they had finally found one, it was still being built and would need a lot of extra work to bring it up to UK standards. Dominic said that the new Residence would not be ready for my arrival. This would mean an eventual extra move of house and that the offices would be very cramped in the meantime.

I was very excited about the prospect of my first ambassadorship and these did not strike me as major problems. Dominic went on to add that in Tashkent the ambassador's car was only a Land-Rover Discovery. In neighbouring Kazakhstan, the ambassador had a Jaguar, and Dominic would be sympathetic if I wanted to upgrade. I said that if I did that, I would prefer a Range Rover to a Jaguar. Uzbekistan was a big country with a lot of desert and mountain terrain.

Finally, Dominic asked me about my meeting with the former ambassador, Christopher Ingham. During the ambassadors' course, I had absented myself for half a day to attend an Eastern Department discussion on Central Asia. This had centred on oil and gas potential, and focused mostly on Kazakhstan. I had, however, had the chance to meet Christopher Ingham. This was the only time I ever saw my predecessor. He was a thin bespectacled man with a slight stoop. He wore a sharply cut, charcoal-grey pinstriped suit and a fawn-coloured Burberry raincoat that he seemed reluctant to take off.

In a tea break during the meeting, Christopher and I adjourned to a small room for a ten-minute private discussion. He wanted to brief me about the staff of the embassy.

Apart from myself, there were only four other members of the Diplomatic Service in the embassy. Jackie ran the registry, which meant archiving the papers, and would do confidential typing for me, though she was also an entry clearance officer, meaning she conducted visa interviews and issued visas. Dave Muir was third secretary and management officer, responsible for logistics, and also an entry clearance officer. Chris Hirst was the third secretary responsible for political reporting and project work. Karen Moran was second secretary and my deputy head of Mission, responsible for managing the office, looking after British commercial interests and for consular work – giving necessary support to British citizens in the country. And that was it.

That is an extraordinarily small team for a senior diplomat to have, both in number and in rank. In Ghana, I managed a whole chain of first secretaries, with second secretaries under them. In Tashkent, even Karen was not an actual second secretary but an acting one. Chris, as third secretary, was in the lowest of diplomatic ranks.

There was also an indication given that there had been some problems with Chris Hirst. Christopher Ingham said that he had received complaints from the Uzbeks about his behaviour, but he had defended Chris and been commended by the FCO for doing so. He added that Chris claimed the allegations against him were being concocted by the Uzbek intelligence services because of his human rights work. This was not implausible.

This meeting left me feeling slightly uneasy but not unduly worried. Whatever the possible issue with Chris, I would take him as I found him. With such a limited number of staff, it would be difficult to provide London with a good volume of quality reporting on political, economic and other issues. On the other hand, I knew I was professionally very capable myself of a high volume of wide-ranging output. I told Dominic that I was much more worried about the lack of qualified political staff in the embassy.

Would it be possible, for example, to replace Karen with a first secretary when she left in 18 months?

'My dear Craig,' said Dominic, 'it is not many years ago that the Tashkent embassy was one man with a suitcase in a hotel bedroom. We still expect our ambassadors in Central Asia to have a bit of pioneer spirit.'

I assured him I had plenty of that but added that I would revert on staffing once I had bedded in.

I visited British American Tobacco (BAT), who were the largest UK investor in Uzbekistan. However, they plainly weren't that interested in meeting me and produced only their head of security for Central Asia, although he did give me a very good lunch at their headquarters at Temple, London. I did a bit better at Rothschilds Bank, where I had lunch with several directors. They handled the sales of Uzbekistan's gold production – it is the sixth largest gold producer in the world. Following my posting as Deputy High Commissioner to Ghana from 1998 to 2001, I knew a great deal about gold and the factors affecting its world price, and that was a valuable lunch.

Fiona and I were guests for dinner at the home of the Uzbek Ambassador, Professor Faizullaev. He lived in a surprisingly modest home in a fenced and guarded estate in Hammersmith. He was a charming man with a very kind wife and pleasant, student-age children. They had prepared for us Uzbek *plov*, the national dish consisting of pieces of lamb cooked in saffron rice and shredded carrot. The rice is plumped up with vast quantities of cooking oil. The food was delicious, although Mrs Faizullaeva complained that she had to use sunflower instead of cotton oil and couldn't find white carrots. The Ambassador explained to us that there were many regional variations of plov, 220 in total. He preferred Tashkent plov to Samarkand plov.

'What kind is this?' Fiona asked.

'London plov,' said Professor Faizullaev. 'It's the 221st.'

It was a very pleasant evening, and there was only one major political point Faizullaev wanted to make. He said that he had been targeted by protestors who had damaged his car and plastered posters on his house, as well as regularly demonstrating outside the embassy. The British government should do more to defend the embassy. Uzbekistan was an ally of the UK and greatly valued this partnership. The protestors were mostly from what he called a terrorist organisation, Hizb-ut-Tehrir, which he said should be banned. It was banned in Uzbekistan. I replied that the right to demonstrate was an important liberty in the UK, but of course his car and home must not be damaged. I promised to report his concerns to the FCO.

As British Ambassador, you are the representative of Her Majesty the Queen. Before you go out to your post, you call on the Queen to talk about your Mission. But this wasn't the case for me. It was Jubilee year, and the Queen had too many public engagements to find time to talk to dull ambassadors. I would therefore be calling on Princess Anne and Prince Andrew instead. I was worried about this, principally because Fiona was to accompany me and I was afraid she would be bitterly disappointed. Fiona is a monarchist; I am not. But in fact she was quite pleased. I had organised state visits for the Queen in Poland and in Ghana, so Fiona had already met and spoken with her. She had not met Princess Anne or Prince Andrew and so was happy to add a couple more royals to her collection.

I had to wear morning dress, which consisted of striped trousers, a long grey frock coat with tails, a grey waistcoat and a top hat. These were hired from Moss Bros at a substantial cost to the FCO. This seemed to me rather a waste of taxpayers' money. I owned a lot of high-quality suits, so why I had to be dressed like an extra from *My*

Fair Lady was beyond me. I could have worn my kilt if they wanted me to look more impressive.

The unit of the FCO which looked after the needs of ambassadors in the UK was called the Heads of Mission section. I asked Hazel, the very helpful lady who ran it, why we had to do this fancy-dress bit rather than wearing an ordinary lounge suit.

'Buckingham Palace did relax the dress code a few years ago,' she said. 'But then an ambassador turned up in a linen suit. The Palace was really shocked, so we had to go back to morning dress again.'

Good God! A linen suit? No wonder we lost the Empire.

At Buckingham Palace, five ambassadorial couples were spread out around the room. Princess Anne and Prince Andrew were brought in, and each was escorted by a courtier around the groups: the Princess clockwise and the Prince counter-clockwise. Fiona and I therefore had separate three-minute conversations with each. The Prince joked that he was unlikely to come to Tashkent with the navy, it being landlocked, but as we were talking, you could see from his eyes that he wasn't really interested and was thinking of something else: probably how quickly he could get away from this boring meeting. In contrast, Princess Anne looked at me very shrewdly. She said she thought the government of Uzbekistan was a real problem. She had visited Uzbekistan with the Save the Children Fund and was concerned about declining standards of health and education and increasing child poverty. As I was to discover, that was the most clued-up observation anyone made to me before I went out to Tashkent.

The last calls I had to make were on FCO ministers. Mike O'Brien was the junior minister with specific responsibility for Uzbekistan. My first appointment with him was cancelled with half an hour's notice. It was re-arranged for the following week, and this time I made it to his office, where I waited for half an hour while his private secretary desperately tried to locate him. Looking exasperated, he said that O'Brien had been meeting another New Labour MP for lunch and had said that he was going for a walk in St James's Park afterwards. He hadn't returned. After half an hour, we gave up and again rescheduled. The third time, the meeting went ahead and O'Brien seemed to me to be a prime example of a New Labour politician: all haircut and presentation. I wasn't too impressed by his recital of a few platitudes about the War on Terror from the briefing the Eastern Department had given him.

I then had to call on Jack Straw. I was ushered through to the

Secretary of State's great room and sat in an ornate chair opposite him as he lounged on a vermilion ormolu sofa. He had my CV in front of him and observed I was not from the usual background of his ambassadors, having been educated at state school and Dundee University. He then asked me about my interest in Scottish folk music and whether I sang. He asked what the main British commercial interests were in Uzbekistan, said I was going to a difficult part of the world and he wished me luck. The interview lasted under ten minutes. As I was walking out, he called after me, 'Oh and, Craig, whenever you get to . . . wherever it is you're going . . . tell them I'm thinking about them.'

That was the extent of my instructions.

CHAPTER 3

London to Tashkent

On 21 August 2002, we left for Heathrow in a chauffeur-driven government Ford Galaxy, with my brother Stuart driving behind in our battered old Renault with the extra luggage. At the airport we drove round airside to the VIP lounge. The luggage was all set out in a long line against the wall, and a man from Alitalia, Uzbek Air's Heathrow handling agent, started to label the cases, swearing volubly in the process.

As we settled into the VIP lounge, I could see that Jamie was taking in everything around him as though memorising every detail to tell his mates at school. Emily, as always, was completely unfazed and seemed to find nothing remarkable, even when I told her that this was a private place where the Queen came before getting on a plane.[2]

Uzbek Air's first-class cabin fully met international standards of comfort *circa* 1970. There were large grey leather seats, configured in three rows of six across: two at each side and two in the middle. The cabin was clean, but the carpet was worn right down with black greasy-looking patches at the entrances to the aisles.

Once airborne, we were offered juice. The hostess appeared with a short rectangular tray with four drinks already poured: three glasses of juice and one of water. When Fiona asked what the juices were, a look of panic crossed the hostess's face, but this was replaced by one of relief as she realised that she had understood the question. They were, apparently, ay-pel and ah-pri-kat.

'I'll have an apricot!' said Emily keenly. She had very much enjoyed living in Warsaw and was very nostalgic about it. I felt she was remembering the apricot trees in our back garden there, and I felt a pang of pain at her uprooting, even though she was cheerfully grinning now. When Emily is happy, her grins are not just a twitch of her facial muscles but a bright permanent feature. The hostess turned towards her and she took one of the glasses filled with a muddy brown liquid, which, now agitated, looked to have the consistency of gritty syrup.

'Does anyone mind if I take the water?' asked Jamie. Politeness and consideration are innate, but Jamie has definitely been polished by his private education. Nobody did mind.

'I don't mind apricot,' Fiona said, taking the remaining glass of mud. This was kind of her, as she knows I dislike apricots and I suspect she herself prefers apple. This left me with the cloudy apple juice. It was a little sharp, but the taste was not bad. It would have been much nicer chilled. Worse, the lack of filtering left not microscopic particles but positive grains that coated your teeth.

Emily declared the apricot juice delicious, draining it all, while Fiona left half of hers. We chatted excitedly about what might lie before us in Tashkent. We really had little idea of what to expect in terms of the sights, sounds and feel of the place.

Shortly after this, a projector came down from under the central lockers and a film started to play on a screen on the central bulkhead immediately in front of me. Jamie moved from his window seat on the left, the better to see, but he soon moved back. If we had been expecting entertainment, we were disappointed. The caption told us that we were watching 'Uzbekistan's 10th Anniversary Independence Day Celebrations 2001'. There followed a long stage show consisting of dancers, acrobats and singing soldiers. It reminded me of the style of Maoist China. This show played continuously on a loop for the rest of the journey.

* * *

A quick word on the history of Uzbek independence, which can largely be applied to the rest of Central Asia: in 1991, when the hardline communists launched a military coup against President Gorbachev, junior Politburo member President Karimov of the Uzbek Soviet Socialist Republic, and the other Central Asian leaders of SSRs within the USSR, supported the hardline communists. They were bitterly opposed to reform and bitterly opposed to the break-up of the Soviet Union, which threatened their harsh and corrupt control over their own fiefdoms.

When Yeltsin defeated the hardliners after the siege of the Moscow White House, the Gorbachev–Yeltsin liberal era briefly triumphed and it became clear to Karimov and his like that remaining in the USSR would mean toying with democracy, capitalism, liberal reform and the loss of their own totalitarian power. They suddenly did an amazing U-turn and became converts to national independence. But they now left the USSR in order to keep the Soviet system, not to destroy it.

That simple fact seemed to escape conservative politicians in the United States of America, and astonishingly it still does. Shortly before my arrival, US Treasury Secretary O'Neill was in Tashkent hailing Karimov precisely as someone who helped bring down the Soviet Union. These short-sighted US Republicans confuse Karimov with Walesa, Havel and others in Eastern Europe who were fighting communism in the name of liberty. Karimov was fighting liberty in the name of communism until it became more convenient to use the name of nationalism instead. After all, the move from Soviet totalitarianism to fascist totalitarianism is not a difficult one. The mechanisms remain the same. It just requires a slight tweaking of symbols and rhetoric.

* * *

My struggles with these problems lay ahead of me as we landed smoothly at Tashkent Airport some time after 2 a.m. It was a six-and-a-half-hour flight and Tashkent is five hours ahead of the UK. When we got in to the dimly lit VIP lounge, a closer peer around revealed that the lighting was so low in order not to wake the staff. We walked forward to a low metal barrier guarded by a green Formica-and-glass booth in which an immigration officer was sleeping, his mouth agape.

I had asked the embassy to let the Uzbek Ministry of Foreign Affairs (MFA) know that I didn't expect them to mount a formal reception at such an unholy hour. Plainly, my fears were unfounded.

It proved pretty difficult to waken the immigration officer, but eventually he came to and with a somewhat resentful air got out of his booth and switched the lights on. He then returned, and I passed our passports under the glass screen to him. He turned to a computer station, which also appeared difficult to awaken, and tapped in our passport details at what seemed inordinate length. As he finished with each one, he stamped it and eventually handed all four back without a word or a smile. He pressed a pedal, the metal barrier opened and we went through.

Two people, a man and a woman, were sitting on one of the sofas in the VIP lounge. The woman leaped up when she saw us. I surmised, correctly, that this was Karen Moran.

'Good evening, Ambassador,' she said, in a cheerful, rather husky voice with a pronounced Midlands accent. 'Or should I say good morning? Well, I am Karen, your deputy, and this is Chris, third secretary and, more importantly, my partner.'

Chris stood up. About 5 ft 11 in. tall, he looked notably strong and well muscled. He carried himself almost unnaturally well, his back rod straight and his head high. His hair was very close cropped, almost shaven, which over-emphasised his jug ears. He had a broad face and forehead but rather small eyes. He broke into a grin. His accent was Yorkshire.

'You did well to wake him up,' Chris gestured with his head towards the immigration officer, who was settling down to sleep again. 'You'll have to wait about an hour for your luggage. You might as well sit down.'

After about 45 minutes, the luggage turned up, wheeled in by two short oriental men on what looked very old luggage trolleys. The cases were piled up crazily and appeared bound to fall off as they were pushed along. Somehow they didn't.

Three customs officials had been waiting for us at a counter. As no one else had come through the VIP lounge, we were the only customers for this particular detachment. They were armed with one of the big luggage scanners that you can put suitcases through. As we moved past, they asked the porters to put the luggage through the scanner, but Chris intervened, thrusting his diplomatic ID at the chief customs officer to within about two inches of his nose. We then swept past at some speed.

Two white Land-Rovers were waiting for us, both with diplomatic licence plates. Karen introduced me to the drivers. Valeri, who was to be 'my' driver, was a short wiry Russian, rather girlishly handsome. He gave me a shy smile. The other, Mansur, was a large, strong-looking man with greying hair and very oriental eyes set deep in a florid face. He had a large roguish grin, strong handshake and carried himself with a swagger. Both looked genuinely cheerful and welcoming; neither spoke any English. It was immediately apparent that neither Karen nor Chris spoke any Russian. Communication in the embassy must be interesting.

As we set off, Emily was delighted with the Union Jack flying from the chrome mast on the right side of the bonnet. This was not the first time I had flown a flag – I had regularly been chargé d'affaires in Accra, for example, and flown the flag when the High Commissioner was abroad. But this was the first occasion I had flown my own flag as Ambassador in my own right. I felt a surge of pride and something of a lump in my throat as I thought about how proud my father would have been had he lived to see this.

It was a dark night, and we couldn't see much of the town as we drove from the airport to the embassy. The roads were all metalled and had tramlines up the middle. A series of colourful lighting displays with snowflake and bird themes were strung across the streets from lamp-posts. There were miles of them, which was rather surprising. The illuminations included giant signs made up of light bulbs atop blocks of flats either side of the airport road. To the left was 'Welcome to Uzbekistan!' and to the right 'Good luck!', which caused some amusement.

It was about a 20-minute drive to the embassy, a two-storey building made of a warm and mellow brick, now bathed in orange sodium light. A couple of large guards in black suits and ties had opened the gates as we swung in, and they now came running to shake my hand and then help with the luggage.

We entered the embassy through the front door, which led into a vestibule with a heavy oak door to our right. A magnificent red Bokhara carpet covered the floor. Karen led the way up a wide staircase and we arrived at a landing, where high French windows led out onto a balcony from which a large flagpole projected. Karen then opened the large doors on our left into the ballroom. This was a beautifully proportioned room some 60 feet in length. The right-hand wall was pierced with numerous high windows hung with extremely heavy gold-brocaded curtains tied with great tasselled scarlet cords. There were two sets of double doors through the wall on the left into the dining room. These openings were again panelled in light oak. The light was from gold and crystal chandeliers, while the furnishings gleamed in mahogany and fine cloths. The overall effect was sumptuous.[3]

Karen and Chris said good night and took their leave as we went through to the dining room. There, the cook, Galina, was waiting. She had prepared for us a lamb casserole with roast potatoes. It was after four in the morning local time, after eleven in the evening UK time. I don't think any of us was really hungry, but she was obviously very worried about how we would receive her food, so I did my best to eat. It was already getting light as we dispersed into our deep comfortable beds and fell asleep.

After a few hours' sleep, I awoke. It was nine-thirty on a Thursday morning, and beneath me the embassy would be working away. I got ready and snatched a quick breakfast, anxious to get downstairs and inspect my domain.

My office itself was disappointing. It was very small – about ten feet square – and a very large modern modular white-wood workstation took up nearly half the space. The windows looked out onto a narrow stretch of lawn and the high but elegant wrought-iron railings that separated the embassy from the street. Half the width of the street was then further boxed off by huge concrete blocks to provide a discrete parking area and to give adequate stand-off for a level of protection against car bombs. The entrance to this outer area was protected by a heavy metal barrier. A further sliding gate then protected the embassy area proper inside the railings. The bar and gate were properly set at 90 degrees to each other, so a heavy vehicle that attempted to crash through the bar would have to turn right very sharply to attack the gate, something most unlikely to succeed with any momentum.[4]

One of the other doors from my office led through into Karen's office – I walked through and said hello, and she inquired brightly how I was. I told her I just wanted to get my bearings for a bit and then would talk things through with her.

I returned to my office and this time opened the third door. This led into a short narrow corridor. To my left off this corridor was a very heavy steel door painted a dull green with a large iron lever to operate the lock, which was protected by a combination dial. This, I realised, must be the registry.

After getting the combination from Karen, I managed the lock, swung open the great heavy door, unlocked the less heavy but still substantial wooden inner door and went in.[5]

The registry is the heart of an embassy. In here is kept the sensitive communications equipment for transmitting back to London and all the top-secret cipher material with which to programme the equipment. A leak from any of our registries could result in unfriendly intelligence services being able to decode all of our international government communications. Also stored here is bugging and counter-bugging apparatus, as well as secret and top-secret documents and confidential files. The registry is the domain of the registry clerk, usually the most junior of the British staff and the most indispensable. Jackie was the registry clerk, although now, and indeed most of the time, she was through in the consular section conducting visa interviews.

The registry was tiny and the equipment was some generations behind current FCO technology. It still operated through the ordinary Uzbek telephone lines and while encryption should render that safe from interception, it meant you were dependent on the Uzbek telephone system. Even without ill-will, that could not always be relied upon, and very often when there was a line it was not of sufficient quality to carry the signal. It could take hours or sometimes days to send a telegram.

I stood in the registry for a while, thinking over the unexpected problems that were starting to come home to me. I then went back to Karen, who took me round the rest of the embassy. There was not much to see.

We went through to the cramped visa and consular section where Jackie and Dave Muir were conducting interviews. Two locally engaged (LE) staff, Shahida and Zhenya, worked in the section. Shahida was Uzbek and dark, Zhenya Russian and blonde. They both had short, layered haircuts and a professional air.

Through a large bulletproof window, I could see the small room – perhaps 12-foot square – that housed the customers. About 20 of them were packed in, but there was a large queue outside the railings of the embassy of people waiting for admission. Dave raised his eyebrows to the ceiling to indicate the hopelessness of the task.

Zhenya was theoretically also my part-time secretary. She dealt with my diary, issued invitations and helped organise functions. But again, she was in fact too tied up with consular and visa work. Her desk and computer were in the visa section, across the other side of the building from me, which was an impractical place to have your secretary.

Accounts and administration were handled by Nafisa and Shadiya, who said hello shyly from behind a mound of papers. Asol, a severe-looking lady always dressed in black, was the receptionist on the main desk.

Off reception, a large office held the commercial section and the Department for International Development. Both had only one, Uzbek, member of staff. The commercial section was run by Lena Son, an ethnic Korean, one of some 400,000 ethnic Koreans in Uzbekistan.[6] Lena Son was short and slim with shiny bobbed hair. She greeted me with a wide grin and turned out to be a real treasure – perhaps the most competent member of staff I have ever had, anywhere. Atabek represented DFID. He too was very impressive. Tall and slim in a well-cut suit, he spoke with great assurance and a slight American accent.

Karen's office was in a corner and could only be entered through Lena Son and Atabek's office or through mine, as indeed the only internal route up to the Residence was through my office. The registry corridor was the only area not accessible to the Uzbek staff. These arrangements were very cramped, and we had to get used to people traipsing through our offices while we were working.

One further wing of the embassy housed the information section, where Chris Hirst worked in a long room lined with beta video cassettes on various aspects of the UK. The cassettes were to be given to TV stations for free transmission. This was surprisingly effective in countries which struggle to fund programme making. They included travelogues on English gardens and series on successful black entrepreneurs in Britain. As propaganda goes, it was not very harmful.

Chris sat at one desk, and the other desk in this cluttered room was empty. I asked Chris who worked there, and he said the position of information assistant was vacant at the moment. He was unpacking more bundles of material from the Information Department in London. On a counter sat an old stand-alone PC that was our only link to the Internet, and that itself was pretty intermittent.

Finally, I entered a room on the opposite side of the corridor from Chris. This was something of a broom cupboard with no natural light. There, my defence attaché, Nick Ridout, was seated opposite his assistant, Vakhida. Nick was a colonel in the Royal Military Police. He spoke very good Russian and had a real interest in exploring the history and geography of the country. He seemed genuinely glad to see me. I was pretty shocked at his office accommodation. All in all, there seemed a great deal to sort out at the embassy.

Having become acquainted with my notably small staff, I arranged to give them a pep talk at the start of the next morning. The main message I tried to get across was that I wanted the embassy to make a positive difference to Uzbekistan – to run projects, provide services and to influence the policy of the government of Uzbekistan, the policy back in London and the policy of international institutions, in such a way that the lives of people in Uzbekistan would be discernibly better for our work.

Over the next few days, it became plain that this would be an uphill struggle. After the staff meeting, I asked Zhenya to stay behind and told her I wanted to pay introductory calls to all the British businesses in Uzbekistan. She seemed startled and asked if I would not prefer them to come and see me. I explained that I wanted to look round the operations, meet the staff and get a feel for what their problems were and whether I could help. I couldn't understand why this perfectly normal request was greeted with such surprise and scepticism by Zhenya. There were only about 30 British companies active in Uzbekistan, so it wasn't a huge task.

The first one I called on was a company called 3C. It was a small developmental consultancy run by a long-term expat, James McGrory. As we neared his office in the car, Valeri was leaning out of the window looking for it. Given how few British companies there were in Uzbekistan, I was surprised he didn't know where it was. As the flag car eventually drew up outside his offices, just off Mustakillik Square, James stood outside on the pavement. He was a strong bear of a man with a ruddy beard, massive shoulders and an even bigger paunch. He looked elegant in a white blazer over a lilac shirt. He had a red carnation in his lapel, which matched his florid complexion, and held a white panama in his hand as he rushed to open the door for me.

He led me up to his office, which was on the second floor and consisted of a couple of rooms leased from the Uzbek state institution which owned the building. He introduced me to the man and woman who comprised his staff and made me a pleasant cup of green tea.

James seemed extremely happy that I had come and said that it meant a huge amount to his staff, who indeed seemed terrified into silence when I spoke to them. James had been there more or less since independence in 1991 and had seen all three previous British ambassadors to Uzbekistan. But I was, he said, the first one to visit his offices. I was incredulous.

James provided advice and assistance to foreign companies looking to invest in Uzbekistan, which was a nightmare of regulation. The laws were so restrictive that, in order to be able to operate, every new venture needed a specific statute, issued as a presidential decree, stating what that venture was allowed to do. This needed to be incredibly detailed, because anything not specifically permitted by the decree would be deemed illicit by venal officials looking to be paid off. After some relaxation in the mid-1990s, the situation had deteriorated further and become such a nightmare that foreign investment had almost completely halted. So business was scarce for James.

Uzbek economic policy was so hopeless that the International Monetary Fund (IMF) had closed their office and left. With this, much of the aid flows had dried up, which, as aid project consultancy was James's other main area, made the overall outlook pretty bleak for him.

James added that the business climate was so poor that the British community in Tashkent, which had numbered a couple of hundred in 1995, was now down to about 40. I was subsequently able to confirm this. The embassy had consular responsibility not just for Brits in Uzbekistan but also for several other nationalities who did not have embassies there, including the Irish, Australians, New Zealanders, Finnish, Dutch and others. Our total list of people in the whole country had declined from over 500 to 120 as economic opportunity dwindled. The French and German embassies confirmed the same picture. The Indian community had fallen from 5,000 to 500. The only community increasing was the American, which had a massive influx of military and intelligence personnel and other workers following the opening of the US airbase in Uzbekistan at Karshi Khanabad in the aftermath of 11 September.

James had given me a lot of food for thought and, importantly, my first real insight into the totalitarian nature of the Uzbek regime. I knew already that it had an appalling human rights record, practised torture, did not tolerate political opposition and had an entirely state-controlled media. Just three days of reading Uzbek newspapers and watching Uzbek TV news had shown me that. Every single TV news item began: 'Today the President of the Republic of Uzbekistan, His Excellency Mr Islam Karimov . . .' There was an astonishingly heavy police presence in the city, with a knot of policemen on every street corner. There was also a palpable air of fear. Everyone was scared, and even the embassy Uzbek staff dropped their eyes and lowered their voices if you asked them about the political or economic situation. In my briefings in London, the FCO had spoken as though this was a South-east Asian model – a highly authoritarian state providing stability in which capitalism was flourishing and society developing. In fact, every day it became increasingly plain to me that this was more like a North Korean model, with government stultifying not just political life but all social, religious and commercial life as well.

Two of the most valuable of these commercial calls I made were on Wakefield Services, a cotton grading company, and Case Tractors. The latter are a US firm but were supplying tractors to the Uzbek market from their factory in Basildon, Essex.

From them, I started to learn something of the Uzbek cotton industry. This is an astonishing story. Cotton plantation was introduced to Uzbekistan by Tsarist Russia to counter the fall in supplies caused by the American Civil War. After 1945, there was a massive expansion, and Uzbekistan produced 70 per cent of the cotton refined by the USSR and its satellites, feeding textile mills from Lodz to Vladivostok. Today, it is the world's fifth largest producer, and second largest exporter, of cotton. The cotton fields are watered by an amazing 40,000 miles of main irrigation canal, with uncountable miles of branches. These open canals and furrows are extremely inefficient – over 90 per cent of the water is lost to evaporation, and this massive out-take of water for the Uzbek cotton system is responsible for over 80 per cent of the loss of supply to the Aral Sea.

More simply put, the Uzbek cotton industry has caused one of the world's biggest environmental disasters, as a whole sea has almost vanished. And that is only the start of the environmental consequences. Cotton is a monoculture in Uzbekistan, and most of the land under cultivation has grown the same crop for over 50 consecutive years. Crop rotation is simply not practised. The result is complete soil exhaustion, necessitating the use of millions of tons of fertiliser. Similarly, keeping the cotton healthy after years of providing the same diet for pests and diseases requires application of pesticides at many multiples of safe levels.

The residue of this vast chemical cocktail is drained off into the Aral Sea or, as the rivers no longer reach it, into the beds of the remnants of the great Amu Darya and Syr Darya rivers, known to the ancients as the Oxus and the Jaxartes. The shrinking Aral Sea is now an ever more concentrated chemical soup, wreathed in clouds of yellow choking mist. Disease levels, and particularly the incidence of congenital diseases, have gone sky high in Karakalpakistan, Uzbekistan's northern province.

The cotton is grown on state farms by a tied labour force. Sixty per cent of the Uzbek population is tied to such farms. As the standard salary on an Uzbek state farm is 2,000 *sum* – that's $2 – a month, they will never be able to find enough money to pay the hefty bribe needed to obtain their propiska to leave. In short, most of the workers in Uzbekistan are cotton slaves, just as surely as Negroes were in the nineteenth-century United States. At Case I was told that in Soviet times over 70 per cent of Uzbek cotton was machine picked. Now it was under 10 per cent, with over 90 per cent picked by hand.

The monopoly purchasers of cotton are two state trading companies. They buy the cotton from the state farm for virtually nothing – the farm gets one-thirtieth of the farm-gate price of cotton in neighbouring Kazakhstan, where the industry has been privatised. As the state trading companies sell the cotton on to the international market at world prices, they are massively profitable. Their offices in Tashkent are clad in shiny blue glass and their executives drive luxury cars. They pay a percentage of their revenues to the state budget, but this is totally non-transparent. The state budget is a secret, as are the revenues of the trading companies. All this leaves massive scope for government corruption, which some members of the Karimov family and their adherents exploit to the full.

As I left James McGrory, he again held the door open for me to get into the Land-Rover and made some remark about it not being a terribly posh car for an ambassador. That reminded me, and as we drove away I broached the subject.

'How old is the Land-Rover, Valeri?'

'Three and a half years, Ambassador.'

'Time to get a new car, then?'

'No, Ambassador, I don't think so.' He gestured towards the speedometer. I squinted from the back at the milometer reading.

'Ten and a half thousand miles! In three and a half years! That's about sixty miles a week! What do you do for a living?'

'It's not my fault, Ambassador. I can only go when the Ambassador tells me.'

When I got back, I spoke with Karen.

'Karen, this is a big country. The flag car has hardly any miles on the clock. How do we get around?'

'Well, the Ambassador often used the Toyota when he travelled – he found it more comfortable than the Land-Rover. And when the Ambassador went on tour, he sometimes flew.'

'Are the flights good?'

'No, but the MFA puts on flights for diplomats sometimes.'

'But wouldn't he send the flag car ahead to use when he got there?'

'No, the MFA will provide a vehicle.'

'Let me get this straight. You are telling me we go around this country on Uzbek government transport and with an Uzbek government escort. How the hell are we supposed to find out what's really happening?'

We had an office meeting every Monday, and I made plain at the next one that I expected we would do a lot of travelling in future, to build up contacts and gather information around the country. Nick Ridout looked particularly happy about this.

On 1 September, Fiona and I had to attend the Independence Day celebrations. These cast a further and lurid light on the nature of the regime. The massive illuminations I had seen on the way from the airport were part of the celebrations for Independence Day. From two days before, the entire city centre, covering several square miles, was sealed off as preparations were made for the celebratory show in Mustakillik Square.[7]

Our invitation to attend the Independence Day celebrations, cast in a formal note from the MFA as instructions rather than an invite, said that ambassadors must be seated by 17.30. We left the embassy around 17.15. I knew that the centre had been sealed off, but I hadn't realised just what that meant. The whole city transport system was suspended. A series of concentric rings of steel surrounded Mustakillik Square. They were formed of trams, trolleybuses, buses and lorries. Each security ring had a single entrance at the opposite side to the entrance to the previous circle, so it was like threading your way through a maze.

The scale of the thing was enormous. We drove around many miles of trams parked bumper to bumper. All the vehicles comprising these rings were jammed up against one another so there was no possibility of anyone squeezing through. The only way would be under, but there were several armed soldiers for each vehicle. The outer circles were mostly trams and trolleybuses, the inner circles mostly buses and army trucks. There were in total thousands of vehicles. I was staggered at the sheer disruption involved in sealing off such a vast area of the city, the inconvenience to people and to businesses, and the crippling of ordinary transport, all for a regime showpiece. It said volumes about the relative importance of state and private sector. I should add that Tashkent is no small city. It has a population of two and a half million and was the fourth largest city in the USSR, the home of much Soviet heavy industry and especially a great concentration of armaments manufacture.

We eventually made it through and were met at the car park by a smooth English-speaking young man from the MFA. He escorted us to our seats in the temporary stadium built for the event, where ambassadors were seated in the order of their arrival in Tashkent. We were seated between the Israeli and South Korean ambassadors, who both grinned. The South Korean produced earplugs, which he said the Italian Ambassador had warned him to bring.

I had presumed that if we had to be seated at five-thirty, it would begin at six. But six came and went, and nothing happened. As did six-thirty. By seven, my bum was getting sore on the plastic seat, and I was getting really angry. By the time President Karimov arrived on the dot of seven-thirty, I was livid.

After some speeches, the show began. On the plane on the way over, we had been forced to sit through a video of the event the year before, several times. This was just the same: ranks of goose-stepping singing soldiers and massed tiny tots with balloons, interspersed with Uzbek folk songs and pop singers. A peculiar note was struck by lines of showgirls who wouldn't have looked out of place in the Moulin Rouge. That cheered me up a bit, which was much needed.

The South Korean was lucky with his earplugs – the volume of the music was incredible. It was like being at a rock concert with your head stuck in the bass bin. The plastic seats vibrated like crazy. It went on and on and on. By the time it finished after 11 p.m. with a firework display, we had been seated for over five hours.

My mood was not improved by waking up the next morning still with a loud ringing in my ears from the pounding they had taken. I went down to work and dictated a formal diplomatic note to the MFA, thanking them for inviting me to their interesting show but saying that it was a gross discourtesy to ambassadors to ask them to be in their seats two hours before an event started. I suggested ambassadors did not constitute a security risk and requested that future invitations indicate not only what time they wished us to attend but also what time the event would actually start. I then copied this note to all other embassies.

This caused a sensation. I did not yet know it, but the Uzbek government routinely treated foreign ambassadors with a lack of courtesy bordering on contempt, perhaps in the tradition of the former Emir of Bokhara who humiliated Stoddart and Connolly for months in the bugpit in 1842 before beheading them. Diplomats in general being wimpish, none of my colleagues had ever raised a whimper before. For exhibiting the remotest trace of a backbone, I was viewed as fantastically daring and backslapped by the entire diplomatic community. Speaking out for the privileges and dignity of ambassadors made me terrifically popular with the diplomatic corps. I was to find speaking out on human rights a different matter.

CHAPTER 4

Diplomacy

Strictly speaking, you are not an ambassador until you have presented your letters of credence, or credentials. These are two letters from your own head of state. One recalls your predecessor as ambassador, and the second appoints you. You have to deliver these in person to the head of state of the country to which you have been appointed.

President Karimov was receiving me and the new Israeli, Japanese and South Korean ambassadors, one after the other. Karen came to support me and make sure I didn't lose the letters. I had decided to perform this ceremony in Highland dress.

I had asked London if I could say something on human rights in addition to the script I had been given on standing shoulder to shoulder against terrorism and the value we placed on commercial and educational relationships. The FCO had surprised me by replying immediately with a couple of pretty strong sentences on the need for Uzbekistan to improve its human rights record.

The reception was held at the presidential offices in central Tashkent – the President lived in a palace outside the city at Durmen and drove in a huge convoy to work every morning, causing massive road closures and disruption. I was shown through to a vast marbled hall. In the glare of television lights, I walked up to Karimov, Karen two paces behind me. We shook hands, Karen handed me the letters from the Queen, and I handed them to Karimov. He then led me through to a side room. There were five Louis XIV chairs for Karimov, his Foreign Minister Komilov, an interpreter, Karen and me. The doors were closed, blotting out the TV cameras, and we sat down to talk.

Karimov was only about 5 ft 7 in. tall but muscular with a short broad neck and a thick jowled face. His oriental eyes were deep-set and his skin sallow. His nose was small and wide, his mouth narrow and thin. He moved easily and seemed very assured. His eyes were less dark than his skin colour would suggest and bright with a shrewd intelligence. He had played for 20 years at the top level of a power politics where if you lost, you died, and many of those who crossed him had been ruthlessly eliminated. He wasn't going to be fazed simply by my putting on a kilt.

'I am delighted to see you, Mr Ambassador,' he said through his interpreter. Interestingly, he was speaking Russian rather than his official language, Uzbek. 'I have always had the greatest admiration for the wisdom of the United Kingdom. You have had many generations to develop that wisdom.'

Subtext: don't expect any rapid change towards democracy here.

He continued: 'One great example of the wisdom of your government, on which I must congratulate you, is that you have just made a derogation from the European Convention on Human Rights to enable terrorist suspects to be detained in the United Kingdom without trial.'

Subtext: don't you lecture me on human rights, people who live in glass houses . . .

'The greatest misfortune in the history of the Uzbek people is what happened in what you call the Great Game. Unfortunately, the British were never able to make any progress towards Central Asia, and their efforts to do so met with some very great historic defeats.'

Subtext: your country doesn't really cut that much ice around here.

'It would have been infinitely better for our people if they had been conquered by the British and not by the Russians. Our whole history of development, and especially economic development, would have been different. As it is, of course, we know only the central planning system. You must realise we are a hundred years behind.'

Subtext: don't expect any rapid changes towards capitalism.

'Of course, the danger of militant Islam is a threat to the very existence of Western civilisation. For a decade, we Uzbeks stood alone to defend the West against Islam. When the allies came to fight the Taliban, it was late. We are still the frontline against Islam. We were vital to the Allied effort against the Taliban. We are a poor country and this cost us a lot of resources. It is natural that we should anticipate that, just as our geo-strategic position was essential for operations against the Taliban, so it will also be essential for operations to reconstruct Afghanistan. Uzbek companies should be fully employed in this work. We are also the frontline of defence for the West against the flow of narcotics. This too is very expensive for us.'

Subtext: give us a lot of money.

There was a lot more of it, but you get the idea. It was a masterly performance. In particular, his opening observation on detention without trial in the UK was very shrewd in pre-empting my own complaints. He was well informed, as our derogation from the European Convention had only just happened. This is a striking illustration of just how much encouragement New Labour's attack on civil rights in the UK gives to dictators around the globe.

I had a number of business points to raise, with which we wanted presidential assistance. These included the establishment of the Tashkent campus of Westminster University, the Oxus mining joint venture proposal and the Trinity Energy oil extraction contract. Karimov had a good mastery of the detail on each, which was very impressive as he had no notes. As things were going well, I threw in the need for the British Council to find larger premises, which Karimov told his Foreign Minister to look at sympathetically. Karimov positively beamed with pleasure when I delivered my message of gratitude for Uzbek support in the War on Terror and made a point of looking out of the window when I delivered my couple of sentences on the need to improve Uzbekistan's human rights record.

He did, however, respond obliquely to this when he gave me what I came to dub his 'Paranoid' speech – I was to hear it several times, and it was the speech he gave to every Western visitor.

Karimov said that Uzbekistan was surrounded by enemies. Afghanistan was still prey to Taliban supporters and their colleagues in the IMU. Following the Tajik civil war, extreme Islamic militants formed part of the government of that neighbouring state. Furthermore, Uzbekistan had to combat a return of Russian influence. Russia had troops in Tajikistan and an airbase in Kirghizstan. Uzbekistan was the region's only reliable ally for the West.

Furthermore, Uzbekistan faced destabilisation from the flow of narcotics through Afghanistan and Tajikistan. A more insidious threat came from China. Sub-standard goods would undermine

Uzbek production. These goods did not comply with safety standards and might be deliberately poisoned. In the light of all these threats, Uzbekistan was obliged to protect itself by measures which were, regrettably, authoritarian.[8]

The first time you heard this litany it was actually quite impressive. It certainly swayed a number of prominent Western officials and politicians, including Donald Rumsfeld and Joschka Fischer. However, I knew enough to distrust Karimov's arguments, and my instincts told me to be wary of him. While he might be a thug, he was a complex and shrewd one with a profound grasp of detail. I also realised that contrary to diplomatic corps opinion, he understood English. Even though he waited for the interpreter, it was clear from his eyes that he was following and understanding what I said. Finally, he was healthy and vigorous. He was widely rumoured to have leukaemia, but he seemed pretty healthy to me.

For the next few weeks, Uzbek television showed pictures of me in my kilt being greeted by Karimov. They put it on between showings of the Independence Day celebrations.

I was still continuing my calls on British companies but having presented my credentials now had further visits to make – on Uzbek ministers and on my fellow ambassadors. This is a protocol requirement but also quite useful as an information-gathering exercise.

I decided to start with my EU colleagues. Three other EU countries – Germany, France and Italy – had embassies in Tashkent.

My German colleague, Martin Hecker, was ensconced in a very large, purpose-built, concrete embassy. He prided himself on a career spent working in the communist bloc and believed this gave him a special insight into the Karimov government. He was tall and spare with a shock of grey hair and blue eyes in a strong face. He spoke of the impossibility of change and said the key skill was to understand the mentality of the Karimov regime and work with them. He stood up and moved to a striking painting on his wall. It was a stable with blurred figures, perhaps indicating a nativity scene. It was painted very cunningly, so that what looked like the interior was the exterior next time you looked.

'This is an illusionist painting,' he said. 'It is very fine. It holds an important truth. What is real is not the specks of paint on the paper. What is real is the impression implanted in your brain. In Uzbekistan, we have an illusion that there is progress. The Americans wish to believe this illusion. But the existence of the illusion is itself the most pertinent fact.

'You know, the only thing we can do in practice from this terrible situation is to rescue individuals. This I have done – artists, musicians, writers. We have given many political asylum.' He reeled off a few names, which at that time meant nothing to me. 'You know,' he concluded, 'when you cannot affect the general, you must concentrate on the particular.'

My ambition remained larger. If we couldn't affect the general, why were we all here?

I then called on my French colleague, Jacques-André Costilhes, whose embassy and residence were in a much grander Russian colonial palace than ours, just a couple of hundred metres up the same street.

While we had local guards, at the French embassy I was saluted by smart French military guards in black uniforms and peaked caps. They escorted me through to the main entrance, where I was shown through a series of plush modern offices. The old palace had been substantially remodelled on the inside. Eventually, I met my new French colleague. A short, black-haired, balding man in his early 50s, eyes sparkling with a wry humour behind brown spectacles, Jacques-André looked on the world with wry detachment and told me that the US had the major interest in Uzbekistan and there was nothing for the EU to gain by rocking the boat.

The French and German embassies each had about 30 diplomatic staff, with counsellors, first secretaries and the full range of a normal embassy. We had just six, all but me very junior. The Italians were on the same kind of scale as us. But my Italian colleague's office was about the size of my embassy, with beautiful thick carpets and expensive furniture. I was shown into his office by three absolutely gorgeous young women, one Italian and two Uzbek, who were a cliché of office sexiness: white low-buttoned blouses exposing a terrific amount of cleavage, hip-hugging short black skirts with stockings and shiny black high heels. I wondered if this was an Italian diplomatic uniform.

I was installed at one end of his cavernous office to wait for the Ambassador, who was preceded into the room by a toy white dog which immediately jumped onto my lap and started slavering all over me, tiny paws on my chest, licking my face. The Ambassador came hurrying over, attracting 'Mitzi' away with a biscuit. He then sat down in the chair opposite me and smiled.

Leopoldo Ferri de Lazara had the most beatific appearance imaginable. He had snowy white hair and wore a spotless white linen suit over a pale-blue shirt with an open wide collar. His smile was concerned and kindly, and he had a perpetual air of being slightly puzzled by where he was and what was going on around him. He looked like someone playing God in an old Jimmy Stewart film. He had previously been Ambassador to Thailand and had met his present wife there. Several of his ancestors had been Doges of Venice – he had brought their portraits in oil, together with a selection of other contents of his Venetian palace, with him to Tashkent.[9]

Now, on first acquaintance, we sat sipping tea from paper-thin antique china as Leopoldo eyed me quizzically. He was refreshing to meet, because he was much less mealy mouthed than other ambassadors about the situation in the country. It was dreadful and getting worse. The Americans, he declared, were stupid if they thought that supporting a dictator like Karimov was a recipe for long-term stability. The problem with the Americans was not that they failed to learn from history but that they never understood the complexity of a situation either at the time or in retrospect. He bemoaned the absence of an EU delegation in Tashkent. The EU Commission had very little understanding of what was happening in the country, and its influence was nil.

Leopoldo gave an attractive and civilised critique but little sign of any spur to action. This was misleading – over the next year he was to become a most valuable and proactive ally.

Things were not to get off to such a good start with the US Ambassador, and the problems began at an IMF meeting hosted by the US embassy.

The Uzbek government had, on the very day of my arrival in the country, done something extremely baffling. It had physically sealed all of its land borders and closed down all the bazaars in Tashkent. The formal retail sector is very little developed, and the bazaars are simply large open-air markets where 95 per cent of consumer needs, from food through clothes to televisions, were retailed. Tashkent had been a major trade centre for thousands of years, and the bazaars were as old as that. Suddenly, they were closed.

The government had cited health and safety reasons for the closure. The border closures they justified first on the basis of preventing the spread of disease, then as necessary to prevent an influx of sub-standard consumer goods.

After a couple of weeks, it had become clear that this was no temporary measure. Word started to come in from the provinces of bazaars being closed down in other cities. The dislocation effects were extreme – about 40,000 people were directly employed in the bazaars and probably a larger number in cross-border trade to stock them.

Eric Reynolds, a very shrewd Scottish consultant who had been working on an EU project on market management, gave me some valuable insights. The formal retail sector was dominated by Prime Minister Usmanov, a very powerful figure whose family owned all the main supermarkets and the largest food importing company, which had a monopoly on many major commodities, for example sugar. There was no formal monopoly, but all imports needed customs approval and no one else would get it. His competition came from the small traders who carried on the time-honoured baggage trade within Central Asia. Wham! All competition had just vanished.

With shop prices at multiples of bazaar prices, and the lack of competition encouraging shopkeepers to jack up prices further, suddenly people in Tashkent couldn't afford to eat.

James McGrory and another excellent British consultant, Peter Reddish, who represented the EU Commission in Tashkent, filled me in further. The Uzbek government was under heavy pressure from the IMF and international community to float the currency, the sum. Previously, it had been much overvalued, but conversion into dollars was very strictly controlled. In other words, you could get a ridiculously large amount of dollars for your sum, if you were a member of the regime and could get permission. Otherwise, you couldn't get any.

While not opening up to free conversion, the Uzbek government had started to devalue the sum. This seriously struck at the perks of regime members, and a trade and retail monopoly was a good way of replacing these. Equally, if free currency conversion did come, meaning that anyone could buy dollars for sum, the liberalising effect could be negated by sealing the borders, thus not allowing anyone but the favoured few to do anything with dollars if they got them.

It was at just this interesting time that an IMF mission came to town to assess Uzbekistan's economic progress. If progress was achieved, Uzbekistan would be eligible for a standby agreement and Karimov could get his mitts on hundreds of millions of dollars of IMF money. That seemed to me undesirable.

The IMF mission was blessed with an excellent Russian economist. We had lunch together, and he shared the above analysis. The term of art for 'corruption' in the IMF is 'economic rent'. The anti-trade measures were a means of transference of access to economic rent by the elite, from currency-access monopoly to trade-access monopoly, he declared.

All of which caused a problem for the United States. Having firmly adopted Karimov as a client, they were trying very hard to get the IMF to agree to a standby arrangement. The US Ambassador had arranged for the ambassadors of the G8 to meet the IMF delegation over lunch. The Russian economist said he expected some pressure at the lunch and asked me to back him up.

I had not yet met my US colleague, who had not attended the Independence Day celebrations. His residence was a huge traditional Uzbek house which fronted straight onto the pavement. Uzbek houses are square in design with a large internal courtyard garden. The US Ambassador, John Herbst, greeted me warmly at the door. He was a tall gangling man with long arms and large hands. He had a fine face with a long thin nose and wore thick black-rimmed spectacles. He had unruly black hair which he would run his fingers through in thought, leaving it sticking up. There was something of the schoolboy about him.

We were about 20 around the lunch table, which had John Herbst at one end and the head of the visiting IMF mission, a Dutchman named Erik with a thick mop of brown hair at the other. Herbst invited a rather nervous lady named Kathleen to make some opening remarks. She was from the US Treasury and worked as an adviser inside the Uzbek Ministry of Finance. She stressed the progress made in devaluing the sum and in building up foreign reserves, and praised Uzbekistan's debt-repayment record.

Invited to give the mission's observations, Erik called on the Russian economist to comment. He agreed progress had been made in devaluation but said that the Uzbeks were nonetheless behind schedule on current account convertibility. But he added that the recent anti-trade measures must be a matter of major concern and raised fundamental questions about the Uzbek government's commitment to economic liberalisation. He was immediately backed up by the resident World Bank representative. This was a grave bearded Englishman named

David Pearce, and he spoke scathingly about the lack of structural reform, particularly on privatisation and utility pricing.

The US Ambassador then suggested the IMF had the choice of saying the glass was half full or half empty. He saw it as half full. If the progress the Uzbeks had made so far was not rewarded, it would be a slap in the face for the reformers in the Uzbek government, who would lose influence. The French Ambassador supported this view and said that a French company had been given an important contract in cotton trading, which was a start to privatisation.

I should explain why we were pontificating in this way. The IMF is governed by a board drawn from the member nations, rather like the UN is governed by a Security Council. The US and the other major contributors from the G8 have the most weight on the board. The IMF staff – as represented by Erik and his mission – would present a report with recommendations, in this case on Uzbekistan and the prospects for a standby agreement. But it would be the board members who made the decision, which is why we were discussing it now. Our home governments would decide on how the board would vote – in the case of the UK, the Treasury and DFID would have the most say. But as Western governments are not full of experts on Uzbekistan, the report and recommendations sent back by their ambassadors in Tashkent following this lunch would have a big influence on the decision.

Erik had a fine line to tread. He had to come up with something intellectually credible and square this with the desire of the IMF's biggest shareholder – the USA – for a positive report at a time when the Uzbek government was busily ruining its own economy. He also had to produce a public statement agreed with the government of Uzbekistan, which was also a member of the IMF.

As the very new kid on the block, I had not yet said anything, which had the advantage that I was able to do some justice to my excellent lunch. Erik was now talking and saying that the Uzbek government was claiming a current economic growth rate of 8 per cent. This brought laughter around the table. Erik then said that they were negotiating a figure with the Uzbek government and thought that their report would say 3 per cent growth.

I was startled into interrupting.

'I'm sorry?'

'Three per cent, Ambassador. I think the Uzbek government will agree a figure of 3 per cent.'

'Well, maybe they will, but it can't be true. I have been visiting a lot of companies since I came, and talking to people active in various areas of the economy, and I haven't met one person who doesn't think this economy is shrinking, not growing.'

'I agree,' said Leopoldo. 'If you wanted an example of how to ruin an economy, then the Uzbek government provides it.'

Erik temporised: 'Well, the difficulty is there are no independent institutions providing economic statistics, and I certainly agree that government statistics can be misleading. But if you are forced to rely on anecdotal evidence, that is not very reliable either. But consider this. This is largely an agricultural economy. Agriculture accounts for more than 60 per cent of gross domestic product. Last year there was a very bad harvest, of both cotton and grains. This year there is a harvest – well, let's not say good, but fair. That already will give you a lot of economic growth.'

John Herbst was eyeballing me in a less than friendly manner and now interjected, saying, 'Well, I think that is a very logical explanation on economic growth. Let us look at devaluation now . . .'

I didn't listen to his next few words because I was perusing rapidly a table of statistics David had passed across to me. What were they? Judging by David's eyebrows, there was a killer fact in here somewhere. What the hell was it? Oh . . .

'I am sorry, John,' I said. 'I just want to clarify something that perhaps I didn't understand on the growth figures. Erik, you said that agriculture was 60 per cent of the economy, so there must be growth this year due to a good harvest, while last year was a bad harvest. Did I understand you?'

Erik, who was trying to eat some of his lunch, looked up and nodded.

'But,' I continued, 'by the same logic, last year there must have been a fall because of the very bad harvest. Yet I see the IMF posted a figure last year of 4 per cent economic growth. Now that just can't be true, can it?'

Erik looked at his papers. 'Well, in logic it would be possible if there was also a very bad harvest in the preceding year.'

'But there wasn't,' said Leopoldo. 'It was a good harvest.'

The ensuing silence was broken by the German Ambassador, Martin Hecker. 'Evidently our young British colleague is an economist. We should be grateful for our number to be augmented in such a fashion. But perhaps we should also remember that Uzbekistan is not Washington or London or perhaps I might even say Berlin. The application of logic does not always apply. Indeed we may say,' he gave a discreet sound between a laugh and a cough, 'that in the situation we have here in Uzbekistan, logic cannot be a suitable diagnostic approach, because the situation itself is not rational. What is required is a more holistic approach, based perhaps on a broader understanding and experience.'

Which, as far as I was concerned, meant: 'Let's ignore the facts.' That is what the international community has done, consistently. The World Bank states that from 1993 to 2003 Uzbek GDP fell from $13.1 billion to $9.9 billion. Yet the IMF has accepted a positive growth figure for all but one of those years and an average growth figure of 4.2 per cent in this period. The best bit is that the World Bank still carries both figures in an impossible combination in its Uzbekistan briefing paper.

The lunch established my reputation for being difficult and outspoken, while convincing me that the US were willing to bend any fact in defence of their ally, Karimov. It also made me very popular with the IMF staff, including Erik, who was used to being pressured by ambassadors to be soft rather than hard.

The following day, I made my courtesy call on John Herbst. There were about 60 diplomats at the US embassy, in addition to all the non-diplomatic staff, the military, the advisers in Uzbek government ministries and a large number of US aid-funded American personnel.

The Uzbek Karshi Khanabad airbase, known as K2, used to be one of the largest in the Soviet Union. It now housed three squadrons of the United States Air Force, guarded by a couple of thousand US troops. Halliburton, the company of which Dick Cheney was formerly CEO, had contractors building the improved airbase facilities and extending the aprons to take more planes, and they were assigned their own US marine guards. Herbst had a big job, an important part of which was keeping the Uzbek government sweet.

The K2 airbase had been useful for supporting US operations in Afghanistan. Now that the Americans had Baghram airbase in Kabul and access to other Afghan airfields, K2 was no longer necessary for this purpose. But the US had been cock-a-hoop at taking over a major Soviet airbase and were now preparing for a permanent stay.

The Pentagon had formulated a new doctrine to ensure control of the 'Wider Middle East'. By that they meant the Middle East as we understand it, plus the Caucasus and Central Asia, which is of course a massive belt of oil and gas resources. This Wider Middle East is to be surrounded by 'lily pads'. These are air bases which have a permanent garrison but the potential to 'open out' – be rapidly expanded to take reinforcement for a massive projection of US military force anywhere throughout the area. The giant airbase at K2 was the easternmost, and one of the most important, of these lily pads. So the US relationship with Uzbekistan was essential to a much wider geo-strategic plan.[10]

To house the vastly expanded US operation, a gigantic new embassy was being constructed in Tashkent. Meanwhile, they had crammed five times more people into their embassy building than it was designed for, and I was escorted through numerous layers of security by US Marines until I met John Herbst in the tiny attic office, overflowing with books, to which he had retreated in the face of a flood of new staff.

John Herbst is a career diplomat, unlike most US ambassadors who are party donors. But no one is going to give a million dollars to the Republican Party to be made ambassador to Uzbekistan. John is a deeply intellectual man who is basically shy and is not one for socialising. But he is a true believer whose heart was entirely in the Bush agenda. This must have helped when dealing with Karimov, as for many others the Uzbekistan regime up close is so obnoxious that it makes them choke. John was particularly keen on the fact that Karimov was such a strong supporter of Israel. On the day I presented my credentials, the Israeli Ambassador told me that Karimov had been a good personal friend of Ariel Sharon for over 20 years.

Now John and I started by going over the economic arguments about the IMF again. He has a disconcerting habit of pausing to consider his reply when engaged in thought about the argument, and these pauses can be really long – about 20 seconds. Most of us cover these moments with empty phrases while we think, but he didn't bother. I had got used to this by the time we got onto human rights.

John argued that the human rights situation was improving. He said that the abolition of the office of censor earlier that summer had been a major advance.

'But what are you talking about?' I replied. 'The media is completely censored. There is absolutely no real news at all – it's the most arrant propaganda.'

'Well, Craig, I don't know how extensive your research has been. But we have a major media project and there have been a couple of articles in the regional press that have been critical of the decisions of regional officials. And Ruslan Sharipov has published articles attacking government corruption.'

'That hardly affects the general picture – they sound like exceptions that prove the rule, from the very fact that you can list the only articles that aren't government propaganda. But the human rights situation is desperate. Do you realise how many torture cases there are now documented?'

'If you are referring to the boiling case, I know you're making a big thing of it, and we are very concerned. But it is an isolated incident. I have never heard of a parallel case. And there has been a real advance on torture. In the Ferghana Valley, three policemen have been convicted of the murder of a detainee. That was after a case which I took up personally with Karimov. That is undoubtedly real progress. Previously officials have been completely immune from any fear of retribution. Nothing will do more to change the behaviour of the police and security services.'

'I still think that is a drop in the ocean. HRW and other NGOs reckon there are some 7,000 prisoners of conscience, held for political and religious beliefs. I must say from my own research I am starting to think that is an underestimate.'

'Yes, but most of those are Muslim extremists. You know, Karimov has a genuine problem that you can't ignore. He faced armed incursions by the IMU. These bad guys really exist. They are not imaginary. You know, we are all caught up in the War on Terror. We didn't want to be. Nobody in the USA asked for the Twin Towers to be attacked. But we find ourselves defending our very lifestyle. And Karimov is part of that defence.'[11]

'Yes, but all the evidence is that the vast majority of those in jail aren't terrorists at all. I don't think they are extremists. Even the ones convicted of membership of Hizb-ut-Tehrir mostly aren't really members. Those who are, aren't violent. The evidence is planted. Most of them are just in jail for following their religion. They aren't extremists.'

'You don't think the Taliban were extreme?'

'Yes, I think the Taliban were extreme.'

'Well, think about it. Most of these guys who are locked up, if they were in power, they would impose the same kind of society.

There are at least some social freedoms here – they would go.'

'Look, accepting for a moment that those in jail do want that – and I think that's open to doubt – if that's what they want, they are entitled to their view, as long as they don't turn to violence to try to achieve it. I don't call them extremists.'

'Well, that's where we differ. A fully Islamic society with Sharia law is extremist. Extreme Islam is itself a kind of institutionalised violence. Do you realise how much women would be oppressed if the Islamists got into power? You know, I had six US congressmen visiting here this week. They were given a briefing on human rights by Mikhail Ardzinov of the Independent Human Rights Organisation of Uzbekistan. He told those congressmen, straight out, that most of these so-called prisoners of conscience – not just most, the large majority, he said, the large majority – ought to be in prison. Now here's another step forward, Ardzinov's organisation has been registered and is fully legal.'

'I'm beginning to see why.'

'That's really not fair. Ardzinov has a very brave record over many years.'

'I look at this another way. People are being locked up because they are Muslim. So are other political dissidents, but most prisoners are locked up for being Islamic. There are no fair trials, and there is a lot of torture in the prisons. We are being seen to support this regime, so we are making Muslims hate us. We are provoking terrorism, not fighting it.'

John looked weary, as though he had heard this all before.

'Look,' he said, 'Karimov's got to keep a tight grip on the Muslims. He also wants to drive forward a reform agenda, but he's facing a lot of resistance from within the governing party. And his biggest problem is his own training. Karimov is a Soviet-trained economist. The problem is, he thinks he understands economics, but all he knows is a lot of false precepts. Karimov is the best Uzbek leader we'll get, and he's not personally corrupt.'

The bit about Karimov not being personally corrupt really did throw me. Herbst was understandably keen to put the best possible gloss on the regime, but this bit about Karimov was so far at variance with all received information that it really did make me wonder just where Herbst was getting his information from.[12]

My next call was on Rustam Azimov, the Minister for Economic Affairs. I wanted to meet him before sending off my telegram about what to do at the IMF. He was touted by the Americans as a leading reformer and with his sharp silk suits and American accent he looked like an Italian banker.

He stressed the progress made on devaluation and foreign currency reserves. I pressed him on why there had been almost no progress on privatisation and particularly annoyed him by describing most of the privatisation as false, involving shifting of assets between entities that were all ultimately state owned. He replied with a barrage of statistics that were patently untrue – I wondered how on earth he could trot them out with a straight face, but I suppose it was Soviet training.

He got pretty angry when I questioned why the borders were closed and simply denied that this was the case. I told him I had visited several border crossing points myself, as had other EU embassies, and they were indeed shut. He looked at me levelly.

'You are mistaken,' he said. 'They are not closed. They are controlled.'

He really got angry when I asked him when there would be a move to privatisation in the cotton industry. No country, he declared, would allow the privatisation of its most important industry. I told him that statement was simply wrong and further pointed out that Kazakhstan next door had privatised its cotton industry, resulting in a threefold increase in production very quickly. Azimov became very quiet and intense.

'That is untrue. Any increase is due only to criminals smuggling Uzbek cotton.'

'I don't think that's true. As you know, the cotton is mostly sold through the Liverpool Cotton Exchange. The figures on increasing Kazakh production come from the traders. Anyway, privatisation is the answer to smuggling. Cotton sells for the market price in Kazakhstan, that's why it gets smuggled there. If you had a market price here, it wouldn't be smuggled.'

'Ambassador, this is not Poland. Privatisation here would lead to mass unemployment and social collapse. You know, I am a Director of the European Bank for Reconstruction and Development [EBRD]. I am the longest-serving director. Let me tell you this. Poland only survived privatisation because it received $18 billion of economic assistance from the West. We have received almost nothing.'

It was very much Azimov's style to blind you with statistics and his air of great assurance, but yet again he was talking complete rubbish.

Having run the economic section of the British embassy in Warsaw, I knew this stuff.

'I am sorry, Minister,' I said, 'but you're simply mistaken. Poland didn't receive $1 billion, let alone $18 billion. Besides, I don't think it would have helped. East Germany did receive massive transfers, and Poland didn't. Yet Poland grew quicker than East Germany. Other factors are far more important, like labour costs and deregulation. In fact, I would argue too much subsidy can be harmful.'

Azimov sat back, a satisfied look on his face: 'There is no point in arguing with someone who simply follows the dogma of the economic liberal.'

Shortly afterwards came the first anniversary of the destruction of the World Trade Center in New York. I was invited to a commemoration held by the US embassy in the ballroom of the Intercontinental Hotel in Tashkent. I attended with mixed feelings. Of course I felt unalloyed sorrow and even despair at the heartlessness of this terrorist act. Yet the United States was using this horror to provide a screen for pushing its very material interests in oil and gas. In Uzbekistan, this took the form of giving strong backing to a very unpleasant dictatorship. I had, in just one month, seen how that regime operated close up, in the Khuderbegainov trial and in the case of the dissidents boiled to death. I had also seen Colin Powell, astonishingly, certify Uzbekistan's human rights record to Congress as acceptable and seen the US protect Uzbekistan from justified criticism in the IMF over its continued Soviet and increasingly kleptocratic economic policy.

Security was very heavy, and after a long queue for the metal detectors I entered the ballroom and exchanged a few polite but sombre words with diplomatic colleagues. The ceremony itself was simple – John Herbst read out a text about the atrocity and the evils of terrorism, supported by Uzbek Foreign Minister Komilov. A tape was played of a mobile telephone call from the Twin Towers suddenly cutting off.

For the next few days, I struggled with my conviction that, in supporting Karimov, the US had got its Central Asian policy thoroughly wrong and that we in turn were wrong to follow the US. I knew that as Ambassador it was my duty to inform Jack Straw and Whitehall of my view. But I was also aware that my view would be acutely unpopular, especially with my own immediate line manager, Simon Butt, and with 10 Downing Street. I knew that saying what I wanted to say was likely to damage my career pretty severely. I talked it over with Fiona, who said that I should remember my obligation to supporting my children, but she appreciated that my conscience must come first. She then rather sourly concluded that she did not know why I was consulting her, as I always did what I wanted anyway.

* * *

During this period, I was visited by a young research analyst from the FCO. Back in London, he shared an office with Stuart Horsman, the analyst who dealt specifically with Central Asia. He was visiting Uzbekistan as part of his research into regional security issues in the former Soviet Union, and he was most concerned about the threat of increasing Islamic militarism in Uzbekistan feeding through into international terrorism.

I was relieved to find that this research analyst shared my views on the situation in Uzbekistan. He felt that the Karimov regime had no intention of adopting real reform, was completely beyond the pale on human rights and was creating a tinderbox of resentment and reaction through harsh repression. He was the first to point out to me that the neo-conservatives in the Bush camp, particularly the so-called intellectuals of the religious right, were talking of a United States–Israel–Uzbek axis driving a military wedge into the heart of Islam – thinking picked up by Donald Rumsfeld in his lily-pad policy of air bases surrounding, in effect, the Muslim world.

He told me that many of the research analysts despaired of our blind support for Bush in Central Asia, which had somehow been subsumed into the US notion of the 'Wider Middle East'. The policy of backing nasty dictators was bound to rebound on us – it always does – but they just couldn't see it.

I had always found our research analysts to be very bright, with a strong reputation in the academic world and a lot of personal integrity. It was therefore beyond me how they had signed up, as they must have, to the claims in the soon-to-be-published dossier on Iraqi Weapons of Mass Destruction (WMD). I asked my visitor whether there was knockdown evidence I was unaware of. He said he reckoned that the claims were indeed the rubbish it seemed. There were no Iraqi WMD. History has proven him right.

* * *

On 16 September, I locked myself in my office and spent the first half of the morning writing a long telegram on the IMF and Uzbek economic policy, specifically stating that we should oppose, within the IMF and other international financial institutions, attempts by the United States to get an easy ride for Uzbekistan, particularly as they were based on false claims about progress in economic reform.

I pointed out that in 20 years in power, 11 of those in charge of an independent country, Karimov had overseen extraordinarily little economic liberalisation and there was no reason to believe that his views had now changed. During my time in Uzbekistan thus far, I had only met two people who seemed to believe that he actually intended to introduce genuine market reforms: the US Ambassador and the MFA press spokesman. I had experience of working on economic affairs in post-communist transition countries and developing countries, and it was clear to me that Uzbekistan was not in transition and showed no signs of developing. I was therefore unable to see how the IMF could possibly approve this so-called reform programme.

During my rounds of courtesy calls to my diplomatic colleagues, I had been told separately by the World Bank and EBRD representatives, and individually by the French, German, Italian, Slovak, Czech, Polish, Indian, Pakistani and Russian ambassadors that, post-9/11, a political deal had been reached in Washington that in return for American use of Uzbek air facilities the Uzbek economic programme would be given IMF approval.

But if such approval were to be given when unmerited, this would affect real lives – especially the poor of Uzbekistan. There were African levels of poverty in this terribly unequal and appallingly governed society, and the situation would continue to deteriorate unless there was real economic reform. That in turn would breed more Islamic fundamentalism. I closed by saying: 'You do not encourage real reform by applauding fake reform. The poor of Uzbekistan should not become more victims of September 11.'[13]

I then drank a cup of coffee, went to the loo, stared out of the window and sucked on my pen before starting my follow-up telegram. Once I began, it came fluently, and my fingers on the keyboard could not keep up with my thoughts. It contained in a few paragraphs the concentrated essence of a month's experience in Tashkent, a month's thinking and soul-searching.

This telegram was my declaration of dissent from our current policy. I argued that the US was playing down the human rights situation in Uzbekistan and that this was a dangerous policy: increasing repression combined with poverty would promote Islamic terrorism. Support for the Karimov regime was therefore counter-productive.

To support my argument, I quoted *The Economist* of 7 September 2003, which stated that: 'Uzbekistan, in particular, has jailed many thousands of moderate Islamists, an excellent way of converting their families and friends to extremism.' I stated that there were between 7,000 and 10,000 political and religious prisoners, and that terrible torture occurred frequently. I mentioned specific cases of female dissidents incarcerated in lunatic asylums for demonstrating for human rights, pointed out that there were no legal opposition parties, and argued that 11 September was being used as an excuse to attack democratic opponents under the guise of counter-terrorism.

Taking a deep breath, I directly criticised the US State Department for certifying Uzbekistan's human rights record, a precondition for the flow of large amounts of US aid. The United States was accepting sham reforms: for example, the claims that censorship had been abolished when the media was still totally servile to the regime. I jibed at the US position: 'State Department call this self-censorship: I am not sure that is a fair way to describe an unwillingness to experience the brutal methods of the security services.' I pointed to strict Internet controls and suggested that Uzbekistan remained a totalitarian state.

I countered US claims of improved accountability for the Uzbek security services, citing the Uzbek response to the Avazov boiling case – the authorities had suggested that the burns were caused by a fight over a tea kettle. To really hammer my point home, I said that support for a ruthless dictator like Karimov undermined the Bush–Blair noble rhetoric: 'If Karimov is on "our" side, then this war cannot be simply between the forces of good and evil. It must be about more complex things, like securing the long-term US military presence in Uzbekistan.'

I even went so far as to point out that 11 September had also been the anniversary of the overthrow and murder of the democratically elected President Allende of Chile and suggested we should have moved on from the disastrous policy of US-backed dictatorships.

'Above all,' I concluded, 'We need to care about the 22 million Uzbek people, suffering from poverty and lack of freedom. They are not just pawns in the new Great Game.'[14]

It is important to understand the background to this telegram. We had just fought a war in neighbouring Afghanistan and were gearing up towards another in Iraq. Tony Blair had staked all on standing 'shoulder to shoulder' with George W. Bush, and the War on Terror and the righteousness of the US cause were unquestionable. I was going way out on a limb.

After I had sent it, I walked through to Chris Hirst's office. Chris was squatting on the floor, going through some documents in a cupboard. I handed him the telegram, saying he might like to look at it. He looked dubious, but his interest grew as he read, and he became increasingly absorbed. After he finished, he handed it back, shaking his head.

'Well, what do you think?' I asked.

'Pretty long for a resignation letter,' he said.

It was not many days before the attack from my line management came, in the form of a letter from Simon Butt. He was concerned, he wrote, that I was 'over-focused on human rights' to the detriment of the balance of UK interests in Uzbekistan. He was also most concerned that I was discussing human rights cases in open email correspondence and making comments about the Uzbek government, in emails and on open phone lines, which were likely to be intercepted by the Uzbek security services and thus damage the UK–Uzbek relationship. My performance was causing concern and would be closely monitored.

CHAPTER 5

The Ferghana Valley

I was determined to set an early example to the staff of getting around the country and wanted to travel to the Ferghana Valley. This high valley, a fertile flood plain where tributaries from the great mountains combine to form the Syr Darya and Amu Darya rivers, nestles in the foothills of the Himalayas, beneath the High Pamirs and the Tien Shan, the Heavenly Mountains. It was considered a likely ethnic and religious flashpoint.

The Ferghana Valley is very heavily populated, home to over ten million people. The five countries of Central Asia together have a land area substantially greater than all of Western Europe. Twenty-five per cent of the entire population of this vast region live in the Ferghana Valley, which has a land area similar to Belgium.

It is, in a very real sense, the heart of Central Asia. It ought to be the economic powerhouse of the region. To explain why it is not, I have to explain something about the crazy geography of Central Asia.

The Ferghana Valley is split between Kirghizstan, Tajikistan and Uzbekistan. The borders of these three countries, and not just in the Ferghana Valley, intertwine and convolute as though they were a jigsaw cut by a one-armed alcoholic. In the Ferghana Valley, there are seven enclaves of Uzbekistan entirely cut off by surrounding countries.

This is the difficult bit to grasp: the borders are deliberately nonsensical and specifically designed not to create viable economic units, and in particular not to have any political, cultural or ethnic coherence. The names Kirghizstan, Tajikistan and Uzbekistan might give the impression that they are the ethnic home of the Kirghiz, Tajiks and Uzbeks. In fact, nothing could be further from the truth. They are quite deliberately not that. For example, the major Uzbek town of Osh, in the Ferghana Valley, is over the border in Kirghizstan. The centres of the great Tajik culture, Samarkand and Bokhara, are not in Tajikistan but in Uzbekistan, even though 90 per cent of the populations of those cities remain Tajik-speaking – although they are now subject to drastic Uzbek government attempts to choke the language out.

The Soviet Union was in theory just that – a Union of Soviet Socialist Republics. Kirghizstan, Uzbekistan and Tajikistan were three of them. But whatever the theory, Stalin had no intention of allowing the republics to become viable entities or potential powerbases for rivals. So they were deliberately messed up with boundaries that cut across natural economic units like the Ferghana Valley and cut ethnic and cultural links.

* * *

After two weeks in Tashkent, we had said goodbye to Jamie, who had returned to boarding school in the UK. This was always a wrench. I was worried about Emily and very much hoped that the Tashkent International School – largely US government funded – would prove adequate for her age group.

Fiona was keen to accompany me on trips and see as much of the country as possible, but at this stage we couldn't leave Emily behind. We decided that I would undertake a five-day tour of the Ferghana Valley, with Fiona and Emily accompanying me for the first two days and then returning for Emily to start school.

I asked Chris to organise the visit. I told him I wanted to call on the local authorities and to visit major companies, with a special emphasis on businesses in which there was a British interest, and also projects financed by the EBRD. I also wanted to visit any British or EU aid projects and call on consular nationals who fell under my protection. On top of this, I wanted to visit universities and call on opposition or human rights activists.

This was a pretty tall order for Chris to get organised at a fortnight's notice. The logistics of travel in Central Asia are complicated and the authorities obstructive. I was interested to see how he performed. In fact, he pulled it all together brilliantly.

I was going to need an interpreter. My Russian was quite good, but my understanding of Uzbek, Tajik or any of the other languages spoken in Uzbekistan was virtually nil. As I was going to be holding meetings outside governmental circles, I would need someone with a good range of language skills.

Normally, an embassy would have its own in-house interpretation capacity. The information assistant would be the usual person called in. But the empty desk in Chris's office was where the information assistant should have been. When I asked Karen, it turned out that this position had been vacant for months and there was no recruitment process in progress.

There is always huge downward pressure on FCO budgets. I arrived under instruction to cut the local budget cost by 5 per cent and, as 80 per cent of local budget went in staff salaries, that was tough. On top of which, you don't have freedom to manage. Rates of local pay are set in London as a result of a convoluted comparison with detailed analogues for each job. The system is administered at great cost by London-based civil servants. So you are told by London what you have to pay and also how many people you must employ and at what grade – your 'approved establishment'.

The embassy in Tashkent was, in every respect, under-staffed and under-resourced. At the collapse of the Former Soviet Union, we made a policy decision to set up in the new republics but never made a fundamental rethink of resources. So these embassies just got by on a shoestring.[15]

What bothered me now was that, within a petty resource allocation, we hadn't filled a key position for supporting our political and PR work. It wasn't only interpreting – Chris should have had his assistant organising my tour now, while he got on with other things, and so I pressed Karen to get on and recruit.

Karen told me that Vakhida, Colonel Nick Ridout's assistant, had been Chris's last assistant and had moved to the defence section. Muttering under my breath about the bloody Ministry of Defence poaching our staff, I went to ask Nick if I could borrow Vakhida for a few days. I found Nick outside in the embassy garden, puffing away on his pipe, panama on head, wearing red cavalry trousers and a long jacket that looked borrowed from Wild Bill Hickock. He readily agreed that she could join me for the start of my tour, but he needed her back to interpret at meetings and she would have to return with Fiona and Emily. We would therefore have to find another interpreter for my last few days in the valley.

While it is not difficult to find Russian–English interpreters in Uzbekistan, getting someone to interpret between English and Uzbek, Kazakh or Tajik is much harder. This is because the educated elite can't speak the native languages and those who do will very rarely have had the chance to learn English, certainly not up to good interpretation standard.

As we set off for the Ferghana Valley, it was a bit of a squash in the Land-Rover. Mansur was driving rather than Valeri, who spoke only Russian. Fiona, Emily and I were on the back seat, with Vakhida in front with Mansur. Vakhida was a very pretty girl with short, layered dark hair and a dark complexion. She always dressed smartly in a high-buttoned blouse and skirt, with sensible shoes. She came from Karakalpakistan.

We headed out of Tashkent and into the countryside on good metalled roads. The landscape was dry and dusty, much of it an angry red. We drove through the dilapidated iron-making town of Angren, and after a couple of hours we were heading up the escarpment on a sharp, winding mountain road formed from concrete slabs. White water rushed by in the valley floor below, while the mountains were jagged, inhospitable and largely uninhabited. It had been 40 degrees centigrade in Tashkent and wasn't cool here, but the peaks were still snow capped above us. Our ears popped as the road wound up and up. Finally, it dived into low tunnels that had been smashed through the mountain, shortcutting another 800 feet of elevation on a twisting climb over the original pass.

At the end of the Soviet Union, when the borders of Uzbekistan, Kirghizstan and Tajikistan changed from administrative internal borders to international borders, the main road from Tashkent to the Valley repeatedly crossed the Kirghiz border. That ancient road ran through Khojand and was taken by Alexander the Great after his two-year sojourn in Samarkand, where he married Roxanne. It was on this ancient road that he decided finally to stop his incredible drive east and turned south over the great mountains of the Hindu Kush to India. As he turned, he founded in the neck of the Ferghana Valley the city that marked the end of his empire – Alexandria Eschate, Alexandria the Farthermost.

Nowadays, the ancient main route Alexander had trod led through

Kirghizstan, so the Uzbek government had upgraded an alternative minor route within Uzbekistan and cut the tunnels at the top.[16]

Entering the valley, the first thing that strikes you is the sheer weight of military and police presence. We had passed a dozen or more police barriers on our way from Tashkent to the valley, but we had been waved straight through most of them. Here, we were held up at both the entrance and the exit of the tunnel while our passports and the car documents were inspected. Then in the valley itself, the number of checkpoints was much greater, including the entrance to and exit from all the towns and villages.

The soil was notably darker here, the mountain air fresher and, while it was still warm, the temperature a few degrees lower. What first strikes you, travelling along the main roads into the valley, is the neatness. The villages consist of trim, single-storey, whitewashed cottages fronting onto the street. The roads are lined with flowerbeds, glowing yellow and red in the summer sun. The fields are filled with endless rows of dark green shrubs. The valley presents a façade of rural contentment.

We stopped in the city of Kokhand, which in the nineteenth century was the seat of a Khanate ruling over the valley, its power spreading down onto the Uzbek plain. We were met here by local government representatives, headed by the town *Hokkim*, or Mayor, and we looked over the ruins of the Khan's palace, an ancient cemetery and the surviving madrassah, all of which were very fine.

Afterwards, the local authority representatives took me for my first formal Uzbek meal. I wasn't fully prepared for the sheer volume of food. The table was loaded with grapes, pomegranates, walnuts, almonds, raisins, sultanas, dried apricots, mulberries and plates of cold meat. These were followed by bowls of soup containing thick hunks of lamb on the bone, then grilled liver, then lamb kebabs. These alternated lumps of meat with great gobbets of fat, crisped on the outside but gushing liquid fat as you bit into them. Finally there was plov, fragrant and wonderful. Our hosts had started the meal by breaking the roundels of *non* bread and handing it round. This little ceremony was always performed at mealtimes, with the host or father of the family breaking the bread. I realised that when Christ did it, he was not initiating but following a tradition.[17]

I was becoming used to the very guarded way that everyone spoke in Uzbekistan. One of the few times the conversation had sparked into life was when we discussed football. The Hokkim said the best teams in Uzbekistan were all in the Ferghana Valley. I commented that there must be great rivalry between the fans. His face lit up, and in a lively voice he started on an anecdote, 'Oh yes, I remember when . . .' Then he recollected himself, the smile left his face, and he said in a dull tone, 'I remember that the President says that sport is an important factor in building a healthy nation and uniting our youth.'

We drove on to Ferghana city itself, police cars in front and behind, sirens blaring as we approached any crossroads. There were policemen everywhere, and they all saluted as we passed. Night had fallen by the time we pulled into the car park of the Zigurat Hotel. A gaggle of men in black suits were waiting to greet us. While they sorted out the rooms with Vakhida, we were ushered through to a feast set like the last one. Had I been on my own, I would have politely sat through it, but as things were I explained that we had just been royally entertained in Kokhand. At our hosts' insistence, we sat for a little soup, after which we were obliged to make a show of eating plov, but we managed to keep it down to 20 minutes.

This time, our hosts did not sit with us, but a couple of dark-suited men stood watching us eat. At one stage I got up to go to the loo and was astonished when one of them followed me inside. He stood by the washbasins and then followed me out again.

After this dinner, we took a rickety lift to our room on the fourth floor. Mansur had already put our luggage in, but our hearts fell when we saw the interior. It looked dirty, decorated in brown and a grey that was meant to be white. A dark patch spread from the ceiling to the wall, damp to the touch. The bedclothes felt cold and moist. But it had been a tiring day, and we just climbed into the bed and pulled the covers over all three of us. I told Fiona about the man following me into the loo. She giggled, got out of bed, opened the door a crack and peeked out. She came back and reported that two men in black suits were standing at one end of the corridor and one at the other end.

'Are we being protected, or watched?' she asked.

'Both,' I replied.

The next morning, the room looked even grottier, and Emily's feet were picking up dirt from the carpet. There was no hot water and only a trickle of cold. We went downstairs for a breakfast of tea and cold pancakes stuffed with cottage cheese. The same men in black were still around, looking like they had been up all night. I had a brief conversation with the receptionist. He spoke excellent English with a slight Liverpool accent, and, much to my surprise, he said he had studied there.

Vakhida had come to our room in the morning and explained apologetically that the accommodation was provided by the *Hokkimyat*. She would see what could be done about improving it.

We set out for our first meeting of the day, at a large square that was also the site of a war memorial. Here, the regional Hokkim came to meet us. There were television cameras and a row of schoolgirls in bright silk costumes. They presented me with bread and salt. As primed, I broke the bread, sprinkled on salt, handed a piece to the Hokkim and then ate myself. This was greeted with much enthusiasm and backslapping.

The Hokkim left us in the charge of one of his deputies for the day, and we went first to a silk factory in the neighbouring town of Margilan. Ferghana is a modern industrial town, of which the oldest parts are the Russian cantonment. There is some splendid colonial architecture, with Russian houses from the end of the nineteenth century, from the ornate governor's mansion down through distinguished officers' residences to rows of barracks. There are also public buildings, including the exquisite pink baroque theatre and assembly rooms, now an Uzbek army officers' mess. The parquet flooring inside these buildings is fabulous. I was struck by how universal colonial architecture is. You could be in Simla or Singapore.

Margilan and Ferghana have grown into one large conurbation, but Margilan was an ancient Uzbek city. It is the centre of the silk industry, and 25,000 workers were employed in the textile mills in the early 1990s. The inefficiency of the huge state-run factories, combined with Karimov's anti-trade measures, had reduced output and staff, but the silk industry remained the mainstay of the town.

We were not visiting one of the main mills but a small private venture that had received assistance from the British Council. The owner greeted us effusively at the gate and proudly showed us his factory. He had started with hand spinning and looming but had now acquired two power looms discarded by one of the state mills. We were too late in the season to see the worms feeding on mulberry leaves, but we saw rows of women seated on low stools, boiling and unravelling cocoons and spinning the threads.

The power looms were not yet working, but a large hall housed several dozen hand looms, each producing a strip of cloth about a metre and a half wide. The complex patterns required a great deal of tying and knotting. Sunlight streamed through, hitting the bright strands of silk. The brilliant colours were the product of artificial dyes, but we visited a hut where a happy dyer, his face streaked with purple, sat amid crucibles and bubbling pots, peering into a small kiln. He was experimenting with producing natural dyes from local plants and minerals, a skill that had been lost in the Soviet period.

Most effort went into producing cloth in Uzbekistan's famous Atlas design. That is, famous within Uzbekistan – the design doesn't travel well. It consists of very bright clashes of many colours arranged in huge jags across the cloth. This is hard either to export or to sell to tourists, and the British Council had paid for designers to work with the factory to produce examples that had more chance in a Western market. The owner proudly showed me some of these designs – they were single pastel colours with an edging in a complementary shade. Given the very high quality of the silk and the prices – $5 a square metre – the factory was now having some success.

They were opening a new carpet-making facility and this was what the new natural dyes were to be used for.[18] In the carpet shed, young girls sat in pairs on the floor in front of looms, knotting very intricate patterns. One worked the left of the carpet, one the right. Consulting a cardboard pattern, they threaded silk through a fine cotton mesh and knotted each thread in place before deftly trimming it off with a sharp knife. I looked at the back of the frame, amazed by the intricacy of the work in that half light.

'One hundred and twenty-one knots per centimetre,' explained the proud owner.

'How long does it take to make a carpet?'

'A small carpet, one metre fifty centimetres in length, will take two girls four months. We can run two shifts and do it in two months.'

'Aren't they a bit young to be working like this?'

'Ah no, they are at least 16. They have to have small fingers for the work.'

We next drove out to the town of Rishton, where fine ceramics have been produced for at least 600 years. The traditional floral patterns in green and blue are striking examples of Islamic art. The designs are much finer and more intricate than Iranian or Turkish pottery, with minute hand-painted detail arranged into wonderful swirls of geometric patterning. We bought a great deal.

I had asked to visit one of the Uzbek enclaves within Kirghizstan, and we set off for Shakhimardan, one police car behind and two in front. The Ferghana Valley is so large that the great mountains around the rim are mostly just a distant presence. It was a long drive south before we started to climb into them. The scenery was idyllic and Alpine. Wooden houses with steep pitched roofs spoke the universal language of mountain architecture. Shepherds started appearing on horseback. They were Mongol-looking men with bright red and yellow saddlecloths, wearing white felt hats with black trim.

We carried on up the road until it became a track, then petered out to a footpath. It was an idyllic spot, where the valley narrowed and the tumbling stream ran in a narrow gorge between huge boulders it had brought down in spate. A crazy-looking cable car with bright plastic four-man carriages ran up the centre, its cables sagging sadly between rusting pylons. A mossy track meandered up the valley floor beneath it.

We had stopped by a pretty white house. On inspection, it was large and ambitious, but it was situated down a gully from the track, next to the rushing river. On one side was the gorge wall, and two other sides were surrounded by thick trees. The house was therefore dark and dank. It was the Hokkim's residence in Shakhimardan but evidently had not been used for some time and was sparsely furnished. Outside, there was a narrow terrace alongside the river, where trees had forced their way up through the stones and overhung the torrent with their shading branches. Here, a couple of large iron beds had been installed.

Most of inhabited Uzbekistan comprises a series of oases in the desert, and the Uzbeks love running water. The country is full of fountains and artificial pools, many of them very ancient and endowed with mystic qualities. Wherever there is running water, the Uzbeks place their huge beds, up to four metres square. In the summer, they sleep outside in them, the river cooling the air and offering respite from the fierce heat. In the daytime, they love to lounge on them, sipping green tea with lemon or mint. This we now did. Our host picked perfect pears, ripe yet firm and full of intense taste. He cut off slices with his penknife and handed them to us.

Shakhimardan means 'king of men' and we visited the tomb of Ali, after whom it is named. He was the son-in-law of Mohammed, had grown up with him as a kind of younger stepbrother, and had been his first adherent. He had stood by Mohammed in his battles, and it was the repeated passing over of Ali, when the first Caliphs were selected (he became the fourth), that led to the growth of the Shiah and their split with the Sunni. This split still rends Islam today. Ali had been the only male allowed to move freely in Mohammed's household, and the only person to assist Mohammed in removing the vast array of idols from the Kaaba.

To both Sunni and Shiah, Ali is a major figure, and his tomb is as significant as the tomb of St Peter would be to Christians. Unfortunately, like Christian relics in medieval Europe, Ali's tombs multiplied, and there are seven of them, three in Uzbekistan alone (the other two are at Khiva and Nurata). But Shakhimardan became a major religious centre for Central and South Asia. Pilgrims travelled for thousands of miles to pray here.

The mausoleum has been repaired with bright new brickwork, and the simple tomb inside neatly re-cemented and whitewashed. One toothless old lady was praying at the entrance, and ragged strips of cloth fluttered from trees outside, tied there by devotees. A long flight of brick steps, also new, led down into the valley.

A major religious shrine was not what the Soviets wanted. They co-opted the site for their own saint, Khakimzade Niyazi, known as Khamza. A poet and playwright, he had pioneered socially conscious Uzbek literature before the revolution and had become chief Bolshevik propagandist in Central Asia thereafter, leading the campaign to free Uzbek women from their Muslim veils (whether they wanted to be freed or not). He became a Soviet martyr and hero when he was killed in 1929.[19]

Khamza's resting place and museum are just above the tomb of Ali on the hill, dominating it and providing an alternative narrative to the Muslim one. The current government of Uzbekistan resolved the dilemma between these narratives by closing the enclave. Other than escorted diplomatic visitors and the few residents, no one can now enter the enclave of Shakhimardan lest the past resonate too loud. Standing on the hill, looking down from the tomb, I asked the Deputy Hokkim why the valley was closed off.

'It's for safety reasons,' he said. 'When the river is strong, water comes very quickly.'

Peering down into the valley, there was some evidence of erosion and a wooden chalet by the river bank had been damaged. But nothing more than you would expect from any mountain river in spate.

'Is that all?' I asked.

'Perhaps we should go back,' he said. I was beginning to realise that in Uzbekistan truth was a precious commodity, to be mined with difficulty.

We arrived back at the Zigurat Hotel to find the Hokkim himself waiting for us on the steps.

'I understand that the accommodation here was not suitable,' he said. 'Pack and we will take you somewhere better.'

Much relieved, we quickly packed and then all set off again. With our car and escorts now merged with those of the Hokkim, it was quite a long convoy. All the sirens wailed continuously to underline our new prestige. Policemen held up the traffic at all the junctions, and judging by the queues, they had been doing so for some time. A short distance outside the city, we drove through some wrought-iron gates and pulled up at a substantial mansion. White-jacketed staff emerged and carried our bags inside. High ceilings, ornate plasterwork and gilding, imitation Louis XIV furniture, crystal chandeliers and large oriental carpets: this was the President's residence in Ferghana, and very nice it was too. Mansur was in the drivers' quarters, but Emily and Vakhida each had their own state room, complete with chandeliers, mirrored walls and jacuzzis with controls like the flight deck of the starship *Enterprise*. Fiona and I had the presidential suite, which you could get lost in.

The next morning, gilded furniture was taken out onto the sweeping lawn, where white-gloved attendants served us pancakes, fruit and yoghurt. I kissed Fiona and Emily goodbye. Mansur then drove them to the airport to fly back to Tashkent, while I went in the official car with the Deputy Hokkim for a further meeting with the Hokkim. Vakhida would follow them on a later flight.

We were now entering the business end of the programme and discussed possibilities for British investment in Ferghana, which I had to say were not bright unless the Uzbek government instituted substantial currency and trade liberalisation and economic deregulation. The Hokkim assured me all these were coming. He noted that my programme said I would be calling on a local human rights activist and cautioned me not to believe stories from such an unreliable source. For my own safety, he suggested, I should allow the police to accompany me to the meeting. I expressed thanks for his concern but declined the offer.

The Hokkim smiled and did not press the point: he had fulfilled his duty by this ritual sparring. He added that he thought my programme was too full. As my host, he would suggest that I cut out the visit to the university, where protocol would detain me a long time. I said that I was keen to go, as the British Council had given support to English language teaching there. I would see how the programme had panned out.

We visited a shoe factory that wanted investment; this used local leather at least in part and was quite an impressive operation. It had been privatised in 1995 and had reduced its labour force from 4,300 to 300, while doubling production. We next toured a brewery, which had received a loan from the EBRD for a new bottling line. The loan had been disbursed, but the new plant not yet arrived. At the time, I did not find this particularly suspicious. The beer, named Ferghana, was really awful – they used a mixture of local wheat and imported malt but didn't add hops. Nor did they have a master brewer. There was a chief scientist, and the beer at various stages of production was subject to scientific analysis, but the concept of taste did not seem to be employed at all.[20]

The human rights activist was named Abdusalom Ergashev. Mansur had rejoined me with our car, and he dropped me at the door, the rest of the convoy waiting politely at the top of the street. Mr Ergashev was a bearded man with a grave manner, and he looked Russian rather than oriental. His beard was worthy of comment because they are very seldom seen in Uzbekistan, being regarded as a sign of Islamic activity and therefore potential political dissent. A beard alone could get you into an Uzbek torture cell, where you could be forced to sign up to a confession of membership of a terrorist group.

Ergashev was plainly suspicious of me. He had himself spent several years in jail after being, he said, falsely accused of charges of sexual assault. I was later to learn that the Uzbek government routinely concocts such sexual charges to silence and discredit opponents, but this revelation made me at first a little wary of him and our conversation was guarded for a while. But I found him considered, organised and impressive, while he also warmed to me. He told me stories of torture and disappearance, and of the more mundane apparatus of repression. In particular, in an economy and society dominated by the state, dissidents and all their relatives would lose their jobs.

I asked Ergashev how many people from Ferghana were being held as political or religious prisoners. He replied that there were about 370 from Ferghana city itself. He had documented most of these cases. The large majority were religious Muslims – about 30 were non-religious political dissidents. Most were convicted under Article 159 of the criminal code – conspiring to overthrow the government or constitution of Uzbekistan. Many had also been convicted of firearms or narcotic offences and of membership of Hizb-ut-Tehrir.[21]

I asked if we could do anything to help with his work. He said he would appreciate a new personal computer or help with fixing his old one. I promised to assist.

* * *

I should explain something of Hizb-ut-Tehrir, the Party of Islamic Liberation. This movement started among the Palestinian diaspora in North Africa but was to find its greatest popularity in Central Asia. The central tenet of HuT is that a united Caliphate should be established to rule over all Muslim lands, as in the early days of Islam. In short, they wish to establish a divinely guided theocracy. How they aim to achieve this is unclear. They are against violence but also against democracy and participation in politics. They seek to obtain their objective by prayer, example and religious proselytising. In Uzbekistan, they have several thousand adherents.

There is a state-authorised Islamic organisation in Uzbekistan that uses about a fifth of the traditional mosques for Friday prayer, at which the mullahs read out messages dictated by the government. The remainder have been closed. Observing the ritual of prayer five times per day is discouraged by the government mosques, as is fasting at Ramadan.

Unsurprisingly, the state religion does not fulfil the spiritual needs of the pious, and there are thousands of underground mosques, normally just a room in somebody's house where a few meet to worship. Possession in private homes of religious literature, including the Koran, is likely to lead to arrest and torture, as is observing regular prayer.

After Uzbek independence, Saudi money paid for a resurgence in religious teaching, but this was suppressed from 1997 and put down with great thoroughness after the bombs in Tashkent in 1999. One result of driving the Islamic movement underground was that many of the teachers were not especially educated. In this milieu, Hizb-ut-Tehrir started to gain supporters. It was particularly attractive because, in an atmosphere where there is no democratic opposition, no free media and no dissent allowed, HuT might be the only anti-Karimov voice heard, especially in rural areas. As poverty and desperation increased, given a choice limited to Hizb-ut-Tehrir and Karimov, the religious group started to look attractive.

So, the idea of Hizb-ut-Tehrir spread through the Uzbek countryside like a drumbeat of opposition. Many of those who call themselves adherents have no contact with the central leadership, largely London-based, or with anyone who does. HuT did not evolve as an organised cell structure in Uzbekistan – it is more an idea than an organisation. In consequence, local aberrations arose. For example, many HuT adherents in Uzbekistan believe they should have four wives and may smoke tobacco.

Despite all this, HuT has produced a number of followers in Uzbekistan of genuine belief and courage. Avazov and his companion, members of HuT, were boiled to death for refusing to recant these beliefs. My best estimate is that about 1,000 of Karimov's prisoners genuinely consider themselves adherents of HuT, although over 4,000 have been convicted of membership. HuT supporters in Uzbekistan perhaps number 8,000, although the large majority of these have no practical contact with the organisation. But they assume a much wider importance because not only HuT themselves but also, paradoxically, the Karimov regime, work to exaggerate their role. Karimov needs a radical Islamic enemy he can point to in order to justify continued repression and to frighten people with the bogeyman of a Taliban-style government. HuT fills this need and therefore HuT leaflets are routinely planted on political dissidents of all persuasions.

It is not only Muslims who are persecuted in Uzbekistan – any kind of religious enthusiasm is frowned upon. Baptists and Jehovah's Witnesses, for example, are singled out for persecution. Chris and I were to come across a case of a Jehovah's Witness convicted of possession of a store of banned literature. The police listed this literature, chiefly copies of *The Watchtower* and *Awake!* But in the middle of the list appeared several Hizb-ut-Tehrir leaflets, which the police had routinely planted on the 'extremist' without realising the contradiction.

* * *

After leaving Ergashev, I said goodbye to Vakhida, who left in a police car for the airport. I would be without an interpreter for the rest of the day but would be joined by a professional one in the morning in Namangan. I judged we still had plenty of time to visit the university and told Mansur so. He was standing smoking and chatting with the escorting policemen. They looked dubious and called the Deputy Hokkim, who had repaired to a nearby *chaikhana* (or tea room) while I was with Ergashev.

'Please, Mr Ambassador,' he said, 'it is late, and it is dangerous to drive to Namangan after dark.'

'It's not that late. An hour at the university and we can be away by five.'

'But I believe we are not expected now at the university.'

My hackles were beginning to rise.

'Well, think what a pleasant surprise it will be for them.'

The Deputy gave a wan smile, and got back into his Nissan Maxima, which had dark pleated curtains over the windows. I climbed into the back of my Discovery; it seemed strangely empty now with only Mansur and me in it. The police cars started off and we followed. After about 20 minutes, we were heading out of town.

'Mansur, where are we going?' I asked.

'This is the road to Namangan, Ambassador.'

'Is the university this way?'

'No, Ambassador.'

'Do you know where the university is?'

'Yes, I think so.' I had explained to the embassy drivers that, within reason, they should always reconnoitre the day's calls in the early morning or the evening before.

'Then stop.'

'Sorry, Ambassador?'

'STOP! We're going to the university.'

Obviously impressed by the drama of the moment, Mansur slammed on the brakes and we slewed to a halt. The lead police car and the Hokkim's Maxima carried on ahead of us, turning round a corner. The police car behind had to brake quickly, and the doors opened as the police got out to see what the problem was. Mansur, having halted, was turned round looking quizzically at me.

'The university, Mansur. Drive to the university.'

'OK, sir.'

It was a wide road, and Mansur spun the Discovery round. We sped off, leaving the puzzled policemen standing in the street staring at us. Mansur had worked out we were giving the escort the slip and drove like crazy through the streets of Ferghana. The escort caught up with us again just as we pulled up in front of the university. I waited for the Deputy Hokkim on the steps. He simply gave me a slight shake of the head. I wanted to go straight to the English department, but he insisted that we should first call on the Rector. I was happy to concede that one.

The university building was a large brick edifice that would not have looked out of place in any British provincial university. The Rector was sour faced and unwelcoming, and we endured 15 minutes of stilted conversation over tea. We then walked down to the English centre, our footsteps echoing off the vaulted ceilings. The most striking thing about the university was that it was so devoid of life – there seemed to be virtually no one around.

In the English language centre, I met two charming old ladies who taught there. They showed me with great pride the books they had been given by the British Council and explained their cataloguing system. The only thing that worried me was that the books all appeared to be neatly on the shelves as opposed to being used by students. I asked them where everybody was, which brought a moment's silence and no real answer.

The authorities had not wanted me to visit the university because of its resemblance to the *Marie Celeste*. I was later to discover the answer to the question, where has everyone gone? They were all in the fields picking cotton.

Even the massive labour forces held on the state farms are insufficient when it comes to harvest time, so more forced labour is drafted in. Staff and students are brought in from colleges and universities, which are effectively closed for the entire autumn term. An able-bodied university or college student will expect to spend three months in the cotton fields. Older schoolchildren will do the same, and even children as young as eight might expect to spend two or three weeks in the fields. Civil servants and factory workers can also be drafted as the size of the harvest and weather conditions dictate.

Conditions can be appalling. The workers sleep in the fields, or in rough barracks. Sanitation is poor, food consists of a bare gruel and water is taken straight from irrigation canals. The harvest regularly lasts through into October or early November, when temperatures can drop below freezing. Each farm and each region has its quota to produce in the five-year economic plan, and managers and hokkims were under extreme pressure to fulfil their quota.

Those drafted in for the harvest are not paid, but they are, for the most part, very successfully brainwashed by constant propaganda on television and radio, in newspapers and on banners and posters about harvesting the nation's 'white gold'. It is chilling to hear a bedraggled ten year old in a field talking about the patriotic duty to pick cotton to fund the nation's independence.

We now left the deserted university and headed to Namangan. Our earlier escape had rather deflated the police escort, and they didn't use their sirens so much – or perhaps they decided I didn't deserve it. After about a 30-minute drive on a good dual carriageway, at a point in the middle of nowhere, we stopped for our Ferghana escort to hand us over to our Namangan escort. I shook hands with the Deputy Hokkim and thanked him. He surprised me by asking if I could send him a copy of *Mission to Tashkent* by Colonel Bailey.

Lt Col Frederick Bailey had journeyed to Tashkent with two companions in 1918 to make contact with the soviet newly installed there and with the numerous counter-revolutionary forces that remained active throughout Central Asia until 1922. His main interest was to keep an eye on any potential threat to British India that might be brewing, from the Bolsheviks, from Islamic *badmashis* or from the large numbers of Austro-Hungarian prisoners kept in Tashkent by the Tsarists and released by the Bolsheviks. He arranged for the provision of British subsidies to some of the anti-Bolshevik forces.

This was a last throw of the nineteenth-century Great Game rather than an early move in the Cold War. Bailey was undoubtedly very brave but achieved nothing. He broke a leg and spent 18 months in hiding, much of it holed up in a beekeeper's hut in the hills. He also adopted a series of Monty Pythonesque disguises.

Bailey's mission had a firm place in Soviet demonology as an example of Western perfidy, and schoolchildren were taught about him throughout the Soviet Union, although obviously it meant more to those in Uzbekistan. His book, *Mission to Tashkent,* is a ripping yarn but leaves out much of what he was doing for reasons of official secrecy. His adventure therefore comes over as even more fruitless than it actually was. I was not surprised that the Deputy Hokkim knew of Bailey – he remains a bogeyman figure – but I was surprised he knew of the book. When I returned to Tashkent, I sent him a copy.

CHAPTER 6

'A True British Gentleman'

The Ferghana police cars were white with sky blue and light green stripes, the Uzbek national colours. The new ones from Namangan were light blue with a green stripe but equally keen on using their sirens and flashing blue lights. We swooped along the road and into the city of Namangan.

It was early evening as we passed through a very quiet town centre, with all the shops shuttered. Climbing a hill, we passed through gates between fortified guardhouses and entered a large compound. The drive wound through a large equestrian complex, where a number of Arab thoroughbreds, bays and greys, were exercising in a paddock. The road spiralled up to the crest of a hill, on top of which stood a mansion in classical style. Across an extensive lawn from this stood a large new square brick building, with lines of tall slim windows. To my disappointment, we swept past the mansion and stopped at the new building, the Hokkimyat guest house.

I climbed out of the car. From this hilltop, lights spread out to the horizon in every direction – a reminder of just how very populous the Ferghana Valley is.

I was shown to my room, which reminded me of a student hall of residence. The room was tiny, with a cubicle containing a shower and toilet. The bed was under three feet wide, the mattress thin, the sheets stiff and the tartan blanket scratchy. I looked at the manager in some amazement. He affected not to notice and told me dinner would be served upstairs in the dining room in half an hour; the Deputy Hokkim would be joining me.

Mansur arrived with my bag and looked at the room, shaking his head.

'Not good, Ambassador,' he said.

'No, but at least it's clean,' I said.

I thought for a moment. Why was I worried? I had slept under the stars in Africa often enough, and here I had a bed, shower and loo. But nonetheless I felt that more respect should be shown to a British ambassador.

I was glad to take a shower and change, and was looking forward to dinner. I went upstairs and found the restaurant, where a single table was ready. There were just two covers set, each for nine courses. The cutlery was gold plated. Each cover also had a water glass, vodka glass and four wine glasses of different sizes, all of them crystal and gold rimmed. A two-foot-high gilded equestrian centrepiece of the Emperor Babur had fruit piled around it. My feelings of neglect dissipated.

The Deputy Hokkim arrived about ten minutes late. A short, ball-shaped man with a fringe of longish black hair around a balding pate, he wore the regulation black suit and white shirt. He patted at the back of his neck with a white handkerchief as he bounded up the steps two at a time. He had a friendly open face and a broad grin as he held out his hand to shake mine, then realised he still had the handkerchief in it.

'Ah, Mr Murray! Sorry to be late. I had a meeting with the Hokkim about the cotton harvest. The President is not happy we will meet our quota. He has sent two presidential counsellors here to warn the Hokkim! Of course, it's seven years since a hokkim was last shot for not meeting his quota, and he had been smuggling personally. Or was it his son? I forget. Anyway, things are more civilised now. Still, it's worrying. I am the Deputy Hokkim for Islamic Affairs and External Relations. Of course, you are an experienced diplomat, so you know that means KGB. Only now we say SNB. Your career has been very good. Did you like Poland? Did they teach you to drink vodka? I served in Poland. Oh, the Polish women! Can we take off our jackets and ties?'

I was rather bowled over by this greeting, and there followed one of the most enjoyable evenings of my life. The meal was tremendous, every course of it, and I was hungry, having had a busy day and not eaten since breakfast. The wines were very good, from Georgia – it was the only time I saw wine other than the execrable Uzbek stuff at official functions. There was a superb well-aged oaked red with the *shashlik*, and a fine dessert wine served with honey cakes. We had a very frank discussion, where I was promoting economic reform and he social stability. We then moved on to more important topics – football and women – and eventually, after finishing three and a half bottles of wine between us, we got on to the vodka toasts.

We started with the Queen and President Karimov, and then moved on to the Hokkim and Tony Blair. We then pledged to friendship between our two countries. My host made a flowery speech about the eyes showing the soul, and that he could see in my eyes I had a good heart. We were getting maudlin by this stage, and I was quite touched, though I later found out that this was a standard Uzbek compliment.

With each toast, we drained our glasses in one go. He was quite impressed by my ability to drink vodka but not by my style. He showed me that the arm should be cocked with the elbow raised to the same height as the mouth, so the forearm was horizontal. You then flick only the hand, without moving the arm, to toss it down. This was the approved Soviet military fashion. You should try it next time you drink with the KGB – they'll be impressed.

The vodka glasses were made of slim-stemmed fine crystal, with the actual container part conical. The meal had been served by three waitresses, blonde and not ethnically Uzbek, which is unusual in Namangan. They wore little black skirts with white aprons and were both efficient and distracting. Every time we drained our glasses in a vodka toast, they were immediately refilled. But four or five toasts in, I noticed something. My glass was always filled right to the brim, so I had to lift it carefully. My host's glass was filled only halfway up – and the glass being a cone, it meant it contained about a sixth as much as it did when filled to the top.

We drank a couple more bumpers, and then I had an inspiration. It was my turn to make the next toast. I rose to my feet and said, 'I feel we are becoming true friends. Our nationalities and positions are not important. As men, ordinary men, we understand each other. In Scotland, we have a tradition – when we are drinking a toast, we pledge our friendship by exchanging glasses.'

I reached across the table and picked up his glass, handing him mine: '*Slainte va.*'

We drank and sat down again. I had, of course, made this story up.

'An interesting tradition,' he observed. 'Perhaps its origin lay in people poisoning glasses?'

'Oh yes, probably,' I replied airily. 'Dropping like flies from poison all over the place, I daresay. You just can't trust some people.'

The waitresses, though, were cute in more ways than one. For the next toast, they part filled *my* glass, and his to the brim. He then insisted on again observing the Scottish tradition, with a glint of genuine humour in his eye. I decided we should switch to a venue where the dice were less loaded.

'My friend, let's go look at Namangan,' I said. 'Maybe a bar or nightclub where we can meet some women?'

'You know, Namangan is not Warsaw.'

'I know, but there must be somewhere.'

'OK, we can try.'

He had the obligatory Nissan Maxima, in black. He yelled at the driver to get out of the car and got into the driving seat himself. I got into the front seat beside him and we set off into the city. It was only about 11 p.m., but Namangan had the deserted air of 4 a.m. We drove quite a way until we came to an outside bar; the tables and chairs were still out in the courtyard, but the bar itself was shuttered up.

'Shit!' he said, throwing the car into a screeching reverse turn. In any Western country, he would have been ten times over the drink-driving limit. We drove around to two or three more bars, with the same result. Finally, he got out his mobile phone and made a number of calls, then turned to me with a smile.

'There is one place, and tonight they have a dancer!'

We drove off again, winding our way through the city. Finally, we entered between high walls into the yard of a large house, which loomed above us in complete darkness. He got out of the car and had a piss against the yard wall. I followed suit. We then walked round the back of the building, feeling our way in the darkness. We climbed a short flight of concrete external steps with an iron side railing, he opened a door, and we went in. We passed down a pitch-dark corridor – I was beginning to feel just a trifle nervous. Then my host simply vanished. For a few seconds I felt around, wondering where he had gone, panic just starting to rise, when an arm seemed to come out from the wall and pull me in.

Behind a carpet hung on the wall was an opening, and on the other side of that was a bar. There were about eight tables around a dance floor, with a few disco lights mounted. Beside us was a bar counter from which a grizzled old man with a bulbous nose dispensed beer and vodka. There were about a dozen men in the place, all of them in military uniform. At the other end was a low stage on which a dancer was performing.

I decided to switch to beer. There was a choice of Ferghana and Zolotoya Bochka – Golden Drum. Having tried Ferghana, I decided to give Zolotoya Bochka a go. To my surprise, it was quite good. My companion stuck to vodka.

The dancer was performing a traditional Uzbek dance. She was tall and slim, and carried out the complicated arm and wrist movements with neat precision. She wore a long tunic of atlas cloth over pink trousers. The only flesh exposed was her hands and face. It was doubtless very good, but not what a boozed-up randy Scot was looking for.

The Deputy Hokkim looked at her raptly.

'What do you think of her?' he asked.

'She's OK, but the costume's a bit dull.'

'Don't worry. There will be a new costume for each dance.'

I cheered up, thinking we would be in for a prolonged striptease. In fact, her subsequent costumes became increasingly all-enveloping. I half expected her to finish off with her hat and coat on.

After she finished work, my host made a good attempt to persuade the dancer to join us for a drink. She declined, and I was a bit disconcerted when asked if I wanted him to compel her. I attempted to say something very gallant about such a charming lady having the right to choose her own companions, but my Russian was starting to collapse – it gets much more fluent after drinking, but after a bit more drinking goes into rapid decline. I made about four attempts to say this, causing her to laugh very prettily, and then I just gave up and said, 'No.'

'I knew it,' he said. 'I have met a true British gentleman.'

We felt our way back out through the darkness and had another piss against the wall. My clothes reeked of bad tobacco smoke. Then we got into the car and drove back to the guest house.

Once inside, we wandered to a basement, past a swimming pool and down a corridor. The Deputy Hokkim fished in his pocket and found a key with which he opened a door at the end. Inside was a full-size Russian billiard table. This is much like a snooker table but with an important difference. The pockets are significantly smaller and less rounded. The balls are also bigger. As a result, it is physically impossible to pot from an angle – the ball will only enter from head on. This affects the whole strategy of the game.

I am rubbish at pool or snooker. My new friend had an idea to make it more interesting. He produced a vodka bottle and two glasses.

'Each time one of us pots a ball, the other has to drink a glass of vodka!'

I have no idea how it happened, but I won convincingly with some really good play. I had a lucky early pot with a blind belt at the pack, which by chance lined up the next ball perfectly. I slotted that one in and then, to my own amazement, cut in a really difficult one. These three quick vodkas really knocked the stuffing out of my opponent, who started to visibly stagger. I suppose it might have been the calming effect of the drink, but I played incomparably better than I normally can. We played two games, and I only had to drink two vodkas in the first and none in the second. The poor Deputy Hokkim was completely slaughtered by the end, and I left him in a chair in the billiard room. It was approaching four o'clock and time for bed.

I found a figure asleep in a chair outside my bedroom. It was Mansur, who had been worried about me and was awaiting my return. I assured him I was OK and asked him to attend to the Deputy Hokkim. Then I showered and went to bed.

I breakfasted at eight, feeling remarkably good. I was glad that there was no sign of any police escort. I wondered if this was because the Deputy Hokkim was still indisposed. Our professional interpreter had turned up, an impressive young man, and so we headed out towards the Nestlé factory.

Nestlé had established a plant for producing pasteurised milk in cartons and water in plastic bottles. They had tankers collecting milk from farmers all over the valley, a very welcome injection of private-sector cash into the economy. The MD was a likeable Australian, Martin Woolnough. Their plant was a haven of cleanliness and efficiency.

Nestlé has received a lot of criticism from health lobbies over the years, with some justice. But their operation in Uzbekistan is a definite asset. Pasteurised milk and safe water are both sorely needed in the country, particularly as TB and other diseases are reaching epidemic levels. Unfortunately, Nestlé were finding it extremely difficult to market the milk. Many Uzbek families, even in the heart of Tashkent, have one or two cows in their courtyards or on the road verges, and if they don't, they buy their milk from a neighbour who does. To get anywhere close to the price competition of the informal sector, Nestlé were selling the milk at a loss while they built up the market.

I was surprised to find that the greatest cost of a carton of milk was the carton itself – later that day I was to find the same thing true when I visited an EBRD-funded juice factory. The reason is the very high cost of the patented Tetra-pak technology. The Swedish family who own the patents are among the top five wealthiest in the world.

Nestlé had found, to their own surprise, that the bottled water was their big money spinner. While the water came from their own boreholes, it was not mineral water and they treated it. But it filled a much-needed demand and production had soared, causing them to open an extra line. Unfortunately, it had stopped working the day of my visit. The new ban on imports meant that they had run out of the plastic blanks from which the bottles were expanded.

Given their huge reserves of hydrocarbons, the Uzbek government had invested in a plant to produce plastics, polythene and polyethylene from natural gas. It had opened that summer, at a cost of $1.2 billion. The equipment was largely American and Italian, and export financing had come from those countries. The Uzbek government had, however, refused to accept a large number of expatriate experts to run this plant. In consequence, when opened that summer, the plant had blown up.

We were now to visit another example of economic madness. The EBRD had invested €26 million of equity, not loan, in a woollen textile mill, and we now drove there. The total value of the investment in this mill was over €70 million (as compared to about €23 million Nestlé had invested in their very impressive factory). The wool factory was in a small town outside Namangan, housed in a series of huge buildings.

The assistant manager and a small delegation were waiting for me, and they took me into a vast manufacturing hall filled with textile machinery. I have always been fascinated by the complexity and ingenuity of such machinery, and there was certainly plenty of it. But there was one major problem – it wasn't doing anything. A single machine in a far corner clanked away rather unhealthily, producing dark brown wiry blankets. None of the combing, spinning, washing, weaving or dyeing equipment elsewhere was working.

The assistant manager was a tall Uzbek with high cheekbones and a good pinstriped suit. He was accompanied by a young Turkish engineer who represented the foreign investor.

'It's not very busy, is it?' I observed.

'We are running at about 10 per cent capacity,' said the manager.

The young Turk said something in Turkish to my interpreter, who passed it on.

'Really 1 per cent, Ambassador.'

I looked around me and observed, 'If that.'

I pointed to the unappealing blankets. 'Is there a customer for those?' I asked in Russian.

The manager replied in Uzbek, through the interpreter.

'The Uzbek army.'

'Will they actually pay up?'

'Maybe, one day.'

I looked more closely at some of the plant. The spinning machinery appeared brand new, but the power looms looked ancient, despite being thickly coated in new green paint.

'The factory is two years old?' I asked. They agreed.

'And this equipment was all sold as new?'

'It is new,' said the manager.

'If this lot is new, you must have been paying someone for the last two years to go around hitting it with a sledgehammer.'[22]

We went out into one of the big sheds, where bales of wool were being unloaded. In the corner, there were untidy heaps of brown, tangled fleeces, with the consistency of wire wool. In contrast, a lorry was unloading big bales of fluffy white fleeces. The manager was beaming with delight.

'Now we will get the factory working properly,' he said.

'Is this wool local?'

'No, it's from Australia.'

'I beg your pardon?'

'It's from Australia.'

'Why don't you use local wool?'

'It doesn't fit the machines.'

'But I thought the whole point of this project was to develop local agriculture.'

He gestured at the dark fleeces in the corner. 'We tried. It doesn't fit the machines.'

We went to the factory shop, where there were bales of suitings in wool, polyester and blends of the two. These had been produced as samples with imported raw materials when the equipment was first installed. Some of the material was very good, and I thought about buying some. We drank tea, and I felt sorry for the sad assistant manager and his young sidekick. There was a general manager, a tremendous swell who lived in Tashkent on a big salary and never visited the plant. My sympathy for this sad pair elicited more and more of the true story.

They showed me the consultancy report, in English, on which the investment had been based. This said that there were plenty of sheep providing fine-quality wool in the Ferghana Valley, and the plant would take up to 60 per cent of the valley's wool production. The truth was, the assistant manager said, that the plant's capacity was three times the wool production of the whole of Uzbekistan. On top of which, the wiry wool of Uzbek sheep was totally unsuited to producing suit material. The young engineer said that it wasn't just a question of producing bad-quality cloth, the machinery wouldn't take the local wool at all, whatever adjustments he tried to make. Only the blanket-making machine would work, fed with string-like local yarn.

The feasibility report had been produced by the same Turkish company which supplied the machinery, which was also the foreign investor and part owner of the plant. This was an incredible conflict of interests. However, rather than stay and manage the plant, after the commissioning the Turkish 'investors' had disappeared, leaving behind their most junior assistant engineer as a kind of hostage. The poor lad had not been paid for two years.

There were three investors: the Turkish company, the EBRD and the Uzbek government. Obviously, the Turks had made their cash on the supply of over-priced machinery, much of it disguised as new. The project was bogus from start to finish. I was astonished that the EBRD had fallen for this.

But it got worse. The EBRD had now given a new loan of €5 million on top of its equity investment of €26 million. The loan was to pay for wool to be flown in from Australia to feed the plant. This was commercial madness, but the purpose was political. In May 2003, the EBRD was going to be holding its AGM in Tashkent. Finance ministers from all the world's major countries would be flying in. The EBRD did not want the embarrassment of an obvious white elephant project, so the factory would be functioning during the AGM.[23]

We left the sad factory and went on to a meeting with a representative of Erk at a village just outside Namangan. Erk was the major opposition party that had been banned some years previously. The village was intensely rural, and we entered the house through a yard where children were setting out cowpats to dry as a store of fuel for the winter. I met a gentle old bearded man, who served me tea from a blue-and-white porcelain teapot. The women in the village were heavily veiled, and the tea and cakes appeared from behind a curtained serving hatch. This was the first time I had come across purdah in Uzbekistan.

My host said that the Namangan district had long been a centre of Islamic culture. It did not have any particular holy sites; it was simply the culture of its people. He explained that Erk did not want to establish an Islamic state or Sharia law. They did, however, want a state where it was possible for those who wished to follow Islamic customs to do so. He seemed very old but assured me with a calm serenity that he expected to live long enough to see democracy come to Uzbekistan.

I asked my standard question about the number of people from that district who were religious or political prisoners. He took me aback by saying that, from that cluster of villages alone, there were about 400. Responding to my look of shock, he said that about one in five of the young men of that area had been taken in. They were kept mostly in Andijan prison. In Namangan province, he believed that about 90 per cent of the population would vote against Karimov given the chance. He did not believe the opposition would turn to violence. This was not due to a creed of non-violence, but the security forces were too numerous and well armed. But people were getting poorer and poorer, and Karimov's end was coming. He spoke with dignified assurance, and I was left to ponder the mystery of why this grave old man was left alone by the authorities.

We next had an hour's drive into Andijan. This had the air of a much bigger city than the others in the valley, with office blocks, large retail premises and wide multi-lane roads packed with cars. We were headed for the offices of Mercy Corps. This was the site of the British government's largest aid project in Uzbekistan. It cost about £120,000, which was peanuts compared to my previous projects of tens of millions of pounds in Ghana. The money came from the British government's Conflict Resolution Fund, and the project was extremely effective.

As I entered Mercy Corps' office, I encountered several groups of local middle-aged women wearing brightly coloured dresses and headscarves, grinning at me and displaying rows of gold teeth. In rural Uzbekistan, everyone has gold teeth.

The project offered micro-finance – small loans to enable women to set up in business. The loans were very small – about $60 on average – but they were enough to purchase a hand loom, or some livestock, or some trading goods. The finance worked at a very low rate of interest – about 2 per cent – and the repaid money went to start new projects.

Mercy Corps administered the project on our behalf, and they reported that there was a bit of a crisis at present because many of the loan projects involved trading with nearby Kirghizstan, and the border had just been closed. Others produced products which were sold in the bazaars, and they had also just been closed.

The young project leader was most impressive. She timidly suggested we go out and meet some of the loan recipients and seemed both surprised and delighted when I enthusiastically agreed. We visited a small village outside Andijan. One lady produced hand-loomed textiles and another embroidered clothes. Both of them had started from scratch and now employed staff. Another lady had bought moulds and sugar to produce boiled sweets, while her neighbour had started a small bread bakery. In total, Mercy Corps believed about 14,000 people in 3,000 families were dependent on income from this project, and many more received direct economic benefit. It was an astonishing success for such a small investment. Chris Hirst and Karen Moran deserved much of the credit.[24]

Over 90 per cent of the loans had performed, but some of this benefit was now at risk due to the Uzbek government measures of border and bazaar closures, which appeared expressly designed to bankrupt their own population. I felt a real anger at the way the regime had done so much damage to the efforts these ordinary women had made to improve their lives.

The next morning, we headed in to Andijan again, where my first meeting was with the Hokkim. There was again a local TV crew, and the Hokkim made a flowery speech about bilateral relations. He said that there were 72 Uzbek–British joint ventures in Andijan. (We only knew of two, and I presume this was just another propaganda statistic.)

I visited one of these joint ventures next, a company called QuickStop owned by Jitendra Patel. They had a factory in Tashkent, which I had already been round, manufacturing plastic sacks for cement. Their Andijan factory made paper from imported wood pulp. I met Jitendra at the plant, and he explained that they were trying to convert the machinery to operate on local cotton waste. Cotton-made paper is very high quality – banknotes are made from it. He also explained that the company name, QuickStop, came from his UK business of food outlets in railway stations.

But Jitendra, too, had a tale of the problems of business in Uzbekistan. He had founded the Uzbek company with an Uzbek partner. Jitendra had later bought out the partner for a very large sum, but the partner had now won a judgment from an Uzbek court awarding him the company. The Uzbek court had refused to accept British court documents certifying that the payment had been made to buy out the partner. This was the first of numerous cases I was to deal with of foreign investors being mistreated by the Uzbek courts.

I called back on the Hokkim to discuss the situation with him and explained that the future of the paper plant was in danger. He seemed genuinely concerned and promised to raise the matter with the President. He confided that the difficulty was that the partner was a very important man who had broken the law by accepting payment into a Swiss bank account. This could not be admitted by the court. I was surprised by the Hokkim's openness in discussing this.

I next had a lunch appointment with a human rights activist, a doctor from the local hospital. Our arrangement involved meeting him on a certain street. I walked up and down for about 15 minutes, increasingly convinced this was not going to work, but finally he turned up, a short old man in a threadbare jacket. His two incisors were gold. He insisted on taking me for lunch in a little local courtyard restaurant and ordered *osh*, which turned out to be Tajik for plov.

He said that over 1,000 people from Andijan were in jail, but the city had the proudest record of opposition to the government. Unlike Namangan, the people of Andijan were more secular, but the opposition was fuelled by economic discontent and by anger at being cut off from the neighbouring Kirghiz city of Osh. I was now convinced that the total numbers of political prisoners in the country were larger than anyone had credited.

There was a remarkable incident during this lunch. After we had been there about ten minutes, two men, both wearing leather jackets, came and sat at a table near the entrance.

'I see the SNB have found us,' said the doctor. He stood up and walked over to them. He spoke to them quietly in Uzbek, and they got up and left.

'What did you say?' I asked.

He grinned. 'I said that you were the British Ambassador and you asked that they leave.'

I next called on CAFE, a Christian NGO. They worked out of a courtyard house, of which two wings were dedicated to English language teaching. They held regular classes, but equipment was very basic and their stock of donated books was not very appropriate to teaching. I was later able to get the embassy to provide a good supply of teaching materials.

But their main efforts were concentrated on public health education. The head of the project was an impressive American doctor who had produced an educational book which CAFE had translated into Uzbek and distributed widely in the villages. It covered basic healthcare questions on matters such as childbirth and contraception, and tackled many local superstitions. The doctor said that disease levels in the Ferghana Valley were much worse than official statistics showed. Infant mortality was worsening. Normally, local wisdom was not to be underestimated, but here there were a large number of problems. For example, in much of the valley the water table was very high, and cesspits were dug into it. A high percentage of local wells were contaminated.

I was most impressed by CAFE but went on from there to a very different call, on the Daewoo factory. This was the great totem of Uzbek modernisation and Karimov's drive for self-sufficiency. I was impressed by the factory. I had presumed that it was simply an assembly plant where knocked down Daewoos were bolted together.[25] But this was a real manufacturing operation, with the bodywork pressed from steel rolls and much of the drive train and fittings locally manufactured. The engines were flown in from Daewoo Germany.

Daewoo had originally owned an equity stake but had sold out, and it was now a licensed plant, 100 per cent Uzbek government owned. The plant had a capacity of 220,000 vehicles a year, but in

2001 it had produced around 40,000, and now in 2002 it was working much less. As we walked around, the management tried to tell me that the staff had finished work early that day for plant maintenance, but I didn't buy this. When I left, I asked roadside cigarette sellers, who eke a living by buying packets of cigarettes and selling them individually. They said that the plant had not been working for five weeks.

The management were very proud that Daewoo Uzbekistan were the biggest exporters of new vehicles to Russia, selling 14,000 vehicles there in 2001. As they retailed in Russia for about $6,500, however, below the cost of production, this was perhaps not a great economic achievement.

This call concluded my programme in the Ferghana Valley, but for my last evening I decided to change plan and move back to Ferghana city itself. We arrived and checked into the Zigurat Hotel, much to the surprise of the management.

I had told the young receptionist that I would be back, and he had contacted two of his friends who had also studied in the UK. We met up around eight-thirty and went to the city's most expensive restaurant, which was a great treat for them. We had a good meal and a lot of wine, and chatted up the waitresses.

They had studied in the UK under the Uzbek government's UMID study programme, under which about 300 students a year went abroad to study, most of them to the UK. On return, they had to work for the government for five years. As there was great resistance in the Civil Service to bright, young people with new ideas, many of them were given meaningless jobs like hotel receptionists and railway conductors. This receptionist had a British MBA.

After dinner, we returned to the Zigurat Hotel, in front of which a marquee had been erected housing a bar. This had a brightly lit stage, and as we approached from outside, we could see the figures of belly dancers silhouetted on the canvas. We went in, sat down and ordered beers, but before long the SNB showed up, six of them, and stood looking menacingly at us. My companions took fright and left. It was a downbeat end to a fascinating visit to this famous valley.

CHAPTER 7

Cry Freedom!

The heavy baggage had arrived, and Fiona had been getting the apartment into shape, although much remained packed, as we would be moving again, around Christmas, to the new Residence. But we were now able to give our first dinner party and experimented on the British staff of the embassy and British Council. This went well, although Galina the cook was very nervous, and Fiona had to do a lot herself.

We were then ready for outside guests, and our first official function was to be a reception for Chevening scholars. All round the world, the FCO funds a very small number of overseas students to come to the UK; the idea is to identify future movers and shakers in their country. Done properly it requires a lot of effort, but overall the scheme is very successful. In Uzbekistan, we only had funding for three scholars a year, but past participants included a deputy governor of the Central Bank and two members of the President's inner office.

It is standard practice to 'see off' the new Chevening scholars with a reception and invite past scholars to it. I decided to augment this by inviting all the UMID scholars, present and past, plus anyone else we could identify who had studied at a UK university, plus the staff who were setting up the Westminster University campus in Tashkent, plus our key Uzbek government contacts in the field of education. The British Council were extremely efficient in providing a guest list of several hundred. Many of the past scholars were in the provinces, but about 120 people turned up, which made it a tight squeeze as they mingled, drank and chomped canapés in the opened-out space of the ballroom, dining room and balconies.

Fiona and I had routinely hosted gatherings for many hundreds in Accra and Warsaw, but plainly this was much more than Galina had been used to in Tashkent, and there were a few hiccups. Serving staff were rounded up from the embassy maids and other families, and off-duty guards were the barmen. They were apparently used to this job, but I was puzzled by the fact that none of them knew what a gin and tonic was.

The Uzbek Minister of Higher Education attended. He passed on one little snippet to me. When the UMID scheme started, the majority of students had been sent to the United States. However, they had come back 'infected' with bad social and political habits. Karimov had therefore decided that most students should instead go to the UK, where society was more conservative. President Karimov had a very high opinion of the UK. I wondered what peculiar impression Karimov had of student life in the UK, which is a great deal more infected with both politics and debauchery than your average American university.

Neville McBain, the tall, handsome ex-army major who was Director of the British Council in Tashkent, said that the problem was that over half the UMID scholars weren't coming back at all. They stayed in the UK as illegal immigrants. This broke the terms of their UMID contracts, under which they had to come back and do government work for five years after graduating.

The parents would be held responsible for their non-return. However, many of the parents were from extremely wealthy regime families – the selection process was often corrupt – and they could escape punishment by the same means they obtained the scholarship. Retribution was taken against less wealthy parents, usually in the form of them losing their jobs, but even by working in a Pizza Hut in the UK the absconder could easily send back more funds than the family had lost.

I made a little speech wishing our new scholars well and reminding them that the university experience was much more than formal learning. Social interaction was important, too, and I had learnt more in the pub than in the lecture theatre. Uzbekistan is overlaid with a very pompous Soviet culture, and the Uzbeks were amazed to hear someone in authority speak like this.

I was delighted to meet my friend from the Zigurat Hotel again. He had made the long journey to Tashkent by bus. Following our night out, he had been picked up by the SNB and taken in for questioning. They had asked him if he had known I would be returning to Ferghana that evening and what I said. He replied that I talked a lot about football and chatted up the waitresses in the restaurant. In the marquee, I had said that I preferred Golden Drum to Ferghana beer, and that I quite fancied the belly dancer in the white, but the one in red was too fat.

At this stage, his inquisitor had struck him, declaring that he was lying because ambassadors don't talk like that! They had wanted to know my views on various political subjects, so he had made it all up. He hoped I didn't mind. I assured him I didn't mind at all. It could do little harm to feed rubbish to the SNB.

I presumed they already knew what I thought, because I was pretty open about it anyway, directly to ministers and to other contacts. I saw no need to hide my views on Uzbekistan's appalling political and economic system; in fact, the wider they were propagated the better.

All the policy points I have written of here had been relayed back to London in official classified telegrams. But for many years I had also been used to a close working relationship between department and embassy by email. I had operated in this way whether posted abroad or working in London. In my previous job as Deputy High Commissioner in Ghana, I had a very close working relationship with the FCO's Africa Department and would exchange emails many times a day in a continuous dialogue.

The Eastern Department was different and seemed determined to hang on to the stilted working practices of a previous century. Above all, they were obsessed with the need to prevent the Uzbeks from knowing what we were thinking. The Eastern Department was formerly named the Soviet Department, and the old Sovietologists remained steeped in the paranoid culture of the Cold War. I was frequently rebuked for sending communications by unclassified email. I replied that I knew my emails were almost certainly being intercepted and that if the Uzbeks found out this way about my views on the bazaar closures that was all to the good: it would save me the effort of telling them.

Chris now received the pathology report on the Avazov case, and we immediately distributed copies to the UN, OSCE (Organisation for Security and Cooperation in Europe) and the EU, and I started to brief the media. The medieval horror of boiling someone to death was so powerful an image that in death Mr Avazov could play a real part in undermining the terrible regime which so cruelly killed him.

A new arrival in Tashkent was a formidable lady named Sikeena Karmali, a Canadian of Indian origin (Asian, not North American). Sikeena was here to open an office of Freedom House, a US NGO devoted to human rights and economic freedom. John Herbst was quick to point out to me that Uzbek agreement to the opening of this NGO was another example of progress. The fiercely bright Sikeena had called on me and invited me to speak at their opening.

I had been looking for a platform from which to make a declaration of the real state of affairs in the country. I wanted to fracture what I believed had become a conspiracy of silence by the West on human rights in Uzbekistan and to outline a distinctively British position in favour of democracy and reform which made it plain that we did not simply follow the United States. This invitation to speak presented the perfect opportunity.

I sat down and drafted a speech, setting out in pretty stark terms our concerns about human rights in Uzbekistan. I then sent it to HRPD in the FCO, copied to the Eastern Department. I knew I could expect strong support from HRPD, whose head of department, Jon Benjamin, was a genuine believer in human rights and who had joined the service on the same day as me.

In London, the clouds started to gather ominously. Simon Butt decided to trump HRPD by going straight to the top. On 16 October 2002, he emailed Sir Michael Jay, Head of the Diplomatic Service. I later obtained a copy of this email and Sir Michael Jay's reply by formally applying under the Data Protection Act.

The government has specifically threatened, both by letter to me and in testimony by Jack Straw to the Foreign Affairs Committee, to sue for breach of copyright if I publish any of these documents. I would not shy from this, but the publisher understandably does not wish to be open to incurring potentially substantial legal costs. I am therefore obliged to paraphrase what they say. Simon Butt wrote: 'We are fast developing a problem with Craig Murray' and quoted the following from my proposed Freedom House speech:

> This country has made very little progress in moving away
> from the dictatorship of the Soviet period . . . no effective

105

brake on the authority of a President who has failed to validate
his position by facing genuine political opponents in anything
representing a free and fair election.

Butt said that this was bound to make the Uzbeks very angry indeed.
Sir Michael Jay's reply, also of 16 October, strongly supported Simon
Butt.

Interestingly, the last five lines of Butt's minute were heavily blacked
out before the document was given to me, on grounds of national
security. But a friend who has seen the whole minute tells me that they
refer to representations against me from the United States.

Following that exchange, Charles Hill, Head of the Central Asia
section of the Eastern Department, was charged with formally
responding to my draft speech. In a letter of 16 October 2002,
faxed to me, he said that he doubted that I should make such
a speech which risked 'antagonising the Uzbek authorities'. He
said that I had failed to take note of the difficult Soviet legacy
the Uzbek government had inherited, or of the genuine Islamic
threat which they faced, and he suggested I make a more
conventional speech, based on past FCO pronouncements and
data already published.

Plainly, this was a crucial moment. Either I was going to conduct our
relationship with Uzbekistan using the traditional quietist approach
favoured by the Eastern Department, or I was going to break new
ground and try to have some impact. This speech would set the tone.

I therefore decided to let Charles have it with both barrels. I faxed
him straight back, offering to make amendments but expressing
astonishment at his unimaginative and cautious reaction to the
appalling human rights situation in Uzbekistan. I suggested that if
the FCO were not prepared to pay heed to my first-hand observations
on the situation, there was little point in our having an embassy in
Tashkent. I condemned the classic public school and Oxbridge-
influenced FCO house style as 'ponderous, self-important and
ineffective', and suggested that the way to maximise our influence
was not to kowtow but to be tough. I mocked his suggestion that I
should acknowledge the Uzbek government's difficult Soviet legacy,
suggesting the Karimov regime *were* the difficult Soviet legacy, and
attacked his mention of the 1999 Tashkent bombings as evidence of
the terrorist threat, pointing out that all serious commentators in
Uzbekistan believed those bombs to have been in fact the work of

the Karimov regime or of feuding factions within it. I even suggested we might see more such government-planted bombs in Tashkent shortly, blamed on terrorists, to justify continued repression and try to take off some of the pressure for reform.

Charles had suggested I drop emotive words such as 'brutality' and 'outrage'. I countered: 'Actually I think that outrage is absolutely the correct emotion at learning that someone has been tortured to death with boiling water. If your reaction at seeing photos of this is not to be outraged, but to wonder precisely which UN Convention contains provision against torture by boiling water, then I am sorry.'[26]

I made a number of amendments as requested by Charles, including adding sympathetic words about the difficulties the Uzbek government faced, then I sent the new draft, pointing out that the speech was to be made the next day and asking for a finalised text rather than comments.

Tashkent is five hours ahead of London, and I was still involved in these exchanges after midnight. In the ambassador's flat above me, Emily was playing with her nanny, Laura, a Tartar. There are about 600,000 Tartars in Uzbekistan, a population deported by Stalin from the Crimea.[27]

Emily was still awake watching videos: she could twist anyone round her little finger except her mum. Fiona was back in the UK for Jamie's half term. Laura was a very pretty girl with a spectacular figure. When I came in, they both jumped up and wished me happy birthday. It was now 20 minutes into 17 October 2002, and I had just turned 44 years old.

That evening, I was due to give the speech at Freedom House at 6 p.m., and by 5.30 p.m. the text had still not arrived. The Eastern Department were negotiating with research analysts, HRPD and DFID, all of whom were fighting hard on my side of the argument. Finally, the text arrived just after six, and Karen immediately whizzed off to make a hundred photocopies while I read it through. I was delighted with the result.

Karen and I climbed into the Discovery, and Valeri raced to Freedom House's new office. We arrived about half an hour late, but I need not have worried, as it was a scene of chaos.

The offices were a standard Uzbek courtyard house, and the meeting was planned for the garden, where rows of plastic chairs were set out. Unfortunately, it had started to bucket down with rain shortly before our arrival. Indoors, there was nowhere with enough space to host a large meeting. After a lot of milling around, it was decided that the speeches would be delivered from the large landing, on which an improbable number of TV and radio crews were setting up. The audience were crammed in standing behind them, and on the stairs, and in the hall below. This extraordinary set-up added to the sense of theatre and helped give what happened next its dramatic quality.

The speakers were hemmed in behind a bank of microphones, blinking in the TV lights. Sikeena gave a brief welcome and then introduced the US Ambassador. John Herbst welcomed the Uzbek government's permission for the establishment of Freedom House as a further sign of positive reform. He cited the abolition of censorship and registration of Ardzinov's NGO as more examples of progress and praised Uzbekistan's cooperation in the War on Terror. The German Ambassador next seconded these remarks in his usual cryptic fashion. Then I was called.

There were a fair number of Uzbek human rights activists in the audience, and they set up an expectant murmur as I walked to the microphone. Because of the cramped conditions, and because some of the auditors couldn't see the speakers, there had been a buzz of background chat. But this died away as people caught the drift of what I was saying, and despite the inelegance of sequential interpretation into both Russian and Uzbek, by a few minutes into my speech you could have heard a pin drop.

This is what I said:

> I am most happy to be here today to join in Freedom House's Open House. This is a welcome addition to the resources available to the community which is working to improve basic human rights here in Uzbekistan. The organisers are to be congratulated on the initiative, as are the US government for their assistance with finance.
>
> Ladies and gentlemen, I am a Scot, and proud of my race. Our national poet, Robert Burns, notes in his great poem 'The Author's Earnest Cry and Prayer' that 'Freedom and whisky gang the gither', which for those whose Scots is a wee bit rusty means 'Freedom and whisky go together'. Well, we all know how difficult it is to find real whisky in Tashkent. It does exist, but mostly on diplomatic premises. There is still a lot of wisdom in old Robert.

It is also a great pleasure to see such a gathering of those promoting human rights in Uzbekistan, both from outside and inside the country, and from both governmental and non-governmental sectors. I am also pleased to see representatives of the media here today – I trust I will see these proceedings fully and openly reported.

Let us have no illusions about the size of the challenge we face. We must all agree that independent Uzbekistan had a great handicap to overcome in the very poor legacy on issues of freedom from the Soviet Union. But nonetheless this country has made very disappointing progress in moving away from the dictatorship of the Soviet period.

Uzbekistan is not a functioning democracy, nor does it appear to be moving in the direction of democracy. The major political parties are banned; parliament is not subject to democratic election; and checks and balances on the authority of the executive are lacking.

There is worse: we believe there to be between seven and ten thousand people in detention whom we would consider as political and/or religious prisoners. In many cases they have been falsely convicted of crimes with which there appears to be no credible evidence they had any connection. Reputable human rights groups such as HRW and Amnesty International have brought to our attention specific instances where the same crime is used serially to convict a number of people. There appears to be a belief that such persecution of an individual can be justified by labelling them as an 'Islamic extremist'.

Now, with the US and other allies, the British government remains in the very forefront of the commitment to the war against terrorism. And we are most grateful for the invaluable assistance rendered to the coalition by the government of Uzbekistan in respect of operations in Afghanistan. We acknowledge that we face the same global threat.

Nobody should seek to underestimate the genuine security concerns of the government of Uzbekistan and the difficulties it has faced in countering those who seek to use religion and the problems of poverty to promote terror. Uzbekistan's strategic situation has put it in the forefront of countries struggling to deal with problems such as terrorism and narcotics trafficking.

But let us make this point: no government has the right to use the war against terrorism as an excuse for the persecution of those with a deep personal commitment to the Islamic religion and who pursue their views by peaceful means. Sadly, the large majority of those wrongly imprisoned in Uzbekistan fall into this category.

But it is not only Muslims who suffer; the British embassy yesterday observed the trial of a Jehovah's Witness being prosecuted for pursuing his beliefs. It should not be a crime to practise your religion, nor to tell others about it. And a number of those imprisoned are ethnic Russian human rights defenders, colleagues of some of my audience. I would like to say at this point how deeply I admire you on a personal level. I am very conscious that I stand here in a very privileged position, in the literal sense. You, on the other hand, daily risk persecution to stand up for the rights of your fellow citizens. You have my deepest respect, and one day your countrymen will be in a position to show you their gratitude.

Uzbekistan is to be congratulated on a good record of ratifying key UN Conventions on human rights; unfortunately, there appears to be a gap between obligation and practice.

World attention has recently been focused on the prevalence of torture in Uzbek prisons. The terrible case of Avazov and Alimov, apparently tortured to death by boiling water, has evoked great international concern. But all of us know that this is not an isolated incident. Brutality is inherent in a system where convictions habitually rely on signed confessions rather than on forensic or material evidence. In the Uzbek criminal justice system, the conviction rate is almost 100 per cent. It is difficult not to conclude that once accused by the Procurator there is no effective possibility of fair trial in the sense we understand it.

Another chilling reminder of the former Soviet Union is the use of commitment to lunatic asylums to stifle dissidents. We are still seeing examples of this in 2002.

Nor does the situation appear to be getting any better. I have been told, by people who should know, that there are significantly more political and religious detainees now than there were this time last year. From my own meetings with human rights groups from across the country there appears to be a broad picture of a reduction in the rate of arrests in the first half of this year but a very substantial increase around August. Just last week saw another highly suspicious death in police custody in Tashkent. There is little sign of genuine positive change in human rights.

And that is what we want to see: genuine change. By that I mean change which actually increases the liberty of Uzbek citizens in their daily lives. Uzbekistan's international obligations require genuine respect for human rights. For example, officially censorship has recently been abolished. But you would not tell this by watching, listening to or reading the media, which is patently under strict control and contains no significant volume of critical comment or analysis of central government policy.

Let me give you an example. In August, the government embarked upon a series of closures of major bazaars in Tashkent and subsequently across Uzbekistan. I witnessed it happen in Namangan, for example. This is not the forum to address the motive for those closures or the rights and wrongs of this action. But it was a radical action, effected with some degree of physical and moral resistance, and closed off the retail outlets through which the majority of manufactured goods are sold in this country. It directly affected the livelihood of an estimated 50,000 people. Furthermore, I have in the last two weeks visited a number of factories in Uzbekistan that have halted production and laid off their workers because their distributors have been put out of business by the bazaar closures.

As I say, I make no comment on the rights and wrongs of this, though I note that the IMF has recommended that these issues be reversed, not least because of the resulting increase in inflation. But everyone in this room knows this has been a burning political issue in the last two months. Yet one could have watched Uzbek television or listened to Uzbek radio solidly throughout this period, and read the newspaper every day, but still have gathered almost nothing of the flavour of what I have just told you. There is little reporting of basic facts and almost no free debate. I trust that the proceedings of this event will be fully and fairly reported.

What then are the components of the real change we wish to see? They are not difficult, but they require political will. I believe that people are born with an instinct for liberty, and that freedom and democracy come naturally to people everywhere, once they are given the chance.

Giving people freedom does not mean that anarchy and instability will follow. Indeed, it is repression which by allowing no outlet for pressures in society risks causing resentment, alienation and social tension. Uzbekistan's partners and friends want to see a country which is stable, free and prosperous. For that to come about there needs to be change – releases of political prisoners; registration of political opposition parties and human rights groups; the opportunity for people to express their opinions in free elections and through a free media and the right to free assembly; and to practise their religious beliefs without fear of persecution. Deeper economic reform is needed also. We are ready to support that process of change, and by embarking upon it Uzbekistan will be able to transform its standing in the international community and earn the goodwill and increased support of partners whose engagement is at present limited by the problems I have addressed today.

I thank you for your kind attention.

This was stuff that just didn't get said. The diplomats wouldn't say it, and if any of the Uzbeks present had made a speech like that they would have been straight into the torture chamber. While I had been making the speech, I had glanced occasionally at John Herbst and watched his facial muscles grow increasingly rigid. I had in effect contradicted everything he had just said and challenged the whole carefully constructed US illusion about Uzbekistan.

In case you think I am exaggerating, it is worth quoting David Stern, a seasoned US reporter on Central Asia, who was present:

Three months after British Ambassador Craig Murray delivered a speech in Uzbekistan, diplomats and analysts are still debating how Murray has changed the tone of relations between Britain and this former Soviet republic. Murray caused a sensation for doing one small thing that very few people seem to have done here: he told the truth.

Uzbekistan, which sits north of Afghanistan, became a critical ally to the United States and United Kingdom in the autumn 2001 campaign to oust the Taliban from Afghanistan. Despite this elevation in status, though, the country has made only marginal improvements in its record of repressing dissidents. At the opening of the Uzbekistan offices of Freedom House on October 17, Ambassador Murray, with top Uzbek officials and diplomats present, delivered the diplomatic equivalent of a salvo . . .

The shock value of these statements, as well as others discussing widespread torture in Uzbekistan and the government's refusal to convert its currency or foster cross-border trade, cannot be overstated. In one fell swoop the British diplomat stripped away the euphemisms that characterize much of the West's relationship with Uzbekistan . . .

Analysts point out that what the ambassador said was in essence nothing new . . . Most of Murray's statements are common currency among foreign diplomats and businessmen in the privacy of their homes and workplaces. Yet his speech stood so far apart from official parlance that it struck some listeners as provocative. 'You could have cut the tension in the room with a blunt knife,' said one of those present.

The irony of Murray's speech, some say, is that it caused friction between the US and British embassies, the two foreign representations that are most concerned with democracy and human rights in Uzbekistan. US Ambassador John Herbst was present at the Freedom House function and had delivered, according to observers, a typical American take on human rights in Uzbekistan, that problems exist but progress has been made. After this predictable address, Murray delivered his broadside. 'The British ambassador's speech was an embarrassment for the United States. It showed up the crack in the shield and many thought that he upstaged [Herbst],' said someone who was present . . . Even if that analysis proves accurate, though, the stridency in Murray's words has emboldened some other critics of Karimov. 'To me the fundamental question is not why did he say this, but why the other ambassadors didn't?' said one Western observer.[28]

I had achieved precisely what I set out to do. I had irreversibly shattered the conspiracy of silence and brought to international attention the brutality of the Karimov regime. I had also made it very plain that British foreign policy in Central Asia was not subservient to US foreign policy.

At least as long as I had my job.

The US reaction was immediate. They had apparently already been trying to undermine me through official channels in London. They now set about a full frontal attack. Another journalist present at Freedom House was Michael Andersen from Danish Radio. He published this account:

> Many Western diplomats in Tashkent were disgusted with the US policy, but their governments kept them 'on message'. That is until Craig Murray arrived. At 44, Murray was Britain's youngest ambassador, with a promising career ahead of him. With the waistcoat of his three-piece suit barely concealing his pot-belly, his thick glasses and unkempt grey hair, he looked like a quirky professor from a softer, more decent era. Uzbekistan shocked him. 'At the Foreign Office, they prepared me with language lessons, but nobody ever mentioned the 10,000 political and religious prisoners,' he said.
>
> In October 2002 the US ambassador gave a speech in which he praised the close relations between the US and Uzbekistan and argued that Uzbekistan had made 'some progress' on 'democratic reforms and human rights'. The broad smile he bestowed on his new British colleague as he handed over the microphone quickly disappeared. 'Uzbekistan is not a functioning democracy,' said Craig Murray, adding (and contradicting what his US colleague had just said), 'nor does it appear to be moving in the direction of democracy.' He then described, in detail, the case of the two boiled prisoners.
>
> 'Murray is a finished man here,' one US top diplomat told me over lunch the next day. 'A shame that Blair could only find an alcoholic to send here,' another remarked.[29]

Karen had done an excellent job of dishing out texts. After the speeches, the other ambassadors left, but I stayed on for wine and nibbles and went out to a restaurant with some US NGO staff afterwards. When I got home, I turned on BBC World to see the news and was amazed to find that my speech was the third item. It had been a busy couple of days, and I kissed Emily goodnight, then went to bed exhausted. I still hadn't opened my birthday presents.

I was shaken awake at 6.30 a.m. and shocked by the sight of a bearded man looming over me. I got on my spectacles and, as my brain started to find its gears, realised that it was Richard Conroy. Richard was a very pleasant but rather shy Englishman, now an Australian citizen, who ran the UN office in Tashkent.

'Craig, wake up. Wake up, Craig,' he said. 'Where's the speech?'

'I'm sorry, Richard?'

'Your speech last night. I need a copy. Where is it?'

'I don't know. Karen had the copies. Hang on . . .'

Richard turned his back as I got out of bed and pulled on a dressing gown. He was apologising incoherently for the intrusion. I wasn't bothered, though surprised.

Kofi Annan was flying into Tashkent that morning. He had been visiting a neighbouring state and last night had seen my speech reported on BBC World. He had asked for a copy to be ready for him at the airport, where he would be arriving in just under an hour.

The only copy I had was the one I had read from. It wasn't in my jacket, and we found it lying scrunched up on the kitchen table. On Richard's inspiration we ironed it. I then opened up the embassy downstairs and we photocopied it, resulting in a passable copy.

'I could kiss you!' yelled Richard as he dashed for his car. Fortunately, he didn't.

That evening there was a state banquet in honour of Kofi Annan at the Durmen residence. I attended in my kilt. After the banquet, Karimov and Annan ceremonially processed from the hall, past the rows of ambassadors and ministers standing at their tables. Then, remarkably, Karimov stopped at my table, pushed past several people and sternly held out his hand for me to shake, making the gesture more theatrical by standing well short of me with his hand held out so I had to take two paces forward to grasp it. He then returned to his march out. He didn't acknowledge anyone else.

After he had gone, I was besieged by other ambassadors asking me what this meant. I could only surmise he was demonstrating publicly, or specifically to Kofi Annan, that he could take criticism.

The banquet finished at 10 p.m. Only undrinkable Uzbek wine had been served, so I decided to try the Ragu. This was renowned as the expat bar, but I had not been there yet. As I entered in my kilt, I saw there was only one customer in, seated on a bar stool at the end of the bar. I asked the two pretty bar girls for a pint of Murphy's stout. They giggled and ran into a back office.

Some months later, the owner of the bar, Raj, told me about this. 'They called up and said that a man in a skirt had just come in and asked for a drink, and what should they do?' he said. 'I told them if his money's good, I don't care if he's naked.'

CHAPTER 8

The Embassy

The new Residence was being leased from the Uzbek Ambassador to Azerbaijan. It was a large imposing building that looked like it should be in *Dallas*, with a white balustraded double staircase sweeping up to the large double entrance doors. The garden was enormous and contained a very substantial swimming pool. The FCO had leased the house before it was built and had accordingly had a say in its design. One of my more flippant inputs had been to request a water feature. This had been provided, with a fountain spouting continuously from the mouth of an amphora lying on its side. The fountain splashed into a pool, which cascaded down a series of terraces until it narrowed into a channel and drove a large water wheel. The water then continued in a narrow stream running down the centre of the garden, crossed by a picturesque arched wooden bridge, until it concluded in a pond and moat surrounding a decorative pagoda.

It was lucky that the garden was so impressive, because much of the entertaining would have to be done there. The biggest drawback to the new residence was that the lounge and dining room were small. They would hold about 60 people maximum. They opened through onto a large marble terrace, which then led down to the garden. I had been told that you could entertain outside eight months a year, but now in mid-October evenings were already a bit chilly.

The lounge, dining room, kitchen and study were on the ground floor. There were two floors upstairs, containing five bedrooms, all with en suite bathrooms. Three of the bedrooms had very large dressing-rooms adjoining. Downstairs, the basement was enormous, extending under the terrace. Here, there was a very large second kitchen, ideal for functions. There were storerooms and a laundry, and a big basement room we used as a playroom. There was also a Turkish steam bath, with marble floor, walls, ceiling, benches and fittings, and a separate large sauna in pine, together with associated showers and plunge pool, and an eight-person jacuzzi. Outside, there was an external or 'summer kitchen' containing large gas-fired plov boilers.

A practical drawback was the lack of loos and a cloakroom. There were eight loos in the house, but five of these were in bedrooms and a sixth was a staff loo off the downstairs kitchen. There was only one on the ground floor. Even pressing into use the one at the bottom of the basement stairs, two loos were not enough for a large function.

There was also no cloakroom. Tashkent is very cold in winter, and 60 people coming to a cocktail party strip off a lot of heavy gear. We had to press the sauna into service as a cloakroom on occasion.

The house was built by a local contractor, but it was being finished, in terms of boilers, air conditioners, generators, wiring, alarms and other technical aspects, by a Northern Irish contractor named Alex Platt. He, with his team of Irish and Polish workers, was a welcome cheerful presence on the social scene. They introduced me to a pleasant little bar called Lionheart, just around the corner from the embassy. It was very basic, serving just beer and vodka to a local clientele, mostly of student age. You could take your own music to play on the stereo, and I took in Queen, Supertramp and The Beatles.

I met two interesting girls there. One Russian girl named Lucy was an extremely talented artist who sold delightful miniatures around the bars. She also designed and made her own clothes, which were original and striking. She was 19, liked vodka and flirting, and would use her powers of seduction on American soldiers to sell her paintings, flirting and teasing outrageously until she had clinched a sale and then pulling away rapidly. This was a high-risk strategy, and I had to rescue her at least twice from soldiers who had understood they would get more than just a painting for their money.

Lucy was a tremendous pool player and would rook money that way, too. I can see her now, winking conspiratorially at me as she bent her body sensuously over the pool table for the benefit of her next victim, arse stuck out to distract him, pretending she didn't know how to hold the cue. She had a delicious upturned nose and wide smile. That Christmas she was to declare to me that she'd painted a picture for my present but found an unexpected customer and sold it to him instead. So, she had decided to sleep with me. Looking at me from the side of her eyes, she said that usually she charged $300 for sex, which was much more than she got for the painting, so this was a better present.

I laughed and told her that I would rather wait till she had a painting for me, and she giggled and hugged me. Sadly, I saw Lucy deteriorate over the next two years: she sold fewer paintings and more sex. Her face bloated and her eyes got redder and narrower. She drank more and the sparkle left her. I never did get that painting.

The other girl I met was Nilufar. She was short, beautiful and vivacious with a perfect figure including the most wonderful neat bum. She always wore figure-hugging jeans and a T-shirt. She seemed a fixture in the bar, sitting there at the end of it, cigarette in hand, chatting to Dima the barman. Dima had long dark hair, wisps of beard and sported a red bandana. He affected a very cosmopolitan air but had never left Tashkent.

Nilufar was extremely intelligent and very much her own woman. The first three or four times I offered to buy her a drink, she turned me down flat. In the end, I had to buy the whole bar a drink, in which she didn't object to participating.

Other than Alex and his staff when they were in Tashkent, the only other expatriates who frequented that bar centred on a humorous man called Bob. He was a 50-year-old American, short and balding with a pot belly. He worked for a company called Premier Executive, who operated commercial flights in support of US operations in Uzbekistan. Two of his colleagues also drank in that bar: they were essentially ground crew. Their company ran small executive jets. This did not surprise me at all, as I could think of numerous ways that kind of logistic support would be needed by the large US presence in Uzbekistan, with its major construction projects at the new embassy and K2 Airbase. I was, however, surprised to learn that they sometimes flew Uzbek prisoners back to Tashkent from Baghram airbase in Afghanistan.

Nilufar was extremely feisty and determined not to be impressed by my being an ambassador. She came from a wealthy Uzbek family, and her father was a retired KGB colonel. Nilufar and I used to argue a lot about politics, and these conversations used to spread to embrace the whole bar. I was surprised when one female student told me that things in Uzbekistan had got much worse since Soviet times. I argued, saying that she was romanticising the Soviet Union. Communism had been an awful system, and the Soviet Union had collapsed simply because it didn't work.

I had been strongly ideologically opposed to the Soviet Union, and while I had recognised how awful the Karimov regime was, I had not yet fully come to understand that indeed this was something much worse than the Soviet Union. Since independence, there has been steadily less personal freedom in Uzbekistan, while living standards have plummeted as Soviet institutions have collapsed without any compensating individual economic freedom. The brain drain of professionals and Russian nationals has been disastrous, and positive aspects of the Soviet legacy, like universal literacy and good roads, are fast collapsing.

A number of students were taking part in this conversation. One tall ethnic Russian with striking long ash-blonde hair was just completing her Ph.D. thesis in mathematics. She told me that her worry was the examination on the works of President Karimov. I was astonished. She explained to me that every educational course in the country, from elementary school to Ph.D., includes compulsory study of Karimov's execrable books.[30] She added that she had to submit a paper entitled 'What the Independence of Uzbekistan Means to Me'. She said, with a bitter smile, that what it meant was that the police had been able to rape her three times in the last year. Yet again, I was astonished.

This is seldom commented upon. Of that group of five girls, four had been raped by the police, some several times. The police do it because they can. People are continually stopped by police for their papers, and pretty girls are fair game. There is no justice or redress in Uzbekistan. An alleged problem with their documents, a threat to plant narcotics or charge them with prostitution is enough. The police have a girl to play with. This evil is extraordinarily prevalent. It has become accepted as one of the standard hardships of life in the country. Nobody even seems to get very angry about it. They are more concerned to hide the shame – a girl must be a virgin to marry.

There is an incredible practice prevalent throughout Uzbekistan. Girls have their hymen sewn back up before marriage, so that the blood-spotted bed sheets can be displayed. This is not an urban myth – the World Health Organisation estimates that 40 per cent of urban Uzbek girls have their hymen stitched up, and I met a British anthropologist researching it. I also met a gynaecologist who performs the operation, but 90 per cent of such procedures are 'back-street' jobs carrying a serious risk of infection.

All of which gave me some pause for thought. I had been fortunate to have a number of extremely enjoyable relationships, ranging from a few hours to several years, with a number of beautiful and fascinating women on my travels. Some of these had been genuine long-term relationships, as complex as any other in their mixture of intellect, romance and physicality. I was always prone to falling head over heels in love.

But these relationships had one thing in common. Whether in Central Europe, Russia, the Caribbean, Asia or Africa, there had always been a startling economic gap between the girl and me. I was much richer than them, or anyone whom they might normally meet. Plainly, beautiful girls do not normally fancy greying, pot-bellied weaklings with bad teeth. Was this a continuum – to what extent was what I might do with these Uzbek girls before me equivalent to what the Uzbek police had done to them? Is consent the only criterion, or do you have to consider the motives behind agreement? On the other hand, have not wealth and authority always attracted women to men?

The question troubled me, and that conversation with those Uzbek girls resulted in a distinct change in my social behaviour.

* * *

On the political front, all was quiet for a couple of days after the Annan visit. Then on Sunday morning I received a summons to go immediately to the Ministry of Foreign Affairs to see Foreign Minister Komilov.

I called Karen to accompany me. I was fully expecting to be declared *persona non grata* and asked to leave the country. We arrived at the Uzbek Foreign Ministry and squeezed into the tiny lift. It is a typical Soviet administrative building with rows of identical doors leading off long straight corridors.

After that meeting with Komilov, I reported back to London. In my telegram, I noted that, in sharp contrast to my introductory call on first arrival, when he was bewilderingly rude and walked out after five minutes, Komilov was at pains to be friendly, and the meeting lasted about an hour. He spoke Russian this time and used an interpreter. As his English is fluent – better than that of the interpreter – this seemed strange until I noticed he was speaking from a text that was written in Russian. He clearly needed to be able to say that he had stuck to the letter of the script from a higher authority.

Komilov said the government of Uzbekistan took issue with my speech at Freedom House but trusted this would not affect other areas of cooperation between us. He noted the speech had caused debate in the media. We must realise the sensitivity and ambiguity of the issues involved in fighting the danger of Islamic fundamentalism. Eighty per cent of Uzbekistan is Muslim and it would be suicidal for the Uzbek government to act against Muslims. He did not agree that there were any political prisoners or that there was religious persecution. He suggested that the tone of the speech differed from the tone of his discussions a month before in the FCO, where there seemed to be a different view. He would be seeking to contact the FCO again to confirm this.

Komilov had noted the different approach of our two governments to Hizb-ut-Tehrir. He claimed that hidden arms had recently been found in Kirghizstan and Kazakhstan, which showed this group was not peaceful. They had already shown us HuT leaflets calling for jihad and advocating the kamikaze use of aeroplanes (we believed these HuT leaflets to be probably forgeries by the Uzbek security services, as nothing like them was ever discovered from any other source). HuT had acted aggressively towards the Uzbek embassy in London. He said the HuT members currently in jail were not political prisoners but criminals. However, he reiterated, he wanted our relationship to be cooperative and not based solely on contentious issues. He would welcome increased dialogue.

In response, I said I had noted his comments about a difference in tone between London and my speech but made it plain that every word had been cleared by the FCO. It was a considered speech of which he should take account.

I told him that the repressive approach to dissidents, including those who want to see moves towards a Muslim state, was breeding real resentment. There was no legal political opposition and, in the absence of legitimate outlets, this build-up of grievances could lead to further terrorism. We feared that, as well as failing to meet international standards on human rights, the Uzbek approach was counter-productive.

Komilov replied that the Uzbek authorities preferred to deal in concrete instances not allegations of thousands of prisoners. Uzbekistan is a large sovereign country and entitled to do things its own way. In particular, no country had the right to tell it to become a less secular state.

I countered that we had not and would not comment on how secular a state Uzbekistan should be; that was for the people of Uzbekistan to decide, preferably through a free and fair political system. But just advocating a less secular way of life should not be cause for imprisonment and maltreatment.

Foreign Office telegrams are an art form in themselves. They are normally beautifully phrased and say very little, being lengthy exercises in temporising, with an extra emphasis on special pleading on behalf of the host government. My telegrams were so different that they were attracting real attention. Throughout my whole career I had been longing for the day when I could be an ambassador and send my own telegrams, without someone above me toning them down. I was now receiving many congratulatory emails and letters from colleagues, including some from ambassadors much senior to me. One message ran: 'Well done! In these dangerous and difficult times, it is our duty to call it as it is, not say what others want to believe.' A simpler message read: 'You must have balls like a sperm whale.'

One fellow ambassador sent me a postcard of Oscar Wilde, with a Wilde quotation: 'Anyone who tells the truth is bound to be found out sooner or later.' That proved to be prescient. His message began: 'We have been reading your telegrams with equal measures of astonishment, agreement and enthusiasm.'

Suddenly, my stock in Tashkent was very high. In my first fortnight, I had accepted an invitation to a dinner to celebrate the 60th anniversary of the state tractor factory. All the ambassadors were invited, but I was the only one to turn up apart from the Belgian Honorary Consul. We were completely ignored and left to find our own place on the bottom of many tables. I learnt that the rudeness shown to the diplomatic corps at Independence Day was typical. The Uzbek authorities were as contemptuous of the outside world as they were mindful of minor hierarchies among their own members. Just as in Soviet days, who appeared in official line-ups with the President, and in just what position, mattered minutely. The third assistant engineer at the Nukus cotton ginnery outranked any ambassador. In consequence, other ambassadors had just stopped going to all non-compulsory events.

They missed some treats. I was invited to a concert at Tashkent Conservatoire and enjoyed a superb performance of both Gershwin's *Rhapsody in Blue* and *An American in Paris*, featuring a young Uzbek pianist who had won that year's Conservatoire competition. The orchestra really was first class, and I was amazed to learn that these were the first performances of Gershwin in Uzbekistan.

I was again the only ambassador to turn up. There was nothing prepared for me, and I was left to find a place in a concert hall that was overfull. I had made the mistake of going to the main entrance, whereas the concert hall is entered by a side door. It was 6.30 p.m. and just getting dark. A very pretty young student with long red hair and bright red lipstick saw me looking confused. She wore jeans and denim jacket, while everyone else was in either Western formal or Uzbek traditional clothing.

She took me by the arm and led me round the great modern building. It was quite a walk, but in her company most enjoyable. She spoke almost no English and was a native Uzbek speaker whose Russian was not fluent. She told me that her name was Tamara, and she was studying concert piano and composition. Her father was a professional musician. As I had plans to use music in my diplomatic effort, I was very glad to meet her. I was even more so when the great romantic climaxes swirled up in *Rhapsody in Blue* and her bosom heaved while she looked at me with wide eyes.

After my Freedom House speech, however, I discovered I was suddenly somebody. I was quickly on the top table wherever I went. Komilov came and sat next to me at functions. More to the point, I started to be able to get things done. The assault on the private sector continued, with new bans on cash transactions. These forced transactions through the state banks, which quite simply stole people's money. Any transaction over $500 would bring a visit from the tax police, who had a whole heap of anti-enterprise weapons. It became clear that there was a definite intention to eliminate private wealth and economic autonomy outside of the regime families.

Part of this was an assault on foreign investors. Jitendra Patel was typical in facing attempts by the Uzbek courts to take his company from him. At least 11 British companies were in similar positions. One UK company owned a 60 per cent stake in a cottonseed plant in Jizzak. They found the doors locked against them, as, without their knowledge, a court had re-assessed the asset value of the joint venture and awarded a 70 per cent stake to the local government. Other foreign companies were being deliberately bankrupted, for example by not allowing them to export product. The government would then claim the assets.[31]

The extraordinary thing about my new hard-man status was that I could intervene in such cases and actually be listened to. In most cases, the local Hokkimyat was the key government entity dealing with investors. I was soon zooming round the country in the Discovery, meeting with hokkims and shouting at them. The browbeating seemed to work and I was able, generally, to suspend the action against British firms. After 10,000 miles in its first three years, the Discovery put on another 15,000 miles in my first three months. All this activism on behalf of British business was to prove crucial to me in my coming trials.

The head of the OSCE in Europe was a Turk named Ahmet Erozan. The OSCE had originally nominated a British candidate, Simon Hemans, but the Uzbeks had refused to accept him, as they did not want the OSCE to be active on human rights. The OSCE had then rather spinelessly produced a panel of candidates for the Uzbeks to choose; they plumped for a Turkish diplomat, thinking he would be most unlikely to trouble them.

They could not have been more wrong. Ahmet Erozan was a big hearty man with a naughty grin and great passion for life, a passion for his work and a passion for helping ordinary people. He took over the office from an ineffectual Romanian. Erozan transformed it into an effective and hard-hitting unit, and did so remarkably quickly.

Now he sat in my office, savouring his tea, stretching out his legs before the sofa, hands in pockets, grinning his broad grin: 'You see, my friend, you have balls. They don't expect that in an ambassador. The others crawl to them. Of course, I have balls,' – he patted them expansively to illustrate his point – 'but no one expects them in a British diplomat. Of course you are Scottish – *Braveheart*!

'I am a Turk,' he went on. 'You know, my people are close to the Uzbeks. I can understand their language, it's like old country Turkish. But I understand their culture. I know their mentality. Other diplomats are polite and listen. They may try to explain but not to argue. I tell you this – the Uzbeks have nothing but contempt for the ambassadors in this town. They despise them. They think they are weak!'

Can't say I blame them, I thought, but just tried to maintain a noble William Wallace-type bearing.

'But you are different. You just refuse to play by their rules. You tell them to their face what you think. You know, you would be surprised at some of the people in this town who admire you. Believe me, I know. Of course, you realise most of your Western colleagues hate you.'

Ahmet obviously needed no lessons from me in straight talking. He carried on, 'I hear you told Azimov to his face that his statistics were lies?'

'Pretty well,' I said.

'You probably don't realise just what you have done. All their lives, nobody ever dared talk to these people like that. Uzbeks would be beaten and imprisoned, Western businessmen are grovelling for favours, and diplomats simply don't. Take Azimov. You know as leader of the Uzbek Communist Student League he denounced his fellow executive members. Some of them disappeared completely. No one has stood up to him since he was 18. He's been spouting his rubbish for years. No one ever challenged him. Then you. This society is based on raw power. Suddenly they find you've got the big balls, and you're pushing them around.'

I had been wondering about this: 'But what's my leverage? Is it just bluff and psychology? Or do they want something I am threatening? They don't seem too bothered about an IMF loan, for example.'

'Mostly it's just basic psychology. They respect the bigger balls. But Karimov cares about international reputation, and they are very keen to host the EBRD AGM in May – that's a big prestige thing for them.'

Reputation was bringing businessmen with problems, and ordinary Uzbeks whose relatives were imprisoned or tortured, flooding to my door. Every NGO and journalist was coming to me for straight-talking analysis of the situation, and I was making friends among members of the Uzbek elite, many of whom were engaged in political bet hedging. All this was enormously helpful to me in picking up information on the country.

I was getting very busy. A small triumph to savour was when, before some official event, I received a call from the Ministry of Foreign Affairs Protocol Department. Ambassadors had been instructed to be in their seats over an hour before the function started. But I could turn up ten minutes before, as long as I didn't tell anyone else!

* * *

I was learning that I had seriously underestimated Karen. She had concentrated on commercial work and, with the help of the excellent Lena, she had an encyclopaedic knowledge of the workings of the Uzbek commercial sector. With Dave Muir tied up continuously in immigration work, Karen also kept much of the mechanism of the embassy turning over and coped with the appalling burden of bureaucratic returns back to London. She could handle any task with tremendous energy and despatch. Chris also was a great support, and he seemed to welcome the new tempo I brought to the embassy's work. He was very capable, though lacking in confidence. For example, he had not been allowed to send off his own telegrams on politics and human rights before. I gave him his head, and he was very good.

On the other hand, the working atmosphere in the embassy could be poisonous. The relationships between some of the UK and Uzbek staff were strained and formal, and I had the impression that some Uzbeks were treated with scant respect. This was a pity, because they were good. Part of the trouble was the lack of the normal senior and middle level British staff in an embassy. To put it at its most basic, Colonel Ridout and I were the only university graduates among the UK staff. The Uzbek staff were almost all graduates, even most of the guards. Relationships sometimes seemed to be ruled by mutual contempt.

* * *

In early November, we had a trade mission visiting from the London Chamber of Commerce. This consisted of a dozen or so representatives of companies hoping to export to Uzbekistan, ranging from British Aerospace to a one-man trading firm. We provided an excellent programme of meetings and managed to get everyone who requested it in to see the senior minister in charge of their sector – an unheard of level of access.

We held a reception for the mission in the garden of the unfinished new Residence on 5 November. It was getting pretty cold for this, but I had ordered large gas-fired patio heaters, which were spread around the terrace. We had about 250 guests, including senior Uzbeks and contacts relevant to the specific business of each company. The evening was a great success and, being 5 November, concluded with a fireworks display.

All this was proving too much for Galina, whose nerves couldn't cope with catering on this kind of scale. I learnt from Alex Platt that the original residence cook was Galina's sister, a first-class professional chef. She had married Alex's foreman and moved to Northern Ireland. The job had then passed to her sister Galina, a teacher who couldn't particularly cook. As the embassy hadn't previously done much large-scale entertainment, that hadn't really mattered. Unfortunately, Galina now resigned. We replaced her with Lena, a short bouncy Russian who could cope with pretty well any demand.

The trade missioners were a fun bunch and included one friend of mine. I had known Bryan Harris as a very successful businessman in West Africa, where he dealt in agricultural machinery and drinking water treatment. He was now coming out to look at the Uzbek market.

The trade missioners introduced me to a person and to a place. Both had a major effect. One businessman invited me to dinner with his key Uzbek contact, an oligarch named Zokirjon Umarov. He lived in a village outside Tashkent, off the Samarkand road. I had not realised how far away it was, down narrow country lanes. Dinner was well advanced by the time I arrived, but I could not help but be entranced by the huge villa tastefully furnished with modern oil paintings and antiquities. These included wooden carvings from Khiva, illustrated volumes of poetry from Samarkand and ceramics from Afrosiyab. He was a genial host, speaking broken English, and insisted he would invite me again.

The other introduction was to the Safar Club. This was right above the Lionheart bar, a nightclub where the clientele sat in curtained booths, eating and looking out at the dance floor where showgirls belly danced or occasionally pole danced in bra and knickers. The belly dancers would go round the tables, squeezing into the booths and performing right in front of you while you tucked a note into their bra or knicker elastic. It was all very demure compared to Western lap-dancing clubs – it became a regular haunt of mine, and I never saw so much as a nipple. But you could invite the dancers or waitresses to sit in the booth with you. The drinks and food were reasonably priced, but certain items – non-alcoholic cocktails and chocolate – were ludicrously expensive. The girls would request these and get a 10 per cent commission on them. The unwary could spend an evening with a girl, feeling confident she had drunk only fruit juice, and then get a bill for several hundred dollars. The answer was to buy the girl beer and slip her ten dollars direct. This was fine with the girls, but sometimes the management could get shirty.

Some of the missioners took me out to this club, where we had a very jolly table. There was a ten o'clock curfew on bars, and you entered the club by knocking on a nondescript door. It opened a crack, and if the doorman ascertained you were safe, a beautiful girl would lead you down a corridor and up two flights of steps, the pitch darkness broken only by the flicker of her cigarette lighter. You then pushed through heavy felt curtains and emerged into the bright lights of the club. A couple of the businessmen knew the pitfalls of ordering and warned the rest of us. It was a fun time.

* * *

Once the trade mission left, I was immediately confronted by two staff crises. The first was astonishing. I received a complaint about an allegedly violent dispute between Chris Hirst and his neighbour. This proved difficult to resolve, as both sides gave markedly different accounts of the events. Chris flatly denied the allegations made against him by his neighbour, but I was aware that this was not the first time there had been problems. Chris told me that he thought the complaint had been instigated by the SNB and this was certainly a possibility given his work on human rights issues. I suggested that he and Karen move out of the area and pointed out that their house wasn't large enough to do the scale of entertaining I wanted my deputy to be taking on. Also, after they left the following year we would need a new house anyway, as they would presumably be replaced by two separate officers, not a couple.

The next day, I had to deal with another problem, this time involving two of our locally engaged staff, Valeri and Zhenya. In this instance, Karen brought me the news that there had been a serious breach of accounting procedures. When challenged, Zhenya and Valeri admitted it – Zhenya arrogantly, Valeri quiet and shame faced. I reluctantly agreed that this had to be a sacking offence.

I would miss Valeri but had to admit I hadn't warmed to Zhenya. She had been recruited direct from the KGB and maintained some of those attitudes. I wasn't really sure how far I trusted her.

I now needed a new secretary, and I decided we would get two people – one for me and one for the visa section – rather than split the job as Zhenya had done. My office and the visa section were both getting exponentially busier. We advertised the jobs in the local papers – another new departure for the embassy – and got the most tremendous response. Karen and I selected a dozen secretaries for interview, and we set aside a day to do it.

The moment the first candidate walked in the door, she had the job. She had the most extraordinary classical beauty, a perfect face framed by long blonde hair. She spoke near fluent English, typed and took shorthand, and had previously worked for a Turkish commercial company. She had married the boss and was now divorcing him. Karen agreed she was the best candidate, which I found a very useful defence when Fiona first set eyes on Kristina.

To replace Valeri, we promoted one of the guards, Dima, to driver. He was a slight but very handsome man. Karen worked out a new shift rota to try to reduce the overtime. This meant that there was no longer a designated flag car driver, though in fact Mansur became more and more 'my' driver. We eventually ended up hiring a third driver, Farhod, as the embassy got increasingly busy. I also had a personal driver, Konstantin, paid from my own pocket, to drive my private car, a Mitsubishi Montero, and to look after Fiona.

Fiona was also increasingly busy. We were averaging three functions a week at home, ranging from afternoon tea through dinner for 16 to cocktails and canapés for 300. In addition, she had taken on the job of chairman of the board of Tashkent International School. This was no sinecure. With the greatly increasing presence of US government personnel, the school was rapidly expanding and needed new premises. Acquiring property in Tashkent was very complicated, and the scheme was likely to involve a multimillion-dollar contract for building and/or renovation. Fiona was tackling all this with her usual mix of energy and brusque acuity.

Meanwhile, we received a welcome addition to our British staff in the shape of Sergeant John Agnew of the RAF, as assistant to Nick. It now became even more urgent to get the defence section out of their cupboard, and we anxiously awaited the completion of the new Residence so that the embassy could expand into the apartment above. We had been hosting parties there while it was unfinished but still hadn't been able to move in, as the hot water and heating systems were still not in place.

CHAPTER 9

Merry Christmas, War is Coming

Eventually, the EU mechanism clicked round, and it was finally agreed that EU ambassadors would deliver a démarche over the boiling deaths and the Khuderbegainov trial. Komilov had been kicked upstairs from the Foreign Ministry to be a presidential adviser, and his smooth deputy, Sadyk Safayev, had been promoted to Foreign Minister. Safayev had been Uzbek Ambassador to Washington, and the US embassy viewed him as a reformer, though I never saw the slightest evidence of it.

EU démarches were normally delivered by a 'troika' of three nations. As there were only four EU ambassadors in Uzbekistan, we all went.

Jacques-André Costilhes, for the French presidency, delivered the démarche in a tour de force of Gallic insouciance. Every nuance of tone, every scrap of body language seemed to me to spell out a plain message: 'I am very sorry to waste your time with this, Minister, and this has nothing to do with me, or with France, but I have to read out this rather embarrassing statement. We are civilised people and I will do this quickly, for form's sake, then you can reply while I listen politely, then we can all go home.'

Safayev said that in the case of Avazov and Alimov, an official investigation had revealed that they had died in a fight over a samovar, which explained the scalds. As for Khuderbegainov, he was astonished that the European Union was concerning itself with a violent terrorist.

Before we left, Jacques-André asked if any of his colleagues had anything to add. I said that in the Khuderbegainov case the problem was the lack of any kind of fair trial, whether he was a terrorist or not. In particular, the allegations that the accused and witnesses had been tortured were not taken seriously by the courts. We were worried about the prevalence of torture in general and the reliance of the legal system upon confessions. Over 99 per cent of trials ended in conviction, which threw doubt on the fairness of the system.

'Ambassador, all our countries have different legal systems. Your system is perhaps very clumsy. Unfortunately, in the United Kingdom many innocent people are accused and, of course, acquitted. Under our system, only the guilty are accused. That is why they are not acquitted. You must allow us our own tradition.'

My French and German colleagues laughed at Safayev's little sally. They had been shifting uncomfortably when I was speaking.

The lack of fair trial was a continuation of the Soviet system, although the use of physical torture had increased. The KGB had largely used the most intense psychological pressure; brute physicality was a hallmark of the Uzbek regime. More and more cases came to me. Plain beating was commonplace, as was the smashing of limbs by a blunt instrument and the application of electric shocks, generally to the genitals. Drowning was pretty common. More so was asphyxiation, and one technique was widespread throughout the country – they would strap on a gas mask and then block the filters. I presume that the advantage of this was that it would suffocate without bruising. I also came across several cases of the use of chlorine gas.

Most common of all was rape and sodomy. Any young woman arrested was bound to be raped, whether she confessed or not. Men were most often raped with objects such as bottles, though they could be brutally sodomised as well. A neighbour of a good Uzbek friend of mine was arrested and died in agony a week later after being anally raped with a broken bottle. Raping someone in front of a relative is a very common method of extracting a confession.

Homosexuality is taboo in Uzbekistan, where it is illegal. Gays are seldom prosecuted but often brutally beaten. Many are blackmailed by the police. But I could not understand how macho policemen, who would hate gays, could then rape prisoners, and not just with objects. I asked Zokirjon to explain this.

'They don't see it as sex. It is power. To humiliate and give pain.'

'But these policemen come.'

'Yes, but it's not sex; it's power. It's not a man; it's just a hole. They are not gay. Call one gay and see what they do to you.'

I was unconvinced – plainly there was a lot of weird repression in this society.

Chris had put a huge amount of effort into a court reporting project. There were no transcripts of trials in Uzbekistan, so the British government had paid for computers to be installed in courtrooms to make recordings of proceedings that could not be tampered with. We employed the American Bar Association and an NGO called CEELI (Central and Eastern European Legal Initiative) to manage the project. A pilot had started in the Ferghana Valley and was due to be rolled out across the country. I was sceptical.

Chris organised a meeting with the ladies from the American Bar Association to persuade me to support the next phase. Their hearts were all very much in the right place, but I asked, 'So, how many trials have been monitored so far?'

'Over a thousand now, Ambassador.'

'And how many acquittals have there been?'

Consternation.

'Well, it is difficult to be completely certain, but we don't believe there have been any actual acquittals. But the point of the equipment is to provide a record. It can be used for appeal.'

'Well, how many have been acquitted on appeal?'

'Well, none yet, but probably most of them haven't completed the appeals process. We believe the existence of the equipment in the court may be leading to a change in courtroom behaviour, with more respect paid to the defence. There could be a reduction in the severity of sentences and in the use of the death penalty.'

'Can you quantify that?'

'No, Ambassador, not yet.'

I concluded it was too early to justify spending on the next stage. What particularly worried me was that the scheme was being quoted, not least by the Uzbeks, as evidence of reform, while it was giving nothing but a veneer of respectability to an unjust system. Better sham trials seemed of limited use and arguably pernicious.

In November, Professor Theo van Boven, the United Nations Special Rapporteur on Torture, paid an investigative visit to Uzbekistan. Everyone was somewhat baffled as to why the Uzbeks had agreed to let him in. It was understood that the US had persuaded Karimov that a well-managed visit would burnish the country's image.

There appeared to be little to fear. Van Boven's programme had been negotiated with the Uzbek authorities. But much of it depended on input from Chris direct to van Boven's office on the most notorious torture centres to visit.

Van Boven arrived in the late afternoon and his official programme started the next morning. But that first evening, we gave a reception for him in the Residence, to which we invited human rights defenders and relatives of torture victims. It was harrowing. The façade of the cocktail party did not last long before van Boven's team got out their notebooks and started taking down case histories. Soon little knots were forming all over the apartment. Fiona switched the supply of drinks to relays of coffee, and I bustled round directing staff to interpret. Under gentle and expert questioning, details came out that I had not heard before. I found tales involving children especially harrowing; at one stage I retreated to my office to recompose myself. I learnt of the placing of healthy dissidents into TB wards so they contract the disease. Uzbek prisons are riddled with drug-resistant TB. I recall Dilobar giving details of her brother's case to a researcher, seated at Fiona's dressing table as he perched on the edge of our bed, notebook on knee. When van Boven eventually left, the researcher with Dilobar had still not finished his notes of this case. He needed a few more minutes, and Chris offered to run him back to his hotel when he finished. Chris and I agreed that, after hearing all that horror, we both needed a drink, so I went along, too. It turned out neither Chris nor the visitor knew which hotel he was in, and Chris drove his Land-Rover to several, cursing under his breath, until he found the right one.

After we finally got rid of our visitor, Chris headed for the Lionheart Bar and something quite extraordinary happened. He put his foot down and started driving in a manner I can only describe as manic. He gunned the Land-Rover up to full speed, ignoring red lights and causing one car to swerve violently to miss us at an intersection. Even more worryingly, he drove straight at a Lada that was moving quietly along in front of us. He went straight for it, travelling about 50 miles an hour faster than it was. Just when it seemed we must collide, he slammed on the brakes and pulled inside, missing it by inches. Having passed it, he pulled back sharply in front and slammed on the brakes, bringing the Land-Rover screeching almost to a halt. The whole time he stared ahead, his face purple and knuckles white on the wheel.

'Fuckers,' he spat out. 'Fuckers, fuckers, fuckers, fuckers. Fuckers, fuckers, fuckers, fuckers. Uzbek fuckers.'

This was counterpointed by my attempts to break in. 'Chris!' I yelled. 'Chris! Chris! Speak to me, Chris!'

I put my hand on his arm. He slapped it away, leaving his hand on my chest. He was much more powerful than me. But he seemed to see me, and he brought the car to a stop in the fast lane.

'Yes, what is it?' he asked, tetchily.

'Are you OK? You seemed to get madly aggressive.'

'I don't know what you're talking about. Do you still want that drink?'

'Yes, but calm down.'

'OK. Lionheart Bar, isn't it?' He drove off sedately. 'I think van Boven learnt a lot today.'

He's not the only one, I thought. But I said, 'Yes, the evening went very well. Thanks for all the slog you put in.'

We pulled up at the Lionheart Bar, and I bought Chris a drink. He then turned to me and said, 'This place is full of bloody Uzbeks.'

I smiled an apology at Dima, who shrugged. But Nilufar had heard.

'I'm a bloody Uzbek,' she said.

'Fuck off, I don't talk to prostitutes,' said Chris.

Several people stood up. I put my arm round Chris. I could feel his muscles flexing.

'Chris, you're tired, go home,' I said.

'Do you want to go to Safar?' he asked.

'Good idea,' I said. At least I might get him out of here before a fight started. But once we were out of the door, I discovered that he didn't mean the Safar upstairs but Safar in the park. There had been five of these Safars, under the same ownership, but they were being closed down one by one by the Uzbek government. The one in the park was reputed to feature actual stripping. I told Chris I didn't want to go to the park, and he stormed off into the night.

I went back into the bar to apologise. Nobody held it against me. I paid for the beers poured for Chris and me, gave them away to a couple of students and made the short walk home. I was really worried about what I had seen from Chris. He normally had an old-fashioned Yorkshire courtesy, but now I had seen this mad rage.

In judging the events of that evening, you have to take into account that both Chris and I had just been through extreme trauma. We had gathered together a group of people who gave direct evidence of terrors so harrowing that Stephen King could not imagine them – every kind of physical and mental torture, involving loved ones of those we were listening to. I still have nightmares now. Imagine your children raped in front of you, or healthy prisoners being deliberately locked up in a dark room with those dying of TB. I am not going to recount some of the physical detail. I reacted with tears; Chris with anger. Chris was dealing with this subject matter every day and working at a level far above his grade. His behaviour seemed to me far from inexplicable, but it did give me cause for concern.

The next day I pressed Karen over plans for them to move. If there were problems in a new district I would know whether or not Chris was the problem. What would then be the solution was another question.

* * *

Van Boven's visit was stunning. Against the protocols, the Uzbek authorities refused to let him enter the SNB holding centre in Tashkent, the most notorious of all the torture sites. He visited Jaslyk gulag, but the Uzbeks deliberately messed around the transport so a day's inspection was shortened to an hour. We obtained definite intelligence material proving that the Uzbeks deliberately delayed and obstructed him. I pointed out to London that we were about to invade Iraq based on much less concrete evidence of obstruction of United Nations inspectors.

Van Boven produced a report which said that torture in Uzbekistan was 'widespread and systemic' and 'used as a routine investigative technique'. The Uzbek government were furious and the Americans much embarrassed. John Herbst argued that it was a mistake to report in such strong terms, because now the Uzbeks would be wary of such visits. I suggested that visits which pulled their punches were of no use anyway. The diplomatic climate was changing in my favour. The diplomatic corps could write off reports from HRW as unreliable; they were not a part of official reality. But a UN report certainly was.

The OSCE were preparing a workshop to be held in the Intercontinental Hotel. It was a teach-in on the international legal position on torture, which is banned in all its forms, much as is slavery. The course included the definition of torture and explained how judicial mechanisms might be used to prevent the infection of the justice system by torture evidence. Uzbek ministries and law enforcement agencies were all supposed to participate at very senior level, but in the event they all sent low-ranking representatives. Here, I met Professor Douwe Korff, who teaches international law at London Metropolitan University. He gave a powerful presentation, setting out that it was against international law to obtain or use information gathered under torture.

Just before this, I had been most concerned by intelligence material we were receiving from SIS (better known as MI6). I had been reading the regular flow of this material, and as I got to know the country I had been increasingly concerned at the gap between the information it contained and the truth. The intelligence material came to MI6 from the Uzbek intelligence services, via the CIA. It just made no sense compared to the facts on the ground. The content of one report reminded me of the statement to which the old man at the Khuderbegainov trial had been obliged to sign up.[32]

Mostly the material just said it came from 'A friendly security service'. Sometimes, but not always, it specified 'From detainee debriefing'. I had seen enough of the routine methods of the Uzbek security services to be pretty sure that this stuff was hot out of the torture chambers.

After meeting Douwe Korff, I was convinced that what we were doing was not only wrong but illegal. That provided the leverage I needed to get us to stop it. The trick, I decided, would be to get the question above officials and put squarely before ministers. A telegram from an ambassador expressing concern that ministers were acting illegally would have to be put before them, rather than filtered out by officials who prepared the ministers' red boxes of daily material.

Before drafting a hard-hitting telegram, I wanted to make quite sure I was on firm ground and would not be making a fool of myself. I therefore asked Karen to go and see her US opposite number, David Appleton, to check with him that the CIA did not have procedures in place to ensure that any material they received from the Uzbeks could not come from torture. She returned and reported that David was not available, so she had met another senior member of the Mission. He had said that, yes, come to think of it the intelligence probably did come from torture. He had not thought of that as a problem before, and he commented to Karen that it was an indication of how far 9/11 had shifted moral perceptions.

So, confident I was on safe ground, I sent off my bullet. I can't reproduce the telegram, because it was classified Top Secret. But it said that we were obtaining intelligence material from the Uzbek security services. It was probably obtained through torture, which the Americans, who supplied it to us, were not denying. We should stop getting it on legal, practical and moral grounds.

Legally, we were in contravention of the UN Convention against Torture, Article 4 of which banned 'complicity' in torture. To obtain such intelligence on a regular basis undoubtedly made us complicit. I said that in supplying this intelligence to ministers, I was afraid we might be putting ministers at risk of breaking UK and international law.

Practically, I said, the information was useless. It was not just wrong, it presented a deliberate distortion. It all had a common theme: it aimed to exaggerate the Islamic threat to Uzbekistan with the aim of justifying continued support to the Karimov regime.

Morally, the argument was self-evident. Torture is simply wrong. In resorting to receiving information through torture, we were demeaning ourselves and abandoning the very values we claimed to be defending in the War on Terror.

My intention had been to get attention at the top of the FCO. I succeeded. Foreign Minister Jack Straw, Head of the Diplomatic Service Sir Michael Jay and Head of MI6 Sir Richard Dearlove held meetings to discuss it. But I had seriously miscalculated when I had believed that British ministers would reject material obtained through torture. What I achieved was to increase to sizzling point the hostility towards me at the senior levels of the British government and particularly from the intelligence services.

I had failed adequately to take into account that I was only seeing the torture material from Uzbekistan. In the War on Terror, it had been decided to relax our taboo on torture, and we were accepting material from the torture chambers of Egypt, Pakistan, Jordan, Saudi Arabia and a number of other countries including even Sudan and Syria. The British government was even to argue in court for the right to use torture material as evidence. The government won this right in the Court of Appeal in November 2004 but lost to a unanimous judgment of seven Law Lords on 8 December 2005.

I had not accounted for the possibility that Blair might be prepared to condone others applying Tudor standards of barbarity. I am glad that the Law Lords upheld the values of civilisation, but I still find it incredible that the government were prepared to argue, before the highest court in the land, for the use of torture material.

* * *

Samarkand was the target for my next regional visit, and I would be setting off with the new team of Dima and Kristina to accompany me. On the way back, we would be visiting the town of Jizzak. It was a dark and cold late November day. I had wanted to leave at noon, but pressure of work kept me back. When I finished work, it was about 4 p.m. and beginning to snow quite heavily. Several of the staff advised me not to go, but I didn't see any great danger in the late autumn weather.

The road to Samarkand ran through a bit of Kazakhstan, and with the border closures a 50-mile section had been sealed off. Ordinary traffic had a two-hour detour, but diplomatic vehicles could still get through, and it was an easy three-hour drive. As we joined the main Samarkand route from a slip road, I realised the snow was getting heavy and the light had taken on an ominous purple tinge. There was already a foot of snow on the verges, and with very little traffic the slush on the carriageway was substantial.

By 30 miles outside Tashkent, we were in pitch blackness, and the wipers could not cope with the weight of snow piling on the windscreen. Dima had slowed down to about 20 miles an hour.

'Dima,' I said, 'we'll have to go quicker or we'll just get snowed in. Take a chance on it.'

Dima sped up to around 50 miles an hour. The snow was falling just as heavily, but at that speed the rush of air blew it past the car. We got along fine, bar the odd skid. Poor Dima had huge difficulty in working out where, in the tumbling chaos, the road was. Again and again, our luck held.

Then it didn't. Suddenly light pierced the darkness and a military guard post loomed, one of the permanent checkpoints on the road, this one marking the boundary of Syr Darya and Jizzak provinces. By the time we saw the floodlit checkpoint through the snow, we were less than a hundred yards away. Dima slammed on the brakes, and as we were now travelling on top of a thick carpet of snow and ice, that was a big mistake.

The wheels locked and the vehicle slewed round. It continued on the same trajectory straight down the highway but was now speeding along sideways like a one-ton curling stone. We were hurtling at 40 miles an hour into a concrete barrier, which was going to strike exactly at the rear passenger side where Kristina was seated.

She screamed. Instinct took over, and I unclipped my seat belt and threw myself over the top of her, bracing myself against the door that would take the impact, my feet pushing her across the other side. I cursed myself – what a stupid way to die.

I had heard that Land-Rovers were famous for their flimsy bodywork, which offered no protection in a roll. But the new Discovery must be fearsomely well built. The concrete edge slammed into the rear passenger door, which jacknifed, bending outwards. But the side protection absorbed the shock, and the door only came in some inches, pushing me on top of Kristina, by no means the worst thing that had ever happened to me.

The left side windows had smashed; we were shocked but unhurt. I felt embarrassed about my unnecessary heroics.

'I was worried I was going to lose you there, Kristina,' I said. 'It was a lot of money and effort to recruit you. I'd hate to have to go through that again.'

Kristina grinned fetchingly, but Dima was now in tears. With windows missing and the door not closing, it was suddenly incredibly cold. I got out into the storm and looked round the car.

'It doesn't look too bad,' I said. 'Unless the chassis's twisted.'

The soldiers had not appeared out of their hut. Probably presuming that no one would be travelling on a night like this, they had left the barriers open. Dima was still sobbing. Kristina was getting into the front seat to comfort him. I stopped her and first swept the shattered glass off the seat with a copy of *The Economist*. I had presumed Dima was just in shock, but when I got back in my place and asked him to try starting the engine, he whispered quietly to Kristina. She looked back at me.

'Dima's sure he'll be sacked for wrecking the car,' she said.

'Don't be stupid,' I replied. 'It was entirely my idea, both risking the storm and travelling so fast. Dima has done a great job. Anyway, it's only a car and we're still alive. Dima, stop worrying!'

The storm was so fierce that the soldiers still hadn't noticed we were there, only 20 metres from their hut. I ploughed over and banged on the door. The soldiers were eating sausage and drinking vodka. They were very cheery and full of concern. They got the door shut and taped plastic fertiliser sacks over the broken windows. We set off again into the night.

I decided we would give up on Samarkand and head for Jizzak, which lay a few miles north of the main road, about 30 miles ahead of us. It was a long 30 miles. The car's heating coped better than I expected, though ice was forming on the inside of the damaged door.

Just after we turned off for Jizzak, the car slowed to a halt. It had been misfiring for a while. Dima was completely dispirited. I know nothing about engines. It had clearly snowed very heavily here, but now just tiny crystals were falling, sparkling like diamonds in the headlights. The road temperature gauge had been showing minus 18.

The orange lights of Jizzak glowed tantalisingly on the horizon, reflecting vividly off the glittering white landscape. Dima got the bonnet open. I realised we had a couple of minutes to get the car started before the diesel froze solid. I opened the carburettor and poured Kristina's lighter fluid into it. I had seen it done in Chicago and, amazingly, it worked. The engine started with a bang but wouldn't engage gear. Still, we had the heating on and big jerry cans of diesel; we could survive the night here if we had to. Kristina had her luggage open and was trying to put on all her clothes. She then had an idea and phoned the human rights activists we were to meet in Jizzak. They readily offered to come out to the rescue.

Forty minutes later, they arrived in a battered green Lada. Rescuing an ambassador was a great adventure, and they were very cheerful. Their leader was Bakhtiyor Hamroev, a pleasant short man in quilted Uzbek gown and lacquered hat. They made light work of getting the vehicle going again. Bakhtiyor said there was a private hotel in Jizzak, and we followed them through the deserted streets, snow banked up against the low houses. I was sceptical, but the Bek Hotel was a delight. It had about eight large bedrooms. There was no gas, and the city's district heating and hot water plant was down, but the rooms had electric fan heaters and individual immersion boilers.

It was still only 10 p.m. I telephoned Lena Son at home in Tashkent and asked her, provided snow wasn't still falling heavily, to get Mansur down to us with a replacement vehicle. I also asked her to start work on cancelling the morning's Samarkand programme and bringing forward my Jizzak appointments.

The bathroom had new Italian fittings and tiling, and I ran a deep bath, unscrewing all the little shampoos and gels and tipping them in. I then closed my eyes and soaked.

I emerged to find what looked like every policeman and official in Jizzak in the lobby, and three Formula One pit crews and the engineering corps of the Uzbek army outside working on the car. Amazingly, everyone, including the city officials, seemed to be taking direction from Bakhtiyor. Who needs breakdown insurance when you have human rights activists? I was whisked through to the restaurant, where we had a very good meal indeed, with French wine and real whisky. I was amazed.

Dima was still considerably shaken and a bit tearful. He still couldn't believe he wouldn't get the sack. Lena called back to say Mansur would set off at first light. She had already had considerable success in changing programmes.

I slept very well. Lena had arranged for us to call on the Hokkim of Jizzak at ten. I was at breakfast at nine. By 9.45, neither Kristina nor Dima had appeared. They eventually turned up just after ten. I quickly hustled Kristina into a car the Hokkimyat had kindly put at my disposal, and we left Dima to await Mansur.

The Hokkim was very welcoming. He was the youngest hokkim in Uzbekistan, the same age as me. We exchanged pleasantries and then discussed the problems of the disputed cottonseed factory. He started by saying it was all down to independent courts. I told him straight that I wasn't interested in playing games – I knew as well as he did that the courts weren't independent. Unless he got a grip, I would be raising the matter with the President. This distinctly worried him.

I was interested in two other factories in Jizzak that had received EBRD loans. One was a pipe extrusion plant, to which the Hokkimyat took us. It wasn't working because of the failure of the huge polymer project, but it did exist. Which was more than you could say for the winery. The Hokkim looked completely blank when I asked him about it, and called in his Director of Industry. He confirmed there was no winery in Jizzak, nor had there ever been. There were no grapes in the province's agricultural production plan. This was pretty weird, as the EBRD loan for this non-existent winery had been given out in full some two years previously, and interest was being repaid on schedule.

We had lunch with the Hokkim, after which we went back to the hotel and met up with Mansur, who had turned up in the old dark-green Toyota Land Cruiser, which he preferred in the snow for its greater wheelbase and wider tyres. Mansur cheerfully set off back to Tashkent in the damaged Land-Rover. It looked awful, but the chassis was basically OK.

After lunch, we met Bakhtiyor and other human rights activists at his flat. This was in a standard Soviet block, about eight storeys high, built of crumbling concrete. I walked gingerly over sheet ice to the entrance and up the dank crumbling stairs. The bottom couple of flights were covered in ice. The tiny flat currently had no heating, water or electricity. The electricity had been off for a couple of days. The apartments of Jizzak had no public heating, gas or running water and little electricity all that winter.

About 200 dissidents had been arrested in Jizzak in the previous few months. They had documented 84 of these cases. Jizzak had long been a centre of opposition, and while they didn't want to estimate the total number of political prisoners from there, it certainly amounted to several hundred.

We set off that evening for Samarkand, passing through the Gates of Tamburlaine, a pass where he allegedly installed massive iron gates to guard the major road from Tashkent to Samarkand, Bokhara and Balkh.[33] When we arrived in the city, there was not so much snow but the cold was incredible. We were booked into a small hotel, the Malika, which had no heating in the absence of gas. It was late when we arrived, and so we just had dinner and went to bed.

We called the next day on the Hokkim of Samarkand, Ruslan Mirzaeyev. I had to wait after breakfast for Kristina and Dima who turned up late again. The day before I had made allowances, but now I made plain that this was not what I expected. But although we arrived at the Hokkimyat some ten minutes late, Mirzaeyev was later. We were shown into a reception room, where we waited in extreme cold for perhaps 20 minutes. Eventually, Mirzaeyev turned up, having evidently come from somewhere heated. We went into a meeting room and sat down at a long table, with Mirzaeyev flanked by five or six officials on one side and faced by Kristina and me on the other. There were small bottles of mineral water on the table which had frozen solid. On some, the tops had been forced off and sat atop little columns of ice rising from the bottles; on others, the bottle itself had split, and spilt ice was frozen to the side like wax on a guttering candle.

Mirzaeyev was in a fur-trimmed long leather coat and kept on his Soviet-style military fur hat. I wore my grey cashmere coat, climbing boots and sheepskin-lined leather gloves. Kristina's beautiful face was framed by a huge fur collar. It was all pretty surreal, especially as Mirzaeyev launched into a 30-minute speech. This was not the normal hokkim's speech about the regional economy and investment opportunity. It was instead Karimov's 'Paranoid' speech, with a piece added on at the end about the impossibility of privatising the cotton industry. Some specific points in this were plainly direct responses to my meeting with Azimov. The government of Uzbekistan is an efficient despotism.

I had two specific points to push, one on tax problems affecting British American Tobacco's factory in Samarkand, the other requesting support for the festival of British music I was planning to hold in Uzbekistan in May 2003. I wanted Samarkand to be the second city for this. I was asking the Hokkim if they could provide the venue, publicity and meet local costs of accommodation and food. He readily agreed, saying he was delighted by this opportunity for cooperation. He would make sure there was a full audience for every concert.

Something about the way he said this alarmed me. I said that we were not intending an admission charge, but we needed to publicise the events in local media so that people could come if they wanted. We didn't want an audience to be compelled. The Hokkim smiled and said he understood.

Mirzaeyev spoke with great energy, occasionally striking the table with the open palm of his gloved left hand. He had the assured swagger of the bully. He had previously been Hokkim of Jizzak, during the period of the most notorious of Uzbekistan's human rights abuses before the boiling deaths. Several old ladies involved in an agrarian protest had been mown down by combine harvesters. In 2004, he would be promoted to Prime Minister of Uzbekistan.

In the evening, we had an invitation to the home of Professor Mirsaidov to meet with a group of Tajik dissidents. Professor Mirsaidov was a retired professor of Tajik literature at the University of Samarkand. He and his friends had wanted to start a centre for Tajik culture, where the language, music and heritage could be celebrated. Naturally, this had been banned. He had gathered in his home to meet me a selection of a dozen dissidents from Samarkand, all of whom seemed to move in and out of jail regularly. The plates of steaming soup were welcome in the biting cold, as was his traditional Tajik wine made from raisins. It tasted sweet, nutty and complex, rather like a good Madeira.

The Tajik civilisation of Samarkand and Bokhara was one of the world's great cultural flourishings, producing the *Thousand and One Nights*, the *Rubaiyat of Omar Khayyam*, the invention of algebra, the medicine of Avicenna and the astronomy of Ulugbek. Over 90 per cent of the population of Samarkand still speak Tajik, but they are falling victim to Karimov's nationalist Uzbek policies.[34] Over 80 Tajik schools had been closed down in Uzbekistan since independence. There were now only 12 left. The Tajik newspapers had also been closed and Tajik radio broadcasting stopped.

All government positions now required Uzbek language examinations, as Uzbek had replaced Russian as the state language. Legislation had been passed with deadlines reserving different grades and categories of public jobs for Uzbek speakers at different times. University teaching in all subjects was to be in Uzbek by 2005 – a major problem when the large majority of lecturers were ethnic Russians and Tajiks. Less than 40 per cent of university lecturers were native Uzbek speakers.

There is a deeper problem. The cultured population of the cities had always been Tajik. The literary heritage of the region was almost entirely Tajik. Printed Uzbek literature is, historically, almost non-existent. There is very little to found a culture on. There are only one hundred and forty books in print in the Uzbek language. Six of these are by Karimov and another forty are propaganda publications of his government. Many of the rest are educational textbooks or public health literature, much of it donor funded. Of Uzbek literature per se, the bulk is Soviet propaganda material of execrable quality, including poetry, plays and some terrible operas. There are three Uzbek novels in print, all of which fall into the propaganda category. Of modern Uzbek plays, seven times as many are banned as currently available. The best living writers in the Uzbek language are all long-term political prisoners.

This is a major disaster. A Soviet achievement was that 99 per cent of the Uzbek population was literate in Russian and most had some familiarity with Pushkin and Gogol. Now a significant proportion of young Uzbeks, especially in country districts, scarcely understand Russian, and bringing Russian literature into Uzbekistan is illegal. In 2003, the Uzbek government refused a gift from Russia of four million school textbooks in a variety of subjects. There are dilapidated street stalls selling books in Tashkent but, in what used to be the fourth city of the Soviet Union, there is now no bookshop. Karimov is leading his people into the deepest ignorance on the planet.

I was told that Mirzaeyev had redoubled the crackdown on Tajik. School closures had started again, and a community newspaper, published by one of the guests, had been shut, the printing equipment confiscated. There was a purge of teachers at Samarkand's universities. Trade and employment had been badly affected by border and bazaar closures.

A very impressive young local from the Institute of War and Peace Reporting, a British NGO that did invaluable work within Uzbekistan, had a lot of documented material on recent arrests. He also told stories of the cotton harvest. The previous year, not only the doctors and nursing staff but all the walking sick from Samarkand's hospitals had been sent out into the fields, resulting in several deaths.

Time and again, I was struck by how delighted such dissidents were to meet me. Trapped in a world of crippling injustice, the idea that anyone outside cared at all was a great relief to them. Whether or not in practice we could do anything to help remained to be seen.

The next day, we paid a call on a local medical NGO, which occupied a crumbling courtyard house in the centre of the city. There was a lot of building rubble and several empty or part-plastered rooms. They were doing up the premises as funds came in, which was slowly. The embassy had given money previously, as had Chris Hirst from his own pocket. There were pictures of Chris on the wall.

I was shown a newly but sparsely equipped operating theatre, the pharmacy and a couple of wards containing women swathed in bandages. The centre was a cross between a hospital and a women's refuge, but there was something deeper that the Director, a female surgeon, was not telling me. After the tour, we sat hunched in our coats in the Director's office. There was no heating or water, and the diesel for the generator was almost finished. Temperatures throughout the hospital were a long way below freezing, and the patients had been hunched under thin blankets. The bread and fruit I was offered in the office were frozen solid. I immediately handed over what cash we had, both mine and the embassy's, and Dima was sent with a hospital staff member to search for diesel and electric heaters.

I had to become brutally direct with my questioning to get the full story from the Director, but this is it.

The hospital deals with victims of self-immolation – women who have tried to burn themselves to death. Generally, they cover themselves in blazing cooking oil in the kitchen. This is the traditional means of female suicide throughout southern Uzbekistan. This centre alone had dealt with 230 cases, just from Samarkand, in the past year.

Only a minority of such cases get to the centre. Most such attempts are successful. If they are not, the family will either quickly kill off the woman or leave her to die slowly in the home to avoid the disgrace. The government hospitals will not accept such cases, nor will the government acknowledge the existence of any such problem in Karimov's Uzbek 'paradise'.

In Uzbek culture, marriages are arranged. After the wedding, the girl becomes effectively a domestic slave to her in-laws. The mother-in-law will immediately retire from all housework once she has a daughter-in-law. The girl will have to rise at 4 a.m. to milk the cow, clean the house and prepare breakfast. Then she will go to work in the fields, weave or do whatever else is needed to support the family economy. She will probably be regularly beaten, severely, by any member of her husband's family. In the evening, she will have to prepare a large meal and will frequently be subject to rape, not just by her husband but also by the other men of the family.

I was appalled at this picture. The Director said that these were traditional features of Uzbek life but had been worsened by a general brutalisation of society by Karimov following the destruction of traditional societal mechanisms by the Soviets.

The scale of the thing was just awful. The Director estimated that if 230 managed to make it to the centre, over 1,500 tried suicide this way in Samarkand alone every year. Across Uzbekistan, it might be many thousands.

It is difficult to conceive. Just how miserable do you have to be to set yourself on fire? And if thousands reach that stage, how many tens of thousands or hundreds of thousands of women lead absolutely dreadful lives but cling on to them? I left the centre with a feeling of real despair.

Our next port of call was the British American Tobacco factory just outside the city. It felt very solid, new and clean. It had its own heating, electricity and water, and was providing them free to local communities. It was ridiculously comforting to sit in an office with British square-pin plug sockets.

We were taken on a tour by the Chilean production manager. It was a large standard cigarette factory. I like going round such places – I find the dexterity of the machinery astonishing. I have never smoked, but I like the smell of raw tobacco.

BAT is the largest foreign investor in Uzbekistan, having put in $300 million of their own cash. They are also the country's biggest taxpayer. But they have never made an operating profit, let alone any return on capital, and in 2001 they had to write off, in their UK accounts, $48 million of sum earnings they were not allowed to convert into hard currency. They are now trying, unsuccessfully so far, to avoid further operating losses and sit things out, hoping for better times.

Their biggest problem is competition from smuggled cigarettes on which no tax or duty is paid. Over 60 per cent of cigarettes sold in Uzbekistan are smuggled, nearly all from Korea. Given Uzbekistan's tightly controlled borders, this would be impossible without official complicity, and indeed cigarette smuggling is controlled by a coalition of the most powerful people in the land, so BAT have problems. What is worse is that the Uzbek government are deliberately trying to bankrupt BAT Uzbekistan (UzBAT). Gulnara Karimova, the President's daughter, has reportedly already done a deal for a joint venture with the Koreans to take over BAT's factory when they are gone.

BAT have other problems. Their cigarettes are made with 90 per cent Uzbek tobacco, with imported varieties used to blend. The Uzbek tobacco farmers all have plots leased from state farms. Even though the farmers pay for the lease of the land, UzBAT were only allowed to pay 40 per cent of the tobacco price to the farmer. The other 60 per cent had to go to the state farm and Hokkimyat, for the senior officials to steal. This meant that it was very difficult for the farmers to cover the cost of their leases.

UzBAT had in 2003 just managed to negotiate the amount paid to the farmers up to 50 per cent when the Uzbek government brought in a regulation that the payments to farmers could no longer be made in cash but had to be made through a state bank. This provided yet another avenue for state officials to rob the farmers, and indeed at the 2004 harvest, six months after UzBAT had made the payments into the state bank in full, not one farmer had received a single cent.

I got to know the UzBAT staff well, from the head, Rene Ijsselstein, an expressive Belgian, down. Without exception, they were passionate, not just about making the company successful but also about tackling poverty and injustice and improving the terrible lot of the Uzbek farmers. It is deeply unfashionable to say something positive about a tobacco company, but that is the truth.

We headed off back to Tashkent. About 20 miles outside Samarkand, we stopped at a small town where DFID had put money into assisting a cooperative of private farmers with marketing strategies.

In the mid 1990s, Uzbekistan had embarked on some limited agricultural privatisation. Azimov had claimed to me that about 40 per cent of the country's agricultural produce was now privately produced. That was, as usual, a large exaggeration, and I had learnt at BAT something of the reality of 'private' farmers' lives. Here, I was to learn more.

In this town, several hundred farmers had been allowed to lease plots of 11 hectares each. But they were told what they had to grow on 95 per cent of this land and given quotas of how much they were expected to produce. On the remaining 5 per cent of the land, they could, in theory, grow what they want. But the quotas were almost impossible to meet, so in practice they had to devote all their land to this. The fines for not fulfilling a quota could exceed the payments for what they did produce.

In the last year, they had been ordered to produce cotton, tomatoes and wheat. The payment for the cotton had not materialised: that was usual. The tomatoes were to be delivered to a puree plant that was a joint venture between the Hokkimyat and a Russian firm, Baltimor. After they delivered, the Hokkimyat had taken over the plant from the joint venture, saying it had gone bankrupt and that the new company did not owe the farmers anything. As for the wheat, they had been told they would be paid not in cash but in fertiliser. This they had to collect themselves from a state plant in the Ferghana Valley, over 300 miles away in the mountains! They had no means of doing so and knew that even if they turned up, there was no chance of their docket being honoured by officials without hefty bribes, which they didn't have the funds to pay.

All this was explained by a very dignified and well-educated lady who was paid by DFID to organise the cooperative. I asked how on earth people lived. She pointed to the frozen vegetable patch in the garden. The farmer next to her just grinned and pulled back his sleeve, to show his emaciated arm.

* * *

149

Back in Tashkent, it was time to organise the staff Christmas party. There were over 60 staff plus partners, guards being the largest contingent. We couldn't afford a restaurant for so many and decided to hold it in the new Residence. This was almost ready. The embassy was in the poshest bit of Tashkent, near the homes of Karimov's daughters, so it always had heating, electricity and water. In the rest of Tashkent, those were in short supply that winter. This included the new Residence, which had no gas for heating. I went down two days before the party. It was minus 11 Celsius actually inside the building – and that was at midday.

Packing so many people in would warm it up, I decided, and there would be lots of hot food and plenty to drink. The kitchens weren't yet fully operational, so we had arranged for the Intercontinental to deliver eight turkeys while we did the veg and puddings. Fiona and Lena the cook went into overdrive.

The day before the Christmas party, I was approached in my office by Lena Son and Atabek. The local staff would not come to the party, they said, if Chris did. I knew relationships were bad within the embassy, but this was amazing.

'Look, Lena,' I said. 'This has been an incredible three months. We have all achieved so much. Now it's Christmas. I am inviting you. And I am inviting everybody. Nobody is forcing you to come. But if you don't, I shall personally be very insulted.'

Everyone did come, and we had a great evening. Even though the temperature inside never did get above freezing, coats were removed and there was a lot of dancing. Jamie came for Christmas, Emily was delighted to see him, and we spent a happy Christmas Day. Hugo Minderhoud, a very bright Dutchman with ABN AMRO bank, and his wife and children were our guests.

* * *

Just before Christmas, I received instructions to call on Safayev, outline the WMD dossier to him, and seek his support for an invasion of Iraq. Fortunately, I did not have to say anything about WMD, as he was positively eager to express unconditional support for an attack on Iraq. I left him a copy of the dossier I didn't believe in, wondering what the New Year would bring.

CHAPTER 10

Iron in the Soul

It was a very hard winter. Throughout the country there was no gas and no district heating, and there were intermittent power cuts.[35] My immediate concern was for the embassy staff, many of whom had no alternative heating or cooking facilities in their homes. I instructed David Muir to get in extra stocks of diesel for all the domestic generators and order several dozen electric heaters to be flown in by air.

I had to fly to London for a conference of British ambassadors on 2 January 2003, which was a waste of time. It was just a PR exercise in the lead-up to the Iraq war. The main purpose was the television news pictures of Tony Blair and Jack Straw addressing the massed ranks of their ambassadors. But it was nice for me, because it was like slipping into a warm bath of back-slapping and handshakes. My punchy telegrams and criticism of the War on Terror had been going down well with most of my colleagues.

The first meeting I had in London was with Linda Duffield, whose FCO title was Director of Wider Europe. She was Simon Butt's new boss and the woman who would countersign his staff reports on me. Linda is a severe woman with short grey hair. I had arranged to call on her, and when I entered her office Simon Butt was there, too. A heavy atmosphere hung in the room.

'Sit down, Craig,' she said. 'Simon tells me that he has areas of concern about your performance, and, from what I have seen, I must say I am concerned, too.'

'OK. Nice to meet you, incidentally.'

This was ignored. Simon started up.

'I think our worry is that you are antagonising the Uzbeks to the stage where they will pay you no attention. You are also causing real damage to our relationship with Uzbekistan. I was most concerned, for example, that you told Komilov that every word of your Freedom House speech had been cleared with London.'

'Why not? It was.'

'You know that's not the full story. You railroaded that speech through junior staff.'

'That's simply untrue. I sent the draft to you and to John Macgregor [Linda Duffield's predecessor]. I even copied in Michael Jay on the correspondence. In fact, I seem to recall you complained I was going over your head.'

Linda intervened: 'I want to make myself perfectly clear. Had I been in this position at the time, I would not have approved your making that speech in those terms.'

Her head shook and she seemed to tremble with suppressed outrage. 'No ambassador should ever make such a speech. That is the job of politicians. Your job is not to undermine UK–Uzbek relations. You seem to lack any sense of proportion. You need to ensure that your focus on one important issue, human rights, is not at the expense of other objectives in Uzbekistan. You also need to act in concert with others, particularly your EU and US colleagues. I understand there are management problems inside the embassy.'

I was really getting angry.

'I am sorry,' I said, 'but you are completely wrong on all points. I put much more effort into commercial work than into anything else, and we have transformed the performance of the embassy in that regard. And we are not losing influence with the Uzbeks; we have more than ever before. Standing up to them is important – they take no notice of conventional diplomacy. I think you've been very badly briefed. Look, Linda, why don't you come out and visit Tashkent and see for yourself?'

She replied, 'I have a very large area of responsibility, and because of you I am already spending more time on this than I can afford. The PUS [Permanent Under Secretary] has agreed that Simon will come out to visit shortly. He will report back to me. I will try to follow up with a visit at a later date.'

Plainly my difficulties were going to get still worse.

My next meeting was with the Personnel Department to discuss the problems with Chris Hirst. He and Karen still had not moved to a new house, and I wanted to know if I could compel them to go. The meeting was chaired by a nice man with the splendid name of Rufus Legg and included staff of the Personnel, Health and Welfare, and Security departments.

The answer was yes, I could compel them. But I also explained that part of my intention in moving them was to work out if the problem really was bad neighbours or whether it was Chris. Since I had proposed the move in November, further direct observation had led me to worry. They promised to get back to me on this.

A couple of days after I got back to Tashkent, I received an email from the Security Department. The details contained within it suggested that the FCO had been aware for several years that there was a potential problem with Chris. I wondered at the sense of appointing him to such a difficult and stressful post, and I couldn't understand why I had been told nothing apart from Chris Ingham's brief comments, which had emphasised that the policy was to defend Chris. I told Karen I wanted them to move house very quickly indeed.

* * *

On my return to Uzbekistan, one of my first actions was to visit a major new British commercial interest in Uzbekistan called Oxus Mining. They owned a 50 per cent stake in a joint venture with the Uzbek government to open a new gold mine.

Uzbekistan is the world's sixth largest producer of gold. This is produced by a huge state-owned conglomerate, the Kombinat, which also produces uranium and other metals. The gold comes largely from the Murantau mine.

Oxus were planning to open their new mine at Amantaytau, some 40 miles south of Murantau. They had, however, run into difficulties raising the cash they needed for the project.[36] Time was running out and things were looking very hairy for Oxus. A visit by the British Ambassador would enhance their prestige, show political support and help disguise the desperate scramble for finance going on beneath the surface.

It was a tough two-day Land-Rover journey to Amantaytau, in the middle of the Kizyl Kum desert. There I met Richard Wilkins, the ebullient Welsh director of Oxus. I was accompanied by Lena Son and driven by Mansur. Richard had started up a successful gold-mining joint venture in Tajikistan, but this was bigger potatoes. He was under a lot of pressure and kept breaking off for long anxious phone calls.

The mine site was a series of cabins in the middle of the scrubby red sands of the desert. There was a small friendly staff of British geologists and mining engineers. They were all extremely enthusiastic about the prospects; their investigations of gold yields had got them really excited. Several of them had been working on this dusty site for years.

I met the head of the Kombinat, Mr Kucharski, an enthusiastic Ukrainian miner. The Soviets had brought in Ukrainian engineers who dominated the senior ranks of the Kombinat. Many of them had been there for 30 years. With Kucharski, I visited the Murantau mine. The second largest hole in the world, it is visible from space. It was fascinating to watch the giant ore carriers wend their way down the slopes of the great crater until they became tiny specks far below. They are extending the pit down to over half a mile and starting to build great bucket conveyors to bring out the ore at an angle of 45 degrees.

Still more spectacular was the ore mill. In a hall the scale of which makes the brain reel, you stand on a gallery and look down on huge cylindrical mills turning, pounding the ore inside against their load of heavy spherical steel balls. This hall is a mile long and contains 36 of these giant mills in a line. The noise is unbelievable. You feel it can't be real; it must all be done with mirrors. As you walk along and discover the true scale, it becomes disorientating.

The mine produces one and a half tonnes of pure gold every week and is so large that it is worth the while of the world's largest mining company, Newmont, to operate a joint venture with the Kombinat just to process the tailings. These are spoil heaps of ore which have been processed but which are still rich enough in gold to be worth reprocessing. Newmont move this powdered deposit from the huge spoil heaps, bulldozing it onto conveyors which run for miles, and pile it into a great hill. Cyanide is pumped through this hill, leaching out the gold for processing from the resultant cyanide lake.

This is another EBRD-funded venture, and indeed loans totalling $165 million made it the EBRD's biggest investment in Uzbekistan. I was therefore keen to see it before the EBRD AGM. But the project raised a lot of questions in my mind.

The EBRD call it 'the lowest cost, most efficient secondary mining operation in the world'. That is true. It produces 13 tonnes of gold a year. But it is only a tailings operation to process the spoil – the expensive mining has already been done. The technology is cheap and basic. The claimed total investment was over $300 million, with $140 million put in by Newmont. I just couldn't see it. I couldn't even see that the total capital cost would amount to the $165 million loaned by the EBRD. Oxus were building an entire new mine and mill, not just a tailings operation, for $40 million.

I gave a dinner for the Oxus staff at the sports stadium in the mining city of Zarafshan.[37] It was a jolly affair – the long-term engineering staff's guests included one British and several local wives. The experts all agreed that the capital costs of the Newmont joint venture were overblown and seemed delighted that I had noticed.[38]

After dinner that night, Richard Wilkins lost his company. The phone calls had been getting more intense, and this normally shrewd but affable man had started sweating heavily. After dinner, we found him leaning on the fence of the stadium car park, swearing softly and staring into space.

Oxus had failed to raise the $21 million required that day. In consequence, they had now fallen to a hostile takeover by a South African company, which Oxus ironically had intended to employ as a contractor to carry out the excavations.

Richard was convinced, with good reason, that the Amantaytau project would be massively profitable. He had worked on it for many years and done the extremely difficult negotiation to bring the Uzbek government on board. To lose it at the moment the deal should have been completed was very bitter indeed.

The chairman of Oxus, Roger Turner, was out on his ear. Richard and he had started Oxus's adventures in Central Asia ten years previously, and Richard was terribly upset for his friend. Richard was being kept on as a front man.

The next day I checked with British Trade International. We were still considering Oxus a British company. The South African company that had bought them had a British office. Oxus HQ would still be in the UK. My visit therefore took on a new priority – the tricky job of persuading the Uzbeks that the change of ownership did not affect the joint venture.

The next day, we visited the mining operation at Uchkuduk and looked at a revolutionary piece of technology patented by the

Kombinat for mechanically grading lumps of ore by gold content. Uchkuduk is right at the end of the roads and water pipes into the desert. Some of that water is put to good use, because here the Kombinat has built its own brewery. Using the finest imported malt, and Czech and German equipment, they produce a range of beers including dark live ones. We drank an excellent strong winter ale called, in English, 'Old Nick'. It was a strange thing, sitting in the middle of the Kizyl Kum drinking real ale.

We travelled on through the desert and visited the weird moonscape of the Kombinat's phosphate operation, where massive digging machines crawled over the scarred white earth. It was well below freezing, and a vicious wind whipped across this wasteland, colouring the desert with white dust for 50 miles around.

We then saw something of the uranium mining operation. I don't pretend I understood this. Over a huge area of desert, water is forced into the sands through vertical pipes. There is a great web of these all over the Kizyl Kum. The water running through the sands picks up the uranium, which is then processed out. The bit I don't get is how water dispersed into the sands of the desert, over a great area, can ever be collected again.

Our discussion with Kucharski was held over a long formal lunch. Kucharski was flanked by his senior staff, and I by the managers of Oxus. In Uzbekistan, no enterprise is possible without government support. Kucharski therefore may have given much more weight than it merited to my declaration of British government support for Oxus. By the end of the lunch, the ice had been well and truly broken and we were into jokes and vodka toasts. It had been a fascinating few days, and effective in helping see Oxus through this crisis.

* * *

On return to Tashkent, I accepted an invitation from Zokirjon Umarov to dinner at his palatial home. I was glad I did. We had a sumptuous meal and got on very well. At this meeting, and others with his friends over the next few weeks, I learnt a great deal.

Zokirjon is an Uzbek aristocrat. His family used to own much of Bokhara. They were an important family before the Russians came, and moved effortlessly from Emirate to Tsarist service. Zokirjon had in his hall an oil painting of his great-grandfather, a distinguished man in turban and oiled beard, wearing the glittering star of a Tsarist order on his breast. The move from Tsarist to Soviet service had been less smooth initially but ultimately very successful. Zokirjon had been the number two in the KGB operation in Afghanistan during the Soviet–Afghan war. The Soviets had used Uzbeks against the Mujahideen in exactly the same way the US used the Uzbeks of the Northern Alliance against the Taliban ten years later.

Zokirjon was full of good stories about this. At one time he had been caught in a group of officers with a major Soviet general in an advanced post pinned down by Afghans. The officers had drunk their way through a crate of vodka. When it was finished, the General called an aide-de-camp and ordered him to send back a helicopter for another crate.

'But, General,' said the orderly, 'the hills are full of Mujahideen with Stinger missiles. That is why we aren't taking you out by helicopter. It could be shot down.'

'Good point,' said the General. 'Better send three helicopters to bring a crate of vodka each. One should get through.'

Zokirjon told me much else that was of more practical use. He and many others in the Uzbek elite were thoroughly fed up with Karimov, who was making the business climate more and more impossible for the private sector. Zokirjon himself had his major business interests in Russia and France, and his family in the US, but when in Uzbekistan he faced a constant stream of supplicants from his extended family, his village and others with a claim on him who were unemployed and in desperate straits.

He told me that Karimov's personal fortune came chiefly from 10 per cent of the production of the Murantau mine, which he had been taking for more than a decade. He took his cut as ingots, flown to Rothschilds bank in Switzerland. Meanwhile, his daughter Gulnara was taking an increasingly firm grip on the range of government contracts and had been the chief beneficiary of what privatisation had occurred, for example in telecoms.

Karimov was very keen that Gulnara should succeed him. She could control her father, and she was concerned that any other successor would break agreements and take her business and property empire from her. Karimov had decided firmly against economic liberalisation and would be increasingly distancing himself from the USA. He was looking to Russia and China for investment. Uzbekistan's massive gas reserves remained the key asset, and it looked increasingly likely that these would mostly go to Russia's state-owned Gazprom.

* * *

Around this time, our Ambassador in Tajikistan, Michael Smith, sent a telegram reporting information he had picked up that alleged that the IMU had decided to kill John Herbst and me, and had in fact already dispatched a 25-man team of undercover operatives from Afghanistan, specifically in order to kill me. I replied, in a widely copied telegram: 'Only 25? I am insulted.'

This spread like wildfire throughout British government circles and did more than anything to enhance my reputation. I still get reminded of it occasionally. In fact, it had been a pretty easy gesture, as I had never believed in this information anyway.

But I also sent a more serious telegram saying that I was worried about the new Residence. The embassy and the old apartment had bulletproof windows. The new Residence didn't. It had many very large windows and was substantially overlooked by other buildings and nearby hills and mounds. I received an astonishing telegram in reply. There was no money for bulletproof glass. I should therefore 'plant quick-growing conifers . . . to screen the house'.

I wondered just how fast they thought conifers grow and had this mental vision of al-Qaeda coming to get me while I backed up the garden planting trees in front of them. I went back with some rejoinder and received further advice to keep the curtains closed.

Much more important, I had not received a substantive reply to my telegram about torture and intelligence. In February, I saw yet more dodgy intelligence, specifying it came from detainee debriefing, so I sent a further telegram repeating the arguments.

At the start of March, I was to attend an EU meeting in Brussels to discuss policy towards Central Asia. I received a pretty terse summons to travel to London afterwards to attend a meeting on the torture intelligence question. This I did.

I was firmly expecting to be sacked. I had concentrated hard on the Brussels meetings and I have in any case a useful facility for putting off apprehension: sufficient unto the day is the evil thereof. But unfortunately, the day came, and when facing an unpleasant meeting I probably feel more scared than most people. I hope that

I hide this beneath a veneer of sangfroid, but I doubt it. My hands don't shake but my palms go horribly sweaty.

I walked over from my London hotel to a small café, named Le Club, next to St James's tube station. Here I had sausage, bacon, fried eggs, fried tomato, toast and tea for about £5. The order was taken at the counter by a particularly chirpy Italian in a white chef's tunic, and when I wandered over to collect it a few minutes later, a very pretty girl, with long sandy hair tied back, insisted I go back to my table while she brought it over. She spilt tea on me, but the thought was nice. I read *The Guardian* and watched the crowds scurrying out from the Underground, heading for work. The breakfast was excellent, but I could not lift the anxiety that gnawed at me. 'The prisoner ate a hearty breakfast' kept piercing into my train of thought.

I really did not mind losing my job from the point of view of personal position. Britain was about to enter an illegal war in support of extreme right-wing corrupt American Republicans and to the advantage of the oil and weapons industries. Did I want to represent this? No, I didn't. But the clichéd position of so many married men in middle age came home. I was trapped. Trapped by my need to provide for Fiona, Jamie and Emily, not to destroy their happiness. If I left the FCO, how would I make money for them? Jamie would certainly have to leave his private school, with his Standard Grades looming. Fiona did not have my experience of personal poverty, and I did not think that she would take to it.

But despite these concerns, I discovered to my surprise that I had started off being scared of being sacked, and my train of thought had wandered to the opposite position of musing about resigning.

My brain started to race, and the excuses for staying on piled up – the individuals facing persecution I might be able to help, the need for someone on the inside arguing the case for integrity.

I found myself gazing idly through the window at the passers by with a vague kind of love. They were a mixed bunch these Londoners going to work – ethnically, religiously, sexually, politically mixed. I loved my countrymen, their tolerance and resistance. As often happens, the legacy of my upbringing kicked in, and I started thinking about the Second World War and how proudly, how indomitably, we had stood up to fascism. Those Londoners had the hell bombed out of them, nightly, as was also the case in Coventry, Birmingham and elsewhere – even Sheringham, for pity's sake. The US had stood by and watched for two years. Only when they themselves were attacked at Pearl Harbor did they join the war against fascism. Why then had we rushed uncritically to instant support the moment they had been attacked from the air at the World Trade Center? The death toll of 9/11 did not equal Coventry, let alone the London Blitz.

I pulled myself up. I did not like this line of thinking. The resentment was perhaps natural but the logic poor. If they had behaved badly, did it follow that we should behave badly now? What were the parallels between the war on fascism and the war on al-Qaeda? Let me think. Yes – the point was that Saddam Hussein was nothing to do with al-Qaeda, and I knew, as did so many others in Whitehall, he did not possess weapons of mass destruction. There was no line of justification from the Twin Towers to attacking Iraq. And in the wider War on Terror, there was no excuse for torture, for abandoning human rights, for betraying the values we claimed to be fighting for. And that is what we were doing.

I glanced at my watch. Wow! I had been in the café more than an hour, lost in this reverie. It was five to ten; I would be late. I paid quickly, leaving the startled pretty girl a tip of what I had saved by not breakfasting in the hotel – it might, I mused grimly, be my last chance to be generous. I hurried across the park to the Foreign Office and found myself queuing for a pass behind a large number of people arriving for a conference of some kind. I had forgotten I would need to get a pass to get in and certainly had not allowed for the 15 minutes it took. So I arrived late at Linda Duffield's office. She was waiting at the top of the three stairs that led up from the third-floor corridor to her office, cheeks sucked in and looking even crosser than usual beneath her severe haircut.

'You're late,' she said.

'Yes, I'm sorry,' I replied meekly.

'The PUS apologises,' she said, brusquely. 'An urgent meeting has come up and he can't now see you this morning. He has asked me to brief you.'

She led the way into her room. Two people were seated at the round polished mahogany table.

'You know Matthew and Michael.'

It was a statement not a question. I did not in fact know Matthew, although I knew of him. Matthew Kydd, Head of Whitehall Liaison Department, the link between the FCO and MI5, MI6 and other shadier organisations. A long-nosed, sharp, refined face. Impeccable grooming, neat whitening hair. Firm handshake.

Now, Michael I did know. Sir Michael Wood, FCO Legal Adviser. His was a friendly face I was particularly glad to see at that moment.

Michael's appearance is highly deceptive. Curly hair cut short, small spectacles on a string round his neck, a pedantic manner, smooth and rounded. He is fastidious and extremely careful and accurate in speech. A prissy, almost effeminate manner, a bit like a maiden aunt. Not only does this hide a muscular shrewdness, it also hides the only man in the FCO who can drink me under the table.

Yes, I was very pleased to see Sir Michael.

The atmosphere in Linda's room was tense and unpleasant. Even Michael did not look me in the eye. Everyone was seated ramrod straight. The mirror-like varnish on the mahogany was misting around my sweaty hands. Linda started in formal, clipped tones: 'The PUS asked me to say that he considers it unfortunate that you did not raise these matters, as invited, in person with William Ehrmann when you were back for the Heads of Mission Conference. The PUS does not think it is wise to commit such matters to paper.'

I said nothing. Linda went on: 'The PUS wishes me to assure you that your concerns have been given full consideration at the highest level. He has discussed this with Jack Straw, and C [Sir Richard Dearlove, head of MI6] has given his views. Both the FCO and MI6 have taken legal advice on the question that you have raised. Michael, could you outline the legal position.'

Michael looked distastefully at the papers before him. 'I am not an expert on the UN Convention on Torture, but I have studied it quite carefully in the light of Craig's telegrams. I cannot see that we are in material breach of any provision simply by possessing, or indeed by using, information obtained under torture and subsequently passed on to us.

'It does appear that under Article 15 such evidence would be inadmissible in a court of law, but that is the only restriction on the use of such material arising from the convention. I therefore see no legal obstacle to our continuing to receive such information from the Uzbek security services. Arguably, we are further distanced from any acts of torture by the fact that the material comes to us via the United States.'

He coughed discreetly. 'That is my view of the legal position. I make no comment on the morality of the case.'

'Michael,' I asked, 'a number of prominent public international lawyers have told me that in this case, when put as a hypothesis, possession and use of such material would be in breach of the convention. I have spoken to, among others, Françoise Hampson and Douwe Korff. Why would they take that view?'

'It is hard for me to say,' said Michael. He took off his spectacles and held them in front of him; he studied them, screwing up his eyes, as though they might hold the answer to this question. 'There is certainly nothing on the face of the convention that I can see, and I am not sure I have seen anything published, that would cover the case.'

'But you know Françoise?'

'Of course.'

'Speak to her.'

Linda interjected, her mouth set so firmly that wrinkles appeared all round it.

'I think we have the legal view and that is very plain. Michael, could you be so kind as to write to Craig to confirm it?'

'Certainly.'

'Good. Now, Matthew, could you give the view of the security services?'

Matthew purred in: 'Certainly, Linda. The view of the security services is that this intelligence material is operationally useful.'

'But it's nonsense,' I interrupted. 'The intelligence is crap. It exaggerates the strength of the IMU and is full of false information about so-called links to Bin Laden. It's just stuff the Uzbeks want the Americans to believe so that they will continue to give the Karimov regime military, financial and political support.'

'On the contrary,' – Kydd again, still more silken – 'I can assure you this has been considered at the very highest level, and there is no doubt that this is operationally useful material.'

'Thank you,' said Linda, herself still more clipped, 'I think that clears this up. We needn't detain you gentlemen. Could you stay a moment please, Craig.'

After Michael and Matthew had left, I stood. I was not in the mood for any cosy chats. Linda went on, 'The PUS wants you to know that he realises these are difficult times for many in the service. He discussed your telegrams in person with the Secretary of State and with C. This question of torture is very difficult. He wants you to know that both the Secretary of State and he lose sleep over it.'

'Look, I am at the sharp end. I see the twisted limbs, meet the parents who have seen their children raped and murdered in front of them. I don't think they are that bothered about Jack Straw's sleep pattern.'

'We really do understand why you are upset. But we need to know that you are on message. Do you understand the position? You are a civil servant, and I should not have to remind you that you act on behalf of the Secretary of State and in accordance with policy set by ministers.'

Suddenly, I felt very weary.

'Don't worry,' I said. 'I understand the position perfectly.'

I walked to the lift in something of a daze. But as I came out into the daylight of the FCO quadrangle, I was struck by a revelation. It had been a carefully planned and rehearsed meeting designed to put me in my place. But they were more scared of me than I was of them. This meeting had been a defensive exercise. They were in the wrong, and I reckoned they knew it.

I flew back to Tashkent deeply depressed and worried. This had a profound impact on me. I had served my country for 20 years, proudly, in the belief that being British entailed certain fundamental decencies of behaviour. Rejecting torture was one. I now found that I was mistaken, and either the British government had never stood for, or had ceased to stand for, those basic values. I was profoundly disillusioned. The whole purpose of my working life seemed to have evaporated.

A few days after my return, I received by fax the promised written clarification from Michael Wood:

13 March 03

UZBEKISTAN: INTELLIGENCE POSSIBLY OBTAINED UNDER TORTURE

1. Your record of our meeting with HMA Tashkent recorded that Craig had said that his understanding was that it was also an offence under the UN Convention on Torture to receive or possess information under torture. I said that I did not believe that this was the case, but undertook to re-read the Convention.

2. I have done so. There is nothing in the Convention to this effect. The nearest thing is article 15 which provides:

'Each State Party shall ensure that any statement which is

established to have been made as a result of torture shall not be invoked as evidence in any proceedings, except against a person accused of torture as evidence that the statement was made.'

3. This does not create any offence. I would expect that under UK law any statement established to have been made as a result of torture would not be admissible as evidence.

Signed
M C Wood
Legal Adviser

So there we had it. Torture by proxy for intelligence purposes was legal. If the so-called evidence that resulted could not be used in a court, that was of little worry – the government had instituted indefinite detention without charge in the UK, on the authority of the Home Secretary, citing 'Intelligence material'.

That evening, I went to Safar to unwind. The girls were delighted to see me again, as I had a reputation as a generous and respectful customer. I drank Chivas Regal and ate some chicken. A girl called Dilya danced for me, and two or three of the girls came to sit with me. Normally, I laughed and joked with them, but this evening I felt down and distracted. Then, gazing out of the booth to the dance floor, I saw her.

She wore matching embroidered purple knickers and bra. Her body moved sinuously as she danced, her upper and lower torso wonderfully articulated by a slender supple waist of extraordinary flexibility. Her body shape was perfection itself. All the girls in that club were great dancers, but she made the rest look clumsy and contrived. She was like a swan among ducks, a comparison all the more apt for her long graceful neck and proud carriage.

She had a shaggy mane of highlighted hair, and she looked out at me with large dark eyes. As I caught her glance, I felt she was drawing me in to her very soul. Her lips shone with a liquid gloss, and they were parted in a way that was both sexy and innocent. She looked lost and anxious, like she really didn't want to be there. She defied the impossible by exuding, at the same time, such ripe sexual attraction and such innocent vulnerability. Her body invited sex while her eyes screamed, 'Save me.'

I had been chatting with a very nice hostess called Lena, a heavily built and down-to-earth girl who managed the floor. I asked her who the girl was.

'I had noticed you looking,' said Lena. 'She's new. Her name's Nadira.'

After finishing her solo dance, Nadira came belly dancing around the booths. I gave her $20. She then returned to join the others on the dance floor. She was intensely distracting – my eyes were continually drawn back to her. Eventually, one of the girls drinking in the booth with me stood up and firmly drew the curtains, blocking the dance floor from view. Nadira was looking directly at me as the curtains closed her out.

I couldn't get her off my mind and eventually convinced Lena to get her to join me. Lena agreed in return for a playful kiss, which left me covered in bright red lipstick. I later learnt that the management had to prevail heavily on Nadira to come to me, and she was pretty horrified by this lipstick-smeared man when she did.

She told me she was an English language teacher from Samarkand. She had quit because her teaching job paid a theoretical $21 a month, but the pay seldom arrived, on top of which the director of the school was trying to force her into sex. She hated working at this club but had little choice. Her parents were actors, working for a state company, and had not been paid for months. They didn't know where she was working. She also had two younger brothers to support. One was at school, the other had worked in the bazaars before their closure and was now unemployed.

All of which sounds like a line but proved to be true. I never doubted her. My instinct told me this was a girl I could trust, who would return the love that was overwhelming me. But she refused to give me her address or phone number.

'Where can I find you?' I asked.

She smiled and replied, 'Here.'

I astonished her by saying that I wanted her to give up the club and be my mistress. I explained I could not marry her, as I was married, but I would keep her. I gave her my card and urged her to phone me.

The next day, I told Kristina and Shakhnoza, the young student from the Tashkent Westminster University campus we had employed part time on reception, that if a girl called Nadira phoned, they should put her through straight away, whatever I was doing. They looked suitably mystified. All morning I stared at the phone, but it rang less than usual and it was never her.

It was a terrifically busy time at the embassy as we prepared for the British Music Festival, the EBRD AGM, the Queen's Birthday Party and a visit by Simon Butt. I didn't get a chance to get back to Safar for a few days. When the opportunity finally came, Nadira was not there. I bumped into an expat acquaintance, who seemed to find it difficult to understand why one girl was not as good as another, but eventually we succeeded in persuading Lena to find Nadira's phone number for me.

I rang this several times, but nobody ever answered. I did not know it, but after she heard I had come back asking for her number, Nadira had started to telephone me. She rang several times but had not been put through, as my protective staff demanded to know what her business was before interrupting their Ambassador. I was really itching to meet her.

In fact, Nadira had only decided she would see me again after being persuaded by her flatmate, Nargiza. Nargiza wasn't sure what an ambassador was but was pretty clear that I must be rich, and she pointed out that it would soon be Nadira's birthday. At the least she might get an expensive birthday present out of me. If I was boring or tried to insist on sex, she could drop me. On this basis, Nadira decided to meet me again.

We were finally able to get together, but not until I had dealt with Simon Butt's arrival in Uzbekistan and the astonishing events that followed.

* * *

By this stage, the British government was hell-bent on war. This must have been pretty obvious to everyone from the rhetoric and the newspapers, and obviously over a million people from all over the UK realised it with sufficient urgency to travel to London and demonstrate. In the FCO, we had known George Bush was planning to attack Iraq even before 11 September 2001. The only question had been when.

Despite being in Tashkent, I was seeing a great deal of internal government communication on the issue, copied to me because Uzbekistan was viewed as one of the few highly dependable allies the UK and US had and particularly valuable as a 'Muslim' state which could be claimed to support the war. But I also knew of the hollowness of the claims of Weapons of Mass Destruction.

For a year from August 1991, I had been Head of the FCO section of the Embargo Surveillance Centre. For much of that time, I literally lived, slept and ate in an underground bunker in central London. Our job was the real-time monitoring of Iraqi attempts at arms procurement. We reported every morning direct to Thatcher and later Major. I knew what we could and could not know, and how tightly we had sewn everything up. We had a handle on not just the demand for weapons but on potential supply, physical movements of kit and transfers of money all over the world.

This was ten years ago, but I had never lost my interest or contacts. Before going to Tashkent, I had a chance to speak with a senior colleague in the Middle Eastern Department. I had put to him that surely our claims on Iraqi WMD could not be true as they were a mix of the unlikely and the unknowable. He replied, with typical bluntness, 'Of course not, it's bollocks.'

He was telling the truth. The elegant cover-ups by Hutton and Butler failed, whether accidentally or not, to call the right people or ask the right questions. Ministerial desire railroaded the civil servants into producing what they knew to be rubbish on the Iraqi threat. Some civil servants were (and are) scared. Some cynically didn't care if it was true, so long as it helped their career. Others, perhaps the majority, took the view that they were civil servants and it was their job to give the democratically elected government what it wanted. Almost nobody took the view that there was an overriding obligation to tell the truth, particularly if the consequence of lies would be a war in which tens of thousands of people, the large majority completely innocent civilians, would die.

More people in the Foreign and Commonwealth Office had difficulty with the notion of going ahead with military action in the absence of United Nations authority. It was hard to disguise the fact that this represented acceptance that the United States, as the sole superpower in the world, can disregard international law and institutions whenever it pleases: a situation which I fear will last until a resurgent China begins to flex its gigantic muscles in about 2015. Then, of course, it might get worse.

Both the Americans and Uzbek government in Tashkent had an increasing swagger as the troops built up in the Gulf and war loomed larger and larger, now dictated by a military timetable. Robin Cook published an excellent account of the cruel machinations in London in this period.[39] As I watched with horror from Tashkent, I was struck by the increasing gap between the official telegrams I was receiving and the obvious reality. The Foreign Office chose to salve its conscience over the catastrophic demolition of the authority of the United Nations by a collective act of self-delusion.

One telegram in particular I will never forget. Sent to all concerned diplomatic posts shortly before the UN was expected to meet to consider a 'second resolution' on Iraq, authorising the use of force, it was an almost incredible exercise in deluded optimism. It said we were confident of obtaining the second resolution. It suggested that Putin and Chirac would pull back from threats to veto because they didn't want to damage the authority of the United Nations. This was an argument Tony Blair was continually deploying at this stage. It was appallingly hypocritical. It was the rapist's argument: 'I am going to do it by force anyway, so why don't you consent' or Hitler's argument in securing the Munich Agreement to annex the Sudetenland.

Anyway, the telegram breezed confidence that Chirac and Putin would defer. It also explained that we would obtain the key votes of French-speaking African nations on the Security Council, following an emergency mission to Africa by Baroness Amos.

This was laughable. We have virtually no influence in Francophone Africa, which we have largely ignored in terms of politics, commerce and aid for a century. On the other hand, France has retained far more influence in Francophone African states than we have in Commonwealth African states.[40] The chances of anyone breaking into this relationship would be slim, but Baroness Amos? She is a prime example of a Blair loyalist making it to high ministerial office without anyone ever having voted for her. The Africans did not take kindly to being lectured on democracy by someone who came to power without ever facing the electorate.

This doomed venture was made even more cynical by the fact that she was suddenly discussing the possibility of assistance programmes in countries where we had almost no record. But as it was, no one was interested. Not only was it too blatant an effort to buy votes, there was nothing really substantive on offer.[41] This futile mission ended with her being treated with scant courtesy and coming home empty handed.

There was a very short period between the hopeless telegram telling us that a second resolution would be forthcoming and the explanation that it had been miraculously discovered that one wasn't necessary after all. Apparently, a combination of the first resolution, specifically not authorising force, and 13-year-old resolutions authorising force in the first Gulf War would be good enough. This remarkable bit of news was not accompanied by the actual legal opinion that set out this doctrine.

I considered the criticism I would have come under had I made such a great error of judgement as lay behind that telegram stating that we were confident of obtaining the second resolution. It had been spectacularly deluded and had very quickly been objectively proven to be so, as we had to give up even trying to put the resolution forward to the Security Council. I was under daily threat from the FCO for errors of judgement that were debatable and, even if true, insignificant by comparison.

Events now unfurled in astonishingly quick time, and I found myself watching in horror the 'Shock and Awe' bombing of Iraq graphically displayed on our TV screens. I knew enough, from my insider's view of the first conflict, not to believe the propaganda about the clinical accuracy of our weapons. Thousands of women and children were dying, as the world now knows. The doublespeak amazed me – one news bulletin had an expert explaining that, unlike last time, weapons were now so accurate they could take out military targets and miss civilians next door. Much lower down in the very same news programme, it was reported that two of our missiles, aimed at Baghdad, had hit Syria by mistake.

In the very early stages of our invasion, I saw on BBC World a speech by George Bush justifying the attack. Having seen what I had of the real motives and methods of US foreign policy, I was just appalled at the sanctimonious crap. I could contain myself no longer and the next day fired off another telegram to Jack Straw, copied widely to our embassies around the world.

From Tashkent, I said, it was impossible to believe that US foreign policy was about freedom. It seemed to be about oil, gas and hegemony – and in Tashkent, the US saw supporting Karimov as the best way to pursue these ends. This could not be squared with our policy in Iraq. Why were we going to war to remove Saddam Hussein while subsidising Karimov?

I continued: 'I was stunned to hear that the US had pressured the EU to withdraw a motion on Human Rights in Uzbekistan which the EU was tabling at the UN Commission for Human Rights in Geneva.' It was obvious to me that we were practising double standards.[42]

I was fully aware that this telegram would be met with great hostility within the Foreign Office establishment. It was the only widely copied internal FCO document that questioned our uncritical support for Bush and the true motives behind US foreign policy. Though carefully drafted to reflect on US policy in Uzbekistan, and thus stay within my legitimate sphere of comment, it was correctly interpreted as an attack on the morality of the invasion of Iraq itself.

The initial reaction was muted. I received a telegram from Peter Collecott, Head of FCO administration, instructing me not to copy my telegrams so widely, allegedly because of complaints from Gulf ambassadors. Otherwise, he threatened, telegram minimisation procedures would be activated. This meant I would be electronically prevented from sending on the FCO network.

It is worth noting that thus far, and indeed until the attempt to get rid of me the following August, my concerns had not appeared in any media, nor had I said anything in public not specifically approved by the Foreign Office. I was exercising my duty to give my views on policy and warn, through internal communication, of the dangers I saw brewing. Only those very close to me knew I was deeply personally troubled by our support for Bush and the turn the War on Terror was taking. It was not I who chose to make my views on all this public. I was still operating as a conscientious civil servant, to the best of my ability.

CHAPTER 11

Murder in Samarkand

Two days before the end of March 2003, Simon Butt came out to visit Tashkent. I had been keen to show him some of the reality on the ground, in the hope that I could convince him of how bad Karimov was and of the dangers of supporting him. I was also keen that he should learn at first hand, particularly from the British business community, how active the embassy was.

I held a meeting with him on the morning of his arrival and briefed him in particular on the situation with Chris, who to my pleasure had finally moved. Since the van Boven visit, there had been no further worrying symptoms from Chris, or complaints against him. Chris and Karen would that evening hold the first reception in their new home, for Simon to meet Tashkent human rights activists. I also briefed him on the more positive aspects of UK–Uzbek cooperation, knowing this would interest him most, including the forthcoming British Music Festival, the support we were lending to Westminster University and our efforts to encourage female participation in the Chevening Scholarships programme. He said very little but recorded what I said in minute handwriting, apparently word for word, on little pieces of card.

Simon had a separate meeting with members of locally engaged staff, without me present. I had been concerned he would be trawling for complaints about me, but that was not the result of the meeting. Rather to my surprise, the LE staff presented him with a list of complaints of bullying and harassment against Chris Hirst.

It was notable that all the specific accusations related to events that occurred before my arrival. Chris once again denied all the charges and suggested that the complaints had been prompted by the Uzbek security services. The staffing problems I had inherited were clearly intensifying, and I realised that action would have to be taken soon to resolve the situation.

Simon made a series of calls on ministers that day, including Trade Minister Elyor Ganiev, who gave him the usual stream of ludicrous figures – vast increases in economic growth, imports, exports, private agricultural production, state agricultural production, automotive production, textile production; in fact, an economy could never have done so well. I was rather alarmed that Butt meticulously recorded all this information as though it had some meaning – I even saw him write down the claim that UK exports to Uzbekistan equalled $420 million in 2002. Our own figures were about 10 per cent of that. Butt took the standard FCO non-confrontational approach and didn't challenge any of Ganiev's statements; he said we were concerned by trade restrictions and border closures but did not come back on Ganiev's assertion that trade was booming and that the borders were not closed at all. I was surprised by how seriously he appeared to be treating Ganiev's remarks.

His meeting with Foreign Minister Safayev followed the same pattern. Throughout their discussion, Butt's pen scratched away as he filled acres of card with his tiny detailed notes. Safayev gave the standard Uzbek spiel that reform should not go too fast in Uzbekistan's precarious geographical position, surrounded as it was by enemies and a true bastion against the evils of drugs and terrorism. Butt stayed on message by lauding Uzbek cooperation in the War on Terror and over Iraq, and was full of praise about all the help they had given the coalition. He was delighted with cooperation on counter-narcotics. We had, he said, noted improvements in human rights and in some areas of economic reform but hoped that the pace of liberalisation might increase. He then assured Safayev that finds of Weapons of Mass Destruction in Iraq were sure to be imminent. He also confirmed that Clare Short would be arriving in May to chair the AGM of the EBRD and said that this senior ministerial visit was evidence of the very good relations between the UK and Uzbekistan. He hoped that Safayev would soon be able to accept Jack Straw's invitation for an official visit to the UK.

Safayev seemed delighted by this easy ride, as indeed he had good reason to be. The British Foreign Office sees no distinction between diplomacy and brown-nosing. I told Simon Butt in the car as we pulled away from the Uzbek Foreign Ministry that this kind of performance undercut my position; that I had given clear messages on human rights and the urgent need for economic reform, but he was now giving the impression London did not place much weight on this. He replied he felt he had been quite firm in saying that we would like to see quicker political and economic reform. By FCO standards, doubtless he had.

I was very pleased to see Abdusalom Ergashev at the early evening reception at Chris and Karen's new house, as he had recently been arrested and held for several days. He was as cool and collected as ever but most concerned that his sons had been taken in by the SNB and beaten. This was part of a pattern of reprisals against dissidents' families with which I was becoming familiar.

Following the reception, we hosted a dinner at the new Residence, where we had ourselves just moved in, for Simon to meet members of the British business community. This was something of a disaster – the table looked beautiful, set for ten, the silver sparkling and Minton china shining, while Fiona had done lovely things with flowers and candles. We stood in the lounge drinking with those guests who had arrived, while we waited for others to do so. After forty-five minutes, we were still only seven and I was beginning to get agitated.

Lena Son had organised the guest list and was with us, although the invitations had actually been sent out by Kristina, who wasn't. I made desperate shoulder-shrugging gestures towards Lena, who took the hint and went to the hall, extracting her mobile phone from her handbag. She returned a few minutes later and whispered to me, 'It's OK – I spoke to Kristina, and they are definitely coming. Doubtless they will turn up soon.'

They didn't, and, after a further ten minutes, pre-dinner conversation was flagging, while Lena the cook appeared at the kitchen door to signal that something was drying out as a result of the protracted delay. I made further frantic signals at Lena Son, who again retreated to the hall. This time she called the numbers of the missing guests themselves. She came back to report. Two, including Jitendra Patel, were not currently in Uzbekistan. Jitendra had been absent for a fortnight, so it seemed very unlikely he had accepted. The third guest very often failed to honour invitations anyway. Lena suggested we start to eat.

One of the great juggling acts of diplomatic life is to arrange the placement for a formal dinner, when the final number of guests very seldom equates to the number who said they were coming. By definition, you are largely inviting important people, who are busy and therefore prone to last-minute changes of itinerary. They also tend to think normal rules of etiquette do not apply to them and will occasionally turn up plus sister or accountant as an additional and unexpected guest. You then come to the problems of placement, which despite being a perfectly straightforward English word, in Her Majesty's Diplomatic Service is always pronounced in French.

When I first joined the Diplomatic Service, I was given a booklet, written by Lady Somebody, on placement. This told you where to seat people if you had a minister, senior judge, bishop other than a bishop member of the House of Lords, baronet, major-general and a Bavarian margrave to dinner. The answer depended in part on the shape of table you had, and all the various possibilities were listed in particular detail. This is all nonsense to me, but some people take it very seriously. I would declare as we went to the table that I had not followed placement rules, with a self-deprecating reference to not understanding them. This only failed with the Germans, who would take this as an invitation to work out the rules properly and re-arrange everyone into formal order while the soufflés sank.

As this meal was in honour of Simon Butt, he was clearly the senior guest, and I was delighted to obey the rules and place him on Fiona's immediate right, i.e. as far away from me as possible. What was worrying me was that we were not going to have enough guests in between. I whispered to our steward Alijon to clear three covers, which he did as discreetly as you can move twenty-one pieces of cutlery, twelve crystal glasses, three serviettes and three Minton side plates. As he spread out the remaining covers, we were left with Fiona and me at the ends, three guests on one side and two on the other, which on a 14-foot table looked pathetic.

Fortunately, James McGrory can both look and sound like a lot of people at the dinner table, and Richard Wilkins was also in fine voluble form. The chardonnay was consumed without obvious relish while the leek and stilton soup and then the potted Arbroath smokie were tackled, but the claret started to be thrown down with great abandon as we came on to the roast. The six bottles I had asked Alijon to open in advance were plainly not going to be enough, so I told him to open the rest of the case.

Richard was bullish about the prospects for Oxus. While not underestimating the difficulties of the market, he believed Oxus had the experience, and years of work in building up contacts, which would pull their project through. Everyone else was very downbeat, particularly about the clampdown on private entrepreneurs and trade. There were tales of government interference and corruption, with James putting down his great bull-neck and stating that the Uzbek government was determined that only regime members would make money, in a tone that defied anyone to disagree with him. Simon did his best to pick up on any remark that gave an opening to comment positively on the Uzbek government measures, but the businessmen were not with him.

He turned the topic to the invasion of Iraq, which had been underway for eight days. He said that while there had been some public opposition to the war, it was plain that, now it had started, the majority of people supported it. He was scathing of Clare Short for her vacillation on whether to resign and suggested this indicated that politicians realised the war would become popular. Speaking as one with his ear close to the centre of power, he said airily that Tony Blair no longer had any time for the Liberal Democrats. Blair had been 'sickened' by the 'shoddy opportunism' of Charlie Kennedy in opposing the war. Simon confidently predicted that after a short successful war the Prime Minister's standing would be enhanced, enabling the Blairites to take a much firmer grip on the Cabinet, while the Liberal Democrats would suffer major electoral damage, largely at the hands of the Tories.

As he spoke, Simon kept shooting me glances, well aware that these were the opposite of my own views.

The treacle pudding was received with great enthusiasm and washed down with a little Sauternes. Then port and stilton, followed by a walk out onto the terrace for a little malt whisky. Eventually, the guests melted away and Fiona went off to check the kitchen.

Simon indicated to me that he wanted to talk, and I led him to armchairs at the end of the lounge. Once seated, he lit up a cigarette, and Alijon quickly appeared with an ashtray, after which I motioned him to leave us alone for a while.

'Not a very good turnout for dinner,' he commented.

'No, it was disappointing,' I replied. 'But the quality was good, and I thought that they made some interesting points on trade and monetary restriction.'

Simon blew a cloud of smoke and stared at it, licking his thin lips. 'Interesting decision to hold a dinner with expatriate businessmen. It might be thought that when expatriates don't show for dinner with their Ambassador, that is a sign he does not enjoy the respect of the business community.'

'I think it is more a case that the business community is very small because the economy is so bad, and a couple of people were out of the country.'

'I noticed you had to remove the covers. That hardly seems good planning.'

'I am afraid there was a mistake in my office.'

'I am afraid that does not say much for your management of the embassy.' He paused, 'Your secretary is called Kristina, isn't she? Didn't she make a serious mistake recently on a diplomatic note?'

Unfortunately, this was true: in translating a diplomatic note from English to Russian, Kristina had missed a 'Not' and we had therefore sent a note to the Uzbek Ministry of Foreign Affairs saying the opposite of what we meant to say. It had been quickly corrected, but Kristina had been given a verbal warning; damn Simon for getting hold of this titbit. I had to be careful: obviously someone was reporting back to him from within the embassy on even little items of information that might be used against me.

'It's really pretty serious that I was not able to meet a larger group. I will expect you to take action with Kristina and to report to me what you have done.'

He reached for another cigarette; he smoked a phenomenal number throughout the evening, but I noticed each was only smoked halfway down.

'Now then,' he said heavily, plainly coming to the main item on his agenda. 'There is serious concern about you in London. That telegram you sent really made people very angry, right at the top of the office. It is pretty off to send a telegram of disagreement just as British troops are about to go into battle. Bluntly, the view in London is that you are unpatriotic.'

I offered no response, so he continued, 'I was asked to send you a pretty stern reply, but I told the PUS that there was no point in initiating a correspondence. I thought it better to warn you in person that you really are pushing things too far. I have told you before that you must make more of an effort to adapt yourself to the current priority of security cooperation. If you can't do that, maybe you had better leave Tashkent.'

'Well,' I began, 'I am not in the least going to apologise for the telegram. It needed to be said, and indeed a number of British ambassadors from around the world have contacted me to say so. As for lack of patriotism, I am British, not American, and that telegram was largely a critique of US foreign policy. I didn't sign up to promote US foreign policy.'

'But you did, like it or not.' Simon was lighting a cigarette from the previous one. 'The Prime Minister has made it plain that we stand shoulder to shoulder with the US in the War on Terror. We are embarking on a war, and London has better things to do than to read over-emotional telegrams from you.'

Now I was getting angry, and my voice grew steadier and more deliberate. 'I am sorry if I get emotional about people being boiled to death, or children being raped in front of their parents,' I said. 'I don't know how else to react. If you don't get emotional about it, I feel sorry for you.'

'I really think,' said Simon, coolly, 'that, if you cannot understand the wider picture, we will have to withdraw you. In the meantime, your telegrams are likely to be stopped by the communications centre. There is a war on and the systems are busy.'

'I am telling truths you don't want to hear. US policy in Central Asia is disastrous. It's crass to prop up Karimov while claiming the need to topple a dictator in Baghdad. It is my duty to report back my analysis and advice, and I will continue to do that.'

'You have lost the attention of the top of the office. Nobody cares what you think any more.'

'That is a pity. But I am still going to tell it as I see it.'

I stood up to go to bed, rather taking Simon by surprise. I waited for him at the lounge door. He stood up and followed me, taking a few steps before, turning back, he picked up the ashtray and took it with him up the stairs to the guest suite.

I crept into Emily's bedroom. Her feet were on the pillow, her face, covered by long strands of tousled blonde hair, peeked out from under a mound of soft toys. I stooped and kissed her forehead, and, without her apparently waking, a small hand snaked around my neck, holding me briefly with surprising force. I crept out again and into my own bedroom. Fiona was already in bed. I gave her a hug: 'Thanks for the wonderful dinner, darling.'

'It's a pity so much was wasted. Three guests didn't show. It's that bloody Kristina. She's useless.'

'Hang on, we don't really know what happened yet.'

'Yes, we bloody well do. Lena told me. Kristina said people had confirmed and half of them weren't even in the country. So much for your dolly-bird secretary. Even if you aren't screwing her, everybody thinks you are, and that suits you and your bloody ego!'

The next morning, while Fiona and I were taking breakfast, the electricity flickered and the generator automatically coughed briefly into life before normal power was restored. Fiona suggested Simon was recharging himself from the mains.

I then went outside to where the car waited, with Mansur tramping up and down in his big quilted jacket and Kristina standing by the back of the car in a thick white jumper with a large roll-up neck that framed her face. I was struck anew by just how exquisite her beauty was, how classical. As she said 'Good morning', a little cloud of vapour sprang from her mouth and hung in the cold air. I thought how pleasant it would be to thrust forward my face and be enveloped in the little warm mist of that pretty exhalation.

Sadly, there was no escaping the need to discuss the previous night's dinner-guest debacle, and I wanted it out of the way before Simon appeared.

'Kristina, about last night.'

'I know, Craig. I am sorry, I am really sorry.'

'But why did you put people down as accepted when they hadn't?'

'I don't know. I really don't know why I did it. It has been just so busy, and it takes so much time to phone round. It's not just a question of phoning – secretaries don't know when the boss will be in, don't know if they are allowed to tell you he's away, they say they'll get back to you and then they don't. In the end I just guessed.'

'But you've never done it before. And of all the parties, to pick the one for Simon Butt . . . You know what he thinks of me.'

'I know. I'm sorry. Will I lose my job?'

'Of course not, but I'll have to give you a written warning.'

Kristina looked utterly crestfallen. I squeezed her hand.

'Look, you know I think you're great. This was totally out of character, and I am sure it won't happen again. Now let's forget it.'

'OK, Craig.'

Silence hung between us for a while. Some tendon in the strong relationship between us had been cut and would take a little time to heal.

It was now gone 8.30. Mansur came up to me with his customary opening in English: 'I'm sorry, Ambassador, but . . .' This was always followed by a stream of Russian. This morning he was getting worried – our first meeting was with the Regional Hokkim of Samarkand at 11 a.m. Less than two and a half hours to Samarkand was really pushing it.

Simon came out of the door carrying his case – he would be going on to Tajikistan by road. Michael Smith, our Ambassador in Dushanbe, would be making the mountainous journey to Samarkand to pick him up. I was looking forward to seeing Michael, a thoroughly decent man. Simon's case went into the back, joining the overnight bags of Kristina, Mansur and me, plus the jerry cans of diesel, the satellite phone, the medical kit with its sterile needles, gauzes and blood plasma, and the emergency rations of champagne, mineral water and tinned corned beef that I always carried on journeys.

We set off with Kristina in the front passenger seat, me behind her and Simon behind Mansur. As the heavy gates swung open, Mansur positively gunned the engine and roared out down the narrow lanes. As he bullied his way through the morning traffic and out of Tashkent, I felt Simon stiffen with disapproval beside me.

This got worse as we hit the dual carriageway. Mansur got the speedometer up to 90 mph, which took a fair amount of cranking in a Tashkent-maintained Discovery fuelled by Uzbek diesel. He mercilessly tailgated anything in the fast lane, almost making contact on numerous occasions, particularly with the passenger-crammed minibuses that were, as ever, oblivious to what was happening around them. At the numerous police and army checkpoints, we slammed on brakes with a terrific screech and burning of tyre rubber, not to stop but to go through slowly enough so they could work out who we were and hopefully not shoot us. Simon was sitting rigid. I rather like this sort of thing, and I had a great deal of confidence in Mansur's ability.

We arrived at the Hokkimyat at 10.55, a feat on which I loudly congratulated Mansur. We were taken to a waiting room, where Simon and I sat while Kristina bustled off to organise things. Simon took the opportunity to tell me to tick off Mansur about his driving – it was very bad for the image of the embassy to be seen to drive recklessly. I replied mildly that we had set off rather late. Simon said he had been surprised that I had not said anything to steady Mansur in the car. I said that in local culture it would not be acceptable to shame Mansur in front of Kristina. Besides, I added, I had not really noticed the driving because I had been giving profound thought to Simon's very sensible words of the night before. Simon looked at me quizzically, but I affected not to notice, gazing upwards as though once again engaged in this improving meditation.

At about 11.15, the Hokkim arrived with a small group of accompanying officials. We all shook hands and went through to the same conference room where Kristina and I had met him in December. Mirzaeyev launched with characteristic energy into a fulsome introduction. He said he was delighted to see me again – I was the 'good friend' of Samarkand. It was also good to make the acquaintance of such an important person from London as Mr Butt.

There followed a discussion very similar to the one I had three months previously, with Mirzaeyev talking of great strides in farming and industrial development. Simon prompted him with what I regarded as non-challenging questions, and the meeting had the sense of going through the motions. At the end, I mentioned to Mirzaeyev that we hoped we would receive full cooperation on the Samarkand events in the British Music Festival in May. He instructed officials to make sure these were well attended, which again rang a small alarm bell within me.

The meeting over, we then embarked on a tour of the antiquities of Samarkand. I was delighted by this opportunity, as on my own visit to Samarkand I had gone through a packed work programme that left little time for sight-seeing.

We had arranged to pick up a guide at the Afrosiyab Hotel, and we pulled up outside this concrete edifice, with its Soviet-style interior of heavy glass and polished metal chandeliers and fittings. It was the same style I had seen in the Orbis hotels in Poland, and it could have been anywhere from East Berlin to Vladivostok.

Our guide, Affie, was waiting for us in the lobby of the hotel, and she turned out to be a treasure. In her early 30s, very dark with short cropped hair and heavy black spectacles, she had a profound knowledge of the ancient city and a grasp of history untainted by Soviet propaganda or the current Uzbek nationalist version. Simon too proved a good and well-informed historian, and we had an excellent few hours.

The Registan of Samarkand is breathtaking. Lord Curzon, who knew a thing or two about grandeur, declared it to be better than any of the great squares of Europe. It is marvellous in the literal sense. I can't look at it without my jaw muscles slackening. The verticals appear so effortless that you are unaware of its great height, and the superb blue domes appear almost to float, while the beautiful tile work dazzles the eye.

It consists of three great buildings around a central square. You approach it from the fourth, open, side, and soon the great decorated fronts of the building, the *ivans,* loom high above you, covered in brilliant, decorated tilework which sparkles and glints in yellows, blues and browns, featuring complex floral motifs and beautiful Arabic scripts. At the top of the ivan of the right-hand madrassah, two great symbols stand out, meeting in mirror image: a figure of a tiger under a rising sun bearing the face of a chubby benign god. This was the badge of Tamburlaine – Amir Timur Leng – whose children and grandchildren built this great Muslim complex, in which it strikes a completely un-Muslim note. Living things are not supposed to be depicted in Muslim art, and the sun symbol hearkens back to the Zoroastrian religion of fire worship which had long predominated here, while the god's face seems an echo of the earlier great flourishing of early Buddhism along the Silk Road.

The left-hand madrassah as you enter the square was built by Timur's grandson Ulugbek. A great mathematician and astronomer, Ulugbek built this in effect as a great university where medicine, mathematics and astronomy were taught alongside religion. This period saw the tremendous cultural flourishing that brought the medical discoveries of Abu Sinna – known to Renaissance Europe as Avicenna, and the mathematical breakthroughs of Al Khorezm, for whom algebra is named. Billy Connolly has described algebra as the only thing he learnt in school he has never used, and I have some sympathy, but Samarkand's period of greatness saw a cultural flourishing as great as any in history.

There has been a huge amount of hopeless over-restoration in Uzbekistan, of a sort that destroys the original. This over-restoration was started by the Soviets and has been continued, to their shame, by UNESCO. Only about 10 per cent of the soaring tiles that you now see are original, and most of those which look old and damaged in fact date from Soviet restoration work in the 1970s. But in

Samarkand, the result is so awe-inspiring that I can, if not forgive the over-restoration, at least put it out of mind.

Tamburlaine's tomb was the first port of call after the Registan. Under the Karimov regime, Timur is revered as the founder of the Uzbek nation, disregarding the fact that he wasn't an Uzbek, didn't speak Uzbek and massacred huge numbers of Uzbeks. The Uzbeks then lived somewhere north of modern Uzbekistan, which they settled much later under a dynasty known as the Shaybanids, who replaced and largely eliminated the Timurids.[43] But now Timur is, defying all logic, the reigning political idol of Uzbekistan, replacing Lenin in both a metaphorical and literal sense. In all the cities and towns of Uzbekistan, Lenin has gone and been replaced by Timur. I am told that the very Lenins were melted down to provide the bronze for the Timurs.

With Timur so glorified, no expense has been spared on the restored interior of his mausoleum, a stunning cascade of gold. His tombstone sits on the marble floor, a thin high slab as Muslim grave markers are. Perhaps five feet long, fifteen inches wide and eighteen inches high, it is reputedly the largest piece of black jade in the world.

Simon's enthusiasm was plainly genuine, and I warmed to him a little. We visited the tremendous Shah-i-Zinda cemetery, the steeply stepped street of mausoleums where Timur's generals, senior officials and lesser relatives were buried. It is a terrific complex and contains the world's earliest examples of majolica tiling – that being the name for the brilliant glazes in yellow, light blue, green and brown so essential to Muslim decorative art.

Finally, we visited Ulugbek's observatory, situated on the top of a hill to the north of the city, to the immediate east of the great mound of the ruins of ancient Afrosiyab. This is where Ulugbek made his measurements and compiled his astronomical tables, at least 300 years ahead of anything comparable in Europe. A Soviet dig discovered the circular foundations of the observatory, now marked in the ground by brick. But further they discovered the marble base of Ulugbek's great quadrant, which he used for making his precise measurements of the stars.

After a very enjoyable few hours, we dismissed Affie with thanks and $50, and, returning to work, we drove off to meet with Professor Mirsaidov and his Tajik dissidents.

The Professor was beaming with pleasure as we arrived, waiting expectantly outside his house, surrounded by his large family. He led us inside to where the table groaned with the familiar weight of food and an extra large amount of the homemade wine that I had so praised last time.

I had warned Simon that this was likely to be a two-dinner day, as the Professor's insistence on providing hospitality was most unlikely to be diverted by Kristina's explanation that we were having dinner later in the evening. There were again some ten other representatives of the Tajik community there to meet us, though a slightly different group to the one I met last time. I hoped the Professor would take on board the need to be brief and to the point in his comments.

In fact, the meeting went very well. The Professor's opening spiel was concise and pertinent, and his associates gave their tales of linguistic discrimination and political repression effectively and with convincing detail that stood up well to Simon's questioning. The recent dismissal of the Rector of the university in Samarkand, one of the city's leading Tajik figures, featured. There had been a student protest demonstration, the largest in living memory in Samarkand, and in consequence the parents and other family members of many of the student protestors had been dismissed from their jobs. The role of the Hokkim in the increasingly repressive atmosphere in Samarkand was well highlighted.

We had arrived at the Professor's house about 4.30 p.m., having not eaten much breakfast and done a lot of traipsing around. The wonderful spread of walnuts, almonds, dried apricots, sultanas, pomegranates and sweet pastries was very tempting. Inevitably, it was followed by soup, then kebabs and then plov, and I left sated. I think there was also a genuine warmth between myself and the Professor and his friends, and that Simon had been given pause for thought by what he had heard.

We arrived at the guest house where we would be staying, checked in, and immediately Michael Smith's Toyota Land Cruiser drew into the courtyard, filthy from its long mountainous journey from Dushanbe. We soon drove out again, to the Tomaris restaurant, where we had booked for dinner. We sat on a horseshoe-shaped couch with a central table, and I contrived to get myself and Kristina as far away from Michael and Simon as possible, with the drivers in the middle. It was a shame not to be able to easily converse with Michael, but I thought he should have the opportunity to speak with Simon.

This did not prevent Simon from raising his voice across the table to praise Mirzaeyev. He seemed to regard the regional Hokkim as energetic and go-ahead. I had a much less favourable impression of his tub-thumping bullying style, and I found his claims to be a moderniser as unconvincing as his glib flow of statistics.

At the end of the dinner, I proposed we move on to the Blues Bar. Simon quickly and Michael reluctantly declined. They were making a start at first light for Dushanbe, while Kristina and I had nothing to do the following morning until our 10 a.m. call on the City Hokkim (as opposed to the more senior Regional Hokkim, Mirzaeyev). It was around 11 p.m., and in the Blues Bar we drank some pretty rough Uzbek 'Koniak' and listened to the old Russian in his red shirt and black waistcoat who played Gershwin with as much calm sophistication as you would get in any penthouse cocktail lounge in New York.

We stayed less than an hour before returning to our beds. It was an innocent enough close to the evening but enough for Simon Butt to note in a minute to Sir Michael Jay dated 16 April 2003 that: 'After a dinner in Samarkand, the rest of the party returned to our hotel. Craig, in the company of our young female LE fixer, went off in search of a jazz club.'

The drip, drip of innuendo against me was moving towards full flood. A jazz club with a young female, eh? Shades of Sodom and Gomorrah.

The City Hokkim was a young, very nervous-looking individual in the standard-issue black suit, with a broad build and broad face. Kristina had reminded me in the car that Mirzaeyev had boasted in yesterday's meeting that, in just over two years in charge of Samarkand region, he had sacked three city hokkims and was now on his fourth. This guy had been in post for less than a week, so a little nervousness was understandable.

We outlined the plan for three concerts in Samarkand in early May – a British classical music concert, a concert performance of *HMS Pinafore* and a Battlefield Band concert. We agreed that the first two would be held in the Opera House and the third in one of the madrassahs of the Registan – an incredible venue. We handed over some initial publicity materials and, most importantly of all, assured him that we had discussed it the day previously with Mirzaeyev, who had agreed. At this, the young City Hokkim visibly relaxed. We drank green tea and ate dried fruits while he told officials to do whatever was necessary to help. Remembering Mirzaeyev's words about ensuring the audience, I stressed the need to advertise the concerts well, not just with posters and banners but also using local television and radio, so that we could get a genuinely interested audience. Then we all shook hands and the meeting was over.

I had planned the cultural festival because, with a regime like that in Uzbekistan, the avenues of possible cooperation are limited. Music reaches people directly, whatever governments might think, and it would go some way toward creating an awareness of the UK in an audience which hopefully would include a fair proportion of the educated classes. Even among them, the media in Uzbekistan was so restricted that they only had the dimmest conception of the United Kingdom and then as a sort of adjunct to the United States. There was also a tendency to see the United Kingdom as synonymous with London, something I hoped the Battlefield Band might help to correct.

In fact, I was pushing at an open door. Cultural cooperation was a form of 'safe' diplomacy the Uzbeks were familiar with from Soviet times. They also had no difficulty with my concept that local authorities would meet local costs, as 'culture' was still something done pretty well exclusively by the state. And these were comparatively non-challenging forms of culture – folk music, classical music and opera. So at first all went well, and I felt pretty chuffed as I went on to look around the splendid Russian Opera House and then the stage inside the madrassah courtyard.

Before we left Samarkand, we visited the great market by the Bibi Khan mosque, built by Timur's wife and now being restored to its original imposing dimensions. There is a massive stone lectern outside, which originally held a great Koran, now in Tashkent, the fifth ever made and physically the largest in existence. This is in charge of the state and, over the past five years, twenty-six of the gorgeous and priceless pages have been cut out and sold, individually, on the illegal antiquities market in Germany. Sadly, since the fall of the Soviet Union there has been a massive stripping of priceless cultural assets in this way, to the benefit of members of the ruling regime. It is equally sad that the great mosques that have been restored remain as hollow monuments, devoid of the spiritual activity that was the purpose of their construction.

The great bazaar next to the mosque sells all the wonderful produce of Samarkand. It hadn't been affected by the bazaar closures, and I stocked up on dried apricots, many different kinds of sultana, sugared almonds, walnuts, pomegranates, cumin, wonderfully aromatic fresh purple basil, and saffron from the crocuses of the Tien Shan. I also bought honey on the comb, two kilos of liquid gold carefully weighed and wrapped in waxed paper, mine for the equivalent of 20 British pence. It came with a proposal of marriage from the lady who sold it, which I accepted with a low bow, drawing great gales of laughter from the stallholders, their hair wrapped in brightly coloured scarves, numerous gold teeth gleaming at me.

The return journey was without incident until we reached the road leading to Kristina's flat, where we were stopped by an officious policeman at about our 30th, and final, police checkpoint that day. He was determined not to let the vehicle through, for no apparent reason. This usually meant that either the President or one of his daughters was somewhere within a three-mile radius. We were dropping Kristina and her stuff off first, at a street a few hundred yards from the embassy. There seems no point in having an ambassador's car flying the Union Jack if any little Uzbek policeman can stop it, and while Uzbeks are used to perpetually being ordered around, I am not. I therefore told Mansur to make a point of saying that I was an ambassador and going through to the home of my secretary.

The road was blocked by concrete-filled oil drums, with just enough passage for a single vehicle, now stopped by a lowered red-and-white striped barrier. Mansur underlined the point by revving hard and nudging the Land-Rover right up against this. The policeman covered us with his Kalashnikov and spoke into his radio, then made a cross with his arms in front of him to indicate we could not pass.

Mansur switched off the engine and looked back at me. I asked him to hand me the car keys. I then got out, opened the boot and took out Kristina's suitcase and her purchases. Clutching these and putting the keys into my pocket, I squeezed past the barrier and set off in the direction of Kristina's flat. The policeman looked completely confused, and Kristina came after me calling my name. She caught up 20 yards down the road and took one of the bags from me.

'Craig, thanks for carrying my things, but there's a problem. You've got the keys, and Mansur says the car is completely blocking the road.'

'I know, that's the point.'

I underlined this by walking resolutely on. Kristina was amazed.

'Craig!' she shouted, in mock outrage. We looked back – two cars that would normally pass the checkpoint had just arrived, one from each direction – a police car and, I was delighted to see, a 'T' plated US embassy car that had just come out of the courtyard of the Ministry of the Interior, which Kristina and I were now passing on our left. Blue 'T' plates meant diplomatic technical staff and, in the current instance, almost certainly CIA. A crop-haired dark-sunglassed driver in a short-sleeved white shirt and black tie had got out of the car and was standing with one arm gripping the top of the driver's door, the other waving in my direction with a short-range radio in his hand. I turned my back and walked on.

'You know, Kristina, I could really do with a cup of tea.'

Kristina's flat was surprisingly spacious, with stripped pine floors and light pine slatting on some walls, others white. There were chrome slimline light fittings, glass and chrome tables and a large plasma TV. It felt more Stockholm than Tashkent.

I said hello to her mum and dandled her eight-month-old toddler as best I could – he was the largest and heaviest eight month old I had ever seen, with the build of a prize fighter. Kristina was divorcing her Turkish husband, and looking at Kristina's slim form and the mass of her child, I decided that should I ever meet the father I would quickly establish that I was nothing more than Kristina's boss.

Kristina made green tea with lemon, and we ate sugared almonds and cinnamon cakes from Samarkand. I caught up with the news on BBC World – the allies were still inflicting shock and awe on Iraq.

Eventually, Kristina's mobile phone rang. It was Mansur. The Discovery's anti-theft and immobilisation devices had foiled all the efforts of the Uzbek militsiya to shift it, and they had given in – we could bring the vehicle through. I told Mansur to thank them but tell them I wasn't that bothered any more. I then finished my tea and walked back to the car unhurriedly, passing a fuming line of very self-important Uzbek officials in their Nissan Maximas. I actually got a grin and friendly wave from the CIA. I hasten to say that no ordinary Uzbek would have been allowed to pass anyway and nor would, for example, an ambulance. I was not likely to have inconvenienced anyone who didn't deserve it. It was a smart sanction.

'*Kooda, Ambassador, damoi?*' asked Mansur, his grin even bigger than usual.

'No, not home – the office,' I replied.

I got back to the embassy about three-thirty. It had been presumed I wouldn't be coming in, so there was something of a scurrying as crosswords and mobile phones were put away and everyone pretended to be working. Kristina arrived about half an hour later, and I got up from my desk to ask her something. I walked about three paces when: CRACK!

I pitched forward on to my face, my spectacles spilling onto the carpet ahead of me. Bloody hell! I had been attacked from behind and stabbed or shot in the back of my left leg. I had actually heard it break. It was agony. I rolled over on my stomach, peering around and scrabbling for my glasses. No one around. I must have been shot.

I tried to stand up; I couldn't bear to put any weight at all on the left foot, but there was no sign of blood. What on earth was happening?

I called Kristina, and soon with Mansur and Dima under my armpits I was being carried out of the office and back into the car. We drove to the international clinic, where an orderly was waiting for our arrival with a wheelchair – Kristina had plainly recovered her usual efficiency.

Dr Reimers, the cheerful lady doctor from the Marshall Islands, was looking at my left calf muscle: 'Mmm, looks swollen.'

A tape measure was produced – it was six centimetres greater in circumference than my right calf muscle.

'Mmm. Something wrong there. Can't take any weight at all? Does it hurt if I . . . ?'

'AAAAGH!'

She had flexed the foot at the ankle. 'Mmm. That's not good. Need any pain relief?'

'All I can get.'

She gave me an injection of morphine or something similar and then got out her textbooks. The fact she was willing to look things up in front of you, rather than pretend omniscience, increased my confidence.

'I think you've snapped a calf muscle. It's more like a sports injury, and I'm not an expert. What does it say here? "Typically the patient pitches forward. An audible snap may be heard. Very often the patient has the initial impression of having been struck forcibly from behind."'

'Yes, that's a perfect description.'

'Thought so. One more thing to check. This may hurt.'

'AAH! It did.'

'Well, the important thing is, your Achilles tendon is OK – it's the muscle not the tendon. The tendon would have been much more serious. What you need is to rest it and tight support with an elastic bandage. Oh, and for the next 24 hours, lots and lots of ice.'

While an assistant was bandaging me, Dr Reimers left and re-appeared with two crutches, tall and aluminium, of the traditional under-the-shoulder model.

'You'll need these.'

'How long for?'

'Oh, about eight weeks.'

I got back to the embassy towards six o'clock, expecting everyone to have gone home. To my surprise, Karen, Chris, Lena Son and Kristina were lined up on the step waiting for me. I expected some wry comments on my crutches, but they looked stern and worried. Karen spoke.

'It's Professor Mirsaidov,' she said. 'His grandson's been murdered.'

Early that morning, the body of the Professor's 18-year-old grandson, Shukrat, had been dumped in the street outside the family home. The Professor had been trying desperately to contact me while still in Samarkand but had presumed I had been staying at one of the big hotels. He had got through to the embassy and spoken with Lena Son. The simple facts were these: the grandson had left the house at around 8 p.m., shortly after Simon Butt and I had departed. His body had been dumped from a truck in the street in the early hours. The Professor believed the young man had been killed as a warning, in response to our meeting with the dissidents.

They told me this as I stood braced on my crutches at the foot of the embassy steps.

'Oh my God!' I said. 'Does the Professor blame me?'

'No, not at all,' said Lena Son. 'He says that he knows you will bring justice.'

I hobbled a step backwards and levered myself on my crutches back into the Discovery. I put my head in my hands for a minute or two. We then went back into the embassy. I delegated Chris to phone the Foreign Office, while I drafted and sent a telegram outlining the bare facts as we knew them. I made a point of being plain that Professor Mirsaidov's meeting was with Simon Butt, not just me. London would take that more seriously. Simon himself would still be on the tortuous road between Samarkand and Dushanbe.

The response from London was immediate and alarmed – plainly a scandal like this could affect the hosting of the AGM of the EBRD, due to take place in Tashkent under UK chairmanship barely one month later. I was ordered to get down to Samarkand immediately and ascertain what exactly happened, in particular whether the murder could be positively pinned on the authorities, and if so whether it could be positively linked to our meeting with Mirsaidov.

It was now after dark and I was pretty tired and in pain from my leg, so I told Mansur to be ready to go down to Samarkand with me at first light and Lena Son to accompany us as interpreter. I didn't want to make Kristina leave her child again so soon. I then had to explain to Fiona that I would be leaving again straight away. I did this hurriedly on first arrival, as soon as I met Fiona in the living room. Only after I finished did I realise that I had not explained why I had appeared on crutches with a bandaged leg.

Fiona was sympathetic but reckoned I should have told the Foreign Office I had hurt my leg and could not go back to Samarkand.

The next day, my leg hurt even more as I eased myself into the car, and the many potholes on the Samarkand road caused agony. Around 10 a.m. we arrived at the Professor's home again. A more sombre family group greeted us as old friends, and Professor Mirsaidov led us to an upper storey room.

The corpse had been buried immediately, in accordance with Muslim custom. But they had managed to take extensive photographs before burial and even make a video. The photographs showed that the elbows and knees had been smashed and the back of the head stove in. In addition, the right hand looked like cooked chicken, with skin and flesh peeling away from the bones. I recognised this and the tide line around the wrist – immersion in boiling liquid. There was also matted blood around both eyes.

Professor Mirsaidov showed me the official post-mortem report, which noted none of this physical damage at all but gave cause of death as asphyxiation by vomit as a result of an overdose. It was not possible, the Professor declared, pointing to the photos. I tried to be exact and rational in the face of the old man's dignified grief.

'Well,' I said, 'there could have been also a drug overdose, but, if so, it wasn't necessarily self-inflicted.'

I went outside to speak with Mansur. A small crowd had gathered in the narrow street, mingling with the neighbours and family who had come to condole. I asked Mansur, who was a Tajik speaker, to see what he could pick up from them: perhaps someone had seen or heard something. I then returned to the Professor, who confirmed that his grandson had simply left the house in the evening and been dumped back in the early hours, tortured and dead.

He said there had been a lot of blood around the body. So it was either still alive or very recently dead when it was dumped. After the body was found – about 5 a.m. – the police had come. They had hosed away the blood, swept the street and taken the body away for autopsy before returning it some hours later. The family had moved the body inside and taken the photos I had seen before the police arrived. No one had seen the police make any investigation of the scene before washing and brushing away any evidence. The police had not taken any photos. I asked whether the family had called the police or whether they had just turned up. The Professor was uncertain. He hadn't called the police; he didn't know whether anyone else had. To the best of the Professor's knowledge, nobody had seen anyone abduct his grandson.

I asked whether the lad had any history of drug use. The Professor told me something I was to hear again and again that day. Samarkand was directly on the main route for heroin trafficking out of Afghanistan. They came to Samarkand either straight from the border crossing at Termez or through the mountains of Tajikistan. Heroin in Samarkand was substantially cheaper than beer. The grandson, Shukrat, like the large majority of his age group in Samarkand, was unemployed. He had scratched a living from the international bazaar trade before the government closed it down four months previously. He was not a *narkoman* but had probably tried heroin. Almost every young person in Samarkand had. There were now two or three young people with desperate addiction problems on this very street – and the same was true on any small street in the city. I asked if this led to problems with HIV and AIDS. The Professor's jaw muscles tensed, and he added a curt '*Da.*'

He then expounded a bit more. Opium had been part of traditional Tajik and Uzbek life for generations. It was drunk, in small quantities and very dilute form, in tea. It was used for headaches and period pains and to provide mild recreation. Only in recent years had Afghanistan started to export predominantly heroin rather than raw opium, and the culture of injecting heroin was a completely different one. It was devastating his community. He grew misty eyed, and I observed that he could articulate his grief for his community in general but was so tightly buttoned-up over what must be a profound grieving for his grandson in particular.

I asked if he had been concerned about his grandson and drugs. He said not particularly – he had said that it was likely his grandson had tried them because they were so very prevalent. He had not said that he definitely had. I asked if he had ever noticed injection marks; he said no, definitely not. I asked whether he had noticed injection marks on the body; he said no but given overall levels of damage it would have been hard to tell. I thanked him.

It may seem stupid to be asking these questions about drug abuse in such an obvious case of murder, but I knew that I would have to prove to London that I had given due consideration to the official Uzbek autopsy explanation, no matter how laughable I might think it.

I asked the Professor if I could see the last person to see Shukrat alive. I looked again at the photographs. He was a thin lad with surprisingly blond hair. Given the agonies of his death, the face was restful. Looking at the shattered legs, I recalled childhood images of the Passion. My eyes started to feel hot and tears began to well. Lena squeezed my hand.

In came a small child, looking graceful and grave in his long velvet *chapan* and square black-lacquered skullcap. He bowed and salaamed, and sat on the chair on the side of the table opposite me, his large beautiful black eyes looking at me seriously, though with no obvious sign of emotion. He was Shukrat's little brother and was eight years old.

Lena checked that he spoke adequate Russian and asked why he had come to see us. Because, he replied simply, he was the last person to see Shukrat.

He explained that he had been in the bedroom with Shukrat that evening. They had been sleeping – the rest of the family were busy all day preparing for my visit. He had been hungry, he said, because the family had spent all their money on the banquet for me. He said this in an even tone, without accusation or petulance, and continued to look me straight in the eye. He had asked Shukrat for some money, but Shukrat had said he didn't have any. Then Shukrat had dressed and gone out.

I asked what time.

About 7.30.

Had he dressed casually or carefully?

Children as young as eight years old are forced to work seventy-hour weeks
picking cotton in Uzbekistan's state-owned cotton plantations.
(Courtesy of the Environmental Justice Foundation)

The chances are that, as you read this, at least one of your garments contains
some slave-picked Uzbek cotton fibres, which are exported to textile
manufacturers worldwide. (Courtesy of the Environmental Justice Foundation)

Friends and allies – Bush and Rumsfeld with Karimov, March 2002.
(both © Getty Images)

The much reconstructed Registan of Samarkand gives an idea of the grandeur and scale of the great Islamic civilisation it once dominated.

Tamburlaine's dreaded standard in gorgeous
majolica tilework soaring over Samarkand.

The domed ceiling above Tamburlaine's tomb.

Cultural harmony – the Battlefield Band and the Sherali Juraev Band jam at the Queen's Birthday Party. (Courtesy of Robin Morton, Temple Records)

Kokhand, Ferghana Valley, April 2004. A meeting to unite the democratic opposition to the Karimov regime. Security services had tried to run my car off the road on the way there.

US Ambassador John Herbst and wife at the Queen's Birthday Party, April 2003, with the Uzbek National Orchestra playing Elgar in the background.
(Courtesy of Robin Morton, Temple Records)

Jean Lemierre (centre) and Clare Short (left) are unamused by a garrulous Karimov. President Nazarbayev of Kazakhstan sits between them, President Shevardnadze of Georgia opposite (right of picture). Six months later, Shevardnadze was overthrown by the 'Rose Revolution' and flew back to Tashkent to advise Karimov to crack down on NGOs. (Courtesy of EBRD)

A stricken President Karimov after the critical speeches of Jean Lemierre and Clare Short at the opening of the EBRD annual meeting in Tashkent, May 2003.

Preparing for *Pinafore* – Professor Neimer adjusts his tie while I talk with Mr Choi.

Nadira vamps it up in the Residence. The photographer, Eldar Karimov, fled to the UK and sought asylum after the Uzbek police searched his studio and found photos of the Andijan massacre. The Home Office refused his asylum request and at time of writing, May 2006, he was in Harmondsworth Detention Centre awaiting deportation back to Uzbekistan and a likely terrible fate. The author was desperately working on an appeal – still trying to battle the British government's attitude to the Uzbeks. (© Eldar Karimov)

Banned from entering my own embassy, I host lunch for British businessmen with Gavyn Arthur, Lord Mayor of London, while trying to cope with the strain of the 'secret' allegations against me.

May 2005, Uzbek forces kill hundreds of pro-democracy demonstrators in the town of Andijan in the Ferghana Valley. (© Getty Images)

Carefully: he had washed and shaved.

Had he said where he was going?

To see Nigina.

Nigina?

His girlfriend.

Girlfriend? I had been told he was newly married?

Yes, the child replied, as though to someone very dim. He had a wife. But Nigina was his girlfriend.

Had he said anything else?

No, he had said he was off to see Nigina, and gone out. He had never seen his brother since. They had not allowed him to see the body. At this last comment, the child's extraordinary composure cracked for the first time; his lip began to tremble and water to form in the lower rims of his eyes. Slowly and with visible self-control, he got down from the chair, bowed again, turned and left.

I was close to tears again, too. Hell, I would never have made a policeman.

I turned to Lena: 'He went to see a girlfriend? Well, that's a whole new factor.'

'Yes,' she said. 'You know, it could be the girlfriend's family. Maybe her brothers . . .'

'It might explain the brutality. I should have asked if Nigina was married. Maybe his wife's family?'

'No.' Lena sounded pretty definite. 'It's not considered that big an insult to the wife or anything. But Nigina's family, possibly. Depends who she is.'

I asked to see the Professor again.

'Who is Nigina?' I asked.

'She's a very bad girl. I have made an official complaint to the *mahalla* [district] committee about her. They have spoken to her parents. But she wouldn't stop seeing my grandson.'

'She was his regular girlfriend?'

'He had known her for many years. He had told her it must stop when he married, but she kept calling him.'

'You know that he said that he was going to see her when he left?'

'Yes, I know.'

'Could her family have killed him?'

'No. She was a very bad girl. They knew it. We know them. They don't think it was Shukrat's fault.'

I did not find this exactly convincing but decided to move on. I asked to see Shukrat's wife.

She entered in her *maraka* mourning dress. She wore a light-blue long gown, with a long white veil over her hair and falling over her arms to her waist, with the bottom of her face covered by a piece tucked over. Her eyes were red and raw from crying. Lena continued to interpret, but there was a flicker of understanding in those eyes when I spoke English.

I started by apologising for intruding upon her grief. I explained that the Professor was convinced that her husband had been killed by the authorities in connection with my visit. She nodded. I then leapt in feet first.

'You know that the last thing your husband told his brother was that he was going to see Nigina?'

This brought on a paroxysm of tears. What did I expect? But what else could I have done?

I did not get a direct answer as to whether she already knew this, but she said that she knew of Nigina, that Nigina had been her husband's girlfriend before their marriage, and that she knew he still saw her. He had stopped seeing her for a period after their marriage, but Nigina kept phoning and inducing him to go back to her.

I asked whether Nigina's family might have killed her husband. Taking a deep breath, I added the question of whether her own family, or someone concerned with her interests, might have taken action against her husband because of Nigina.

She smiled wanly. No, that was impossible. Besides, she knew who had killed her husband.

Really? I sat up straight, and soon wished I hadn't, as any movement was now causing me great pain in my left calf. The pain was causing sweat to form on my upper lip, and my shirt felt soaked, bunched and uncomfortable at the small of my back.

She reached into the folds of her gown and produced a photograph of her husband. He was sitting in a restaurant, small, thin, open-shirted and, in this photo, mousy-haired. He had a silly grin on his face. He stood out among the group of four men sitting behind their table, arms around shoulders, with Uzbek champagne and vodka bottles and party detritus before them on the white tablecloth, cheap wood panelling behind. The other three were much heavier and broader built, with sallow complexions, broad faces and a more oriental cast to their eyes. They wore leather jackets, chunky watches and gold jewellery. Gold teeth shone.

'They killed him.'

'Who are they?'

The photograph had been taken just a couple of weeks earlier at a birthday party for one of Shukrat's schoolmates. She indicated one of the group. He was SNB; the other two were drug dealers. They had befriended Shukrat, who had known them at school, but she said Shukrat had told her they had not been special friends. In the last two weeks, however, he had been out with them several times to expensive bars and restaurants, and they had paid for him. She had begged him not to trust them, but Shukrat had told her not to worry. Now, she concluded simply, they had killed him.

I asked why, and she said she did not know. But she was sure it was them. She stood up to leave. On an impulse, I asked her if she had Nigina's phone number. She did not flinch but calmly wrote it down for me.

'Need a girlfriend in Samarkand?' Lena inquired after she had gone. We needed some gallows humour, and it was appreciated.

'I take it you mean Nigina and not the widow?'

'Of course.'

'No thanks. I wonder if Nigina's crying her eyes out now, too? My leg's killing me. I need a drink.'

As if by magic, the Professor entered bearing a bottle of his homemade wine, followed by two ladies of the family with tea and mineral water. I looked out to the spreading grapevine, supported on horizontal wires to shade the whole courtyard, now budding with new life. After they left, I turned to Lena. 'What do you make of all this, Lena?'

'Well, the SNB connection could add weight to the Professor's claim of a political killing.'

'Yes, but on the other hand, there's a drug connection again. Of course, the two could be linked – maybe he had learnt too much about the authorities' involvement in drug smuggling? Maybe they hadn't realised his family links to the opposition until I came, and then they had to get rid of him? I don't know.'

The dead man's mother came to see us next, of her own volition, but she kept bursting into tears and beating her breast. She did not appear to have anything new to add, and I was anxious not to upset her. Finally, I saw the neighbour who had discovered the body. About

4 a.m. he had been awoken by the sound of a truck in the narrow alley. The house across the street rented out PA systems for parties, so large vehicles would quite often come at strange hours, and he hadn't thought much about it. About 5 a.m. he had opened the gate of his courtyard and seen the body. He had touched it: still warm and not stiff. There was a great deal of blood, mostly from the back of the head.

We spoke with Mansur – he had picked up that the whole neighbourhood knew of the affair with Nigina, but nobody seemed to think that was the cause of death. He had also learnt that there was a major drugs problem in the community but that Shukrat was not thought to be involved. A son of the man who found the body was an addict. He confirmed that when the police arrived they had very quickly hosed down any evidence. They had taken great care to brush away any tyre tracks – one of the neighbours said that he had asked a policeman why they were spoiling this evidence and had been asked by the policeman whether he wished to die, too. The neighbours took it as read that the authorities had done it.

I stayed to eat plov with the family, which was done in heavy silence. Then I took up my crutches and hobbled away. The Professor's parting words were, 'Karimov is truly the heir of Amir Timur as he claims. My grandson died as a warning to his opponents.'

I hobbled painfully to the Land-Rover and we went to the Afrosiyab Hotel. I lay on my bed for a couple of hours and by the end of the afternoon I felt up to confronting the authorities. Professor Mirsaidov had given me the address of the District Procurator dealing with the case, and we drove there. At the reception counter, I showed my green Ministry of Foreign Affairs diplomatic accreditation card, and after being checked by about six officials in ascending order of seniority, I was finally shown in to the District Procurator himself.

He wore grey-and-blue military camouflage uniform and was a sharp-eyed man of strongly oriental features, with bushy eyebrows and a lined forehead. He looked me in the eye: 'It is most unusual for an ambassador to honour a mere District Procurator with a visit. To what do I owe this honour?'

'I am here in connection with the murder of Professor Mirsaidov's grandson.'

A flicker of recognition – he certainly knew of the case.

'I was not aware that the Professor had such powerful foreign friends.'

'I think you will find he has quite a strong international reputation.'

'Really. Samarkand should be proud of him. I did not know the outside world took such an interest in Tajik literature.'

His eyes narrowed. He continued, 'The death of the grandson is most unfortunate. A drug addict, you know. Very sad case. An overdose. Very sad. It seems to have turned the old Professor's mind.'

I lost my temper. Coming clumsily to my feet on my crutches, I took the photographs of the body from Lena. I slammed down a photo of the smashed back of the skull on the desk in front of him. I positively shouted at him, 'Perhaps you can explain how that happens as a result of a drug overdose?'

I slammed down more photos, slapping my palm hard on the desk each time. Concerned officials started to arrive behind me. As each photo hit the desk, showing the boiled hand, smashed arms, broken legs, I yelled, 'Explain that! And That! And That! And THAT! Go on – tell me that's a drug overdose.'

I stood over him, and the Procurator motioned for me to sit down, which I did.

'Ambassador,' he said, 'to an amateur the sight of any dead body is grotesque. You can easily misinterpret.'

'Procurator,' I replied, 'since I came to Uzbekistan, I have seen more of these kind of photos than I would have ever imagined. This evidence is pretty plain.'

He shifted his ground: 'This dead young man was not British; why do you care?'

'We have a strong interest in human rights in Uzbekistan. Besides, I had a meeting with Minister of the Interior Almatov last December. It was very friendly and he invited me to visit any police station or prison at any time and inquire into any case.'

'Unfortunately, this office is under the Procurator-General, not under Mr Almatov. I am not authorised to speak with you.'

'Are you personally in charge of the case?'

'Yes.'

'Did you attend the scene?'

'Yes.'

'Why were the police allowed to wash away all evidence at the scene?'

'It was not necessary to conduct forensic investigation.'

'If you persist with this story of drug overdose, I will make you known as a liar throughout the world. This could affect the holding of the European Bank AGM in Tashkent.'

I saw the first flicker of fear in his eyes.

'Are you calling me a liar?' he blustered.

'If this case is closed – yes.'

Suddenly he was all comradely bonhomie: 'But who said it was closed? My investigation is just beginning. You and I know how governments work.'

He winked and leered.

'I will report your interest to my authorities. Who knows what will happen? And when this case is . . .' he paused, collected the photos from his desk and handed them back to me, '. . . buried, you will come back to Samarkand and we will drink together.'

It was the best I could do that day for the Professor. I left my card and said I would get back to him.

By evening I was feeling a bit better and we did the discos of Samarkand – well, all three to be exact, one of which had no booze and no customers but insisted on a $10 entrance fee. Lena was great company, and we had much fun with the local youth and my crutches. It was desperately needed light relief.

The next day, we went back to Tashkent. I reported to London that it was impossible to be certain why the Professor's grandson had been killed. Plainly, the autopsy report was a sham. That combined with the efficient destruction by the police of evidence at the scene showed the authorities were deliberately hiding something. This would give weight to the Professor's view that the murder had been committed by the authorities themselves to discourage dissidents from meeting the British Ambassador.

On the other hand, the victim's tangled love life might be the motive. Or it could be connected with his new friends and the drugs trade. The authorities were up to their necks in narcotics trafficking throughout Uzbekistan and might have ordered both murder and cover-up from that motive. At this stage, it was impossible to be certain. I could investigate further, for example by visiting Nigina and her family, or by going to Shukrat's old school, identifying the three men on the picture from the school reunion and questioning them.

London did not want me to investigate further. They were satisfied that there was enough area of uncertainty to allow them to proceed with chairing the EBRD AGM. I was, however, allowed to make a protest to the Uzbek Ministry of Foreign Affairs about the discrepancy between the autopsy report and the photographic evidence. I did this but as usual received no practical response.

About ten days after my return from Samarkand, I was attending a state banquet, I believe for a visiting president of another former Soviet state. As I was milling around in the general gathering over drinks, one of the other ambassadors pulled me aside and asked me what London made of the death of Mirsaidov's grandson; the Professor was telling everybody it was connected to my visit.

I said that it was certainly possible: the autopsy was plainly a fraud and there had been no proper investigation. Something was being covered up.

This ambassador had excellent contacts in the SNB and they were, he said, furious at the killing, regarding it as pointlessly sadistic and counter-productive. It had been done by the Samarkand militsiya on the direct orders of the Hokkimyat. They were determined to stamp out Tajik dissidence in Samarkand.

I thanked him. It was food for thought. It certainly seemed to fit with the regime's explosive style, the school closures, linguistically based job purges and the removal of the Tajik Rector of the University of Samarkand.

I considered what I knew of this ambassador and his character, his motivation for telling me the truth or for misleading me. I considered whether the SNB might have misled him, and why. My conclusion is that he was telling me the truth. The most likely explanation of the death was that the Hokkimyat ordered the killing to intimidate Samarkand dissidents. It fits all the known facts.

That leads me to conclude that, in a sense, I was responsible. Had I not arranged to visit Mirsaidov and the other dissidents with Simon Butt, the lad would probably still be alive now. I continue to worry away at it, but it is some consolation that Mirsaidov does not blame me. As he points out, totalitarian regimes terrify you into inaction by the threat of violence against you or, still more effectively, against others. If for that reason we give in, totalitarianism will always win.

I can appreciate that intellectually, but emotionally I still get hit by waves of guilt. Sometimes they hit me just in the supermarket or on the Underground. I think I will still see those images of Shukrat's corpse, horribly tortured yet peaceful, in my dreams until the day I too die.

I reported back to London what the ambassador had told me, and that I believed him, but they did not seem that interested. In fact, from about this time my influence with the FCO appeared to vaporise; they simply ignored almost anything I had to say.

At the state banquet, as he moved away, the ambassador motioned towards the glass of champagne in my hand. 'If I were you,' he said, 'I wouldn't eat or drink too much here.'

I thought he was being melodramatic, but I put down my glass and found a bottle of Nestlé water with the seal still intact, which I stuck to throughout the evening. At the state banquet, each course was brought individually plated and put in front of you. Members of the visiting delegation, who comprised a third of the guests, were continually leaping up from their seats and beavering off to fine-tune speeches, handle press queries or deal with logistics for the next day's programme: all tasks I knew very well. I contrived to keep taking courses from their empty seats, depositing my plates on a side table.

Anyway, I had no bad effects from that evening. But later I had much cause to dwell on his warning.

CHAPTER 12

Pinafore, Battlefield and Baseball Bat

I was feeling pretty low. Getting so close to the death of Mirsaidov's grandson, combined with the nagging sense that it was my fault, had hit me hard. My sore leg was causing constant pain. I had lost my faith in my own country and in the job I was doing. The issues of torture and intelligence were causing me a real crisis of conscience. I was facing unmistakable personal hostility from my immediate management. Intellectual company was in short supply, and I didn't have any sympathetic senior FCO colleague with whom I could talk over these problems. I had to cope with all of this while living in the landscape of human misery caused by one of the worst regimes on earth.

In novels, people survive a whole series of dramatic and traumatic events and come through them all guns blazing. They never crack up under the strain. I suppose that's why they are heroes and why it is fiction. Anyway, I couldn't crack up yet, as I was about to enter the busiest period of my professional life.

In the next four weeks, we had to prepare for chairing the EBRD AGM, to put on the British Music Festival in five cities, and to run the Queen's Birthday Party with a guest list of over 2,000. I had miscalculated one vital factor. I had been used to working in teams of dynamic and ambitious young graduates, wedded to the job and prepared to give their everything at all hours. Now I was having to bring along less ambitious staff whom I needed to enthuse. I ended up doing much more myself than I expected. I also found it was often the local staff who rose best to the challenges.

There had been changes in staff. Dave and Debbie Muir had left and been replaced by Steve Brown, another ex-army man, and his beautiful ethnic Russian wife from Kazakhstan. Jackie had left and been replaced by Angela Clarke.

I had initiated a major programme of new and better staff housing. We had also taken on quite a number of extra Uzbek staff. Steve Brown had two new assistants, Ulugjan and Lilya. I had finally persuaded Chris to take on an assistant, an earnest young man named Talat. I had signalled to London that if I was going to stay in Tashkent, they would have to put the embassy on a better funding basis and update the communications equipment. One of the issues that had prompted this was a complaint from London that the embassy was not following all proper procedures in accounting, procurement and recruitment. Quite simply, the embassy had never had enough staff to carry out the FCO's bureaucratic requirements.

I am a great fan of cultural diplomacy – reaching the population of a country and presenting them with a connection to the UK through popular events. Given modern communications, with satellite television promoting popular culture worldwide, this may seem anachronistic. British soaps are watched, and British pop music heard, all round the globe. But not in Uzbekistan, where the media is very tightly controlled and the large majority of the population – all except the wealthiest city dwellers – have no access to satellite.

As the fourth city of the Soviet Union, Tashkent had a great tradition of classical music, opera and ballet. I invited the great former ballerina Bernara Karieva to dinner on a couple of occasions and much enjoyed her stories. But she was very sad about the decline of these arts in Tashkent.[44]

If you see Uzbekistan as a post-colonial state, having thrown off Russian occupation, then it is only natural to expect that the coloniser's art forms should disappear – native Uzbek music has a very different tonal base. But it is still sad. The opera and ballet continue, though with sharply declining standards. The new Conservatoire continues some excellent teaching, but the balance shifts evermore towards Uzbek traditional music. In the Soviet tradition, this 'folk' music has been cut off from its roots in communities and is presented in a stultified and joyless state-approved form.

There remain some wonderful classical musicians in Uzbekistan.

The National Symphony Orchestra is first class but seldom gets to play. There are no public orchestral concerts. Very infrequently, the government decides to bring out the symphony orchestra on a state occasion – for example, a concert in honour of the EBRD AGM. But the orchestra is wilting through neglect. Its members receive theoretical salaries of about $12 a month, but they seldom arrive.

My idea, based on experience in Poland, was to put on a music festival using local musicians to play British music. We couldn't afford to bring an orchestra out from the UK, but using the Uzbek orchestra could be both effective and cheap. What we could afford to bring out was a folk band. I chose the Battlefield Band, in my opinion the best and certainly the most enduring of the Celtic revival bands. The final element came together when I was invited to a concert – Handel's *Messiah* – by the local Silk Road Chamber choir. Privately sponsored by South Korean businessmen, they were of the highest musical standard. I am a great fan of Gilbert and Sullivan operettas, which I think are ludicrously underrated in the UK. They too travel well internationally, and this choir could tackle one.

So, in October I had put the plan together. There would be three elements. The Battlefield Band would play in Tashkent, Samarkand, Navoi, Ferghana and finally Tashkent again. The orchestra would put on a programme of accessible British light classical music in Tashkent and Samarkand, followed the next day in each venue by *HMS Pinafore*.[45] The embassy would pay for the performance fees, scores and UK costs. We would ask the Uzbek authorities to cover venue, transport and accommodation.

None of the music in the festival had ever been heard in Uzbekistan before. This would be the first-ever production of Gilbert and Sullivan in Central Asia. This would need the willing cooperation of the infamously truculent Uzbek authorities. Only one of the proposed cast of *Pinafore* could speak English. The orchestra had never so much as heard the music. We needed to make sure that concerts were carried on radio and television to meet a much wider audience. These were just the first of the logistical difficulties we faced. All of which inspired me to rise to the challenge.

Project funding within the FCO has to be won through quarterly competitive bidding. Unsurprisingly, our bid failed. But I persuaded the Eastern Department that, if they were so very keen on cooperation with the Uzbeks, they had better put some money into this. We also raised a good sum from British companies in

Tashkent, thanks to hard work by Karen. Predictably, the British Council Arts Department turned their noses up, sniffily refusing to help even with sourcing the scores. Thankfully, Chris Hirst found most of them on the Internet. For others, we had to get the Uzbekistan desk officer in the FCO, Daniel Grzenda, to go to Boosey & Hawkes in London to collect them and send them out to us by diplomatic bag.

Tamara, the young student pianist I had met at the Gershwin concert, was to prove invaluable, becoming pretty much an extra, unpaid, member of staff. She introduced me to her father, Professor Timur Gulyamov, professor at the Conservatoire. Between them they did a tremendous amount to spread the word and enthuse the local musical community about the festival. Timur invited Fiona and me, with the children, to a lovely traditional meal in his house, after which he got out his *dutar* – a long-necked two stringed instrument – on which he played beautifully to us.

Karen had organised to hire the Uzbek National Orchestra –the rate was $15 per player per performance, plus $100 each for the conductor and director. The orchestra as an institution would get to keep the scores – which were worth a couple of thousand pounds. The initial contract was to play at the Queen's Birthday Party, at two orchestral concerts and two performances of *Pinafore*. We were using a 63-piece orchestra, and the fee for all this was approximately $6,000. I was very excited when, accompanied by Tamara, I attended the first orchestral rehearsal. The orchestra were excited, too, because they very seldom saw new scores.

The conductor, Vladimir Neimer, kindly ran through the whole programme for me at the first two rehearsals before getting down to serious work. He was a tall gaunt man of few words and a fantastic musician whose services were in demand throughout the former Soviet Union. He was dedicated to his orchestra and expended huge efforts on individual tuition. His father had been a conductor at the Volksoper in Vienna, so he took easily to the spirit of this light music. He could be fierce in rehearsal and would bark at the musicians when they didn't give the tone he wanted. I worked very closely with him, in particular on the tempos, and we forged a firm friendship. I got to conduct the orchestra in rehearsals once or twice; there is no more exhilarating experience. Under Neimer's direction, the orchestral concerts were very quickly on track, and indeed in the event were nothing short of superb.

HMS Pinafore was much more difficult, in particular getting the choir to sing successfully in English. I spent more time working on the pronunciation than on the music. Their director, Mr Choi, had said from the start that five months was not enough, but I had swept him along with my usual enthusiasm. From December, I found I was spending an average of two hours every day, maybe more at weekends, at orchestral and choir rehearsals, on top of my usual work. I was starting to regret my impetuosity.

I made extra trips to Ferghana and Navoi to firm up arrangements for the concerts and to choose venues. I had to call on Prime Minister Usmanov to obtain his agreement to the festival, but once that was achieved the local authorities were all eagerness to help.

I had few worries about the Battlefield Band, an extremely professional outfit who had been touring the world for 25 years and could be guaranteed to put on a display of outstanding musicianship and to enthuse an audience. Some of the venues were superb, but there was much to do in terms of arranging publicity and practicalities like lighting and power sockets. I made television and radio appearances on these visits to promote the music and gave out CDs. We had posters, leaflets, banners and other publicity material printed. The highly profitable monopoly on banner printing and banner hanging is held by Gulnara Karimova, the President's daughter, which is why the streets are always festooned with scores of banners advertising state enterprises. Our publicity material was given to the local authorities to put out.

The Queen's Birthday Party was to be held on 28 April at the new Residence.[46] I was determined that we would use the occasion to establish the high-profile role of the British embassy. I wanted about 1,200 guests, so we would need to invite about 2,000 people.

I had announced this to a gobsmacked staff in November. I said that the first hundred names on the guest list should be the most famous people in Uzbekistan, be they actors, sports personalities, newsreaders, singers or whoever. I wanted people to leave saying, 'Wow! Did you see who was there?' This idea was greeted with some scepticism – Atabek said the mafia held a third of the top hundred places – but gradually they warmed to it. I then wanted the heads of the hundred biggest companies, state or private, the hokkims of the regions and the big cities, all our commercial and political contacts, every consular national for whom we were responsible. Every British company was to have the chance to nominate guests useful to them.

We should invite not only ambassadors but also key diplomats from other embassies. Oh, and all the neighbours.

I wanted a programme of entertainment that started at 3 p.m. and finished at 9 p.m. This would kick off with the full symphony orchestra in evening dress playing the British light music programme on the marbled terrace by the swimming pool. It would conclude with a concert by the Battlefield Band, playing to a banked corner of the garden where we would set out 300 chairs in a natural amphitheatre. Food was substantial. There were to be 11,000 canapés, 3,000 shashliks and 100 kilos of plov, served over six hours. There were also to be two large bars, plus a Pimms tent, a British beer bar and a British cheese stall. British Airways flew out much of this. Getting it through customs was a tussle. Lena and 16 helpers cooked the food, while the Sheraton provided bars, glasses and 46 serving staff. We bought and imported marquees. The Hokkimyat provided chairs and tables for 600, spread round the garden. Twelve policemen organised the traffic, and we hired a nearby stadium for parking for 300 cars – it overflowed. Thirty-six soldiers secured the perimeter. And, of course, there were fireworks to close. I love fireworks.

It was a hell of a lot of work. Just collating guest lists and writing invites was a massive task. The Uzbek post is completely unreliable, and the invitations had to be hand delivered all over the country. Karen, Kristina and Fiona produced miracles of organisation.

Jamie was out on his Easter holiday, and from 11 to 14 April I went on a holiday with the family to Samarkand and Bokhara. Returning through Samarkand, I started to feel small stirrings of alarm. I had handed over publicity materials to the City Hokkim when I visited with Simon Butt. Chris Hirst had followed up and delivered much more. But I couldn't see a single poster or banner up anywhere. When I got back to Tashkent, Daniel Grzenda had come out from the Eastern Department at my request, to give us a hand at this busy time. I sent him off to do a John the Baptist routine around the venues, making sure everything was ready. But I then found that our large placard outside the Tashkent Opera House had been taken down. None of our posters or banners had gone up in Tashkent either.

The BBC Monitoring office in Tashkent had very kindly translated *HMS Pinafore* into Russian for me and done a superb job of capturing the spirit of Sullivan's sharp and witty lyrics. My plan had been that the choir would deliver the spoken dialogue in Russian between songs, but sing in English. Now Mr Choi asked for an urgent meeting and told me that the choir could not speak the dialogue. They intended just to do a concert of the songs. I resisted this. A huge amount of effort had been put into translating the dialogue so that the audience could follow what was going on. To leave it out would substantially devalue the experience.

Mr Choi was adamant, however, and he suggested as a compromise that they use a well-known actor as a narrator. He would adapt the libretto and explain what was happening between songs. I was reluctantly obliged to agree.

The next morning, Karen met me at the door of the office. She was always the first one to arrive at work.

'Chris says that the Opera House has been on the phone. They've cancelled the performances,' she said.

Half an hour later, a note from the MFA arrived. All further rehearsals for the British Music Festival were cancelled, it said. The National Symphony Orchestra was needed to prepare for a concert for the EBRD.

I sped round to the symphony orchestra. Professor Neimer shook his head. They had been given the programme for the EBRD concert. It was from the extremely limited officially approved repertoire. Professor Neimer said that they really did not therefore need to rehearse much for the EBRD, and there was nothing to stop them doing both the EBRD and our festival. I therefore wrote and suggested to the Uzbek authorities that if rehearsal time was the clash, maybe they might incorporate some of our music in the EBRD concert.

After sending a note to the MFA, I received a call round to the Ministry of Foreign Affairs, where I met Mr Yusupov, head of the European Department. He explained that it would not be possible to change the programme for the EBRD. All programmes for public performances had to be approved by the Permitted Arts Committee (PAC), which was chaired by the Prime Minister.[47] I asked why our banners and posters had not gone up. Yusupov said that with the EBRD coming, it had been decided it was inappropriate to allow any advertising by a foreign power. There was, he advised, absolutely no chance that this decision would be changed.

The Opera House was now genuinely hosting another EBRD event on the day of our orchestral concert, but Karen and Lena had found and booked another hall, the Railway Palace. Built as an educational institution for the workers of the Trans-Caspian Railway, it had a huge hall with much better acoustics than the Opera. Karen and Lena had also produced new leaflets and were getting them out to universities and libraries. They had persuaded the management of the Opera House that *Pinafore* could still go ahead, the day after the EBRD concert.

It was lucky that Karen and Lena were so active, because Chris's input was now minimal. That lunchtime he had come in dirty and bruised with a bleeding leg. He had, he said, been walking by the canal when a Lada drew up, and four big men with crowbars had got out to attack him. He had, however, beaten them off.

Chris stated that he thought the attack had been organised by the SNB. He then returned home and essentially stopped working from that moment. The incident had obviously shaken him deeply, and while he turned up occasionally, he made little contribution. As we were seriously fire-fighting at this point, however, I was unable to tackle this problem immediately.

Then, on the afternoon of Friday, 25 April, Kristina brought me the following letter, from a Mr Burkhanov, a partially sighted and registered disabled man. It had been delivered by hand to the embassy. He wrote:

> On April 25 2003 at 7.10am when I was going to my work along the Ankhor river bank, which flows along Bainal Minal Street (International), an unknown man with his dog was coming towards me. The dog, without a muzzle and collar, was running 20 metres in front of its owner. The animal came near me and attacked me. It bit my thigh and ankle joint of my right leg, my trousers were torn. I lost consciousness, could not protect myself and felt very bad. I am third category disabled.
>
> The owner of the dog unhurriedly approached me. Instead of giving me the first medical aid, he, on the contrary, suddenly pushed me aside and went on past as though nothing had happened.
>
> Some time later I regained consciousness and . . . called the ambulance.

The letter went on to give Chris's address. I sent Ulugjan to the hospital to check out the story.

The weekend of 26 and 27 April was spent physically setting up the Residence for the Queen's Birthday Party, briefing all the staff involved, dealing with late requests for invitations and rescuing supplies from customs. At 2.30 a.m. on 28 April, the day of the party, I was at the airport welcoming the Battlefield Band, along with Talat. He had assured me that there would be a bus from the hotel waiting to take the six of them and their large amount of equipment. There was no bus, and we crammed them into the Land-Rover and two taxis, arriving at their hotel towards 4 a.m. I left the band so they could grab some sleep and went to get a little myself before the 11 a.m. gathering of staff to prepare for the party kicking off at 3 p.m. Before I went to bed, I loaded 2,000 bottles of beer and many hundred bottles of wine and soft drinks into a series of large chest freezers to get cool by the afternoon. I got to bed around 7 a.m. and was up again at 9.30.

Ulugjan arrived early with Steve Brown. He confirmed to me that he had seen the partially sighted man in the hospital and said that he had no doubt he had been attacked by Chris's dog, which had been out of control. Shortly thereafter, Chris and Karen arrived. Chris quickly argued with Fiona and then went and sat at a table by the wall, where he remained for most of the day, not contributing anything.

The situation was now very difficult. Although we had received more than one serious complaint about Chris, I had to bear in mind that there was a real possibility these were politically motivated and had been trumped up in an attempt to get him removed from his post, thus disrupting the embassy's work on human rights. His efforts in this area had almost certainly not endeared him to the Uzbek authorities. On the other hand, I had personal experience of seeing him lose control of his temper after the van Boven visit and was aware of complaints against him in other postings, though I didn't know how Chris had defended himself against those charges. With the atmosphere in the embassy growing worse by the day, I could see no other option than to send him home once we got through the very intensive next few days. It is worth noting that Chris always denied all of the allegations against him and, as they were never properly investigated, I just do not know where the truth finally lay.

The Queen's Birthday Party was, in conventional terms, the high point of my career. I have said that I had obtained more influence than other diplomats in Uzbekistan. That day was proof of this. The Uzbek government would always nominate a single full minister to attend every embassy's national day. You might get a few deputy ministers thrown in. The Americans were the sole exception: they might get two or even three full ministers. We had seven, which astonished the diplomatic corps – including me. Even more unheard of, we had the President's daughter. Gulnara had never been to a national day before, but she came to that one.

She appeared in mid-afternoon, as the orchestra was in full swing. Fiona and I had spent the first hour greeting guests in the living room as they passed through to the garden. Kristina had been standing by us to interpret where necessary.

After an hour, we had gone into the garden to circulate, and I was called back into the house some time later to greet Gulnara. I led her out into the garden and, as she didn't want to sit, we stood talking on the little wooden bridge over the stream. Then 31 years old, she was charming and girlish, giggling delightedly at my light conversation. It was very difficult to reconcile this with her reputation, especially when the following happened.

A particularly drunken guest came up to me. A fat grey-haired man, he was the Deputy Hokkim of Navoi and rather full of his own importance. Earlier he had asked me for ten minutes of my time. I had said I should be delighted to give it to him, but not on this particular day. Now he was back, drunker and more persistent. He interposed himself between Gulnara and me.

'Mr Ambassador,' he said, 'I have something very important to speak to you about.'

'Not just now, my friend,' I said. 'I am really busy.'

He turned and leered at Gulnara. She shrank back, and I sensed several security men move closer.

'Are you an interpreter?' he demanded.

I grabbed his arm.

'No, she's not an interpreter,' I said. 'I'll come and talk to you in a little while.'

He turned back to Gulnara and pushed her hard in the shoulder.

'But you speak English, yes? You can interpret?'

Gulnara was shaking her head at one of her security men, telling him not to intervene. Michael Timke, the South African honorary consul and a businessman, came past. I put my arm round the nuisance and shoved him towards Michael.

'Why don't you have a drink with my good friend Michael?' I suggested.

Michael is a large well-built man. He is also quick on the uptake, and he firmly but chummily led him to the bar. I turned back to Gulnara.

'I am so sorry about that,' I said.

'Do you think I could get a job as your interpreter?' she giggled. 'Sounds like it might be fun.'

It is of course a truth universally acknowledged that no woman can resist flirting with a man in a kilt. Nevertheless, how many presidential children would react so prettily to being pestered by a drunk? Her reaction did not fit with the stories I had heard about her. Her simple dress belied the $4.5 million of personal jewellery listed in her US divorce settlement. There didn't seem to be obvious darkness behind her laughing eyes. Was she really behind the corrupt acquisition of all those businesses, the closing down of rival companies, the massive bribes from huge energy deals?

Everything at the party went perfectly. The orchestra was superb, and the Battlefield Band got everyone enthused and dancing. They were joined by Uzbekistan's most popular musician, Sherali Juraev. This was received with wild enthusiasm because he is banned by the government from public performance for criticising the President, but on diplomatic premises they couldn't stop him. Nor could we, and the music wound up around ten, even then only because I started the fireworks display.

Gradually people left, and by eleven the party was basically over. Maybe a dozen close expat friends and their wives and girlfriends remained, having a quiet drink and musing over the day. Some very pretty American and Canadian girls from CEELI stripped down to their underwear and jumped in the pool. Two or three others joined them, including Richard Wilkins' assistant, a member of his Uzbek staff who went further and took off her bra. This was going a bit far for the circumstances, so Fiona took her a towel to cover herself. I got to bed about 1 a.m.

The next evening, the Battlefield Band held their first public concert, in the Opera House. It was packed to the rafters, and the music was incredibly well received. They had the audience going wild and received a massive standing ovation and several encores.

Chris then went with them for their next concert in Samarkand, while I caught up a day later in Navoi. Again, the same rapturous reception – indeed, possibly still better. We had then returned to Tashkent, where they had a day off. That evening, we were all guests at Timur Gulyamov's house. All the musicians had brought instruments, including Timur's Uzbek colleagues, and the result was drinking, fun and incredible music-making into the small hours.[48]

The largest cost of the Battlefield Band tour, apart from their fee, was the sound equipment. I had checked with the British Council that there was nothing of sufficient quality available in Uzbekistan. They had therefore brought a system with them, including a 16-channel mixing desk, amps, speakers, monitors, cables and mike stands. Shipping all this by air cost £3,000 in each direction, even at a special reduced rate from British Airways.

Robin Morton, the Battlefield Band's producer, suggested to me that I contact the owners of the equipment, Northern Light of Edinburgh, and discuss buying it second-hand. If we were having more bands out, then it would save these huge shipping costs. I passed this idea on to Steve, who had been in a band and was a DJ. He negotiated with Northern Light and we bought the lot for £4,000 – only £1,000 more than it would have cost to send it back to them. This was to come back to haunt me.

The next day, I had to make a speech to the Institute of War and Peace Reporting on persecution of writers in Uzbekistan and chair a number of EBRD preparation meetings. The day after that, we had the arrival of Clare Short, a full day of meetings, the official opening of the EBRD conference, the final Battlefield Band concert at the Railway Palace and a late evening reception at the Residence for 300 Brits involved in the EBRD conference. These included the British delegation, EBRD staff, the visiting press corps, NGOs attending the meeting and local businessmen. By now, I was definitely knackered.

On 5 May, the EBRD conference closed, and we had the first public concert of British light classical music at the Railway Palace. It was absolutely sparkling – it really took your breath away. *Pomp and Circumstance* was missed out, and from the *Fantasy on British Sea Songs* all of 'Rule Britannia' was cut except the closing phrase of the piece. But overall it was such a huge success, so massively enjoyed, that it seemed a shame to quibble.

Pinafore at the Opera House the next day was not such a success. The narrator was intrusive and told the story in broad terms. Like any Gilbert plot, simply told, it just sounded silly. The soloists sounded under-rehearsed. Worst of all, the male chorus, so crucial in *Pinafore*, was weak and seemed short of several members. It didn't help that the house lights were left fully on and the audience never really settled. Everyone was anxious in the interval. At my insistence, the house lights were off in the second act. The soloists got stronger, and there are a succession of solos and less chorus work. It was well received. The small expatriate community had strongly supported all our events, and while they had been really happy about the Battlefield Band and orchestral concerts, 'Good try' probably summed up their reaction to *Pinafore*.

On the Wednesday, Fiona and I were due to leave Tashkent at lunchtime to attend the orchestral concert in Samarkand. But I received a phone call from Mr Yusupov saying that I was to call on Foreign Minister Safayev at 4 p.m. I said that I couldn't, because I had to be in Samarkand. It was made plain to me that this was compulsory. The MFA would, however, arrange a police escort to get me to Samarkand afterwards.

Every time I was summoned to the MFA, I worried they had decided to declare me *persona non grata*. I consoled myself that couldn't be the case this time, or they wouldn't have offered to escort me to Samarkand. I arrived at the MFA with Fiona and the luggage ready in the car. The meeting with Safayev did not take long. He said that it was a very grave matter and that Chris Hirst had been attacking people in the street. A formal complaint had been made to my predecessor, but no satisfactory action had been taken. He said he had a dossier listing allegations of 12 attacks, including one on an old lady who had suffered permanent brain damage and another on a 12-year-old girl who claimed to have been dragged by her hair down the street by Chris.

These new and terrible allegations shocked me. Although I had not yet given Chris the chance to respond to them, it was clear that it was impossible for him to remain in Tashkent. The Uzbek authorities were obviously no longer prepared to permit his presence and so I said I would ensure that he left Uzbekistan straight away. Safayev, who had been prepared for a fight, looked astonished at my reaction. I noted that among the papers he handed me was a note from the Uzbek MFA of 18 September, eight months previously, which I had never seen.

After I left Safayev, we screamed down to Samarkand, several police cars clearing the way. We went to Samarkand's Opera House, more elegant and with much better acoustics than the one in Tashkent. But we were still in the opening bars of 'Jerusalem' when I realised something was badly wrong. The audience didn't look educated at all – they were all in peasant clothes. They were talking noisily and excitedly, and when the music started just talked louder over it. Some seemed to be eating their dinner. This continued throughout the first half. The Deputy Hokkim was with me and seemed vaguely aware of my increasing concern.

At the interval, I called a meeting with the Director of the Theatre, the Deputy Hokkim and Professor Neimer. I was really quite angry. Against my specific request, I said, it was obvious that the audience were not there voluntarily but had been instructed to come. Plainly, most of them had no interest at all in the music. I had attended concerts all over the world and never seen such disgraceful behaviour. Either we stopped the concert now or we announced that anyone who wanted to leave could do so.

Neimer was fretful. He said he had once been resident conductor in this Opera, and it used to have excellent audiences. He had many friends in this city, but not one of them was here. And where was the Rector of the University? He loved classical music and always turned up to introduce the concert and explain the music to the audience.

I knew the answer to the last question. He had been sacked and was under house arrest.

Before the second half, the Deputy Hokkim lectured the audience on their bad behaviour. He did however say, as I had requested, that anyone who wanted to do so should now leave, and two-thirds of the audience got up and left. He then picked on a young man in the audience, one of very few ethnic Russians present, and ordered him to leave for talking during his speech. The young man stood and argued – he was one of the few who really wanted to be there – but he was taken out by the police. The second half was beautifully played, and the remaining audience were very enthusiastic, but I had lost my savour for the evening.

The next day, I discovered that students and staff at the university had specifically been ordered not to attend the concert. None of the advertising material had been used and nothing had appeared in the local media. Mirzaeyev had simply ordered the poorest mahalla to provide the audience. As this was regarded as a punishment detail, they had hardly been receptive.

The next day, I insisted on seeing Mirzaeyev and gave him a piece of my mind. I asked him to stand down the rent-a-mob for *Pinafore* that evening, and with Professor Neimer I set about going round the university and talking to all my other contacts to whip up an audience. For *Pinafore*, it wasn't quite a full house but not far off, and they were very enthusiastic. The whole performance was much better than in Tashkent, helped in part by the better acoustics. It was the last concert of our music festival and was followed by a party at their hotel for the orchestra and choir. This was great fun, and we all let our hair down. I sang the part of Admiral Sir Joseph Porter alongside Abdumalik and Natasha in the trio 'Never Mind the Why and Wherefore'. It was a riotous evening and a great release.

Now it was over, Mr Choi and Professor Neimer filled in some of the gaps for me. The Prime Minister's committee had banned 'Pomp & Circumstance' and insisted on the removal of 'Rule Britannia' from the *Fantasy on British Sea Songs*. These were decreed inappropriately British for an Uzbek orchestra to perform. They had also banned the Russian dialogue from *HMS Pinafore*, which was considered politically subversive. Singing it in English was OK, as the bulk of the audience couldn't understand revolutionary lines like: 'I always voted at my party's call, I never thought of thinking for myself at all'. But spoken lines, translated into Russian, like: 'An official utterance is generally considered unanswerable' could apparently provoke mass unrest. I thought Gilbert would have been proud to find his work banned by a despotism a hundred years after his death, but the stupid thoroughness of Uzbek totalitarianism was stunning.

That summer, while on holiday in South Korea, Mr Choi had his Uzbek visa revoked and was unable to return to Tashkent. All his effort in building from scratch both the Silk Road Chamber Choir and his furniture company came to nothing.

The next morning I went back to Tashkent and had the difficult task of tackling Karen. She was tearful but said she was relieved it was over. She admitted she had been intercepting letters of complaint about Chris, preventing them from reaching me. This included the Uzbek note of 18 September. She said that while Chris had never struck her, she had felt intimidated and bullied by him. I asked if she had hidden the papers Chris Ingham said he had left for me. She denied this and said he had not left them for me but for her. She proved this by producing them still in a sealed envelope addressed to her by him. I opened it and saw for the first time Ingham's telegram of 28 January 2002 to the FCO. It began: 'Note from Uzbek MFA accuses Chris Hirst . . . of beating two Uzbek citizens and setting his dog on them.' The telegram went on to say that the Uzbeks seemed to have got it wrong and that it was Chris who had been assaulted.

I sent back a telegram outlining developments. London replied, instructing me in effect to get Chris Hirst on the next plane out. They would conduct an investigation in London into his behaviour.

I told Chris that there were more complaints from the MFA that he had been involved in violence and that he was to return to London in the morning. I didn't think he would come back to Tashkent.

Chris breathed heavily and stared straight in front of him, saying nothing, for a very long and tense five minutes. Then he said, 'I suppose that's it, then.'

I handed him his air ticket, and he left.

The next morning, I went with Karen and Chris to the airport to make sure he got on the plane. Both Karen and I tried to make light conversation, which he ignored. He still had that fixed stare, but he went quietly enough.

CHAPTER 13

The Circus Comes to Town

The EBRD held its AGM in Tashkent from 4 to 5 May 2003. The decision had been taken some years previously, when reform had been expected to go rather faster in Tashkent than turned out to be the case. As things stood, the EBRD AGM had acquired enormous significance. The Uzbek government saw it as a tremendous boost to their international image. For the international community, and for NGOs in particular, it had become a litmus test for how the international institutions should deal with recalcitrant dictatorships that refused to reform.

On a more mundane level, for me it also meant a great deal of work. Not only was there a visiting UK delegation to look after but extra liaison duties also fell on our small embassy because the EBRD is London based. Furthermore, Clare Short, then Secretary of State for Overseas Development, was coming out to chair the conference. Any visit by a Cabinet minister puts a great demand on an embassy in terms of extra communications with London, the arrangement of bilateral meetings and press conferences, and the provision of numerous logistics for the minister and their staff.

We became the chief contact point for the EBRD permanent staff in London, of whom some scores of Brits were coming out for the conference. This was also the height of the panic over the SARS epidemic. It was raging not far away in western China and we all knew that even if it had reached Uzbekistan the regime would never admit it anyway.

One female member of EBRD staff emailed me from London: 'Should I wear a face mask in the conference hall?'

'I don't know,' I typed back. 'How ugly are you?'

Sadly, this was not appreciated.

Some of the arrangements the regime made for hosting the conference verged on the incredible. Four new five-star hotels were built and six substantively renovated at incredible speed and a cost to the Uzbek people of well over $300 million. Management contracts allowed them to be called the Radisson, Meridien, Sheraton, Intercontinental, etc. Roads were repaired, tramways restored or ripped out. False shop fronts were put up to cover empty buildings on key routes. Rotten Soviet concrete buildings were given a Meccano external framework that was then plated in blue glass.

The charade to fool the delegates got still more extraordinary. The local food bazaars had reopened and the stall owners and key shop owners were instructed to display goods at one-third of the true price, to give the visitors a false impression of living standards. They had to sell at that price to anyone who looked like a foreigner, though locals got short shrift.

Clare Short had expressed a desire to get out and meet ordinary people, and we had organised a visit to Chorzu bazaar. The Uzbek government had tried to insist she visit Alejski bazaar instead, which they had tarted up as a showpiece, but we insisted on Chorzu. The female among the eight deputy prime ministers turned up unexpectedly at our delegation office, having been designated to accompany the Minister to the market. We had made it very clear in writing that Clare Short wanted a chance to meet ordinary people with no officials around. She made it plain to me that was still what she wanted; she would never meet anyone if surrounded by hordes of Uzbek security. I had to take the Deputy PM aside and explain to her that she did not have to come to the bazaar, as our Minister wanted some private time. She replied it was quite all right, she was very happy to come with us. I had to explain three times, finally quite brutally, that she wasn't wanted.

She looked crestfallen, and then great panic ensued. We were asked to wait five minutes in our delegation office. We agreed, provided it was only five. After twelve, Clare Short's patience snapped and she said, 'Come on, let's go.' We emerged into the tenth-floor corridor where we were told that all the lifts had been closed down for security reasons as the Prime Minister was in the building, so our visit to the market had to be cancelled.

Undaunted, Clare Short headed for the fire stairs, and we fairly bustled down ten flights. At the bottom, we found a group of several police guarding a fire door that they explained was padlocked as an anti-terrorist measure. They said innocently that they had no idea who had the keys. There was, they explained, unfortunately no route from this fire escape to the main exits.

There is a restaurant at the bottom of the building where the food is dire. I had once eaten there as the guest of some Uzbek institution. I had been seized with urgent stomach cramps and had run round the basement areas desperately looking for the loo. I had not found one but had found a small door to the dustbins, which sat in a well with a ramp up to the back car park. I had relieved myself squatting between the bins.

The Lord moves in mysterious ways, and as a result of that unpleasant experience I was now able to thread our way through the service areas to that small door and lead the party out, which must have shown impressive local knowledge. I tried hard not to remember old acquaintance as we passed the bins and walked up the ramp. Immediately, our large vehicle convoy swept up to the bins, led by three police cars with sirens blazing. I travelled with Clare Short but sent my Land-Rover to lead the convoy, a sensible precaution as the convoy several times seemed determined to take us somewhere else.

On arrival at Chorzu, we were astonished to see another large fleet of official cars waiting to greet us. Our official Mercedes pulled up to a receiving line including the Deputy Hokkim of Tashkent, the Minister of Trade and numerous minor officials. There were about 40 of them surrounded by a huge circle of security men. A preceding wave of security had already gone ahead, pushing everyone out of that part of the market so that the official delegation could enter.

By now, Clare was getting angry. She asked me if I had not properly explained what she wanted. Unmistakably so, I replied. She shook hands with everyone then told them, bluntly, to go away. They looked puzzled, so I translated, being even more blunt because of my poor command of Russian. In a huge huff, the senior officials and ministers climbed into their limousines and sped off as Clare Short set off into the market.

Unfortunately, they left behind them a cloud of junior officials and two distinct groups of besuited security men with ear microphones. One group was closely surrounding Clare Short, and she soon managed to see them off herself. The second group was larger and consisted of about 20 men ahead pushing everyone to a distance of at least 50 yards to the side. I chased around and eventually managed to send them away. Then, however, a large number of burly tough-looking men in leather jackets emerged from the crowds around and started to shove people aside still more roughly. They were SNB – secret police – who had been mingling with the crowds but evidently had now been called in to take the role of the open protection team that we had sent away.

Clare Short was by now apoplectic. A particularly large thug looked to be in charge, and I went to him and told him in Russian that the Minister didn't want bodyguards. He made out that he didn't understand me and looked away. I grabbed his arm roughly to get his attention, looked into his eyes and said 'Fuck off' in English. He seemed to get that, and he and his men drifted away. However, they kept appearing throughout the visit, straining desperately to overhear conversations and shadowing us. There was a farcical moment among the clothes stalls where Clare Short doubled back and round in circles in a grim game of tag with them. More sinister, as we left a particular stall or area they would close in on the frightened stallholders to ask what had been said.

We first went to the upper level of the food hall to see the spice market – an incredible sight, with concentric circular rows of stalls displaying great piles of rich coloured spices which scented the air with cardamom, turmeric, saffron, nutmeg, every type of pepper, sweet basil, cloves, allspice, mint and a thousand others. But extraordinarily, instead of their rich variety of Eastern garb, all the stallholders were wearing what looked like neatly ironed green hospital gowns with little green surgical caps covering their heads.

The unlikelihood of this was not lost on Clare Short. Atabek interpreted for her as she observed to a stallholder that his gown was very new. Where had he got it from? The poor man looked terrified; he glanced from side to side for assistance. Eventually, he mumbled that they always wore such gowns for food hygiene. His neighbour was bolder. 'Actually, we just got them today,' he said.

Clare Short enquired if they were free.

'Oh yes, quite free,' he told her. 'A gift from the market authorities.'

And did he think they would be allowed to keep them once the EBRD conference was over?

'I don't know, probably not,' he observed cheerfully.

He was quite right. Two days later the gowns were all taken in again, though where they then went is a mystery. Possibly packed away for the next international conference.

I had been at the airport at 2 a.m. to greet the Minister on her arrival at the newly refurbished VIP side of the airport, known as Tashkent 2. It glittered in marble and gold leaf. More than thirty ministers and at least four heads of state were expected for the conference, each with their own delegation, plus thousands of delegates, EBRD staff, businessmen chasing EBRD contracts, journalists, NGOs and lobbyists. This really was an event on the grand scale.

It was also an event conducted in true Soviet style. It was after 2.30 a.m. that the British Airways flight arrived. I met Clare Short and her small staff on the tarmac and drove with them to the terminal. The senior official accompanying her was Jessica Irvine, a friend whom I had worked with on West Africa and who had been a house guest with us in Accra.

At the terminal, Elyor Ganiev, the Minister for Foreign Economic Relations, was waiting to greet Clare. They shook hands and he led her into a sumptuous side lounge while the baggage was collected. We sat around a marble-topped table piled with fruits and nuts.

Ganiev is a heavily built slow man who looks every bit the ex-KGB operative that he is. He has an unalloyed Soviet style, but I didn't expect to be treated to it at 2.30 a.m.

He rose ponderously to his feet and addressed Clare Short in Russian. He paused for interpretation after every phrase.

'Minister,' he began, 'you are most welcome to Uzbekistan. We greatly value our alliance with the United Kingdom. We are proud to be working with you on Iraq, and we have the greatest respect for the leadership shown by Tony Blair to the whole world in the War on Terror. As your esteemed Ambassador knows,' he nodded cumbersomely in my direction, 'Uzbekistan was already fighting this menace before the events of 2001.

'This is a strong country and we believe that our economic achievements deserve recognition by the international community. We have always met our obligations on debt repayment and never requested restructuring. For this reason, we now believe our currency is strong enough to sustain convertibility. We have devalued the sum by over 80 per cent in the past 18 months and will move to full convertibility by June.

'The basis of our economy is a strong industrial and agricultural base. GDP growth in 2003 is projected to exceed 8 per cent. It is worth noting that in 7 years the Republic of Uzbekistan has seen GDP per capita increase by a total of 50 per cent.

'At a minimum, 327 enterprises will be privatised during this year. Wheat production is increasing by 18 per cent, while the percentage of agricultural production from private farms will increase from 32 per cent to 36 per cent. In the automotive sector . . .'

Clare Short stood up and smiled. In her strong Birmingham accent she said, 'Thank you, Minister. That's all very interesting. But it's 2.30 in the morning, we're very tired, and we're going to bed.' She then turned round and walked out of the room, while we scurried to catch up.

I had been disappointed that she had decided to stay in the conference hotel rather than in the Residence, but she had thought this more convenient as she was chairing the meeting. As we drove to the Intercontinental, she turned to me.

'Is he always like that?'

'No, usually he's worse.'

'Bloody hell! Was any of it true?'

'No, this year there has been a growth in fake economic statistics of 182.7 per cent.'

I had been pretty sceptical about the performance of the EBRD in Uzbekistan. Their investment decisions had been very poor. My discovery of the non-existence of the Jizzak winery was followed up on a subsequent visit to Samarkand with Kristina. Four out of six recipients of small and medium enterprise loans that we tried to visit either did not exist or the buildings at the address were derelict, with no sign of the machinery allegedly purchased with the loan. My research interested the German embassy, who came up with very similar findings.

These small loans, of a few million dollars each, came from a large fund of several hundred million dollars given by the EBRD to three Uzbek state banks. As far as the EBRD were concerned, that was the end of it. It was for the Uzbek state banks to choose and monitor projects to lend to. These Uzbek state banks were certifying the projects were good and were repaying the interest to the EBRD as required. So the EBRD line was that everything was in order.

Except that the Uzbek state banks were intensely corrupt. They were lending the money to regime members, often against forged paperwork for non-existent purchases. The state bank was then paying back the EBRD with Uzbek taxpayers' money. It all got lost in the secret accounting of the completely unaccountable Uzbek state banks. In a minority of cases, the Uzbek state bank was actually receiving interest payments from the loan recipient, even though the project didn't exist. The suspicion was that, in these instances, the capital was being used to finance narcotics trafficking.

On the larger projects, these were almost uniformly disastrous, including the textile and brick factories. Lena Son did some research for me and could not discover a single EBRD project where the partner was not either a minister of the Uzbek government or a very close family member.

Part of the problem was the EBRD office in Tashkent. The three expatriate staff were all Japanese, and they found my criticisms of these projects incomprehensible. Interest was being paid, wasn't it? The idea that they should assess transition effect was lost on them. They were even more astonished when I suggested that they should get out of their office and go and look at some of the projects they were funding. That wasn't in their job descriptions. They viewed the EBRD simply as a commercial bank, but it is not. It is an inter-governmental institution set up to promote the transition of the ex-communist states to democracy and capitalism.

But the EBRD centrally rose to the challenge of holding its AGM in Tashkent. The secretariat of the bank were lumbered with this decision by the member states, but the President, Jean Lemierre, handled it brilliantly.

He first visited in autumn, when the bazaars had been closed and borders sealed. He criticised the Uzbek government roundly for this. The Uzbeks followed up with some even weirder actions – they made all Tashkent's bars and nightclubs close at 11 p.m., except for three – Katacomb, Che Guevara and Wigwam, all owned by Gulnara Karimova. And they made billiards illegal. *Biliardy* was the most popular pastime of the Uzbek youth. There were little billiards clubs everywhere; now they were shut down overnight. The government then announced that it was closing Broadway.

This central Tashkent street has a real name, but everyone just calls it Broadway. It contained perhaps 150 metres of the closest thing most Uzbeks could ever get to fun. It was lined with beer and kebab tents, but there were also a few fairground stalls, involving shooting water pistols at targets or rolling balls into holes. To a Western eye, most amusing were the karaoke stalls. For a small sum, you could stand in front of a television on a table in the street and sing the karaoke song of your choosing, minutely amplified, to yourself and a couple of friends standing next to you, who would hear it mixed with the sounds from the other karaoke tables. There were also a couple of very small carousels, stalls of Soviet memorabilia and a lot of artists selling their pictures to the few tourists among the crowds of curious locals.

This outbreak of fun clearly could not be tolerated. The announcement of the closure was made while Lemierre was in town for a preparatory meeting. He reacted immediately, driving to Broadway with his escort and hapless accompanying Uzbek minister. Seating himself at a stall, he ordered a beer and a kebab. He declared to all who would listen how very much he was enjoying himself and how the delegates to the EBRD AGM were going to love coming here for a beer and a kebab, too.

This was bollocks, of course, as the vast majority of delegates to the EBRD conference never eat out at less than a hundred dollars a head. But as a declaration against the Uzbek government's continued clampdown on the private sector, it was most effective.

The same spirit was shown in the insistence that NGOs be allowed to register for the conference. This was almost negated by the complicity of the Tashkent EBRD office with the Uzbek government. While international NGOs could register with EBRD HQ in London, the Tashkent office were making it administratively impossible for local NGOs regarded as dissident. Once the conference secretariat arrived, I arranged directly with them to register a number of people, including Professor Mirsaidov. They got to have their say on conditions in Uzbekistan, and while of course there was no coverage of this in the local media, it did have an effect on international opinion.

But the real difference the EBRD made was in insisting, as a condition of holding the AGM in Tashkent, that the opening session must be broadcast live on Uzbek TV. The EBRD, at my suggestion, even went so far as to insist on their own interpreters for the broadcast, to make sure that what was said was accurately transmitted.

The significance of this was that, in the opening session, Clare Short and Jean Lemierre both made strong criticisms of Uzbekistan's economic policies and the lack of human rights and democracy. Karimov had viewed hosting this conference as a massive propaganda coup and endorsement of his regime. The Uzbek media coverage had been trailing this line for months and it was also conveyed in the many banners advertising the event. He sat at the top table, on the stage of the great Hall of the People's Friendship, flanked by the presidents of Kazakhstan, Georgia, Kirghizstan and Tajikistan. He was hosting them and senior ministers from almost every Western country. It was the ultimate display of his prestige. And now, at the height of his success, he was being criticised in unmistakable terms by Short and Lemierre. He had been President of the Uzbek Soviet Socialist Republic and then President of Uzbekistan for 15 years. Nobody could do this to him. And it was being broadcast, live and uncensored, on all main Uzbek TV and radio channels, with a massive audience which he himself had ordered drummed up to watch his apotheosis.

I cannot overstate the drama of that moment. Clare Short's points were piled up relentlessly in that flat Brummie accent. Lemierre was sharp and expressive, his tone heavy with Gallic contempt. Karimov first went ashen faced. Then he ostentatiously removed his earphone and tossed it away. Then he placed his head in his hands, covering his ears before slowly moving his hands round to cover his eyes, then allowing his head to slump forward until it almost rested on the table. He remained in this extraordinary posture for ten minutes. At one stage Nursultan Nazarbayev, President of Kazakhstan, put a consolatory arm around him.

All this was captured on Uzbek TV – and captured so well that the producer and director were sacked as soon as the conference delegates had left. But that broadcast was a defining moment. It did more than anything to break Karimov's grip on his people – his carefully cultivated image of perfection was stripped away. It was the moment that the boy shouted out that the emperor had no clothes.

Why did he react so badly in public, rather than put a brave face on it? I can only think it was a mixture of shock and disbelief. But, as my friend Ahmet would say, it gave room for doubt about the size of his balls.

There were so many presidents and ministers in town that mere ambassadors were a long way down the pecking order, and I had a long walk to my car after the session. I had to pass a taxi stand. A gaggle of taxi drivers who had been listening to events on the radio recognised me. They mobbed and hugged me, offering me vodka, and a small crowd gathered to cheer '*Gaspadin* Craig'.

Actually, it hadn't been much to do with me. I had strongly supported, but not initiated, the EBRD insistence on live unedited broadcast. I had no direct input into Lemierre's speech, though I always got on well with him and I believe he valued my views. A few days earlier, Karen and I had been waiting for a draft of Clare Short's speech so I could comment. DFID had sent it to the Eastern Department so it could be sent out on an encrypted fax; there were two specific linked machines, one in the Eastern Department and one in our registry. It was an antiquated system which seldom worked, because it needed higher quality phone lines than we had in Uzbekistan.

The speech didn't come when expected, so I phoned Charles Hill in the Eastern Department. He said he would send the speech but that DFID did not want any changes unless absolutely essential to correct a mistake of fact. It was too late for more general comments. If I had any urgent points, I should send them to him.

I looked briefly through the speech, which was very good. I could see no urgent need for changes, so I went on to other work. A couple of hours later, I had a call from Clare Short's private secretary. He asked why I hadn't commented on the speech. It had been sent to the Eastern Department the day before with the message that she specifically wanted to know what I thought. She had been particularly impressed by my reporting telegrams on Uzbekistan.

I did not tell him that the Eastern Department had been keeping this message from me. It was a pretty easy surmise that they were worried about what the combination of Clare Short and Craig Murray might produce. It was possible, of course, that Charles Hill was personally unaware of the message from Short's office.

I hosted a lunch for Clare Short to meet human rights activists. These included Tamara Chikunewa. She told us about her son, who had been sentenced to death. She had gone again and again to the prison asking to see him. She had been repeatedly denied, but one day she had been bundled into a room and ordered to wait. She hoped that she would finally see her son. Then she heard a single shot. The guard returned and told her, 'You won't see him now; we've just shot him in the head.'

The lunch worked very well in presenting just how grim the situation was. Sikeena Karmali was particularly forceful and impressive, as Clare Short noted to me afterwards. She also made an acid observation that I had invited all the men to speak before any of the women. I had arranged a speaking order by subject and was not aware that it had this effect. I felt quite guilty.

In the car, Clare Short said to me, 'Jessica tells me that you're getting problems from the Foreign Office.'

'To say the least,' I replied.

'It takes ten seconds to tell what kind of government this is. But if we support Bush . . . Anyway, tell me if you need any support. Not that I'll be in much position to give it!'

I was slightly mystified by this last phrase. After the EBRD meeting closed, along with several other ministers Clare Short flew on to a meeting in Kirghizstan to discuss development needs in Central Asia. Ganiev was also present and was there when the Kirghiz government showed the delegates the bridges across the border river in the Ferghana Valley that had been recently destroyed by Karimov to seal the borders to trade. The separated families and the harsh economic consequences had been all too obvious, and apparently Short had absolutely exploded at Ganiev. Good thing, too.

That evening, she returned to London. The next day, she resigned from the government.

CHAPTER 14

Love in a Hot Climate

I felt more and more isolated from London. They had, in effect, sent me to Coventry. I simply stopped receiving any reply to my telegrams, letters and emails. But as the world blackened around me, I had one major solace. I had fallen profoundly in love.

I had obtained Nadira's phone number, but my attempts to get through to her had not succeeded until she finally answered her mobile on Monday, 7 April. Her voice was so gentle and sweet on the telephone, and I was elated when she told me she also had been trying to telephone me. We agreed to meet at 8 p.m. the next day in the Ragu bar. I came from a meeting at the Residence, where we had been wrestling with the logistical problems of the Queen's Birthday Party. I was in good spirits, and as we looked round the garden I vaulted the stream on my crutches several times, to general applause and amusement.

Steve and Ulugjan came with me to the Ragu. There was a camaraderie amongst men in Tashkent, pretty much all of whom had girlfriends as well as wives.

Nadira arrived on time. She looked wonderful in sky-blue jeans and a clinging cotton blouse, and I was taken aback anew by just how spectacular her figure was. Steve and Ulugjan grinned their approval. She asked for an orange juice, and I persuaded her to remove her baseball cap, which she was reluctant to do, as her hair was dirty. She told me that two days previously she had quit her job at Safar, which cheered me up. But she also said she could only stay for one hour, which deflated me. I couldn't shake her from this – she said her flatmate Clara was ill at home, and she had to look after her.

The hour passed quickly, and I then insisted on leaving with her. She said that she lived in a very bad area, that her flat was poor and dirty, and that it would be hard for me to get up the stairs on my crutches. She then appeared to get annoyed and said that I was only coming with her because I didn't believe she was really going home. But I was not going to lose her so quickly, and we went to her flat in a smelly crumbling block at Yunusabad, one of the worst bits of Tashkent. Prone alcoholics and staring drug addicts littered the yard. It was hard to get up the staircase on crutches in the pitch dark. There was almost no furniture in the little flat, and the loo was cracked. Clara was a pretty girl with long lustrous hair. She looked pale and ill and lay stretched out on a sofa under a blanket. Nadira's 15-year-old brother, Sanjar, eyed me with suspicion from under a mop of blue-black hair. The other inhabitant of the flat was Nargiza, a plump traditionally dressed girl with a wild clump of hair and black spectacles. She kept making jokes in Uzbek and occasionally bursting into song. I was a lot more tolerant of this than her flatmates. We drank tea and chatted. Nadira kept flitting around. Clara was, of course, a captive audience, and I talked with her for a while. Nadira had a beautiful short-haired Siamese cat, which sat on my lap as I stroked it. It was two days after Nadira's 22nd birthday.

I felt I had found a refuge from my troubles. I was particularly entranced by the way Nadira made the green tea. In traditional Uzbek style, she three times poured tea from the pot into the bowl, then back into the pot, to brew it. She then handed me a bowl of tea with her right hand, her left placed over her heart in a gesture of respect. I had seen it many times, but she did it with such deft grace and natural feeling that I was really moved. I left around midnight.

I phoned Nadira again the next day, but she said she couldn't come out because of Clara, and that I couldn't come and see her because they had a power cut. There was really no reason why that would stop me, but she so evidently didn't want me to come that I decided it might be counter-productive. I was off to Samarkand and Bokhara for a few days, so I didn't have the chance to see her again until the following Thursday.

I gave a speech to the American Chamber of Commerce, which was hard hitting and very well received by an audience that included all the major foreign investors, American or otherwise. I had been invited to dinner afterwards with Zokirjon. I went to Nadira's flat first and swept her off with me to the dinner.

Zokirjon was delighted to see me and very pleased to see that I had finally got a girlfriend. He was convinced that I needed a lot of sex to help me cope with the stress of my job. He had offered to set me up many times, but I had respectfully declined. I think he had started to think I might be gay. For her part, Nadira was pretty worried about meeting Zokirjon. In Uzbekistan, such obvious opulence can mean only one thing – mafia – and Nadira had few illusions about what could happen to girls in places like this.

Zokirjon was on good form, and we had a pleasant dinner. I had brought wine, and Zokirjon had a bottle of Johnny Walker Blue Label he had bought specially for my visit. I didn't like to tell him I prefer Black Label at about a fifth of the price. We also drank vodka with pickled tomatoes, which is a great deal nicer than it sounds.

After dinner, Zokirjon retired with his companion (he always had a different beautiful girl with him every time I called). He showed Nadira and me to a luxurious bedroom suite on the ground floor. Nadira was now very scared.

'I'm a virgin,' she whispered, once we had closed the door. I put a hand around her tiny waist and kissed her on the forehead.

'It's OK, we don't have to have sex,' I said. 'But I don't want Zokirjon to know that.'

We sat on a large sofa and chatted, just lightly kissing a few times and occasionally throwing cushions at each other. After an hour or so, we said goodnight to Zokirjon – we had to shout this through the sauna door.

Zokirjon had been most worried about my appearance on crutches. He insisted I should go and see his doctor the next day, and he got out a mobile and made an appointment there and then. I felt I had been treated very well by Dr Reimers at the international clinic, and I was reconciled to another six weeks on crutches. I didn't think an Uzbek doctor would be able to help, but Nadira persuaded me to give it a try.

The following lunchtime, I got up into the Land-Rover with my crutches (at which I was getting pretty adept) and gave Mansur the address for the doctor, telling him to swing by Nadira's flat on the way.

We drove to Chilanzar, another cheap dusty suburb of dreary Soviet apartment blocks. My faith diminished further when I found the doctor was based in a small apartment in the middle of this estate. I struggled up the steps to the first floor. An extraordinary little man in a velvet gown opened the door. Short and wiry, with his long wispy beard he looked like the old Chinese sage in a kung fu movie. He led me through to his front room, which was largely filled by what seemed to be an old enamel-topped morgue trolley.

He gestured towards Nadira and said to me, 'Zokirjon told me you were like him.'

He then placed a towel and a pillow on the trolley and indicated I should take off my clothes and get up on it, which I did. He gently unwrapped the strapping from my left calf, and then felt up and down it, pushing his fingers between the layers of muscle. It was intense agony. Then he went out of the room, quickly returning with a candle in one hand and in the other a cylinder which smelt strongly of alcohol and held two dozen foot-long needles with wooden handles. Bloody hell! Acupuncture. What had I got myself in to?

Only the desire not to let Nadira know what a coward I am prevented me from getting up and walking out. Plainly the needles were in alcohol and before inserting each one he sterilised it further in the flame of the candle, so the risk was limited. I decided to go with it.

I had imagined that acupuncture involved sticking the needle in a little way. Not at all. These were going in several inches, and quite a few being pushed right in and out the other side. I watched from the corner of my eye, transfixed in horror, as the first needle went in to the right side of my neck. The next went through the right elbow. It was pushed in to the inside and, amazingly, passed through the joint and came out about four inches on the other side. The next one went right through the top of my left thigh. I didn't know much about acupuncture, but I had presumed it didn't hurt much because it was cunningly directed at nerve points, or something similar. I was swiftly disillusioned. It hurt every bit as much as you might imagine having a large needle stuck through you would hurt. Once the needle was in position, it became uncomfortable rather than painful. But then came the next needle.

I lay on my back with the needles in me for about five minutes. Then he removed them and motioned I should turn onto my stomach. He put needles into my back and buttocks. He now seemed to be trying to manoeuvre each to touch a precise spot within me.

When he hit it, he would twist the needle. He then passed a series of needles into and through the affected calf muscle. After this set of needles were withdrawn, he massaged the muscle strongly and very deeply; it felt like he was pulling the tendon away from bone, but this time it didn't hurt.

The entire session lasted about an hour. When he had finished, he told me to get up. I reached for the crutches, which were leaning against the wall, but he motioned me to leave them. He wrapped up my bandage neatly and handed it to Nadira. I stood to dress and gingerly put some weight on my left leg as I pulled on my underpants. It seemed OK. Once dressed, I slowly and carefully started to walk towards the door.

As I got to the door, he stopped me. He indicated he was very worried about something, and he spoke quietly with Nadira.

'He thinks you are starting a big problem with your heart,' she said.

He motioned to me to unbutton my shirt. He felt between the ribs, just to my left of my breastbone, and then pushed in and withdrew a needle in an incredibly quick movement. It penetrated the chest cavity and went in a good three inches. It only lasted a second, but it was indescribably painful and I was really shaken. He spoke again to Nadira. She looked a bit put out. I was worried.

'What is it?' I asked her.

'He says you have many difficulties, and it will hurt you. To give strength, you should sleep with young girls. At least two.'

'Well, let's go and make a start.'

'No, younger than me. Maybe 16 years old.'

Great stuff, I thought. It ought to be available on the National Health Service.

I walked out the door and down the stairs, Nadira following behind carrying the crutches. Mansur gave a whoop of joy when he saw me walking. My calf muscle was completely healed and behaved normally from that moment. It had been ruptured, a fact that had been confirmed by ultrasound. I have no way of explaining how acupuncture fixed it.

I met Nadira again several times over the next week for a quick drink in the evening and once for dinner. She came with me to a couple of orchestra and choir rehearsals. But the pressure of work was too great to devote the time I would have liked to developing an affair, and we were in danger of becoming just good friends.

Nadira, Dilya, Sanjar, Clara and Nargiza went to all the British Music Festival concerts. For a week or so in the run-up to the festival, I had little opportunity to call Nadira, and when I did she didn't answer. After the opening Battlefield Band concert, I was due to meet Nadira outside and go for a drink with her. But the concert was such a success that the band were besieged by autograph hunters, and packing up all the gear took longer than anticipated. By the time I emerged, Nadira had given up and left. My heart ached with not having seen her for so long, and I went to her flat to look for her. Sanjar answered the door and said she had been called away to nurse a sick aunt. I was worried she was angry with me, so I insisted on entering to check she wasn't in the flat. She wasn't.

In fact, Nadira had been playing me along, and my passionate desire to be with her was scantily reciprocated. Nor was she nearly as sexually innocent as she looked. She was indeed a virgin but had done pretty much everything else. She had a regular boyfriend, a diplomat at the Turkish embassy. He had bought her the Siamese cat and the clothes she was wearing the night of our first date at the Ragu. She was meant to have dinner with him that evening, which is why she had told me that she had to leave at 9 p.m. She had been in despair when I went with her to her flat. Clara wasn't ill, just a good actress. The phone call I thought she had made to her father in Uzbek was to her boyfriend in Turkish.

She also had another boyfriend called Lee, a GI serving with the US forces in Afghanistan. He had been sending her money from his pay packet for months. He was not the first GI to be her boyfriend or to ask her to marry him. He had come to Tashkent on leave the week before our musical festival. While I had been fretting about neglecting her, she had been staying with him in the Sheraton Hotel, making a determined attempt on the world oral sex record. This continued when she was supposedly nursing her sick aunt.

But I was in love and didn't find out any of this for more than another year. When I did, I felt terribly betrayed, which just goes to show what a hypocritical bastard I am. I had told Nadira I was married and could not have a permanent relationship. Yet I expected complete loyalty in return. Nice if you can get it. I suppose we deserve each other.

* * *

Back in the embassy, I had the problem of knowing what to do about Karen. She was due to leave that November anyway but was desperate to stay until then. My initial reaction was to ask her to leave, but the more I thought about it, the more attractive it was to let her stay. She was very good at the job, and I was very short staffed. Soon, however, it became clear to me that relationships within the embassy were so damaged that I would have to ask Karen to leave. That was, I think, a major error on my part.

Chris, Karen and I had been the only British resource doing the main work of the embassy – that is political, economic, commercial and information work. With all three of us there, we had been seriously under resourced. Now I was going to be doing it all myself for the next three months, as well as shouldering the substantial administrative and managerial burden Karen had borne. And I was already knackered.

One thing was plain – with Chris and Karen gone, I was in immediate need of more Uzbek staff to keep the embassy going. There was no time for a recruitment process and nobody to organise one, so I got on the phone.

I got in Nilufar from the Lionheart Bar to man reception. She proved to have charm and efficiency, and is today the Ambassador's personal assistant.[49] I put Dmitri Potemkin from Radio Grand into the information section but effectively gave him large wodges of Chris Hirst's job. Dmitri's English was superb, and I had met him at a number of cultural events. He was a former pop singer and TV presenter, now in his late 40s, who loved and was fascinated by the UK. I judged him to be bright and capable, and it turned out to be a great appointment. As his assistant, I got in my Russian language teacher, Victoria Belyarskaya. A journalist, she proved to have somewhat too much initiative, and that appointment worked less well. But Yuliya Usatova was a brilliant young economist and a really important addition to the team. I broke every recruitment rule in the book (which was to be used against me), but I had a functioning embassy again in 24 hours.

My mother and brother had come out to visit for several weeks. It was great to see them, and provided some much-needed relaxation. Nadira and I were becoming comfortable together, meeting perhaps three times a week. The relationship was still pretty chaste, but it provided what I needed at that time.

On Thursday, 22 May, Catherine Davis from the BBC and Matilda

Bogner from HRW contacted me about another human rights case. The body of another torture victim, Orif Eshanov, had been returned to his parents in Yangiyul, a village some 30 miles outside Tashkent. His case was particularly interesting because he was a member of Hizb-ut-Tehrir and had been beaten to death in Karshi, where the US base was situated.

I dashed down to Yangiyul to see the victim's family, taking Catherine Davis with me. The family were traditional Uzbek, living in a low mud-built house, and they greeted me with great courtesy. Over tea, we discussed the condition of the body, including the fact that the fingernails had been pulled out and genitalia mutilated. Catherine Davis recorded the entire meeting, and it had quite an impact when it was broadcast on the BBC World Service.

Eshanov had been forty-six years old and a father of three. One of the ironies was that his father, a stooped, bearded old man, had been an officer in Stalin's KGB. He discussed precisely what had been done to his son with a disconcerting dispassion.

That evening I had dinner with Timur Gulyamov, which once again was followed by wonderful music. My mother and Stuart were entranced. This time Tamara and her sister played Rachmaninov together on the piano.

Timur's dream was for Tamara to study in Europe. The first step was for her to improve her English. The family had been saving and borrowing money from relatives, but they were still short of a few hundred pounds. I had arranged for Tamara to attend a British Council-approved language school in London for two months and to stay with Stuart. I rather hoped that romance would blossom – Stuart was recovering from a painful divorce – but sadly it didn't. I gave Tamara the extra money needed.

On the day of her departure, Tamara came to the office to see me in some distress. She didn't put it that way, but she had spent several hundred dollars of the money on clothes (mostly on one leather jacket) and now was short. I was rather annoyed, but I gave her the needed cash and a hug goodbye. This, too, was to be used against me.

I had to travel down to Jizzak again for a further meeting about the cottonseed factory. This was Nadira's hometown, so I took her with me. I had lunch with her parents at their flat. Like most of the city, they had had no running water for about a year, but the flat was notably better furnished and equipped than other Uzbek flats I had entered. This reflected all the money Nadira had been sending back to her family.

As we pulled up outside the block, dozens of children had come pouring out of the flats, calling 'Nadira! Nadira!' She burst into a great grin and lifted one or two of the smaller ones up into the air. She explained that since her early teens she had looked after the children of the flats, sitting in the courtyard and making up fairy stories for them as they sat at her feet. As we trudged up to her parents' flat on the fifth floor, young and old appeared at their doorway to embrace her as she went past. This spontaneous display of affection towards her was quite astonishing.

Nadira told her parents that she worked with me as an interpreter, though I am not sure they were much taken in. Her father was a jolly moustachioed man, who seemed happy to meet me. Her mother fussed anxiously over the food, of which there were massive quantities. Her father was a playwright, actor and theatre director, her mother an actress. Various friends of theirs, mostly writers and actors, kept dropping in during the meal to look at me. After lunch, we went up into the mountains on the Tajik border and saw the beautiful shrine at Bakhmal. Here a crystal-clear stream bubbles out of the foot of the mountain into a beautiful rock-pool. Holy fish feed on the nutrition carried up by the stream and disappear into the fissures from which the water flows. There are five of these, and they have cut five channels in the basin, said to have been the imprint left by the hand of a prophet. An ancient wooden mosque still stands on a site whose superstitions predate Islam.

I held Nadira's hand. As I looked at that pure mountain water and then my gaze swept down the fields of grain lying sun-basked in that fertile high valley, my heart rose within me, and I thought, 'What a great place to make whisky.'

I can't help it. Genetic imprinting.

A few days later, first thing in the working day, Sikeena from Freedom House sent another victim round to see me. His name was Mr Atayev, and he was a small farmer from the town of Kitab, south of Karshi. His story was that he and three of his brothers had leased land from the state farm, or *kolkhoz*, there. The kolkhoz now wanted it back. The brothers had refused. As a result, one of the brothers had been murdered and a second jailed for seven years. The third had gone into hiding in Tashkent and was with me now. In the past week, his mother, who was 84 years old, had been beaten up by a mob and their apple orchard destroyed. The local authorities knew he was in Tashkent seeking help. They had told the family that no foreign embassy could change what happened in Kitab.

I decided we should prove them wrong. I yelled to Kristina, 'Go home and pack. We're off to Kitab. Tell Mansur to get ready.'

Kristina immediately got up and walked to the door. She paused, turned back and said, 'The farm workers probably won't speak Russian. Do you know if they speak Uzbek or Tajik down there?'

'Tajik, I should think,' I conjectured. 'It's near Shakhrisabz. Does Dmitri or Victoria speak Tajik?'

'No, I don't think so. Shall I try to find an interpreter?'

'No, there's no time. Let's take Nadira – she can speak Uzbek and Tajik, and every other known language as far as I can tell.'

'Shall we pay her as an interpreter?'

'You mean my company's not payment enough?'

'Not for me, it isn't.'

'But you're not Nadira.'

'Thank God. You're difficult enough as a boss. As a boyfriend you must be impossible.'

Kristina gave me that incredibly beautiful smile and disappeared to get ready for the trip.

Two hours later, we set off for Kitab. Just round the corner from the embassy, I was amazed and delighted to see a small human rights demonstration outside the Procurator-General's office. I got out of the car and shook their hands. They were all friends of mine, led by Talib Yakubov. They knew about the events in Kitab, and when I said that was where I was heading they gave a small ragged cheer to send me off.

It was a five-hour drive to Karshi. Uzbekistan was in the grip of a diesel shortage, and after Samarkand we had to head into a farm, where, for a backhander, they siphoned diesel from a tractor for us. We arrived in Karshi after 3 p.m., checked into a hotel and then sped on to Kitab, a further hour's drive. I had to quell a rebellion in Karshi from the rest of the party, as none of us had eaten all day, but I insisted we didn't have time to stop. I bought bread and cheese to eat in the car. We arrived after 5 p.m.

Driving into the deepest countryside, we looked for our small farm. Eventually, we found it. There was no longer much to see. The cattle stalls were broken and abandoned, the fields overgrown with weeds. There were three cottages close together. One had belonged to the murdered brother, one to the imprisoned. The womenfolk now lived all together in the third.

When we met them, they started pouring out their stories all at once, and it was difficult to grasp anything coherent. It turned out they spoke Uzbek rather than Tajik. One thing they did say was that the kolkhoz had moved recently retired military personnel into the vacated cottages. They had been carrying out a campaign of violence and intimidation.

This was rapidly borne out. As we stood talking in a field, three swarthy men came up to us carrying farm tools in a menacing manner. One stepped forward and prodded me twice on the neck, hectoring me. I didn't understand him, but it was plain he was telling me to go away. He poked me in the chest again, so I slapped him across the face, hard but with an open palm. Surprised, he backed off for a moment. Mansur was out of sight in the car, and I was alone in the field with Nadira, Kristina and the three Uzbek women. Suddenly Nadira was in front of me, yelling angrily in a throaty language and seemingly threatening the three men who stood facing her with mattocks in hand but looking uncertain whether to use them.

I put a restraining hand on Nadira's shoulder and asked her what had happened. She was shaking with fury, 'He said they would beat you dead and rape your women.'

Kristina, who had not previously understood the Uzbek exchange, started to look very nervous and to back down the path. I thought that was psychologically dangerous, so I stepped forward and pushed what seemed to be the leader in the chest, saying loudly that I was the British Ambassador. I had no hope he would understand me but thought that the unknown tongue might give him pause. My heart was in my mouth, and it was not helped when one of the Atayev women said something which Nadira translated: 'She says these are the men who murdered her husband.'

Great. Typical of my planning – end up miles from anywhere in a field, in a slanging match with three brutish murderers, accompanied by two gorgeous women.

Although they looked like they would murder their mothers for a plate of beans, fortunately they were not quite certain if they were meant to murder me. I decided to shout a bit more, and they shrugged their shoulders, turned their backs and walked across to the far side of the field. There they sat on the fence and looked at us, occasionally hefting their mattocks menacingly from hand to hand.

As we talked on with the women, we were joined by two male cousins of the Atayev family and an earnest young Russian who had been sent to the village by a Samarkand human rights group. The story was as I had been told it in Tashkent. The family had leased land from the kolkhoz in the brief spring of liberalisation in the mid-1990s. For a while it had flourished, with cattle and apples. Then the kolkhoz had decided they wanted it back, and what had followed was violence, intimidation and theft or destruction of livestock and crops.

The brother who had been jailed was convicted of stealing his own apples, as the court ruled they should be the property of the kolkhoz, which owned the land. The fact that the brother had paid for a lease was ignored by the court. The family invited me to go into the village and meet the grandmother who had been beaten.

We were not the only group which had been expanding. The three thugs had been joined by others, and shortly a white Nissan Maxima pulled up. Three men in suits and sunglasses got out and joined the small crowd at the other side of the fence looking at us. Kristina had gone to get the car, and Mansur pulled up for us to drive the mile or so to the grandmother's house. But I decided to make a statement. Our group of cottages was at the end of the village, which straggled a mile or so along the road. We had to go to the other end, and I decided to walk. The women all got into the car. I started the long walk down the road between rows of low white cottages, our three new male companions walking alongside me. The Discovery followed just behind. Twenty yards behind that came the three thugs walking, followed by the Nissan Maxima, followed by a small crowd of unfriendly-looking men. The sun was setting directly behind me, and the entire village came to their doors and gates as we walked by. Some ducked inside and closed the door as we reached them. I was being deliberately melodramatic and milking the moment, but it did feel exactly like a Western.

There was a point to this. I was openly defying the kolkhoz authorities in a little world where they were gods. I was showing that the British embassy could even reach Kitab, 20 miles off the Karshi to Shakhrisabz road.

It had been over 40 degrees Celsius that day. It was still very hot and the walk seemed long. We eventually reached the old lady's home. She was standing in her courtyard. She showed me her destroyed vegetable patch and then took me inside the little house with its plain walls of mud and dung. It was totally bare – everything had been stripped out by her attackers. Then in the courtyard she astonished me by pulling down her dress. Her shrivelled breasts, arms and upper torso were covered in huge livid blue and purple bruises, some of which were bleeding. She had been beaten mercilessly with clubs three days ago. She was 84 years old. She stood there defiant, half naked, having moved beyond shame. I was boiling with rage.

We then walked around the corner, and my eyes were struck by an even more arresting sight. It was the Atayev family's orchard. A field stretched down the hill as far as the eye could see, and row upon row of felled apple trees, perhaps thousands of them, lay in terrible death, their black and gnarled limbs looking like a great litter of charred and twisted bodies. The leaves were coming away, and here and there great sweeps of late blossom were browning and giving off the sweet smell of decay. Over each corpse stood, for a headstone, a golden-topped stump. That wanton destruction of so much goodness, that loss of so much potential, seemed a metaphor for all the cruelty and waste of Karimov's Uzbekistan.

I turned to one of the men with me.

'Who did this? Who cut them down?'

'The kolkhoz.'

'I know it was the kolkhoz. But someone had to physically cut the trees. It was a lot of work. Who did it?'

He looked at me as though I was simple. By now most of the village had gathered at the top of the field to see the fun. He gestured towards them.

'Why, the people of the village, of course.'

'Why? Why would they do that? Why chop down their neighbour's trees? For Christ's sake, in a village like this, half of them must be related to your family.'

'Certainly. But it's not their fault. They are poor. The kolkhoz paid them 200 sum each to do it.'

So there you are. Society is so debased that for 20 US cents someone will cut down their neighbour's trees and ruin his life. I was deeply depressed. How could you help such a people who were devoid of any feelings of mutual solidarity and support? I felt that I was trying to save a people without a soul.[50]

It was certainly true that they were poor. The wage for the 16,000 workers on this huge kolkhoz was 2,000 sum – that's $2 – a month. They lived on the vegetables and livestock they could produce in their own little courtyards, usually about 20 metres square for a family. Before I entered the orchard, I had entered a home, asking permission of the astonished lady of the house. There was an old tin stove, a short table, two wooden benches and a few cooking utensils. They slept on mats on a beaten mud floor.[51]

I addressed the villagers in Russian, saying that this destruction was a crime against God and nature. I also said that the world was changing, as my appearance in Kitab demonstrated, and neither the regime nor the kolkhoz would last for ever. One day those who now attacked their neighbours would answer for it.[52]

I asked the family whether they had tried complaining to the local Procurator. The attack on the old woman, for example, was plainly a crime. I was told that the Procurator had actually been there and instigated the attack. When they had tried to get him to investigate the brother's murder, he replied that if they caused trouble he would have them all killed. He was the law in Kitab, and there was nothing anyone could do about it. I decided the Procurator deserved a visit.

The local human rights monitor plainly felt this was all much more than he had signed up for and declined to join us. But we squeezed in two of the Atayev family ladies who had witnessed the District Procurator's threat to kill them all, and Mansur, Kristina, Nadira and I set off with them in the Discovery into Kitab town, to find the Procurator's office.

Kitab was quite a pretty little town, with streets lined with trees providing shade. We entered the District Procurator's office, where we were confronted by an aggressive young man in military uniform demanding to know who we were. It was about 8 p.m., but Uzbek government offices work long hours to keep that great bureaucracy churning. I explained I was the British Ambassador, come to see the Procurator. He said that the Procurator was not in, as he had gone to the site of a bus crash with the Deputy Procurator General of Uzbekistan.[53]

I replied that it was good that the Deputy Procurator General was around, because I was sure he too would be delighted to see the British Ambassador. I spotted an office with the District Procurator's name on it, opened the door, walked in and seated myself behind the desk with my feet on the table. My rather bemused party followed me in.

After we had been waiting half an hour or so, a young man entered with tea. Shortly thereafter, a simply dressed man with heavy grey stubble arrived. He introduced himself as the Managing Director of the kolkhoz. He asked why I had come, and I said I was investigating allegations against him of murder and violence against small farmers. He retreated to the corridor and fished out a mobile phone, then returned and gave me the message that the Procurator could not make it back that evening but could see me in the morning at 8 a.m. I decided this was as good as we could get and agreed. I gave the Atayev ladies money for a taxi and told them to rendezvous there again at 8 a.m. the next morning. I was a bit worried about them but felt that with me obviously around and proactive, they were unlikely to be bumped off overnight. They were giggling with delight. They were astonished that anyone could be in a position to behave this way towards the local authorities. I hoped that the general effect might offer them a bit more protection in the village.

The kolkhoz manager asked if we would join him for a beer and shashlik to talk over the problem. I could virtually hear Nadira and Kristina salivate at the mention of food. I decided there was no harm, and I might get beaten up by my own people if I refused, so I accepted. We walked across the street in what was now complete darkness and sat under a tree on the rough wooden benches of a shashlik stall.

Our host said I shouldn't get too worried about the problems of the Atayevs. The kolkhoz was a huge institution – it had 12,000 hectares. The welfare of the whole was much more important than the welfare of three families. It was one of the top cotton farms in the country, and the head was personally appointed by Jurabekov. Jurabekov was Presidential Counsellor on agriculture and ran Uzbek cotton trading. He was one of the most feared men in the country. Our host was letting me know he had Jurabekov's support. I asked, if the farm was so huge, why was the Atayevs' small portion – less than a tenth of one per cent of the farm – so important? He said it was because it was the patch which surrounded their village, and the kolkhoz needed to expand that village in order to house more workers. The Atayevs had been offered better land elsewhere in exchange, but they had refused. The violence against them was regrettable but nothing to do with him. Of course, if they were interfering with the well-being of the kolkhoz, the kolkhoz workers would get angry. He couldn't control that. As for the murder and imprisonment – well, the law must take its course, the judiciary were independent, at which I said, 'Look, there is no point in talking such bollocks to me,' and he grinned. As for the destruction of the apple trees – well, they were going to build housing there, so they had to go.

He concluded by saying that if I came back to Kitab, I should let him know and stay with him. Looking lasciviously at Kristina and Nadira, he said he could organise the kind of hospitality and entertainment that might be to my excellent taste. But he then added, 'But I don't suppose you will come back to Kitab. Nobody ever does. Tomorrow evening you will go away, and I will still be in control here. That is what matters.'

He got up and ostentatiously pulled a wad of large-denomination dollar bills from his pocket, giving one to the astonished shashlik vendor, who literally fell to his knees and cried in gratitude. When he had gone, we agreed our host had made a convincing villain.

'It is true, you know,' said Kristina. 'Tomorrow you will be gone and he will be here.'

'Keep chipping, chipping, and you'll crack the marble,' I replied. It had been a scorching hot day, and Kristina asked if the sun had got to me.

We travelled back slowly in the blackness of the winding country roads. Every now and then we passed an illuminated nodding donkey, slowly and tirelessly bringing up the oil, and orange flares lit up patches of sky towards Karshi. In the middle of nowhere, we came across a service station that was both open and had diesel. I rummaged in the little plug-in fridge in the boot and got out a bottle of champagne. We sat under the stars on a fence and drank from the bottle, thinking over the day. We got to the hotel at midnight. It was 15 hours since Mansur and Kristina had started work, and I apologised to them.

Mansur astonished me.

'We all love you, Ambassador,' he said. 'There will never be another like you.'

I quickly left and walked away to my bedroom, so they wouldn't see me cry. When I got there, I realised I had turned my back on Nadira and left her with the others. Shortly there was a quiet tap at the door, and she came in. She wiped my tears and kissed me on the forehead. She said, 'I didn't know about you. I didn't understand what you did. Nobody ever cared about or tried to help such country people. May Allah protect you. I will say *dua* for you.'

She slipped out, and I was left alone with my thoughts. I seemed to be engaged on a hopeless personal crusade. I was trying to change a massively entrenched dictatorship by hurling myself against it. What was the point?

The point, I decided, was that it had to be done. Think William Wallace. On the other hand, when they tortured him to death they forced his own testicles down his throat.

With that less than comforting thought, I fell asleep.

The hotel air conditioning was not working. I was so tired I nevertheless slept well, but I awoke with the bed sheets drenched in sweat. I then found there was no running water either. All I could do was towel down briskly. Kristina and Nadira appeared for breakfast around six-thirty, but there was no sign of Mansur. I checked his room, but he had upped and packed. By seven o'clock, I was getting worried, but he reappeared in the lobby, covered in oil. The air conditioning in the car had broken down; he had found a mechanic, but they had been unable to fix it.

This was seriously bad news. We set off back to Kitab, and even as we arrived just after eight it was swelteringly hot. Our two ladies were waiting for us in reception, and we all entered together into the Procurator's office. The District Procurator was there, an untidy old-looking man, together with the Deputy Procurator General, a much younger and better-groomed man with a great deal of gold braid on the shoulders of his green uniform. The two men were sitting at a long table.

There were no greetings or handshakes, and the District Procurator opened aggressively: 'What do you want, Mr Ambassador? We are extremely busy here. I can give you five minutes.'

Plainly, I needed to wrest the initiative.

'Get out of this office!' I shouted.

He was stunned.

'What did you say?' he asked.

'Get out!' I replied. 'Get out of this office! These two ladies will testify that you threatened to kill them. I believe you are already implicated in the murder of one man and were present at the beating of an old woman. You are not a procurator; you are a criminal. Now get out!'

He faltered.

'But this is my office!' He looked appealingly at the Deputy Procurator General for support, but the latter stared fixedly ahead of him. The District Procurator stood up and picked up his cap.

'I have other business to attend to,' he said and left.

My approach had not been pre-meditated, but this was a stunning result. This local tyrant had been humiliated in front of these women and the gaggle of staff and others who were revealed standing in the corridor as he opened the door to leave.

I sat down at the table, unbidden. Kristina joined me. Nadira and the two ladies took a seat on chairs that were standing against the wall.

'An unusual way to behave,' remarked the Deputy Procurator General. 'Tell me, Ambassador, what is your locus in this matter?'

I had got used to answering that one: 'Uzbekistan, along with the UK, is a signatory of a number of international conventions guaranteeing human rights. As a lawyer, I am sure you realise that a state party to a convention has the right to urge compliance on another state party.'

I was relieved he didn't ask me which clauses of which convention I was referring to, because I could never remember that stuff. But he simply nodded and asked, 'And is this an official complaint from the government of the United Kingdom?'

Oh well, in for a penny.

'Yes.'

'And what precisely is the nature of the complaint?'

'Yesterday I met an 84-year-old woman who had been beaten by thugs from the kolkhoz. Perhaps these women might tell you their story.'

And they did, the Deputy Procurator General apparently taking notes of what they said.

'I know of the case,' he said. 'I will look at it when I get back to Tashkent and send the Ambassador a report.'

'Look,' I said, 'we all know the system and how it works. Sadly, there is going to be no major change in the structure of Uzbek agriculture any time soon. But for local officials to get so ridiculously brutal with a small farmer is just going to bring in people like me and cause you a great deal more trouble than the disputed land is worth. Think about it and tell them to leave these small farmers alone.'

The Deputy Procurator General said something non-committal, then the District Procurator returned, now all false bonhomie. When I got back to Tashkent, I tried to persuade Atayev to go back to Kitab and look after his womenfolk and his farm, saying I was pretty confident I had put the kolkhoz off any further radical moves in the short term. But he was too scared and claimed asylum in the United

States instead. We did, however, get the other brother out of prison, which was an excellent result.

Returning from Kitab to Karshi, we visited the United States Air Force base at Khanabad. I learnt a lot of stuff there, but I can't tell you about it because it's secret. The scale of the place, and particularly of the civil works in progress, was vast. I was made very welcome, but plainly they were even happier to see Nadira and Kristina. Can't say I blame them.

We had a late lunch at the base, and then, driving through Karshi again, I stopped at the SNB headquarters where, a week previously, Orif Eshanov had been tortured to death. I registered my interest, while wondering if it was one of the men I met who had yanked out his fingernails. We then embarked on quite an ordeal of our own.

The drive from Karshi to Samarkand takes about three hours and passes through serious desert. The heat was searing – the car's thermometer was showing an external temperature of 52 degrees Celsius. Inside, it was still hotter. Even at the US base, they had been unable to fix the car's air conditioning. I had stocked up with a crate of mineral water, and we were soon drinking it from the bottle, at a temperature that would have been hot for a bath. Even with all the windows open and my head intermittently stuck out of one, I soon began to feel giddy and faint and had a blinding headache. More worrying, so did Mansur. We parked up for a while and rested in the shade of a nodding donkey. After drinking a great deal of hot water, we headed off again. We arrived at the Afrosiyab Hotel after dark. The air conditioning wasn't working in the hotel either, but it seemed deliciously cool.

The next morning, we left at first light to get to Tashkent before it got really hot. As I pointed out, this had the great advantage that we could still do a full day's work when we got there. Kristina and Mansur didn't seem to share my enthusiasm.

CHAPTER 15

Hammer to Fall

Morale was at a particular low in the embassy, with no easing off of the suspicion and distrust between the British and Uzbek staff. To try to tackle this problem, I decided that we would have an embassy away day.

We headed off to the spectacular new resort on the mountain lake at Chimgan, owned, unsurprisingly, by Gulnara Karimova. There we had morning and afternoon workshops where I outlined the global mission statement and objectives of the FCO. We then discussed areas of activity including trade promotion, democratisation or narcotics control and applied them to our work in Uzbekistan, ending up with a decent set of detailed objectives for the embassy. I would never have got the Uzbek staff to open up and play a full part if we had held that discussion in the embassy, but in this environment they relaxed and got very involved.

The second workshop finished at 4 p.m., leaving plenty of time to enjoy the pool, jet skis on the lake, mountain bikes and other diversions. Then in the evening we had a group dinner with plenty of wine and an impromptu disco.

It was on this occasion that we took one of the Land-Rovers down the run of terraced steps that ran within the resort from the hotel to the swimming pool area. The vehicle was driven by Mansur, who was not only sober but is teetotal. The FCO were to make much of this incident for propaganda against me.

* * *

We had in a year brought more international attention to the horrors of the Karimov regime than had been achieved in the previous ten years of Uzbek independence. The Bush administration were extremely unhappy about the exposure of their ally and were about to strike back. The first blow was unexpected.

I had been very pleased to be invited to lunch by Jennifer Windsor, Director of Freedom House, visiting from Washington. I had worked closely with Freedom House on a number of occasions, and cooperation with Sikeena had been first class.

I said as much to Jennifer Windsor, a former senior State Department official, over lunch. She said that she appreciated my input, but there would be a change in Freedom House's operations in Uzbekistan. She explained that a number of influential members of the board of Freedom House approached these issues from a vantage point on the right of the Republican Party, and they had expressed concern that Freedom House was failing to keep in sight the need to promote freedom in the widest sense, by giving full support to US and coalition forces in the War on Terror.

I asked what this meant in practice. Jennifer said that it meant they would be stopping 'advocacy': that is to say that they would no longer be making public statements on human rights in Uzbekistan or publicising individual cases of abuse. They would train activists in documenting and reporting abuse. They would be careful not to work with political opposition figures. They would be 'emphasising human rights over democracy'. The primary activity from now on would be working with the Uzbek authorities, training them on how to respect human rights, rather than standing outside and shouting at them.

I said we were ourselves trying to start some work with the Ministry of the Interior in the same way and hoped we could cooperate. But the Uzbek government seemed very competent at playing along the international community while having no intention of initiating genuine change. The cooperation programmes could then become fig leaves to cover horrors. That was much more of a danger if you simultaneously stopped criticism, as Freedom House were about to do.

This conversation worried me, so that evening I phoned Sikeena. She stunned me by saying that she was packing to leave Uzbekistan. I asked what was wrong. Had she been sacked? She said no, of course not. She was going back to Canada to finish a book. She sounded poised as ever, but there was a catch in her voice. I never saw her again.

One area where the Karimov regime was protected by its alliance with the United States is narcotics trafficking. The United States, Germany and the United Kingdom bilaterally, and the UN and European Union, have all put money into narcotics control. At Termez, where the Friendship Bridge crosses into Afghanistan, they have provided Uzbek customs with every modern facility from sniffer dogs to giant X-rays that can scan an entire container.

United Nations famine-relief vehicles are sometimes stuck for weeks at this border, waiting to get in to Afghanistan. But if you stand there for a little while, you will start to notice the convoys of Mercedes with black windows and of six-ton military trucks which are waved onto a track around the customs facilities and never stopped. They carry 40 per cent of Afghanistan's heroin production. Mostly it is then placed into cotton bales and sent up the railway to the Baltic at Riga and St Petersburg for onward shipment into Europe.

The Afghan end of this trade is controlled by General Dostum, the leader of the US-backed Northern Alliance, which did the bulk of the ground occupation against the Taliban, following on the heels of US carpet bombing. General Dostum reportedly had a predilection for tying opponents to tank tracks then driving on, and for locking prisoners into metal containers in the searing heat and leaving them to bake to death. He thus has the same kind of image problem as President Karimov. The vehicles that are never searched run between Dostum and the Uzbek regime, bringing narcotics out and arms, money and chemicals for heroin manufacture in.[54]

Like human rights abuse, this was one of those things that just never got mentioned. And everyone was engaged in anti-narcotics cooperation with the Uzbek government, providing expensive equipment and training, and pretending they were tackling the problem. In fact, the few interceptions of narcotics by the Uzbek authorities were best characterised as removing private-sector competition.

Customs and Excise in London argued to me, with a straight face, that because the Uzbek authorities intercept negligible amounts of heroin, that proves very little comes through the country. In Tajikistan next door, a great deal is intercepted, so that must be the major route. Of course, this argument is bonkers. The big league avoids Tajikistan precisely because it has effective interception.

In general, I have the highest respect for Customs and Excise Special Investigations Division. Unlike MI6, they are intrepid, reliable and put themselves in personal danger. But they didn't even have anyone in Uzbekistan. We were covered by Stuart, who had to travel from Turkmenistan and was only able to spend one day in Uzbekistan every three months. He was good fun, and we would always have a drink together.

Stuart was proud of his Russian and spoke it all the time with Uzbeks both to show it off and to try to improve it. In the Ragu with me one evening, he turned to Raj, the owner, and asked him a long and involved question in Russian.

Raj looked him up and down, paused, and replied, 'Don't ask me, mate. I'm from Slough.'

* * *

After the departure of Chris and Karen, I had asked Personnel Command to send out someone on a pastoral visit to see if they could recommend appropriate ways to deal with the continuing British/Uzbek staff divide.

A very pleasant young Scot, Colin Reynolds, was sent out in June. He held an opening meeting with all staff, at which I urged everyone to be open and cooperate fully with him. He then held individual meetings with virtually all of the staff.

But something extraordinary started to happen. First Nick Ridout, then Steve Brown, then Kristina came to see me immediately after meeting with Colin. They were mystified. He had asked them almost nothing about relationships within the embassy but had instead asked repeatedly how much I drank and whether I was sleeping around. One by one, almost the entire embassy staff came to see me after seeing him, all pretty angry and anxious on my behalf.

Colin came to see me at the end. He said he was concerned that not all proper procedures were being followed. I said they never had been because the embassy hadn't been resourced to do it. Steve Brown and I were making a real effort to improve on this, but obviously the loss of Karen and Chris had disrupted things a bit. I then said that staff had been telling me he had focused on asking personal questions about me. If I was under investigation, it would have been polite to have let me know.

Colin said that he had been asked to investigate allegations against me, including those that I was alcoholic and that I was, together with an expatriate, renting a flat in the town for shagging purposes. The Eastern Department had shown him an article in an Uzbek newspaper which mentioned these claims.

I said that all these allegations were untrue. Colin said he agreed but had wanted to check out the evidence with the staff before talking to me.

I should say something about drink. I have recounted several drinking sessions because they were memorable. I have always had the ability to drink a great deal, to hold my drink and to get up and go to work the next morning. I did not drink every day by any means – on average, I should think I drank on three evenings a week, and two of those moderately. Sometimes I might go for a couple of weeks without a drink at all. I was never drunk in the office or at work.

But now, the strain of doing the jobs of Chris and Karen as well as my own was getting to me. Shortly after Colin's visit, I found that I was having a drink when I got home, to relax the tension. I had never used alcohol in this way before, so I went to see Dr Reimers about it. She said I was massively stressed and greatly needed a holiday. But with Chris and Karen gone, I just had too much work to do.

For months, I had received virtually no communication of any kind from the Eastern Department. It may be illogical to ascribe a quality to silence, but this was a hostile silence. Furthermore, I was being kept completely out of the loop – for example, a junior Foreign Office minister phoned Uzbek Foreign Minister Safayev to discuss UK–Uzbek relations, and not only was I not consulted beforehand, I wasn't even told when it had happened, leaving me severely wrong-footed when Safayev mentioned it to me.

On 28 May 2003, I had emailed Linda Duffield to complain about how difficult life was with no support or communication from London. She replied on 2 June that London was very busy with other things than communicating with me.[55]

This was followed again by silence for the next three weeks. I had described the silence as 'weird and unnerving' because I felt sure that the Eastern Department were looking for a way to get rid of me and of my uncomfortable views on human rights. Colin Reynolds' briefing to investigate me seemed to constitute part of such an attack. I did not know that, following his visit to Tashkent at the end of March, Simon Butt had already given me an unfavourable report. On 16 April, he had written a minute to Linda Duffield and Sir Michael Jay:

SUBJECT: CRAIG MURRAY, TASHKENT

I visited Tashkent from 30 March-1April. I briefed you orally on my return on discussions with Craig on his performance, and we met with the PUS [Sir Michael Jay] yesterday. This is to record the position more formally . . .

I discussed with Craig his telegram on US policy, sent and widely copied on the eve of the hostilities in Iraq, and another example of his accustomed, rather emotional style. (He has since been instructed, with some of our other ambassadors who have the same predilection, not to copy their reporting quite so widely, following complaints from Gulf Posts.)

Craig was unapologetic. What he had said needed saying. He had again received congratulatory emails from a number of other Posts which had received the telegram. These were issues about which he felt strongly, and which needed to be aired . . . He was not prepared to compromise on principles to further his career . . .

I ought perhaps to mention, without further comment, one further aspect of Craig's unconventional style. After a dinner in Samarkand, the rest of the party returned to our hotel. Craig, in the company of our young female LE fixer, went off in search of a jazz club. I have heard from others that he has patronised strip clubs in Warsaw (where he encountered [name removed]) . . .

Simon Butt

Here, Simon Butt named a political figure. This was an astonishing slur on the man, who, to the best of my knowledge, had never been in a strip club in Warsaw or anywhere else.

So in mid-April 2003, Sir Michael Jay, Head of the Diplomatic Service, was already holding meetings that were setting out the problem – Craig Murray criticising US foreign policy and refusing to stop, even if it threatens his career – and the potential solution – attack him over his personal life. This was followed by that period of hostile silence, then the attack in the shape of the visit by Colin Reynolds, primed with stories about me.

Unfortunately for them, Colin Reynolds was perceptive, experienced and honest. He wrote a report of his visit on 26 June 2003, which he sent to Alan Charlton, the Head of FCO Personnel, and copied to, among others, Linda Duffield and Simon Butt. Again, I am not allowed to publish this document, which is exceptionally frustrating. In it, Colin says that his two purposes in visiting were to follow up on the departure of Chris and Karen and to discuss with me reports received in London about my 'activities outside the office'. Nowhere in this report does he say where these reports were received from, except for a curious reference to the fact that they came by 'a rather circuitous route'.

He criticised me somewhat for not having been aware of the extent of the antipathies between the staff, which was fair enough. My tactic had been, rather than to dig up the problems, to give everyone a sense of purpose and hope that once motivated and very busy they would rub along. It hadn't entirely worked.

But Colin also noted that the staff were 'uniformly positive about Craig during my visit'. They had been taken aback at first by my informality but enjoyed working for me and felt that we had a new high profile and were greatly liked and respected by the business community and others.

Colin also noted that the staff had no concerns about my social behaviour and gave no evidence that I drank too much, nor was there any evidence that I had, as had been alleged in London, a 'love nest' apartment in Tashkent.

Perhaps the most important section of Colin's lengthy minute concerned the relationship between the embassy and the Eastern Department. Colin was neutral in reporting this but very fairly stated that I was bitter about the lack of communication and support. He detailed the fairly recent incident where a British minister had spoken with the Uzbek Foreign Minister by phone without my being consulted or even told. And Colin noted that the Eastern Department and I had serious policy disagreements 'in particular on human rights'.[56]

I was entitled to be confused on the last point. My Freedom House speech had been specifically commended by the government to the House of Commons Select Committee on Foreign Affairs. It was republished in full as an appendix to the FCO's 2003 Annual Report on Human Rights – the only non-ministerial speech ever to be published that way. Yet Linda Duffield had told me I should not have been allowed to make it, and Sir Michael Jay's minute about the draft showed he was against it, too.

This was an early symptom of the fact that while we continued to advocate human rights in public, in private the government was deciding to abandon the concept of fundamental rights as an interference with the War on Terror. They are now pretty open about it, but in 2003 they were still schizophrenic, and I was caught in the middle of that schizophrenia.

The other factor was the Americans. The rumours about me, which the Eastern Department were passing on to Personnel Command, about the source of which Colin Reynolds was deliberately obscure, were being produced by the US embassy in Tashkent. After 20 years in the Diplomatic Service, I had a lot of friends, particularly in the lower grades. A junior member of Jack Straw's private office has told me that what happened next was that a high-ranking policy adviser to Tony Blair, whom he named, came back from a visit to Washington with a message that the US wanted someone to rid them of that troublesome British ambassador in Tashkent.

The *Observer* columnist Nick Cohen has told me that in the autumn of 2003 he had lunch with an FCO minister who said that the instruction to get rid of me came from Number 10. Michael Andersen, the distinguished Danish journalist and Central Asia expert, commented in *The Spectator* that in autumn 2003: 'Sources in the Foreign Office told me that "a systematic campaign" was waged against Murray, partly directed from Downing Street.'[57]

This is consistent with the account published by three investigative journalists from *The Guardian*:

> A senior source said the former ambassador had been put under pressure to stop his repeated criticisms of the brutal Karimov regime, accused among other things of boiling prisoners to death. The source said the pressure was partly 'exercised on the orders of No 10', which found his outspokenness about the compromises Washington was prepared to make in its 'War on Terror' increasingly embarrassing in the lead up to the Iraq war.[58]

I had a holiday in Canada with the family booked for the end of July. I desperately needed this break, but who was to take over? Daniel Grzenda had been appointed to replace Chris Hirst, and it was agreed to bring him out early to do this. It was extraordinary that he would get to be in charge of the embassy after only a day in his first posting, but we decided it would be so quiet in Tashkent in

August that it should be all right. In retrospect, I should have been suspicious that the Eastern Department did seem very anxious for me to get away on leave.

Fiona and Emily had returned to the UK a few weeks ahead of me, at the start of Jamie's holiday, and I had been able to spend a lot of time in the evenings with Nadira. We had really got very serious about one another. I was very sorry to say goodbye to her for a month but looking forward to Canada with the children.

I had seen Colin's report and felt that I had seen off the Eastern Department's attacks for now, although there was no change in their frostiness in the month between Colin's visit and my getting away on leave.

I had one day in London before we left for Canada. I used it to call on Simon Butt, Linda Duffield and Alan Charlton, the Director of Personnel. If I had any illusions that the hostility had died down, they were quickly dispelled.

On my arrival at the department, I received astonishing news. Kristina, Lena Son, Atabek, Yuliya and Nafisa – my five senior members of locally engaged staff – had all been suspended from duty and asked to leave the embassy. This had actually happened the moment I left the embassy building, as I was on my way to the airport. I was astonished and livid, and demanded that they be reinstated.

When I got to his office, Dominic Schroeder was on the phone to Jessica Irvine of DFID. She plainly was furious – Atabek was a DFID, not an FCO, employee. I stepped inside and said 'Is that Jessica? Tell her it's nothing to do with me and I want him back.'

Dominic gave me an unconvincing smile and a thumbs-up but didn't say this. I repeated it. He was telling Jessica that there would be a full investigation and again didn't pass on my message. I decided to do so myself, but though I tried several times that afternoon, I could achieve no more than a message on her answer phone.

Simon Butt denied all pre-knowledge when I met him. He said they would investigate it and I should go on holiday. I said I wanted it fully understood these were valuable members of staff.

The rest of my conversation with Simon was even more worrying. He said that he had been appointed the investigating officer in the Chris Hirst case and that disturbing facts had emerged. He said he had interviewed Chris and found him convincing. He denied all the assaults. Furthermore, Chris claimed I was harassing him because of my personal dislike of dogs.

There were further allegations that I was drinking in bars and had taken Chris to a strip club after the van Boven reception. Also, at the Queen's Birthday Party itself, there had been nude swimming in the pool. That alone could constitute gross misconduct, Simon said. He then said that it had also been alleged that I had no respect from the British business community.

I couldn't believe it. It was becoming all too clear that the FCO were attempting to use Chris Hirst to substantiate their allegations against me, which they were prioritising above the investigation into the allegations against Chris. I replied to Simon, describing the events after the van Boven reception. I suggested that in the circumstances, counter-accusations from Chris might be considered with a little more scepticism. As for the QBP, it had finished and a few friends had stayed on for drinks and a swim. Richard Wilkins' assistant had briefly removed her top.

Simon said he thought this was a major problem.

Chris later resigned from the civil service before the investigation into his conduct had been concluded, and so it has never been established whether or not he was guilty of the allegations levied against him. After my experience with him on the night of the van Boven reception, it did appear to me that he had the potential to react aggressively when under stress, but I never saw him attack anyone. I continue to bear in mind that Chris found himself in a horrendous situation: he was dealing with the reality of human rights abuse by a corrupt regime on a daily basis, undertaking the work of a grade higher than that for which he was qualified. There was also the possibility that the allegations against him were politically motivated. When I arrived at the embassy, it appears that the FCO had been aware of potential problems with one of my core members of staff, yet they failed to fully inform me about what had been going on. Had I been clearly briefed on the situation, I would have been in a position to offer Chris the support he may have needed. Instead, when the problems came to a head, Chris was used as another piece of evidence against me.

Profoundly depressed, I told both Linda Duffield and Alan Charlton that I was considering asking to leave Tashkent. The policy differences were making it very difficult for me to continue in conscience and seemed to be feeding through into persecution. Neither tried to dissuade me; both told me to make my mind up quickly.

We flew to Toronto the next day.

All my instincts were screaming at me to give up the holiday and get on the next plane back to Tashkent. Plainly, something very strange indeed was happening, and I was convinced that the removal of my key staff was the start of an attack on me while I was on leave. But I was both physically and mentally in desperate need of a holiday. It had been a draining year, and I had not had a break of longer than four days in the preceding three years. Fiona and the children were hugely looking forward to the holiday in Canada, and we weren't all together as a family very often. So, fatally, I went.

For the first few nights I couldn't sleep. I had this profound worry about what the FCO were up to. It grew to a constant subconscious nag, an awareness of facing an implacable hostility. Every now and then the hairs on the back of my neck would rise and I would be overcome by a despairing consciousness that people were acting against me, thousands of miles away. It wasn't a psychic phenomenon – it was my mind working on a perfectly rational analysis of the situation and forcing it to my attention while I was constantly struggling not to think about it. I tried not to show any worry, especially to the children, but I think the strain did show, and Fiona certainly noticed I couldn't sleep. I kept telling myself that I would get less stressed as the holiday unfolded, but it didn't work – the feeling just built and built.

Which is a shame, because it was a wonderful holiday. Toronto, Niagara Falls, Fort Henry, Quebec, Sunwapta Falls, Vancouver – it could not have been better for the family. In Vancouver, having crossed the continent largely by road, we were staying at the Royal Towers casino hotel. I had found it on the Internet simply as a good-quality hotel offering an excellent deal. The casino was incidental; it did not bother us and we did not bother it. The room was very cheap – Canadian $85 a night – presumably because they expected you to spend money in the casino. The family were happy and bubbly as we checked in; I had no idea that my marriage would end in that hotel.

At first we were in a cramped room with two double beds. I looked up the Internet booking print-out and went down in the morning to do battle with reception. They upgraded us with great promptness and courtesy. A porter helped move the luggage. By now we had a huge stack, full of souvenirs from all our points of call and presents for all the Uzbek staff. They put us in a beautiful penthouse on the ninth floor.

We went to the tourist information centre, looking for a play or film to see that evening. It had free Internet access, and Fiona logged in to our family address. There was an email for me from Howard Drake in the FCO Personnel Department. It was peremptory. I was to telephone him immediately.

Howard was my 'grade manager'. He was responsible for career progression of the senior grades of the Diplomatic Service. The next morning, I went to our Consulate-General in Vancouver. The Consul-General, a nice man named Laurence, was slightly bemused but lent me his office. I got through to Howard Drake.

I knew Howard slightly. I had once taken over a job from him, either as Head of Cyprus section or Head of Maritime section of the FCO, I forget which. He had big hair, a careful blond coiffure like a minor American politician. We had had a week's handover of the job and got on well. Now he sounded very uncomfortable indeed.

'Thank you for phoning, Craig. How are you?'

'Very well, thanks, Howard. How are you?'

'I am fine, thank you, Craig. And how is your wife? Fiona isn't it? And the children?'

'All fine, thank you, Howard. We have had a good, much-needed, break.'

'Yes, I am sure. Well, Craig, the thing is that you called on a number of people before you left for, er, Canada, and you said that you were thinking of quitting in Tashkent.'

'Yes, that's right. I said I'd think about it over the holiday.'

'And did you?'

'Yes, I did. I think I was just exhausted. I am ready to soldier on now. Actually, I'm looking forward to going back.'

'Oh. That could be unfortunate.'

'I am sorry, Howard?'

'Well, Craig,' he audibly swallowed, 'the thing is that it has been decided here that Tashkent would be better off without you.'

I remember that phrase precisely. Better off without you.

'Well, I don't agree. Have I been withdrawn?'

'Not yet, no. What are your travel plans?'

'Well, we fly back to Tashkent in a couple of days.'

'Are you coming to London first?'

'Only to change planes.'

'Well, Craig, I have to be quite clear. You are not to return to Tashkent. That is a direct instruction from Sir Michael Jay. You are to come back here immediately and to see me. I have to tell you that there are serious disciplinary allegations facing you.'

'What allegations? Who from?'

'I can't say any more on the phone. How soon can you be here?'

'I don't know. I'll have to see a travel agent. Will the office pay the extra costs?'

'I don't know. I suppose so.'

They didn't.

Tashkent is about ten hours behind Vancouver time. The hotel staff were very helpful when I explained I had to make some urgent international business calls at 4 a.m. and didn't want to disturb my family. They gave me the key of an adjacent suite, activating the phone and asking me not to use the bathroom or disturb the bed.

I quickly got through to Daniel. I explained to him briefly that London had told me I would not be returning to Tashkent. His strangled 'What?' indicated genuine surprise. I asked him what could have happened to precipitate this. Daniel sounded pensive and worried: 'Well, I think some things were said when Dominic Schroeder came out.'

'Dominic came out? Why did he come out? And what things were said?'

'He came out three weeks ago to investigate the suspension of local staff. He asked a lot of questions about you.'

'And what did people say?'

'Well, I think some people thought you could give them more support and back their judgement more in management issues.'

'Well, that hardly sounds enough.'

'Look, I think we all just said we should talk it through with you when you returned and sort it out. No one wanted you kicked out.'

A suspicion crossed my mind: 'Daniel, Dominic came out in response to the suspension of local staff. Now whose idea was that?'

'It was my decision as chargé d'affaires.'

'Yes, of course. But what happened exactly?'

'Well, Steve brought me this email from Atabek which was mocking my authority. We looked it up in Diplomatic Service Procedure and decided it was gross misconduct. It said that suspension pending investigation was the first option. So I did that. Look, I said to London that if anyone could show me what I did wrong according to Diplomatic Service Procedure, I would take the blame. As far as I'm concerned, I just followed it.'

'No doubt. Daniel, I am really not worried about that – I have been in the Service for 20 years now and I haven't opened Diplomatic Service Procedure yet. But you didn't know, following Dominic's visit, that I wouldn't be coming back?'

'No, we didn't think that was the outcome at all. We said we had some management issues but just wanted to put them on the table with you to improve relationships.'

'OK, Daniel. Thanks. Don't worry about it.'

'OK, Craig. Look, I'm sorry. What shall I tell the others?'

'Nothing yet. Good night, Daniel.'

'Good night, Craig. Sleep well.'

I didn't. At six o'clock in the morning, I woke Fiona and we went into the bathroom to talk where the children wouldn't hear us. I told her everything I knew. I also told her about my relationship with Nadira. I couldn't think what else the office could be going to throw at me. I didn't want Fiona to hear about it from anyone else. Fiona was obviously very furious but icily calm. She asked if I was prepared to give Nadira up and never see her again. I said I didn't think I could promise that; I was in love. But neither did I want to split up our family. Fiona told me not to be so childish and to grow up. If I didn't end the relationship with Nadira, the marriage was over anyway.

Despite her fury at me, Fiona saw very clearly that the desire of the FCO to remove me from Tashkent was nothing to do with Nadira. Marital break-ups in the Diplomatic Service are extremely common, and my personal history had plenty of entanglements which had never threatened my career. I told Fiona we were most unlikely to be going back to Tashkent.

We couldn't fly back to London the next day and so would be returning only a day ahead of schedule, which the children didn't even notice. We tried to keep things as normal as we could for them the next day and then headed back. It is a long flight from Vancouver to London, especially if you call in at Chicago. It was a 14-hour overnighter, and I didn't sleep a wink.

CHAPTER 16

One Step Ahead of the Shoeshine

I went straight by taxi from Heathrow Airport to the FCO, while Fiona drove home with the children and the luggage. I arrived at the Old Admiralty Building off the Mall and searched through its maze of corridors for Howard Drake's office. I went to the loo to splash cold water on my face, to try to snap my brain back into gear. Looking in the mirror at this man in crumpled clothes, with reddened narrow eyes and two days of stubble glinting grey and russet, I thought I could not have made myself look more disreputable if I tried. It was 21 August 2003.

I was first introduced to Kate Smith, a young lady from my union who was to accompany me at the interview. The union, the Diplomatic Service Association, has since changed, but at that time it represented only the most senior members of the Diplomatic Service, so it was hardly the most radical organisation in the world. It was probably the only organisation accredited to the Trades Union Congress with a majority of members that had attended private schools. It tended to the view that the FCO administration, composed of a fair proportion of its own members, was probably right in most instances. Like me, Kate Smith was on a fast-tracked career. Aged about 30, she had a key role in the Iraq Unit. She sported the usual short-cropped hair, flecked with premature grey. Her smile is very warm and her features elfin, but at this first meeting she was viewing me with ill-disguised reserve, like a barrister defending a mass murderer she is pretty sure is guilty.

We went in together to see Howard Drake.

'Hello, Craig,' he said. 'It's been a long time.'

The hair was still big but thinner, and the blond colour had dulled.

'Ten years?' I suggested.

'Your career has gone well, eh? Ambassador?'

'Well, it is only Uzbekistan.'

'Still, you've done better than me.' Suddenly his mouth clenched and facial muscles tightened, and he said as if with great effort, 'Look, this isn't very pleasant, but I might as well launch into it.' He then started speaking from prepared notes, and as he progressed his voice took on a tone of active hostility. He was getting into the part and didn't look at me very much.

The main reason for the meeting, it quickly transpired, was to ask me to resign from my post. There were apparently serious concerns about my leadership within the embassy, and criticism of my handling of the Chris Hirst case was cited along with problems between UK and LE staff. Howard handed me copies of the reports from Colin Reynolds and Dominic Schroeder, and highlighted Reynolds' assessment of the lack of adequate management procedures and financial controls within the embassy.

Next came the bombshell that there were 'a series of very serious allegations from UK-based staff in Tashkent', some of which apparently related to 'potential vulnerabilities from a security point of view'. These allegations were to be investigated, but in the meantime I was to return to Tashkent only to pack up and leave by September.

I could hardly believe what I was hearing and struggled to fight off the fog of sleep deprivation and jet lag. It seemed clear to me that the Eastern Department wanted me out, but there was no way I was going to resign on the basis of what Howard had just told me. It was one thing to suspend me while investigations were being conducted, but the request for my resignation was the equivalent of finding me guilty without trial.

Howard was plainly shaken by my refusal to resign. He positively went white. The FCO is a very collegiate organisation in which those few in the top levels who don't come from a private school and Oxbridge background survive by acting as though they did. This meeting was a bit like the old films where the army officer is left the revolver on his desk and asked to do the decent thing. I picked it up and started shooting at the bastards. I countered the specific management points made and then made it clear to Howard that I believed I was being singled out due to policy differences with the Eastern Department. I was not a typical ambassador, and I believed that my challenging questions and refusal to gloss over the fact that we were receiving intelligence gained under torture had clearly infuriated members of senior management.

Looking back, I am astonished about how coherent I was. It had just passed 1 a.m. in Vancouver, and I had had virtually no sleep for the previous 72 hours. But I pointed out the major discrepancies between Dominic Schroeder's allegations and Colin Reynolds' report of just four weeks earlier, and I rebutted in detail the claims about my mishandling of staffing problems. I also asked why none of these points on management had been made to me when I had called on Simon Butt, Linda Duffield and Alan Charlton only three weeks earlier.

It became obvious to me that nothing I said was having any impact on Howard at all. So I stopped and asked him if anything I said might change the mind of the Office. He said no, and there was no point in our talking about it. So I asked why they did not, in that case, simply instruct me to leave, rather than ask me to resign. His minute of the meeting notes his reply: 'I reiterated that our hope was that he and we would agree that withdrawal would be the right step. We also had in mind his well-being and dignity.'[59]

When Howard handed me the allegations, I didn't have time to take them all in, but what I read hit me like a bullet. Offering visas for sex, being an alcoholic, financial corruption. How on earth, after 20 years' service, could they produce such lies? These people actually knew me. But why were they so keen to browbeat me into resigning? I drew a simple conclusion. They couldn't sack me. They knew as well as I did that these allegations were bullshit, and they must have been warned off by their lawyers. As soon as I got back to Tashkent, I would start to marshal witnesses in my defence.

Howard read my thoughts.

'If you do go back to Tashkent,' he said, 'you are not, under any circumstances, to mention this meeting, these allegations, or the request that you resign, to anybody at all. Is that plain?'

I could hardly have been given a more sinister instruction.

'Plain but not fair. How do I establish a defence?'

'You don't. The FCO will appoint an independent investigator to determine the facts.'

'In which case I want it noted that I have no confidence in the fairness of the procedure.'

Howard was not open to reasoning and was just carrying out instructions from the top of the office. But I had changed one mind. Kate Smith and I retired to another room immediately after the meeting; she was plainly perturbed at what she had just heard and realised that something strange was happening here. I was being asked to resign on the basis of a series of points which it was acknowledged had never been put to me before and told it made no difference what I might answer. I suggested to her that the Eastern Department had failed to get what they wanted from Colin Reynolds, so had gone out to do the job themselves. The suspension of my key staff while I was still on my way to the airport looked like a put-up job to get Dominic out there to do the business.

I returned to Tashkent with Emily, who had to start school. Fiona was remaining in the UK for a couple of weeks with Jamie until he returned to Glenalmond. From Tashkent, I maintained a correspondence about procedure with Kate Smith, who got ever more helpful, and Tessa Redmayne, acting for the administration. The hostility from London was unabated. So I decided to address the infamous FCO allegations against me. On 27 August I sent an email to all who had received Howard Drake's minute:

From Craig Murray, Tashkent
27 August 2003

Craig Murray – Disciplinary Allegations

It has become clear to me that the allegations contained in Dominic Schroeder's minute of 6 August are colouring opinions in London against me, even though they have not yet begun to be investigated. I would therefore like at this stage to give my initial response, which may also help to get the investigation off to a flying start and go some way to help remind those in London not to pre-judge me:

Allegation 1
That he had facilitated visas for girlfriends, paying money for air tickets, receiving sexual favours in his office in return.
I have never had a sexual relationship with a visa applicant. I

have never indulged in any kind of sexual activity in the office. Even in the broadest sense of the term, I have 'facilitated' no more than perhaps six visa applications in a year in Tashkent. I have never seen a Head of Mission in a visa post do less.

Allegation 2
That he regularly turns up at the office drunk or hungover and late before going home to 'sleep it off', then returning to the office at 16.50 demanding people start late work with him.
Completely untrue. I have never been drunk in the office. I would put my average arrival time between 09.10 and 09.15. I generally work a week of around 65 hours including receptions and officially directed out of office activity.

I have held over 700 meetings with perhaps 1,200 visitors over the year. Nobody has ever claimed they found me not sober and on the ball.

In the course of the year I have returned to the Residence during office hours on perhaps 7 or 8 occasions. Three of these were to attend staff meetings in the Residence on QBP organisation. One was to give a TV interview and one to prepare the staff Christmas Party. I once went home feeling unwell – not hungover – and once to attend to some frais accounting. It is possible that on one of these occasions I returned at 4.50 and asked for some important work to be done, but I have no recollection of it.

If I regularly returned home during the day it would show in the flag car log.

I believe there are medical tests now which show background or long-term alcohol abuse. I would happily take one.

Allegation 3
That he took a girlfriend as an interpreter on an up-country trip after which no note was produced.
I roped in a friend, Nadira Bekhanov, as an interpreter on a (particularly gruelling) visit to Kitab to investigate human rights abuses against private farmers there, which had received widespread publicity on the BBC. It was alleged further acts of violence were imminent so we went at short notice. As we were visiting deep country areas around Shakhrisabz where

Russian would not be understood I needed interpretation potentially for Uzbek and Tajik. The embassy was very stretched as we had lost the DHM and 3rd Sec (Chris Hirst and Karen Moran) while visa section was very busy and needed their interpreters. Kristina Ozden, visits officer and social secretary, was accompanying me and she cannot interpret in Uzbek or Tajik. I therefore persuaded a friend fluent in the relevant languages (and with a master's in English) to come with me.

We held meetings with the farmers affected, with the local procuracy, with the head of the collective farm, and with the national Uzbek deputy Procurator-general . . .

We left at 10am and reached Kitab around 3pm. We first met the victims, then toured vandalised fields, then met the head of the collective farm. We returned immediately to Karshi to our hotel and did not reach it until midnight – a very gruelling day and spent largely outdoors in 45C. The next morning we were up at 7am to return to Kitab. We met the local and deputy state procurators. These were tense and difficult meetings . . .

It is true no single note was produced, but the visit was mentioned in our telno 55 and elsewhere, and particularly in discussions with our OSCE and US colleagues. It resulted directly in a major success – the release of an innocent man from jail. Dmitri Potemkin has been working on this case and can confirm this. Kristina Ozden can confirm my account of the trip, including that Bekhanov was needed for translation, and that this was a very hard-working trip. You can also check the hotel bills and see that our party of four (inc driver) had four bedrooms.

Allegation 4

That he authorised the purchase for £4,500 of the sound system of a band (made up of his friends) which played at the QBP. The equipment is in the MO's cellar, never likely to be used. That $80 bottles of whisky were drunk by the band and paid for by local budget.

There is a wealth of snide innuendo here: I employ my friends, to no good purpose, they are drunks, I contrive an unnecessary purchase deal to give them money.

In early April and late May we held a British Musical Festival in Uzbekistan, with the full support of Wider Europe Directorate . . . It consisted of six concerts by the Battlefield Band (Celtic folk), three orchestral concerts of British light classical music, and two concert performances of *HMS Pinafore*. It covered five cities. The Battlefield Band concerts attracted a total live audience of over 7,000 and were broadcast on national and regional TV and radio. Total live audience for all events was over 10,000.

I had heard the Battlefield Band as a student, but they became friends of mine when they headlined a major (£300,000) British cultural festival 'British Nights in Poland' in 1995, and again in 1996. They have performed many tours abroad for both the Council and Embassies, and are the second biggest selling Celtic band of all time. The Band's website has a very good and entertaining account of their Uzbek tour, with good pictures.

We early ascertained, in collaboration with the British Council, that the sound system was a major problem. There are no systems of sufficient quality available to hire in Uzbekistan. We therefore agreed with the Band that they should organise the hire, from an Edinburgh company, of a suitable large system (the biggest venue had an audience of 3,000). British Mediterranean kindly gave us freight half price, but nonetheless the cost of this was from memory £6,500, the bulk of it in airfreight charges. This was a major part of the cost of the festival.

I have every intention of keeping up a high profile of cultural diplomacy here. Neville McBain, British Council director, and I agree that imprinting a consciousness of the West on the successor generation here has to be a top priority. We have already twice repeated the orchestral concerts to live audiences of over 1,000 covered purely from sponsorship, and I have just succeeded in finalising the sponsorship to cover in full an autumn tour by the Allegri Quartet. Further events are in the pipeline from both the embassy and the British Council (who are now working on a reggae tour) and while it is true that the sound system is currently stored in the MO's cellar while the embassy is refurbished, it is ludicrous to allege that it is 'never likely to be used'.

I therefore decided that rather than pay £6,500 every time we needed to ship out a sound system, it made sense to purchase the one that was already here. The purchase was of course from the equipment hiring company not from the Band. For the record, I had no prior or subsequent connection with the hiring company.

We certainly bought drinks for the band, and quite right too, and used them several times as the centre of receptions for local notables. Any bottle of whisky would indeed cost $80 in Uzbekistan.

I will not continue to give my response to each allegation, but you get the general idea. The rest of the allegations were:

Allegation 5
That at an away day Craig encouraged drivers to take embassy vehicles down staircases.

Allegation 6
That he belittles UK-based staff behind their backs before denying a problem when approached by the officers directly concerned.

Allegation 7
That he has told the DHM not to be serious about an MCS [Management Consultancy Services] review due in mid-September 'we'll promote everyone and they'll be happy'.

Allegation 8
That he 'knows' the SNB (local intelligence service) are watching him but doesn't worry because he is open about his behaviour. But he is scared his wife will 'find out' and divorce him, taking the children.

Allegation 9
That certain LE staff 'dollybirds' are employed in eg visa section at double normal rates 'because he says so'.

Allegation 10
That staff were warned not to co-operate with Colin Reynolds during his recent visit because Craig 'had something' on the FCO.

Allegation 11
That he has twice asked the MO to issue a warning to his own PA which has been rescinded without explanation once the PA has spoken to Craig.

Allegation 12
That he frequently takes the flag car out (with driver) until 02.00-04.30.

Allegation 13
That the May account is not yet signed off.

Allegation 14
That a 5 per cent overspend of local budget in the first quarter is 'laughed off'.

Allegation 15
That no meetings are held, notwithstanding Craig's assertion to Simon Butt that they are.

Allegation 16
That he turned up at the first Commercial contacts meeting three hours late at 21.30, claiming to be the only UK-based officer who did any work, but was 'covered in lipstick'.

Allegation 17
Claims to UK-based colleagues to send e-mails to 'wind Simon Butt up', then complains about Simon's response to Linda Duffield.

Allegation 18
'Admits' to writing 'exaggerated' letter to Peter Collecott about conditions at Post.

Dominic's minute simply stated each allegation, without expanding on it, and claimed that each was supported by at least one member of UK-based staff.

Most of these allegations had no basis in fact whatsoever. I suggested that some of the problem might arise from the fact that for the past three months I had been working with just two FCO staff, both of whom had the very lowest substantive grade in the service, well below diplomatic rank. They simply didn't understand what I was doing. But I didn't believe these allegations had all genuinely been made in the form in which they were now being presented to me. My refutation concluded that the allegations contained so much gossip, innuendo and slant that they did not come over as completely disinterested.

I was to get further evidence to support the possibility that this is what had happened. Many months later, one of the members of the embassy staff reported that they had been sitting having a coffee in a Tashkent hotel when Dominic Schroeder joined them and asked, 'What's the gossip about Craig Murray, then?'

He had seemed jovial, and the staff member had told him some gossip, without any intention of certifying it as true, just in the way people like to indulge in a little mildly vicious gossip against the boss. It now seemed that it had been the germ of some of these allegations.

Dominic Schroeder gave a different account. He told me that he had been surprised when approached by staff with serious and detailed accusations and that he had no choice but to list them for investigation.

The large majority of these allegations could have been cross-checked and dismissed in a couple of hours at most. But I do not believe that establishing the truth was the aim. The aim was to force my departure, as seems to be illustrated by a minute from Simon Pease. On 29 August, Simon Pease of the Personnel Directorate wrote a minute to Sir Michael Jay and to Jack Straw. The first two lines were instructive. It began:

> Allegations have been made about the conduct of our Ambassador in Tashkent, Craig Murray. These allegations came to light during visits by Personnel Directorate and Eastern Department to the Post.

That is of course wrong. Allegations about me were fed to Colin Reynolds of the Personnel Directorate before his visit, not during it. And they were fed to him by the Eastern Department.

Astonishingly, in this minute Simon Pease fails to note the result of the investigation by Colin Reynolds of his own directorate. Colin Reynolds had reported that he 'dug fairly deeply in this area' and went on to clear me of the allegations. This Simon Pease minute gives the exact opposite of the truth, claiming that Colin Reynolds' visit added to the allegations, rather than throwing severe doubt upon them.

My copy of this minute was given to me after I made a legal application under the Data Protection Act. Large areas have been blacked out, allegedly for reasons of national security. This includes blacking out the list of people it was copied to. My source within Jack Straw's office tells me that this is because the list included Number 10, the Cabinet Office and MI6.

But it does show that it was copied to Jack Straw. And there is a manuscript note on the minute dated 1 September from Sir Michael Jay to Jack Straw. It reads:

Secretary of State

> Updates our conversation last week. Gareth Evans has now spoken to me, and written to you. Tony Crombie is content for the arrangements for the enquiry ie Craig Murray to stay away from the embassy. Perhaps we could discuss again at our next bilateral on 3 September.

In his own hand, Jack Straw replied: 'I agree with this approach. JS'

This is very significant. It proves that Jack Straw was actively involved in the attempt to get rid of me and regularly discussing it at meetings with Sir Michael Jay. In fact, my 'Deep Throat' tells me there were seven such meetings. Yet to the media and to Parliament, Jack Straw has repeatedly denied that he had any involvement with the disciplinary allegations or attempts to remove me from Tashkent.

The Gareth Evans referred to is the former Australian Foreign Minister. I had never met Gareth Evans, but he had heard from people on the ground what a good job I was doing. The minute also noted that a blacked-out name had telephoned the Head of HRPD '. . . to allege that policy differences with the FCO over human rights have led to a campaign by the FCO to remove the Ambassador' and that local businesses in Tashkent had written in my support.

Now the truth is that you could remove 99 per cent of British ambassadors from their job tomorrow and nobody would care. Most expatriate business communities would heave a sigh of relief and hope vainly the next one might be better. I can think of nowhere I had served where the local staff would have actively supported the ambassador, let alone former Australian foreign ministers. Did all this interest lead them to conclude that perhaps I wasn't actually a useless, corrupt old drunk? No, rather Pease warned: 'UK Parliamentary and Press interest is therefore quite possible.' In other words, they would have to work hard on the spin – always New Labour's first concern.

They had to be seen to be acting behind a charade of formality. Pease continues, immediately after noting the parliamentary and press interest: 'It is important that we handle the investigation strictly according to FCO procedures. Tony Crombie, ex Moscow, has been briefed on the latest developments and has agreed to carry out the investigation.'

The rest of that paragraph is blanked out – four more lines. It is fascinating to wonder what it said about the conduct of the investigation that has to be hidden.

When Howard Drake first handed me these allegations, I had been severely shaken. It was hard to believe that the organisation I had worked for very successfully for nearly 20 years was now acting against me with such appalling malice. Then I started to cheer up: the allegations were so far removed from the truth, they must be easy to fight off.

But once back in Tashkent, it was very difficult. Because I wasn't allowed to mention the allegations to anyone, I could do nothing to prepare a defence. And Dominic Schroeder had sent his minute to every member of British staff, so they all knew exactly the hymn-sheet from which the office wished them to sing. They all had their careers to think of and were very jumpy. It was hard for them to deal with a boss who they knew was hated at the top of the organisation and likely to disappear any minute. They were at the same time anxious individually to indicate to me that none of them had wanted this to happen. They had made some individual management points when they had been trawled for complaints, not knowing they were feeding into a devastating and unwarranted personal attack alleging corruption.

I was getting more and more agitated about my inability to defend myself. On 26 August, I emailed Kate Smith:

Kate

   . . . For example, one completely untrue accusation against me is that I am habitually late for work and drunk or hungover on arrival. This is easily disproved – I can call as witnesses the cook who prepares and serves my breakfast, the drivers who take me to work, the gate guards at each end of the journey who know what time I leave and arrive, the staff I work closely with. But I am not allowed to contact any of these potential defence witnesses. As I understand the office intends me to leave Uzbekistan very shortly, and as it will be very hard indeed to build my case from outside Uzbekistan, this prohibition seems completely unfair. This is especially so as it does not apply to Eastern Department.

   Craig

I think it is fair to say that Kate was now convinced and started to work very hard on my behalf, which was to be crucial. Howard Drake had given me the deadline of 29 August to voluntarily resign. I had to communicate my decision to Dominic Schroeder. If I didn't jump, the office would decide whether to push me, and Howard had left me in little doubt as to the outcome.

On 27 August, a further blow fell. In reply to my minute refuting the allegations, I received an email saying that Sir Michael Jay had banned me from entering my own embassy. I was still Ambassador but not allowed on embassy grounds. That was plainly an impossible position and could only be the prelude to my dismissal two days later. It would also remove me from my computer and files and make it impossible for me to mount a defence. The situation was becoming absolutely Kafkaesque.

Jay's decision was based on allegations that I had been pressurising staff, following complaints allegedly gathered by phone by Dominic Schroeder. I was given no opportunity to deny these untrue complaints before being banned from my own office. As noted above, that tactic was specifically approved by Jack Straw.

I left my office on 28 August 2003, convinced I would never see it again. I was clearing out and had to explain to Kristina that I had been banned from the embassy and expected to be asked to leave Tashkent permanently the following day. I gave her a brief description of the nature of the allegations against me. She was first incredulous, then reduced to tears. Fifteen minutes later, Kristina, Lena, Yuliya, Atabek, Nafisa, Dmitri and I were all in my office and all in tears. I had now broken the instruction not to tell anyone about the allegations, but I had been punished for that before I had done it, by being banned from the embassy, so I wasn't too bothered.

I left with the declaration from the staff that they would fight this ringing in my ears. As I left for the Residence, they got to work.

That very afternoon, Jack Straw and Sir Michael Jay received a letter signed by 90 per cent of the Uzbek office staff of the embassy.

> 28 August 2003
> His Excellency
> Jack Straw
> Secretary of State
> Foreign & Commonwealth Office
> London
>
> Your Excellency,
> . . . Ever since he arrived in Tashkent, Craig Murray had been the most active and outspoken critic of the Uzbek

government's poor human rights record and lack of economic progress. His famous speech at the opening of the Freedom House was the first public criticism of the Uzbek Government and its anti-reform policies in the run-up to the EBRD Board of Directors in the annual meeting in Tashkent. He has been the main agent for raising the profile and support for civil society reforms and promoting political and economic freedom in this complex environment. Notably, his voice was heard and respected not only by international community but more importantly, by host government. It goes without saying that any positive changes however small and hard fought, bear personal contribution by Craig Murray. He is considered here as the undisputed star of the diplomatic corps and renowned leader of the international business community.

He is not only seen as the most active promoter of democratic and civil society values but also as an ardent supporter of economic liberalisation and regional economic cooperation and integration. His frequent visits to the projects managed by UK businessmen are highly praised both by foreign and local entrepreneurs who, in all honesty, are not used to seeing ambassadors in their premises. He is the first high ranking diplomat to combine effectively his human rights and economic/political duties. He is professionally capable of dealing with the most difficult commercial issues and addressing them in the most appropriate ways at the highest political level. British and local business communities and the Uzbek Government hold his personal views in high regard. His persistent efforts to engage with the government on the need for economic liberalisation in Uzbekistan have had its impact on the minds of local officials. Major British investors such as Oxus, Trinity, UzBAT, Wakefield Inspection Services, British Airways and many others consider Craig's personal involvement as the crucial factor in implementing their projects. In countries with a difficult political environment the importance of personal interventions can hardly be underestimated. Craig is a valuable asset and is good at solving problems and suggesting alternative decisions.

Craig Murray commands sympathy and the respect of the embassy staff and British commercial circles in Uzbekistan. He is admired for his professional abilities and a great sense of humour.

We strongly feel that his departure from this post will not only lower the morale of embassy staff but also reflect negatively on the embassy image in local and foreign institutions present in Uzbekistan.

> Sincerely Yours,
> Atabek Sharip
> Mansur Mansurov
> Kristina Ozden
> Lena Son
> Dmitri Potemkin
> Nafisa Nasyrova
> Nilufar Ibragimova
> Ravshan Salidjanov
> Shadiya Akhunova
> Farhod Babulaev
> Umid Abudallaev
> Victoria Belyarskaya
> Yuliya Usatova
> Dima Yelkov

That seems pretty powerful, especially as unhappiness of locally engaged staff was one of the four reasons Howard Drake had given for my removal from Tashkent. But the FCO were too subtle for this. The Personnel Directorate sent a handwritten note to Michael Jay on a copy of this letter:

> PUS,
> This is potentially valuable as evidence that Murray has put pressure on staff. It therefore justifies your decision to ban Murray from the embassy. There is no reason to suppose that these are genuine views of the local staff.

No reason except, of course, Colin Reynolds' report of six weeks before, which stated: 'The LE staff were uniformly positive about Craig during my visit.'

But that report was now deemed to have backed the Schroeder case, even though it contradicted it. The truth is that I had no idea that this letter was being written. It was terribly brave of them given that five of them had been temporarily suspended just three weeks before as part of the moves against me.

The FCO might have been pleased that they managed to twist the staff letter into evidence against me, but just two hours later the fax machines whirred again in Michael Jay's and Jack Straw's offices, and a letter arrived in my support signed by 15 British businesses in Tashkent, including British Airways, British American Tobacco, QuickStop, Oxus and Trinity Energy. The letter stated that:

> Craig Murray is without doubt the British Ambassador who has put the most effort into promoting British commercial and economic interests, and the only British Ambassador who has had real clout with the Government of Uzbekistan.

The moment this letter arrived, the wheels came off the plan to sack me. Plainly, I could not be an incompetent alcoholic. The attempt to force me out on that pretext failed when the effort to keep it all quiet failed. The Foreign Office had failed to hush up the stitch-up.

But the political imperative to be rid of me was still there. Tessa Redmayne telephoned to say that, irrespective of the outcome of the 18 allegations, I would now face a 19th serious disciplinary allegation: I had broken the instruction not to tell anybody about the allegations.

Meanwhile, those fax machines kept churning. Individual letters of support started pouring into Jack Straw's office. One of the first was from former Australian Foreign Minister Gareth Evans, now President of the International Crisis Group (ICG).

> 29 August 2003
>
> Dear Jack,
>
> I have learned that you are considering recalling your Ambassador to Uzbekistan, Craig Murray. I would normally not even think of commenting on a matter so clearly within HMG's competence but the case is unusual. The man in question is a most prominent diplomat in a specially sensitive area where ICG is deeply involved, and it is the perception of our people on the ground – whose judgement I highly respect – that such a move has the potential to be quite damaging for the British government's image in Uzbekistan and perceptions of its wider foreign policy goals and ideals.
>
> ICG's Central Asia staff based in the Ferghana Valley have considerable experience in Uzbekistan and a good

understanding of the activities of the UK embassy. Murray has a reputation in the country as one of the few diplomats able and willing to make strong representations to a notoriously obdurate government on a wide range of issues, from human rights abuses to economic reform. Of course he has run into considerable opposition from the authorities but he has been extremely influential in gathering support around a more coherent international policy towards Uzbekistan that is shared by at least most European governments, the IMF, World Bank and other international organisations. His forthright approach has been a useful balance to some perhaps over-accommodating aspects of US foreign policy.

The allegations against Murray that we are aware of – and of course we cannot be as well informed as you and your department on all the internal dimensions of this matter – are considered either trivial or unsubstantiated by my senior ICG people, who have personal knowledge of the man and his work in the difficult Tashkent environment. The risk under these circumstances is that his recall would inevitably be viewed by the Uzbeks and many internationals as intimately connected with his strong support for human rights, democratisation, and economic reforms, all avowed aims of UK policy in the region. Murray has been particularly effective in promoting the image of the UK among Muslims in Uzbekistan, at a time of growing suspicion in that community of Western interests.

My people on the ground consider Murray the best-informed Ambassador in Tashkent. He has taken considerable pains to understand how the system works, and has travelled widely throughout the country. He has won influence among Uzbek elites and has been the most prominent member of the diplomatic community for some time. He has significantly raised the profile of the UK in Uzbekistan and gained considerable respect among international organisations, other diplomatic missions and the local population. He has also been, I should frankly acknowledge, extremely helpful to the ICG in helping us cope with some of the pressures to which a key member of our locally-engaged staff has been subjected by the Uzbek authorities.

Ambassador Murray has been a very effective advocate for British foreign policy goals during his year in Tashkent. His recall, for whatever reason, so early in the normal tour of duty certainly carries with it some risks – in both policy and political terms – which I thought it proper to convey to you from ICG's perspective. I simply ask you to ensure that the considerations I have raised are fully taken into account before any irrevocable action is taken.

> Sincerely
> GARETH EVANS
> President
> International Crisis Group

Of course, it was correct but not really helpful of Evans to note that I was providing a useful balance to US foreign policy. It was because of this that Straw wanted rid of me. The British government didn't want US policy balanced, they wanted it unquestioningly backed. This was the War on Terror, black and white, with us or against us.

A letter from Hartley Booth, former Tory MP and now the official figurehead for UK/Uzbek trade promotion, was addressed to me and copied to the FCO:

> 7 September 2003
> Dear Craig,
> I have been informed that there are questions about your performance as British Ambassador in Tashkent. I am horrified, to say the least. As both the Chairman of the official British Uzbek Trade & Industry Council and as Chairman of the British-Uzbek Society, I have had opportunities to see you in operation on behalf of Britain. You have three unusual and special qualities, in my observation and based on the reports I have received.
>
> 1. You have quickly grasped the most complex issues of the posting and formed accurate and sound judgements on them – a quality not always immediately found in outposts such as Tashkent.
> 2. You have been fearless and most helpful to British interests in Uzbekistan by your pursuit of the logical conclusion from your judgements inside the Uzbek government.
> 3. You have gone out of your way to provide help for the brave frontline of British interests that I too am in post to defend and promote. All businessmen I have met and with whom

I have had occasion to discuss you over the past year have said that you have been the best ever British Ambassador in Tashkent from their standpoint.

Please show this to whom it may concern. I will attempt to have this passed to the Head of Department FCO and am happy to give confidential advice to anyone in appropriate authority.

> With Best Wishes
> Dr V E Hartley Booth

Against all diplomatic procedure, letters of support came from staff heading the UNDP, EBRD and European Commission headquarters in Tashkent. The American Chamber of Commerce wrote in my defence.

The reviews were great and just kept pouring in:

I have been in the country for nine years now . . . During this period I have known three British ambassadors before the present incumbent, and I can say without hesitation that Mr Murray is easily the most effective of all four . . .

When he first arrived, Mr Murray made a point of personally visiting each and every British company here, and of spending some time with them genuinely eliciting their concerns and aspirations. This was entirely unheard of, and brought Mr Murray the trust, respect and even affection of the British community. He then set about promoting Britain (through imaginative promotions, concerts, receptions and sponsorships) in the eyes of the Uzbek public (to such an extent that our stock has never been so high) and the interests of British business through constant and effective lobbying of the Uzbek government.

Construction Contracting Consultants Ltd

We have welcomed the honest, open and direct approach that Ambassador Murray and his staff have shown when dealing with the Uzbek government, both on our behalf, and on other important issues such as human rights, property rights, and economic reform . . .

The Uzbeks clearly recognised that by picking a fight with

a British company, they were also acting against the interests of the British government and the British embassy, Tashkent. The Uzbeks do choose their battles carefully and will avoid conflicts with stronger parties. It is therefore essential that UzPEC continue to receive the strong and active support of Ambassador Murray . . .

Uzbek Petroleum Enhancement Company Ltd

I have known the British Ambassador in Tashkent, Mr Craig Murray, since his arrival more than a year ago and in my opinion he is a very intelligent, resourceful and original person . . . Mr Murray contributed to the ongoing dialogue with the government to improve the foreign investment climate and he supported foreign and local businessmen in their efforts to do business in a very difficult economic environment. Mr Murray is a 'Breath of fresh air' in the diplomatic community . . .

ABN AMRO Bank

In order to ensure that the £20 million contract is concluded successfully in our favour, I approached Ambassador Murray for advice. After seeing the documentation he personally took interest in the matter and has been doing everything that the British embassy can possibly do . . .

I have had the privilege of personally knowing all Her Majesty's ambassadors who have served in Uzbekistan so far and I have found H.E. Mr Murray to be the most capable and professional ambassador. He is very compassionate and friendly and always available to promote British business interests in Uzbekistan.

DIL International Ltd

. . . Mr Murray dealt with our issues directly. With his personal involvement he successfully convinced the governor of Jizak region not to overuse his authority against British personnel. Working on 'Jibri' joint venture in Jizak, in another case, with his help we restored our share in 'Ohangaron Rangli Sement' JV after it was taken away by the State Privatisation Committee of Uzbekistan.

Eurocommerce UK Ltd

Dear Ambassador,

I would like to thank you for your assistance in terms of lobbying the interests of our venture 'UzCase Tractor' with the government of Uzbekistan, thereby resulting in a $1 million export contract from the UK.

Case Tractors UK

The role of the British embassy in supporting British businesses and improving Uzbek-British relationships has significantly increased with the arrival of His Excellency Ambassador Murray . . . he had been highly effective in introducing people and facilitating conversations. This directly assisted some important bond finance launches . . .

Carthill Investment Company Ltd

The role of the . . . Ambassador Mr Craig Murray during the last nine months has been significant. Without the strong support and backing of the Ambassador we would not have achieved the very positive results which we have achieved today and continue to achieve . . .

Trade Development

British Mediterranean Airways started operating their flights to Tashkent on 31st March 2003. Mr Craig Murray, British Ambassador, played a great role in this . . .

British Airways

Craig has been an active supporter of the project to establish Westminster International University in Tashkent. Craig took a particular interest in the formation of the students' union. He advised the students on the development of the SU constitution and acted as returning officer at the first SU elections. Craig brought his unique style and flair to this process . . . Craig made a valuable contribution to establishing the ethos of the University. After free and fair elections Craig hosted a reception for the entire student body . . .

University of Westminster

The current Ambassador, Craig Murray, has been particularly active in . . . assisting British companies with their activities in Uzbekistan. The support given to us does not only include assisting with relationships with central government, but also a site visit last November (which did much to promote Oxus in Navoi and Zarafshan), and briefings with visiting bankers, brokers and other members of the London financial community.

Oxus Mining

Our efforts in Tashkent have resulted in significant business for us. We have visited Tashkent frequently over the past twelve months and have received excellent assistance and advice. I have had the pleasure of personally discussing our activities with the Ambassador Mr Craig Murray and have received continued support from him throughout this time.

Geest Overseas Ltd

The current Ambassador has been proactive in helping this British company to lobby the Government of Uzbekistan for liberalisation of the economy and to resolve many Company specific issues relating to taxes, joint venture privileges, issues associated with state prosecutors as well as security issues. Senior Management has immediate and open access to the Ambassador often at short notice. This gives us the confidence to continue to operate in this challenging environment. We know we can count on the embassy and the Ambassador for immediate and sympathetic help in the event of any crisis.

British American Tobacco

I told you it had been a busy year – I am amazed myself by this solid record of achievement in just one year, as well as the action I had taken on human rights and the EBRD and dealing with major staff problems.

The above represent just extracts from a selection. I calculate Jack Straw's fax machine received at least 87 pages of letters in support of me from those with a direct interest.

Plainly, the weight of this material clearly contradicted the story from the Eastern Department that I was an incompetent drunk who didn't turn up to work and did not have the respect of either his staff or the local British community. If the senior management had genuinely been reacting to reports initiated from below, it is inconceivable that, faced with all this, someone at a higher level would not have started sending minutes querying whether Simon Butt and Dominic Schroeder had got their assessment of me right. That this did not happen can only mean that the 'Murray must go' line indeed came from above. In fact, yet again the only senior reaction to this correspondence was not to consider the content on its merits but to accuse me of conspiring to conduct a campaign.

So the office introduced a further refinement. Tony Crombie, formerly of our embassy in Moscow, had been appointed to conduct the investigation. I was informed by Tessa Redmayne that this would be a purely internal affair. Crombie would not talk to, or consider evidence from, anybody not employed by the British government.

The deck was being loaded still further against me. My feelings of helplessness were starting to spiral towards despair. The injustice of it all stunned me. I had put my heart and soul into the job and made a real impact, despite some terrific handicaps. This letter campaign in my support had no stimulation from me at all. Kristina and Lena had started it, and the business community had taken it up with spontaneous enthusiasm. It is truly unusual – other British ambassadors just wouldn't get that kind of support because they wouldn't have given so much of themselves for their communities. The common theme running through the letters was that I was better than other British ambassadors. But if I had done very little and been quietly inactive, the FCO would have been perfectly happy with me. They didn't want me doing stuff. I was meant to be ornamental, not effective.

The 29th came: the date when I was expected to resign. I said I was tired and would like another day to think about it. They said no, I couldn't have another day. Still, I didn't reply until the 30th, and I told them that as I had done nothing wrong, I wouldn't go. They would have to sack me.

After that, it all went eerily quiet. I was extremely busy anyway. The Lord Mayor and Lady Mayoress of London were visiting along with the Sheriff of London and his wife. They had a very full programme, including meeting Karimov himself, Prime Minister Usmanov and the ministers of foreign economic relations and industry. I hosted a number of functions including a briefing lunch with British companies and an evening reception for 400. For this, the Residence garden was beautifully illuminated with thousands of fairy lights and flaming torches, and the entertainment included a chamber orchestra, jazz band, dancers and acrobats.

I had a new deputy now, Carl Garn. He was very pleasant and

efficient but seemed to me not to be very decisive. He found himself thrown into the middle of an impossible position. I had to run the whole mayor's visit while trying to disguise the fact I was banned from the embassy and couldn't approach my own office.

But all of the meetings went extremely well. The Lord Mayor, Gavyn Arthur, had to keep explaining that his was the ancient office of Dick Whittington and confined to the original City and its business interests rather than the much bigger job and area of Ken Livingstone.

He could be rather brusque. He continually asked more and more detailed questions about such subjects as rates of corporation tax or changes in import tariffs. Luckily, I could answer. He also was very good at assimilating and presenting all this various material. He put very firmly to the Uzbek authorities the need for economic liberalisation to promote foreign investment, and he even succeeded in interrupting the famous Karimov 40-minute introductory 'Paranoid' speech. For some reason, all the Uzbeks, from Karimov down, were effusive in their praise of me. They all raved about the music festival in particular with such uniformity that it was plainly part of a central script.

The local business community made sure that the Lord Mayor knew of my problems and what they thought of them. One of the Mayor's ports of call was British American Tobacco. As we left, Rene Ijsselstein, the manager, came up and grasped my hand as I was about to get into the car.

'Look, Craig,' he said, 'try not to worry too much. Anything we can do, anything at all, just let me know.'

At this stage, it was expressions of kindness that I found most difficult; I had learnt to cope with unremitting hostility. My lip was trembling, and I turned my face to look out of the window. Gavyn Arthur said to me, 'Ambassador, you should know I saw Rene's gesture, and I know what it is about. I have noted your complete support from the British business community, and I will make sure my views are known at the appropriate level in London.'

* * *

One of the first things I had done on arrival was go to see Nadira and tell her that I wouldn't be able to see her for a while as I was under investigation, and it was even possible I would suddenly leave the country and never see her again. She found this impossible to accept. I had seemed so solidly wealthy and powerful to her, she didn't believe it could vanish, and she presumed this was just a brush-off after I had reconciled with Fiona on holiday.

Nadira had been having a particularly nasty time in my absence. She had been twice raped by the police. On one occasion she had pleaded with the policeman not to take her virginity, and he had raped her anally. On the second occasion, which had been in a Nissan Maxima, the policeman was a very senior one. He had ignored her pleas and used violence as well as coercion, but luckily he had been unable to sustain an erection.

Nadira was hurt that I had been away, not contacted her from Canada, and now that I was back I was saying that I wouldn't be in touch. I was hurt about the rapes. It in no way excused the policemen, but in one case she had voluntarily entered his flat to go to a 'party' and in the other had voluntarily entered his car for a lift from a bar. Sexual assault is never justified, but I didn't view her behaviour as sensible. So our meeting was an occasion of mutual hurt, misunderstanding and anger. I reacted by withdrawing still further into self-pity. Nadira reacted by going out partying with other men.

So Nadira added to my problems. On 5 September, when to my surprise I was still in Tashkent, I went to her flat, now on the 12th floor of a block at Zhemchuk. I told her I was going away, perhaps for a fortnight, perhaps longer, and gave her $300. I went out to the balcony and looked down. I felt an overwhelming desire to jump, but I was saved by a chance remark from Nadira, who said that from here she saw Karimov drive past every morning. That brought my mind back to the struggle against dictatorship, to which I still had much to contribute.

* * *

I somehow came through the Lord Mayor's visit. I recently met someone to whom I spoke at my reception for the Lord Mayor, and he says that he found me lucid and outwardly fine. But inside I was falling apart, and in fact I have very little memory of that fortnight in Tashkent. The Lord Mayor having flown off on the sixth, and with Fiona returning on the eighth to look after Emily, I could give up the terrible effort to soldier on. I collapsed completely, mentally and physically. The feeling of helplessness, that I was crushed by an unrelenting hostility with no course of action to defend myself, manifested itself in physical helplessness. I lost the use of my muscles and cried continually. Someone got a doctor to me, and they flew me back to London the next day, Dr Reimers beside me. I did not positively want to kill myself, but I had lost the desire to live. It was the viciousness and injustice of the allegations, combined with not being allowed to fight them, that did for me.

CHAPTER 17

Purgatory

It is very difficult to write this next chapter. This is partly because the memories remain extremely painful. But I have probably already lost your sympathy with the explanation of my collapse at the end of the last chapter. It looks pathetic to me as I read it now. But the shock of facing those allegations, the realisation that everything I had worked for was over and my reputation ruined, and the feeling of being crushed by an implacable malevolence, temporarily destroyed my reason. I found myself a psychiatric in-patient at St Thomas's Hospital in London, in a private room in the Westminster ward on the top floor. Diana Nelson from the FCO's welfare section was in charge of my care.

For the first ten days, I was on suicide watch. This involved a burly male nurse watching my every move 24 hours a day, and even following me into the loo. I can promise you, if you are not suicidal before, you will be after ten days of having a large male nurse follow you into the loo.

I was sedated and quietly monitored for the first 48 hours or so, then the consultant psychiatrist, Professor Michael Kopelman, came and sat for with me for three hours as I told him in brief the story contained in this book.

As I spoke, I realised that my story sounded absolutely extraordinary. Professor Kopelman looked at me seriously, even sternly, as I outlined the whole thing: my arrival in Tashkent, my astonishment at the extent of Western support for the regime, my battles with Whitehall over it, the sudden raft of false charges, my inability to cope with having my basic integrity questioned, the appalling helplessness of being faced with these accusations and told that I was not allowed to discuss them with anyone or prepare any defence. I fought back tears as I tried to explain how I felt at having my reputation and life's work destroyed, with no hope of self-defence.

People came under Professor Kopelman's care because they were mad. As I looked at his concerned face, I wondered, does he believe me or does he think I am imagining it? When I finished, he looked at me silently for 30 seconds (which feels like a long time in those circumstances). Then his features suddenly broke into a boyish grin, 'You know what I think, Mr Murray?' he said. 'I can help get you well again, but what you really need is a good fighting lawyer.'

I cannot tell you the relief I felt at finding someone on my side. I said thank you, buried my face in the pillow and had my first real sleep in five days.

The next morning, Professor Kopelman returned to see me and prescribed Venlafaxine, which is quite a powerful anti-depressant. 'This is quite a high dosage,' he said, 'but it will still take around ten days before it really kicks in. I imagine that you will be with us for a few weeks yet, but you will probably stay on Venlafaxine when you leave, for a while at least. Now it's generally a well-tolerated drug, but you must not mix it with alcohol. Also, its most notable side effect is that it can decrease libido. That's no problem in here, but it could be a problem when you leave. Do you have any questions?'

'Yes. Can't drink, reduced sex drive. How is it supposed to cheer me up?'

I can't really describe to you the agonies of those first days in St Thomas's. Mental torture can be as terrible as physical, and I writhed and squirmed and knew no rest. But after three interminable weeks, I calmed. I read a lot of books and started some initial research to write a life of Palmerston. Eventually, Professor Kopelman said that they had decided I was sufficiently recovered to leave hospital for the weekend. We would see how it went, and if everything was OK, we could try a couple more weekends, until it was time to continue treatment as an outpatient. I felt pretty happy at this and made plans to travel north to stay with my sister and her husband for the weekend.

In the hustle of St Pancras Station, I began to feel afraid. The bustle and noise intimidated me. I realised how pathetic this was for a formerly intrepid traveller and managed to pull myself together, stand in the queue and buy my ticket. I know how feeble it sounds, but I had two aborted attempts to join the queue before I succeeded, sheering away at the last moment and pretending I was doing something else. Mental illness is a different country, difficult to explain to someone who hasn't been there.

The weekend was a success, despite the agony of withdrawal I suffered after forgetting to pack my medication, and two weeks later Professor Kopelman released me into out-patient care. I went to live with my brother Stuart in Morley Road, Leyton. This is hardly the most salubrious of areas – indeed, it is one of the least salubrious areas in the UK, with an extraordinary proportion of illegal immigrants and a high unemployment rate. Stuart's flat is the converted top floor of a two-storey house that was pretty small in the first place. Stuart shares this with a fellow Metropolitan policeman, Steve, an easy-going Yorkshireman. My bed was an old mattress squeezed onto the living-room floor between the sofa and the television. We found an old curtain for a blanket and I took a sofa cushion for a pillow, but the moment my head nestled into it I went under and slept like a baby.

The next morning, I called Fiona. She was highly suspicious that Adam Noble, whom the Foreign Office had sent out as a temporary replacement, was intended to take over from me permanently. He had been to look round the Residence, which he had compared unfavourably with his house in Moscow. Fiona was also being pestered almost continually by journalists at this point but referred them on to James McGrory, who had kindly volunteered to deal with mounting interest from the media. She was most occupied at the moment in organising the Guy Fawkes' Night party for the British community. She wanted advice on how much to spend on fireworks and was having little response to her email request to Brits in Tashkent to help supply firewood. On top of this, she was organising the curry lunch for Commonwealth citizens after the Remembrance Sunday service. The defence section had recommended inviting only British citizens, but she was inclined to invite all Commonwealth, as we had done the year before (I agreed with her). All in all, she was kept pretty busy.

Fiona did a brilliant job in this period, refusing to leave Tashkent and the Residence, and continuing to host the functions and perform the social duties of the ambassador. The Foreign Office kept suggesting she might like to come back to the UK, out of a pretended concern for her welfare, which Fiona saw straight through. With journalists now all over the story, the Foreign Office didn't feel able to evict her.[60]

I also called Nadira but as usual got number unobtainable. I sent her an email message from Stuart's laptop and took the opportunity to catch up on my Hotmail – a combination of requests for interviews from journalists and goodwill messages from friends.

Handling journalists was going to be increasingly difficult now I was out of hospital. Three things had kept me in my job – the powerful media reaction in the UK in my favour, the extremely strong reaction of the British business community in Tashkent and the support of the embassy staff. Of these, the media reaction was, far and away, the most important. I was, therefore, very keen not to alienate journalists by non-cooperation. On the other hand, speaking to journalists would give the FCO the excuse it so desperately wanted to sack me; I needed to be able to look officials in the eye and say truthfully that I had not been speaking to journalists. While I had been in hospital and unable to defend myself, James McGrory in Tashkent and a friend Andy Myles in Edinburgh had been voluntarily speaking to journalists in my defence, while Steve Crawshaw of HRW in London gave them background information on the human rights situation in Uzbekistan. It was now time to elevate this to a deliberate policy, to keep this network of media handlers fully briefed and to refer journalists to them.

Thus was born the network of 'Friends of Craig Murray', who appeared frequently in the press and over the next three months conducted a media campaign that completely defeated the government spinning machine.

That machine did its best. At least four journalists told me that they had been warned by the FCO not to support me because I was a hopeless drunk and that, when the truth came out, they would look foolish. The FCO very early on leaked details of the allegations to *The Guardian*. My own friends in journalism have been invaluable in relaying such information back to me, and I also met with the prominent newspaper columnist Nick Cohen at this time. He had lunched with an FCO minister who had been adamant that the pressure to remove me came from Number 10.

I was already well known to a lot of senior journalists, and they simply didn't believe the allegations against me. Virtually every

British newspaper sent a journalist to Tashkent, and they crawled all over the bars and hotels trying to dig up dirt on me. This included the tabloids, who would have loved to run an 'Ambassador sells visas for sex' story. But, without exception, the media concluded from their own investigations that there was no truth in the allegations and that they had been trumped up because of my concerns about the human rights record of an ally of the United States in the War on Terror.

* * *

Stuart was not working the day after I moved into his flat and over breakfast we discussed my next moves.

'You know,' I told him, 'I have half a mind just to pack up my things and go back to Tashkent on Friday. It would wrong-foot them completely. At the moment, they are trying to deny to the media that anything is wrong and are saying I am just back for medical treatment. Well, if I am back in Tashkent, that line's going to make it a hell of a lot more difficult for them to drag me back here again without an enormous uproar in the press.'

'Yes, good plan,' said Stuart. We both knew I was joking.

I next called Andrew Mackinlay, Labour MP for Thurrock and a member of the House of Commons Foreign Affairs Committee (FAC). He told me that, in response to media reports, my case had been discussed informally among members of the FAC. However, members were scared to move because of the death of Dr David Kelly. The government had implied that heavy questioning by sceptical members of the Foreign Affairs Committee may have contributed to his (alleged) suicide. Given that the FCO was briefing that I was mentally disturbed, the Committee, and Chairman Donald Anderson in particular, were unwilling to open this one up in case I topped myself.

Stuart and I went to do some shopping and then went to an Indian restaurant for some lunch and a couple of beers. I was trying just to relax and de-institutionalise myself. When we got back, there was a phone message from Diana Nelson. It said that I was not to return to Tashkent at the weekend but must wait for medical clearance from Professor Kopelman. There was some strain in her normally well-modulated voice. Stuart and I joked that they must have had the flat bugged and heard my reference the previous night to going back at the weekend.

Then it got heavy. Carl Garn phoned from Tashkent. He said that the staff were very excited because of a rumour I was coming back at the weekend. He understood, he added, that I was still undergoing medical treatment. What should he say to the staff? I told him not to worry – I was not well yet.

Next came a phone call from Simon Butt. He asked if I knew it would be a disciplinary offence to return without medical clearance. I just said thank you and hung up. Then the secretary of Andrew George, Diana Nelson's boss, telephoned with the same message. Finally, Professor Kopelman phoned. He had heard, he said, from FCO Medical Advisers that I was planning to return at the weekend. I assured him that I was well aware that I was not yet fully recovered and told him I had no idea how the rumour started.

That bit of course was not true. I had never been serious about the idea of returning immediately to Tashkent, but the humour had been deadpan and might not have been picked up by a listener. Perhaps the degree of panic it was causing showed what a good plan it would have been! Stuart and I had both been aware of the possibility that we would be bugged, but from now on we were particularly careful and held any sensitive conversations out on the street among crowds on the pavement.

You can be bugged very easily. A sound bug can be no bigger than a pin, but it is not necessary to plant one. Directional microphones are very effective and can be used from several hundred metres away if necessary, but it is much easier to use the telephone. Either a home landline or a mobile can be remotely activated to serve as a microphone, bugging the room even though the handset is down or the mobile switched off. The resulting sound can be cleaned up to surprising quality.

We were rather sombre that evening, both as a result of the thought that we were being bugged and from phone calls that demonstrated the continued determination of the government to stop me from getting back to Tashkent. However, as I said to Stuart, things were by no means all black. The position was much better than could have been imagined two months earlier. I was still Ambassador to Tashkent, while the degree of press interest was such that they would now need to come up with something apparently pretty solid to shift me. I did not put this entirely beyond their powers of fabrication, and perhaps they were biding their time until press interest waned, but so far, so good.

For my birthday on Friday, 17 October 2003, I was up in Scotland staying with my cousin Margaret and her family in the idyllic rural village of Braco in Stirlingshire. I had travelled up in order to spend half term with Jamie. A year ago I had been making my declaration for liberty at Freedom House. Now I was a mental patient on a pass. Sadly, one had brought down upon me the wrath that led to the other.

The next morning, there were articles about me in both *The Guardian* and *The Independent*. Both were strongly supportive. The *Guardian* piece was a 'special report' on pages one and two. It was headed 'Ambassador accused after criticising US'. The sub-heading ran: 'The strange case of Britain's outspoken envoy in Uzbekistan who was threatened with sack and faulted for shortcomings after upsetting No. 10.[61] The pressure on the FCO was building.

In the early evening I took phone calls from Andy Myles. He asked if I had direct evidence of US pressure. I said that I had no evidence: when you are attacked from behind your back, by definition you will be the last to know what is happening. But I knew that a number of sources within the FCO and Cabinet Office had been telling journalists that US pressure was involved, and this made perfect sense to me. Andy was particularly excited about contacts with the *Mail on Sunday*. Their reporter, Fidelma Cook, had been particularly sympathetic and seemed to have other good sources.

Early the next morning, Margaret woke Jamie and me and tossed us the *Mail on Sunday*.

'Is there anything about me?' I asked.

'Only on pages 49, 50, 51 and 52,' Margaret replied.

I thought she was joking, but there was a massive four-page story. The front cover of the Review section had a full colour photo, the height of the page, of me in a kilt. A massive red headline screamed: 'Is this the new Dr Kelly?' The sub-heading ran: 'Craig Murray, Britain's Ambassador to Uzbekistan, found himself victim of a string of lurid smears – including drinking and womanising – after he spoke out against torture by the American-backed government. Now he's back in London being treated for depression and friends are asking "Is this the new Dr Kelly?"'[62]

The parallel being drawn was that both David Kelly and I were honest civil servants put under pressure by the Blair government when the truth – on Iraqi WMD or on torture in Uzbekistan – did not coincide with the spin New Labour wanted. It was, I think, a fair parallel to draw.

That evening, a journalist phoned Braco, and, having determined to avoid direct contact with journalists, Jamie and I took off for a few days to a guest house in Aviemore, another of my old haunts. I was very sorry to say goodbye to Jamie at the end of his half term.

My left shoulder suffers from recurrent dislocation, which is extremely painful, and I had undergone surgery for the problem two years previously. Back sleeping on the floor in Stuart's flat, it dislocated again when I got up one morning. An ambulance arrived and while being manhandled down the twisting stairs on a chair, I fell on my shoulder and put it back in again. I was nevertheless taken to Whipps Cross Hospital to confirm all was well. It was here that I first realised I had become a minor celebrity – the doctors and nurses knew who I was.

Two weeks later, Professor Kopelman reckoned I was well enough to return to Tashkent. Knowing they would hate this, I phoned the Eastern Department and told them I would be going on the next available plane. Sure enough, the next morning a letter arrived from Chief Medical Officer Vyv Thornton stating that clearance from Professor Kopelman was not sufficient; I would need to be seen by the FCO Medical Advisers as they had concerns about my shoulder. I was not to get on a plane to Tashkent until I had their approval.

They really didn't want me back in Tashkent. I now needed a specific certification that I was fit to return from the consultant in charge of my shoulder. Thankfully, after my recent visit to Whipps Cross, I had immediately booked an appointment with the surgeon, Professor Povlsen, to check what was happening. As I was a private patient, I got the appointment very quickly, wrong-footing the FCO, and Professor Povlsen confirmed that there was no reason to believe it would dislocate again. He recommended that I do the physiotherapy exercise I had been given and agreed to write to the FCO immediately, giving them clearance for me to go back to Uzbekistan.

Mission accomplished. I left swiftly, returned to the flat in Leyton and started to pack. I called British Airways and made a reservation to return to Tashkent the following afternoon. Now the Foreign Office could no longer hide behind my medical condition, and with the apparent total failure of their investigation to dig up any dirt, despite two months of desperate effort, they would have either to let me back or admit to the media that I was suspended for political reasons.

The next morning, a fax arrived from Professor Kopelman. It was a copy of his letter to the FCO Medical Advisers saying I was fit and well and able to return to Tashkent. I phoned Guy's Hospital, got through to Professor Povlsen's secretary, and she confirmed to me that his letter of clearance had also been faxed. I then telephoned the FCO Medical Advisers office to see if they had received the clearances. There was a sharp intake of breath when I gave my name and a lot of off-stage female whispering noises. Then the voice returned, saying that they would check and call me back. I waited two hours or so, then called again. The records, I was told, were with Dr Thornton. I would have to speak to him. No, he wasn't available at the moment.

I began to smell a rat. I had been medically evacuated several times in the course of my career.[63] Medical clearance to return to post had always been an absolute formality. The whole system was geared to prevent malingering and get you back to work, not to detain you in the UK.

I had quite deliberately manipulated the medical clearances to spring it on the FCO and get back to Tashkent before they could make up their minds to suspend me or take further action. I strongly suspected that they were now striving to slow down the process, on non-medical grounds, while they worked out how to stop me.

The volume of press coverage had been extraordinary and without exception the articles had taken the line that I was a good man being persecuted for pointing out the dirty side of the War on Terror and for exposing the extremely nasty nature of a regime closely allied to the US. I was described as 'colourful' and 'flamboyant', but the allegations of corrupt or dishonest behaviour were ridiculed, described as 'false', 'curious' or even 'trumped-up'.[64]

Journalists from national print and broadcast media were still contacting me every day. I would shrug them off but then tip off Andy or Steve to brief them. I had no doubt that the News Department in the FCO was still under similar pressure, and that is where I now headed. I counted the Deputy Head of the News Department, Andrew Patrick, as among my best friends in the office. Andrew is as honest as they come, and I could talk to him easily.

'Andrew,' I asked, 'are you still getting lots of inquiries about me?'

'God, hundreds,' he groaned.

'What line are you giving?'

'Hang on, I'll print it out for you.' He tapped away at his keyboard and two pages of A4 came out of his printer giving the official line on Craig Murray.

First came the opening statement to give if the subject was raised. It said I had left Tashkent as I was unwell and I was undergoing medical treatment in the UK. There followed a number of possible supplementary questions and the answer to give:

> *Was it true I was under disciplinary investigation?*
> – 'We do not comment on individual staff matters.'
> *What was the nature of my illness, and when would I return to Post?*
> – 'We do not comment on the health or personal circumstances of staff.'
> *Did the FCO support my stance on human rights in Uzbekistan?*
> – 'Yes. As Bill Rammell said to the Foreign Affairs Committee
> . . .'

There were perhaps a dozen more items in this exercise in dodging the question. I read it and looked at Andrew with a smile.

'I am afraid you have to change this, radically,' I said.

'I thought you might say that. Which bit?'

'The basic premise. I now appear before you fit and well. I am no longer gibbering and climbing the trees. My shoulder is healed and I can bowl leg-spin for England again. You see before you a healthy and whole human being.'

'Great,' said Andrew. 'When are you going back?'

'I don't know,' I said. 'Both consultants I am under have sent medical clearance for me to return, but there seems to be some delay in getting medical clearance from the Foreign Office.'

'So you are not fit.'

'No, so I am fit, but the FCO doesn't want to admit it so you can maintain this load of nonsense as the line.'

I handed it back to him. 'But I object to being called sick when I am not, so the next time you tell a journalist I am sick, I am going to contact him and tell him it's not true and send him the medical clearances to prove it. That should give the story some very long legs.'

Andrew looked at me, half wary, half amused.

'I see where you're going,' he said. 'Are you sure you want me to report this?'

'Absolutely. Never surer.'

'OK, what do you think the line should change to, then?'

'How about: *Mr Murray has returned to Tashkent and resumed his duties as Ambassador.*'

'Do you think that's likely?'

'I don't know, Andrew. But if not, you're going to have to tell the truth about why I'm still here.'

'Yes, I got that message.'

'Thanks. Still friends?'

Andrew nodded.

I wandered out of the newsroom and turned right down the high ground-floor corridor to Sir Michael Jay's office on the corner of Downing Street, overlooking St James's Park. In his outer office, I jauntily said hello to his private secretary, Menna.

'PUS in?' I asked.

'Not at the minute,' she replied.

'Anyway, tell him I have got medical clearance and I am going back to Tashkent tomorrow. I just wanted to say goodbye and thank him for his assistance,' I said. Menna looked perplexed as I sauntered out to take the tube back to Leyton.

The next morning, I phoned Medical Advisers again. Once more, the secretaries would not confirm whether the clearances had been received and said I would hear from Dr Thornton. No, he was in consultation at the moment and not available to speak. What time could I see him? He was busy all day. Could I make an appointment? No, not without his confirmation that it was necessary for him to see me.

The secretary I was talking to started by being defensive but progressed to being brusque and downright hostile.

'OK,' I said. 'I'll come in and see him.'

'He is very busy. He doesn't have a spare appointment.'

'That's OK. It'll only take a minute. I only need his confirmation he received the clearances.'

'I cannot guarantee when he will be ready to see you.'

'Don't worry, I'll bring a good book.'

I took Fitzroy Maclean's life of Bonnie Prince Charlie[65] and arrived at Medical Advisers about 11 a.m.

'Hello, I'm Craig Murray.'

'Dr Thornton's busy.'

'That's OK, I'll wait in the waiting room, shall I? Can you let him know I am here?'

'He can't be interrupted.'

'Well, let him know I'm here when you can.'

I climbed back up the half flight of stairs to the waiting room and there then followed a seven-hour charade, during which I repeatedly made my presence known and was basically ignored.

Eventually, I settled into a practice of returning at 45-minute intervals. At 3.15, I was told he had gone out to the American embassy and would not be back until 4.30 p.m. By 4.45, when I was coolly informed that they were not sure if he had returned from the US embassy yet or not, I was starting to get seriously annoyed. When I went back at 5.30 p.m., I found the desks all cleared.

The Medical Department had packed up and gone home, leaving me in the waiting room, without telling me they were going. The sheer rudeness of this annoyed me a lot. It was obvious what the game was – the medical excuse to keep me out of Tashkent had evaporated without warning, there was no evidence against me, and the Administration were desperately searching for a way to stop me. The staff had been instructed to hold the fort and delay me. But leaving me in the waiting room while they slipped out was downright discourteous, particularly when I had waited for almost seven hours.

I decided to confront my personnel 'handlers' on this. First, I went to see Peter Walter and Diana, who were supervising the disciplinary investigation. Their offices were two floors above the Medical and Welfare department. Neither was in. Nor was Howard Drake, my grade manager, whose office was just along the corridor. This was strange – staff in the FCO very rarely get to finish work at 5.30 p.m. Colin Reynolds wasn't in his office, and nor was Diane Corner, the Assistant Director on the disciplinary side, or the Head of Personnel, Alan Charlton. Alan's personal assistant, Margaret, was there. She explained he had gone to a meeting with Jack Straw. I explained to her that I had been left in the Medical Advisers' waiting room for seven hours and then left there when the office closed. I said I knew I was now being kept away from Tashkent on no valid pretext. Alan should know I was hacked off and that they wouldn't get away with it.

I then left Margaret and went over to the main FCO building. I had decided that if the Medical Advisers were being instructed to detain me, there was no point in railing at them; I needed to speak to the people who had instructed them. I arrived at Sir Michael Jay's office. Menna was not in his cramped outer office but about three other minions were. One looked distastefully at my jeans and Arran sweater.

'Can I help you?' he asked.

'I'm Craig Murray,' I said.

That got their attention. Typing stopped and phones were held in mid-air while everyone turned to look at me.

'I want to speak to the PUS. Now!'

There was an uncomfortable silence.

'Er, Sir Michael's with the Secretary of State.'

Less supercilious now – almost awed, which felt good. I turned behind me to look at the whiteboard screwed to the wall next to the door. The PUS's daily diary was always scrawled up there. It was very interesting indeed. Today he had seen Howard Drake, Diana Lees, Simon Butt, Andrew George and Alan Charlton, one after the other. And at the end of the series it said: '*6.30pm S of S re CM*'.

'OK', I said, pointing at the board, 'I'll go and look for him there.'

I walked up the glorious Foreign Office main staircase, the epitome of High Victoriana and imperial grandeur. I went into Jack Straw's outer office on the first floor and spoke to one of his private secretaries. I didn't know him, but he knew me and greeted me by name.

'I would like to see the PUS when he finishes with the Secretary of State,' I said.

He seemed completely unsurprised.

'OK, Craig,' he said. 'Would you like to wait in the ambassadors' waiting room?'

I went out and crossed the wide corridor to the ambassadors' waiting room, a very grand chamber indeed just across the balustraded corner from Jack Straw's office. In this sumptuous area at the head of the main staircase, the walls are covered in massive frescoes. They feature Britannia in different roles, personified by an Amazon with sturdy thighs and baseball breasts. She figures in one fresco as *Britannia Pacifatrix* – Britannia the Peacemaker, dispensing peace – in another as *Britannia Victrix* – Britannia the Victor, looking stern – and in the third as *Britannia Bellatrix* – Britannia the Warrior. She is surrounded by numerous allegorical symbols and by other radiant but lesser damsels personifying other nations, looking like the podium line-up in the Olympic heptathlon, only with a lot more exposed nipple. The overall decorative effect is stupendous, but on close inspection the artist, who donated his services, was a pretty poor draughtsman aspiring to be Frederick Leighton.[66]

I sank down in one of the burnished red-leather easy chairs in the vast room, switched on one of the gold-pillared standard lamps with its heavily brocaded shade and picked a *Guardian* off one of the many highly polished mahogany occasional tables. I had just started on the first article and was contemplating taking my shoes off and sinking them into the thick pile of the Axminster carpet with its Adam shell design when Howard Drake and Peter Walter, the FCO's employment law expert, rushed in, a look of panic on their faces. It was about a minute since I had left the private secretary.

'You asked to see the PUS,' Howard said, as though it was an accusation.

'Yes,' I replied. 'Is he coming?'

'He is tied up with the Secretary of State at the moment.'

'As, I take it, you were?'

No reply came to this; they just stood there looking at me: Peter embarrassed, Howard in a state hovering between apprehension and menace. As they were not making any rational attempt to communicate, I turned back to my newspaper.

'Why do you want to see the PUS?' asked Howard, his indecision resolving into bluster.

'Sit down and I'll tell you.'

'Look, Craig, we don't have much time.'

'That's a pity, it's a long story.'

I turned again back to my newspaper. With a show of reluctance, Howard sat down in a chair opposite me, Peter standing beside him, eyeing me inquisitively.

'Look,' I began, 'I want to go back to Tashkent. As I am sure you have just been discussing with Jack Straw, I have medical clearance from both consultants who are treating me. You cannot claim any longer there is no problem except my illness. But you are messing about with my medical clearance, delaying it on non-medical grounds.

'I have been medi-vacced plenty of times before, and I know damn well that once you get clearance from the consultants, clearance from Medical Advisers is a formality. But for three days now you've been buggering me around. Today I sat for seven hours in the Medical Advisers' waiting room. I called down to the secretaries every 45 minutes to check they knew I was still waiting. But at 5.30 they all buggered off home without telling me they were going, leaving me still in the waiting room. That's not good enough.

'Either you suspend me, or you let me go back to Tashkent. Otherwise, this is going to hit the media still harder. And,' I added gratuitously, 'I am going to report Dr Thornton to the British Medical Association for unethical behaviour in delaying my clearance on non-medical grounds. The media will love that one.'

Howard looked at me warily. 'You must understand that we are primarily interested in your welfare. You have been very ill.'

'Very kind of you. But I am better now. And I want an apology for being kept waiting in the Medical Advisers today.'

Howard said he would pass all this on to the PUS. I felt much better, even though Howard wasn't much of a punchbag. Peter had kept his counsel. After they left, I remained a few minutes to finish perusing the newspaper. As I came out, a small crowd of people were just exiting Jack Straw's office. From Sir Michael Jay downwards, they consisted of everyone who had been dealing with my case, and I could think of no other subject that could possibly bring that precise group together for a meeting with Jack Straw.

It seemed clear to me that Jay's individual meetings all day with these same people must have been part of a massive consultation overseen by Jack Straw. The doctors had been ordered to stall me while they worked out how to stop me.

There was a glorious operatic moment as we paused in that gorgeous palatial setting, looking across the corner of the figured balustrade at each other. Words cannot describe the wave of concentrated hostility I felt directed towards me from that group – and these were supposed to be my colleagues; indeed, some of them had been my friends. What had I done to deserve it? I had insisted on telling the truth and then refused to resign when it had been put to me as the gentlemanly way out.

I contemplated the ironies of the situation. The most reactionary Republican administration in history was giving very active assistance to the group of Soviet apparatchiks in power in Uzbekistan, who were striving with some success to preserve the last remnants of Soviet communism. They were being greatly helped in this by George Bush. He, possibly the most right-wing leader in US history, in turn was supported unquestioningly by a so-called Labour government in the UK. To do this, we had spat on the United Nations, alienated the

French and German opponents of US imperialism, and a Labour government had aligned itself with Silvio Berlusconi.

I am a liberal but was viewed as a left-wing menace by ostensibly Labour ministers while these colleagues, some of whom I knew to hold very right-wing personal views, were delighted at our aggressive and 'Atlanticist' foreign policy. Now they looked at me with contempt but also with puzzlement that they could not make me go away. For a moment, chatter had stopped and we just stared, then I gave a little wave and a grin and walked as jauntily as I could summon down the Grand Staircase, while they resumed their conversations, somewhat hushed now, and several of them put on overcoats or gathered briefcases from the rack in the corridor.

They managed to hold me up for about another week. The meeting had reported to Jack Straw that Tony Crombie to date had been unable to find any substantial evidence against me. He was told to try harder. But fortunately for me, Tony Crombie retained his personal integrity.

My good friend Bryan Harris had returned to the UK, and he kindly lent me a penthouse flat in Docklands, overlooking the Thames. One morning we were driving from there to Stuart's flat to watch a rugby World Cup match on Stuart's satellite TV. Bryan turned on the radio just as the *Today* programme launched into a long and extremely positive report about me from Tashkent. All in all, things were looking up.

CHAPTER 18

What Dreams May Come

I could hardly believe I was really going back. I had won! Most of the serious newspapers covered my pending return as a victory over the Foreign Office, and they were right. The great support from the NGO and business communities, from the British public and media, and from individual MPs and MEPs had foiled their quiet little stitch-up. I also felt pretty clear that once back in Tashkent I could face down any false accusations.

I had impulsively booked a seat on the flight the next day, as soon as the final clearance had come through. I had been in meetings in the Foreign Office until after 8 p.m., then spent all evening answering the phone to journalists and referring them on as news spread. I looked out fondly from the balcony down the Thames to Canary Wharf, thinking it might be the last time I used the flat and saw that wonderful view. I then turned in and quickly slept, exhausted.

The next day, the plane was pretty full, but the BA flight to Tashkent calls at Yerevan, and the large majority of the passengers were only going to Armenia. On this occasion, about 30 were going on to Tashkent, and once the Armenia mob had left us, people began to pick me out and congratulate me on my return, with a steady trickle through the curtain that divided business class from economy. One young Uzbek man had a *Daily Telegraph,* which he flourished in my face, pointing to an article about me. He then grasped both my shoulders and hugged me.

Business class was very comfortable. I had been able to lie out and sleep quite a bit on the London to Yerevan leg, and I read an Ian Rankin novel between Yerevan and Tashkent, getting up occasionally to stretch my legs. The flight was eight hours in total. We had been due in to Tashkent about 4 a.m., but with the Heathrow delay we arrived about 6.30.

When my legs touched Uzbek soil again, I sighed audibly. I hadn't thought I would make it back. Even the greeter from the Uzbek Ministry of Foreign Affairs had a cheesy grin as he formally welcomed me. Entering the VIP lounge, I went to the customs area and looked past it to where Mansur was waiting, positively beaming at the sight of me and giving little skips of delight. With a look that brooked no interference from the Customs officials, he hustled past them and clasped my arms: 'Ambassador! *Ja ochin rad, ochin ochin rad!! Dmitri tozhe, i Kristina, Yulia . . .*'

His voice tailed off then and, re-collecting himself, he retreated back to his place behind the Customs barrier.

Even the little man deputed to collect my luggage seemed to have a spring in his step, and he must have made a positive effort to gather it for once. He reappeared with the bags in only 30 minutes and wheeled them out to the car. Mansur took the Union Jack from inside the Land-Rover and fitted it over its silver mast, commenting that it was good to be flying it for the 'real' Ambassador again.

It was a crisp bright Saturday morning in November. We hurtled round the city bypass at speed and in style, before turning left across the tram tracks and then shooting down a warren of twisting alleys between low houses as we entered the mahalla of the Residence. Mansur beeped the horn joyfully as we approached the big green gates and they swung open, a sturdy guard on each. As I got down from the car, the guards came rushing forward to shake my hand and slap me on the back. They had not even waited to close the gates first, which was a serious security breach, but it didn't seem to matter on this glad morning.

Lena the cook, Reiapa the cleaner and Alijon the steward came rushing down the steps to join in the general jollity. My bags were taken and carried up the steps as I went in to the lounge, where Fiona was waiting for me. She regarded me hostilely as Lena entered the room with me, taking my order for tea and porridge. Once alone,

I embraced Fiona, but she glared at me defiantly through reddened eyes. 'Well?' she demanded, 'what have you decided?'

'Fiona, darling, I am only just back. Let's talk about this later.'

'No,' she said firmly. 'I want to know where I stand. Are you going to give up this floozy?'

'Look,' I said lamely, 'I can't just give her up. I haven't seen her, or you, for months. I need time to think things over.'

'You've had plenty of time!' Fiona was shouting now. 'If you're not prepared to give her up, I want a divorce. It is that simple.'

'Look, I really don't see why we have to get divorced over it. I've had girlfriends before. And I can't just drop Nadira.'

'Oh no! I am not going through that again! I bet everybody in the embassy knows. Don't they? Don't they?' By now Fiona was screaming. Lena opened the door to bring in the tea but beat a hasty retreat back to the kitchen.

'You don't know how horrible it is, everyone laughing at me behind my back. And all your little groupies thinking, "Oh, Fiona, she's just stupid, Craig doesn't care about her."'

'Darling, I don't think anyone thinks you're stupid.'

By now, Fiona's face was crimson, hot tears coursing down her cheeks like tropical rain on a windowpane.

'I must be bloody stupid to have put up with you. I can't stand it any more.'

She sank down on a chair and curled up looking utterly defeated. I felt like a complete bastard. I knelt and put my arm around her, but she shook it off. Fiona lay there like something broken. I knew that I could mend her by simply vowing to give up Nadira and end Fiona's personal nightmare. But that was the one thing I could not do. If I let Nadira go, she would fall back into something even worse than Fiona was experiencing. And I was convinced that my one chance of personal fulfilment lay with Nadira. Even to think of her name gave a dull deep echo from the base of my heart.

Why did Fiona need everything to be so black and white? Why was she forcing on me a choice I wanted to put off when I was just off the plane? An unjust resentment made me feel peevish. I didn't want clarity. For the last ten years, my personal life had been swathed in ambiguity, comfortably cocooned in grey mists of vaporous duplicity. I had a wife I loved, wonderful children and a comfortable and well-ordered home. And I had wonderful, madcap booze-fuelled evenings out, full of wit and wrongdoing, and a string of mistresses. It was like living inside *Die Fledermaus*. It was cosmopolitan and somehow both sophisticated and adolescent. It had all worked so well for me, but only through Fiona's indulgence, her willingness to swallow small lies, to look the other way and to forgive me when caught out.

Now, however, a very public crisis had hit – one which could not be papered over. I was confronted with the reality of all the agony I had brought Fiona over many years now come to a head.

The door opened, and Emily put her head around it.

'I thought I heard Mummy crying.' Then she saw me: 'Daddy! My daddy! My daddy!' she screamed and came running towards me, arms outstretched, the tails of her nightdress flapping. I swept her up in my arms, whirled her round and round, shook her playfully from side to side, her legs swinging, and buried my head in the long warm hair on her shoulder.

The next morning, I woke up with a slight pain in the small of my back. Carl and Kristina came to the Residence separately to brief me on what had been happening in the embassy and bring me papers to read myself back in. By the end of that day, the pain in my back was worsening. I asked Fiona to rub some liniment into it, but she refused, so I got Emily to do it instead.

The following morning, Monday, I woke up and had difficulty getting out of bed at all. The pain in the small of my back was extreme. I struggled to dress, hobbled down to breakfast and ate my tea and toast lying on the settee. I just couldn't get back up again – my stomach muscles seemed paralysed. I rolled onto the floor, put my hands onto the coffee table and pushed myself up into a kneeling position. Fiona had come in and was eyeing me contemptuously.

'I can hardly move,' I gasped. 'I think there's something seriously wrong with me.'

'Good,' she said. 'I hope you die.'

Apparently not forgiven, then.

I got myself upright, and a concerned Lena straightened my tie and handed me my cashmere coat. When I left Tashkent, I was banned from the embassy. I did not recall having been formally un-banned, but I was going to re-enter it now, having got back against all odds. I was going to do so with a straight back, a firm step and a smile on my face, even if it killed me.

I tried to get down from the Land-Rover without any sign of trouble, but the pain made me sweat so much that my clothes were drenched. I had great difficulty bending and unbending my midriff. As I entered the embassy, the staff overwhelmed me in a wave of affection, and I had to endure numerous hugs and slaps on the back. In fact, I too was so elated by the moment that the pain lost its edge. Most of my staff were in tears.

Some things had changed. The flag car was a new top-of-the-range Discovery with leather seats. My office was now upstairs in the former dining room, large and luxurious. Kristina was in the ballroom, which was partitioned by curtains to give a conference room also. The defence section were in my old bedroom, and in the other former bedrooms were Daniel, Dmitri and Victoria. The registry was now more spaciously housed in the former kitchens.

The downstairs staff had all followed me through the embassy to the foot of the old Residence staircase. There they stopped and applauded as I walked up the stairs, and the upstairs staff had gathered on the landing and were applauding, too. I almost didn't make it up the stairs. The pain was incredible. I was willing my body, with every last ounce of courage, to walk up those steps. The pain of keeping my back straight was indescribable. I couldn't breathe, and my vision kept going. My smile must have looked like a rictus. Kristina later told me that everyone just thought I was overcome with emotion.

Finally, I was alone in my office. Kristina brought me a cup of tea. I saw Nick, Carl and Steve. I went through with them the results of the Management Consultancy Review, which had taken place in my absence. Allegation 7 against me was that I had instructed staff not to take this review seriously, but in fact that was the absolute opposite of the truth. I had requested the review because it is the leverage you need to get extra resources. The result was everything I had hoped for. The review confirmed the need for all the extra local staff positions I had created. In my response to London, I could not resist pointing out that the review did not bear out the accusations of extensive management failings at post. Steve Brown deserved much credit for the successful outcome.

I confided to Kristina that I was sick and asked her to phone Dr Reimers to make an appointment for 1 p.m. Nadira lived close to the clinic, and I called on her en route. She was delighted to see me. She felt very distressed because she had not understood what was happening to me in September and had thought I was just making up a story. For the first few weeks I was in hospital, I had not contacted her, or indeed anyone. But finally messages started getting through to her. She had really loved me and in early summer had believed I was going to change her life and rescue her from what seemed an inevitable path to prostitution. She had believed those hopes dashed in September, then they came alive again. Now she mopped my brow as I tried to gulp tea. I had a presentiment this illness might be serious and I might disappear again, so I gave her more money and told her to believe I loved her.

Ten minutes later, I was lying on a bed in the international clinic. Dr Reimers looked really worried and called Dr Ellen and their local staff. I was soon in an oxygen mask. My blood oxygen levels were down. Anything above 95 per cent is normal, and anything below 90 per cent is not sustainable. I was at 88 per cent. Dr Reimers thought it was pneumonia, while Dr Ellen thought it was pulmonary embolism. An X-ray didn't establish which but showed it was very serious and in both lungs. They decided to treat me for both. I was on a drip, and they injected antibiotics into the bag. They put blood-thinning injections straight into my midriff. I was in so much pain, I didn't feel the needles. Jan Reimers said they couldn't give me strong painkillers because I was going to need all my fight.

Then it happened for the first time. I couldn't breathe. Normal breathing happens without effort, and we don't notice the muscles that do it. But I seemed to have lost the use of them. I simply couldn't breathe. The pain in my chest was incredible, growing into an all-engulfing blackness. My body thrashed hopelessly, and I half fell out of bed. Dr Ellen screamed for help. Doctors came running and more injections went in. The oxygen supply was turned up until I could feel real force inside the mask. Suddenly the pain eased and I could breathe again. Jan Reimers had been counting down the blood oxygen reading: '88 – 85 – 78 – falling quickly now – 72 – 77 – 72 again – 65! Christ! 65!'

That had been real panic. It was back up to the high 80s again. Surely I wasn't going to die now?

Jan Reimers was talking to me: 'Ambassador Murray? Craig? Can you hear me?'

I nodded.

'Look, don't panic now. I know it feels bad, but Dr Ellen was right. It's a pulmonary embolism. Now we know what it is, we can treat it. Just a couple of months ago we had an American lady who had it, and she's fine now and back down in Samarkand. There's an air ambulance on the way here from Germany to take you back to London. So don't worry.'

'I don't want to go back,' I gasped.

Fiona came in. She looked worried but seemed more angry than sorry.

'I am not staying this time,' she said. 'Emily and I are finished here. We're going back to London. There's no room on the ambulance. We'll go back British Airways. I gave the tenants notice to quit some time ago.'

Suddenly, she looked close to tears. I found I had nothing to say and no breath with which to say it. She had kept up a tremendous lonely vigil in Tashkent, but it was time to finish it now.

'Yes, I understand,' I gasped.

Fiona melted away. Time passed, then it came again the second time. I gasped and tried to shout out but couldn't. My back arched involuntarily until my stomach was well clear of the bed. My head was banging against the bedstead. Dr Ellen was holding my hand as I blacked out. A few hours later, I came to. Dr Reimers was opening my eyelids and looking into my pupils with a pencil torch.

'Don't worry,' she said. 'Four more hours and the ambulance will be here.'

Everything looked bright orange. I felt nauseous. I was not conscious of breathing at all but could hear myself doing so in tiny very fast gasps. Then the pain came again, and this time it seemed to last and last, even after everything went black. Suddenly the pain took on a different quality, and my lungs seemed like blocks of ice. My feet were freezing, numb and hurting. Where was I? I opened my eyes. My chest didn't just feel pressed on; it was actually strapped with thick luminous-green belts. My back was uncomfortably resting on what felt like a plank, narrower than me. My eyes squinted. Consciousness was returning, and I could see I was in a narrow tube packed with equipment that was plugged in to me by a variety of tubes and cables. It was a plane! I was in an aeroplane, but a very small one. The door was open, and outside was a dark airfield apron, tiny crystals of snow swirling in the arc lights. That feeling of cold was real – it was incredibly cold. If I hadn't been strapped down, I could have reached an arm through the open door.

A man in a bright orange jumpsuit climbed a couple of steps into the plane, sliding the door closed behind him. It was so cramped he had to lean over me to stand beside my stretcher. He tucked the thin blanket delicately over my feet.

'Mr Murray, good morning,' he said jovially. He had a light voice with just a tinge of German accent. 'It is four o'clock on a fine November morning. We are refuelling in Murmansk, in the Arctic Circle. It is 40 degrees below freezing. This is not good. But from now on, your life gets better. You are going to live. Just now, though, sleep.'

He gave me an injection and I slipped away, thinking, 'Murmansk? Bloody Germans. No sense of direction.'

I opened my eyes again. Light was streaming through a large picture window. It was my old room in St Thomas's Hospital, only a mirror image. Professor Kopelman and Dr Reimers were leaning over me, smiling. I was still all trussed up and wearing a large mask that seemed to cover my whole face. Then they were gone.

'Are you awake, Mr Murray?'

It was a pretty young Irish nurse I remembered from St Thomas's.

'Would you like breakfast? Dr Bateman says you can take your oxygen mask off to eat for a few minutes.'

There were Rice Krispies and soggy toast. I was indeed back in St Thomas's. It was three days since I had passed out in Tashkent. I was in the room next to my old one.

I was wheeled down for one of those scans where you go right inside a large machine while dyes are pumped into your bloodstream. An instruction kept coming through an earpiece for me to take a deep breath and hold it, but I could do neither, only breathe in shallow, quick gasps. That afternoon, Dr Bateman came to see me, a cheery, brusque character, trailing a cloud of junior doctors and students. He looked at the scan results.

'Worse than I thought,' he said breezily. 'Multiple bilateral pulmonary emboli. That means, Mr Murray, that both your lungs are full of blood clots. We can disperse them over the next few weeks with blood thinners. But you've had a close call. Wonder what caused it. Any history of embolus in your family?'

Not to my knowledge. Shortly afterwards, Professor Kopelman came in and asked how I was feeling. I told him weak and disappointed after that huge struggle to get back to Tashkent.

'Yes, we've all been wondering about that,' he said. 'Toxicology have run a whole range of tests but not found anything yet.'

An enigmatic comment, but now the crisis had passed I was thinking along the same lines. It was an incredible coincidence that, after returning against all efforts to keep me away, I had instantly succumbed to near fatal illness – and without obvious cause.

Pulmonary emboli can be caused by deep vein thrombosis – DVT – and I developed this 48 hours after flying to Tashkent. But that convenient explanation has holes. DVT normally shows as a sharp pain in a leg or arm – you don't get DVT in the small of your back. I had no leg or arm pain. On top of which, it was only a six-hour flight, plus time on the ground in Yerevan, and I was in a very comfortable business-class seat where I could lie down. I had stayed hydrated, walked around a lot and even worn flight socks. Also, DVT was unlikely to result in both lungs being clogged with numerous clots.

Even if I had developed a DVT, it would still be weird that after the hundreds of flights I had taken in my life it was this disputed return that did for me. I don't buy the DVT theory. I simply don't know what really happened. I am intensely suspicious that when powerful people had tried to get me out of Tashkent, I should immediately almost die on return there.

But it isn't too convincing to shout, 'I have just been released from psychiatric care and now they're trying to kill me.' So I kept my counsel.

All my friends now advised me not to go back again, but I was more determined than ever. It was a mixture of bloody mindedness, of belief I was doing an important job in Tashkent, and of a desire to get back to Nadira. It was also professional pride – I wanted to prove that now, with better staffing levels and better staff, I really could run a good embassy.

My mum came to visit me in hospital, which was a great comfort. I had a very happy childhood. I have two brothers and a sister, and we grew up poor, happy and extremely close. It's the sort of family where just remembering one another's existence makes you feel warm and supported. Fiona and Emily came, and Fiona and I took the first tentative steps towards building a new and different kind of relationship. I apologised for all the hurt I had caused.

After being discharged from hospital, I went back to live in Bryan's luxury flat. Tony Crombie's investigation chuntered on, and I was preparing as best I could to defend myself. Kate Smith continued to be a help. The DSA was affiliated to a real trade union, the FDA,[67] and a real trade union official, Paul Whiteman, had been appointed to help me. Paul was a chirpy fellow a bit younger than me with thinning curly dark hair, an open face and spectacles. He had the weary air of someone who had seen it all before. I met him first with Kate Smith and ran through the story, giving him a mound of papers to study.

On about our third meeting, Paul looked up at me and said with an air of surprise, 'You really are not guilty of any of this, are you? In fact, it's the most appalling attempt at a stitch-up I've ever heard of. And so badly done, too.'

He was now wholeheartedly with me and a great support. I also met Gareth Peirce, the legendary human rights lawyer, now working for those detained for years in Belmarsh Prison, held not only without charge but without even having been told why. I was rather awed to meet her. She too was outraged at my treatment and anxious to help.

In December, I had my interview with Tony Crombie. Most of the charges were very easily answered. The accusation about girlfriends being given visas in return for sex came down to a single person – Tamara. I had rather suspected from the reference to buying air tickets that they were alluding to her, but why the plural 'girlfriends'? The evidence that we had sex was allegedly that I told someone so.

The only surprise came at the end of the interview when Crombie produced rather dramatically a sheaf of papers.

'There is an additional allegation,' he said, 'which, with the allegation of talking about the allegations, makes number 20. Do you know this woman?'

The papers were a visa application. The photo was of a beautiful young woman named Albina Safarova, born in 1985.

'No,' I replied. 'Never seen her before in my life.'

'It says here on the application form,' said Crombie, searching carefully, 'HMA instructs issue. Now why would it say that?'

'Well,' I said, 'anyone can write that. It's plainly not my handwriting, and it's rather extraordinary there's no signature to that note.'

'There is also,' said Crombie, 'a note from the visa officer which says that you instructed issue.'

The note read as follows:

Tuesday November 18, 2003
To: Tony Crombie

Subject: CONFIDENTIAL – STAFF – INVESTIGATION

With regards to the points you raised:

a) The visa issue to Albina Safarova, I did write on the back of
the VAF 'HMA instructs issue.'

b) I was verbally told by — and —[68] that Dermot Hassett
was a contact of the Ambassador. I have never seen them
together, however I think Dermot actually stated on the letter
in question that he was a good friend of the Ambassador, or
words to that effect.

I hope that this clarifies the points you raised regarding the
written statement

   Regards
   [Visa Officer]

'Actually,' I said to Tony Crombie, 'it doesn't say I authorised issue.
It says the visa officer was told I did. You know, I am 100 per cent
certain that I have never even heard of Dermot Hassett. The expat
community in Tashkent is very small. Now why would those two
members of staff tell the visa officer he was a friend of mine?

'Another thought,' I continued. 'Have you ever run a visa section?
No? I thought not. Well, I have. I have never known an entry clearance
officer who would simply issue a visa to someone because they were
a friend of a friend of the ambassador, even if the ambassador told
them personally, let alone someone else saying so. They would at
the very least insist on a signature from the ambassador. And I have
known plenty who would still not accept that. To anyone who knows
anything about immigration work, this doesn't add up at all.'

Crombie looked crestfallen.

'Then how do you explain the letter from Dermot Hassett?' he
demanded. A photocopy of this undated letter was also attached.
Hassett's letter in support of the visa application of his fiancée
included the line: 'I can also confirm that the Ambassador Mr Craig
Murray is also aware of these facts.'

313

'Well, again, anyone can write that. I repeat to you,' I said, 'I have never, ever, heard of Mr Dermot Hassett. What does he say?'

'I am not talking to people outside the Office. This is an internal investigation.'

'Which is why it is useless.'

The interview was over.

'What on earth was that about?' I asked Paul.

Paul looked at me intently: 'Had you really never heard of him?'

'Honestly, not at all.'

'In that case,' said Paul, 'what this is about is that they know they can't put a finger on you on all the other stuff, so they've actually fabricated some evidence.'

A year later, I gave the Safarova papers to Bob Graham, a highly seasoned investigative reporter of the old school. He tracked down Dermot Hassett, who confirmed to him that he had never met me. Astonishingly, he told Bob Graham that the British embassy had asked him to write in his letter that I knew all about it. He had thought it strange, but as he had been told that it would help the application, he had done it.[69] I believe that this was indeed an attempt at the last moment to fabricate evidence against me once it became clear that the original charges wouldn't stick and I wouldn't resign.

Tony Crombie finalised his report and sent it to another senior diplomat, Edward Chaplin, later British Ambassador to Iraq. Chaplin agreed with Crombie's recommendations. The decision was that on 17 of the now 20 charges there was no case to answer.

But nonetheless, the whole affair was my fault. The recurrent phrases that dominated the report were 'poor judgement' and 'failed to show the judgement expected of a senior member of the Diplomatic Service'.

My so-called involvement in the visa case was therefore 'poor judgement', even though I had never even heard of the woman or her application. My remarks on the MCS review, which I had never made, were 'poor judgement'. The report refused to face the fact that the majority of the allegations had no evidence to support them and were plainly both false and malicious. It was all covered in layers of fudge, and if there was any fault, it was mine. I was allowed one read of this report, which was then officially destroyed.

Three allegations went to a hearing:

Allegation 2: That he regularly turns up at the office drunk or hungover and late before going home to 'sleep it off', then returning to the office at 16.50 demanding people start work with him.

Allegation 12: That he frequently takes the flag car out (with driver) until 02.00-04.30.

Allegation 19: That, contrary to instructions, you discussed the allegations with your staff.

It was deemed that none of these potentially constituted gross misconduct, which was strange because, if true, Allegation 2 certainly did. There was therefore no tribunal, just a hearing before the Director of Corporate Resources. Dickie Stagg had taken over this position, which was a major improvement. Dickie is bright, honourable and sensible. Had he been in post a year earlier, I doubt the administration could have done what it did to me without his trying to call a halt.

It turned out that the reason the charges were said not to constitute gross misconduct was that the evidence in both cases related to just a single incident. Staff in the visa section had said that on one single occasion I had told them I was going home to sleep off a hangover. I can't remember it, but it was quite possibly a joke. The car misuse was similar. Paul Whiteman was at the hearing and simply said there was no case to answer. Dickie Stagg agreed.

I was found guilty, however, of talking about the allegations – again, an impeccably Kafkaesque result. I didn't do any of those things, but I talked about being accused of them.

I had to be found guilty of this, because I had already been judged. Sir Michael Jay had at the end of August banned me from my own embassy for talking to staff about the allegations. I had indeed told Kristina, but I felt personally that being in the middle of a nervous breakdown, brought on by these same false allegations, ought to be some defence. The Office disagreed, and I was given a written warning, stating that if I stepped out of line at all in the next 12 months, I would lose my job.

I had a right of appeal, which in a further Kafkaesque twist was to Sir Michael Jay, who upheld the original decision. I made several written requests to Jay and Stagg requesting an investigation into how such a huge raft of untrue allegations had arisen. I especially wanted a formal investigation into the visa case, which I believe revealed a potentially criminal conspiracy to frame me. I was turned down flat. The official investigation had concluded that my own poor judgement was the root of the whole problem.

Simon Butt told me to my face that just because the allegations could not be proved, did not in his view make them untrue. He would be watching me. I explained to him that they had not been tested for proof beyond reasonable doubt. Under the FCO disciplinary system they only had to be proved on the balance of probability, and they had failed even that test.

* * *

For Christmas, I joined Fiona, Jamie and Emily at Gravesend, sleeping in the attic bedroom. We had a busy few days. When a household splits, you need an extra set of everything, and we spent several days shopping for Fiona. Shopping is fun, and these were surprisingly tension-free times.

I returned to Bryan's flat, from where I got medical clearance in mid-January to go back to Tashkent. This time there were no complications. I had taken care to keep in much closer touch with Nadira, and she and Lena the cook had been getting the Residence ready. In mid-January, I set off once again for Tashkent.

CHAPTER 19

Tashkent Again

I had insisted to London that Carl be allowed to run the embassy in my second absence, unlike the first when Adam Noble had been brought in above him. The staff were happy to see me on my second return, but their reception was more muted. I was still not fully recovered and tired easily. Most afternoons, I slept on the sofa in my office. I was also worn down mentally by all these struggles. I was to discover that my experiment – I believe a successful one – in a more dynamic style of ambassadorship, was at an end. I had achieved real influence through my approach but only so long as the Uzbeks believed I had the British government behind me. It was now plain to all that this was not the case. There was real amazement among the diplomatic corps that an ambassador could survive such a determined attempt by his own government to get rid of him, and every bit of the media battle had been pored over in Tashkent. But whereas I had previously been a force, I was now more of a curiosity. My powers of analysis and depth of knowledge were still respected, and I was firmly a hero to the Uzbek opposition. But that could not disguise the grim fact that I had to struggle hard against becoming a lame duck. I was not sure I had the strength or the courage for that fight.

At least my private life had resolved itself, and I was able to enter a new phase of happiness with Nadira. She was waiting for me in the Residence when I arrived and had sat up all night to be sure to be awake when I came in. It was a rapturous reunion. As the weeks went by, I was to learn how truly devoted she was, and her support and kindness became essential to me. On her part, the love I had professed for her offered a dream in which she had never quite dared to believe. It now came true.

* * *

I was sad to discover on my return that I had lost a friend and ally. Richard Conroy had been killed in an aircrash shortly before I got back to Tashkent.

An Uzbek came to see me on urgent business, having travelled from near Termez on the Afghan border. He claimed that Richard Conroy had come down to Termez to meet an important contact on counter-narcotics business. This contact had formerly been an important player in heroin smuggling from Afghanistan, either direct or through the mountains of Tajikistan. He had subsequently fallen out with his erstwhile collaborators in the regime and had written to Richard Conroy offering full evidence of government involvement in the narcotics trade and particularly the personal involvement of senior government ministers.

My visitor's story ran that Conroy had flown down to meet this man in Termez and had been returning with him to Tashkent to formalise the evidence for the United Nations. An SNB agent had accordingly been placed on the plane by the government to shoot Conroy and the informer. The SNB man sat behind them and had killed both with a shot through the back of the head. What the SNB man did not know was that the government had also placed a bomb on the plane, just to make sure.

I thanked the visitor for his information. I told him that from my own sources I had no doubt that the Karimov regime was indeed involved in narcotics smuggling. But I had some difficulties with this version of events.

First, I had heard from many sources the rumour going round Tashkent that Richard Conroy had been shot through the back of the head before the crash, but given that everyone on board died, how did people know what had happened? Had it, for example, been radioed in to the control tower? I found that my visitor, too, could offer no satisfactory explanation of how he could know about the shootings and who sat where.

The second doubt, which I kept to myself, was that this did not sound like Richard. A gentle man, deeply interested in economic development, he seemed to me the last person who would suddenly jet off to meet with an informant from the narcotics trade. The UN had multiple interests in the border at Termez: the crossing was vital for regional development and the flow of humanitarian aid, and indeed the UN, EU and the UK all had various counter-narcotics programmes involving this border. As titular head of the UN effort in Uzbekistan, Richard could visit the anti-narcotics project. But to become operationally involved? It just didn't sound like Richard at all.

I thanked my visitor, who left a long letter which he stressed was highly secret and must not fall into the wrong hands. Once translated, it turned out to say no more than he had told me. The visitor promised that he would get back in touch with more evidence, but he never did.

After he had left, I asked Steve Brown to come and see me. Steve had been heavily involved at the time of the air crash and had helped Jan Reimers to identify the corpse of Richard Conroy and that of one other person for whom we had consular responsibility.

This had been very dreadful. The corpses had been badly charred and were laid on the floor in a hangar. The Hokkim of Tashkent had tried to stop the identification effort and instructed that each grieving family be given one corpse, or collection of remains, each; it did not matter which. Steve Brown and Carl Garn had done a terrific job standing up to him and insisting that our protected nationals must be identified.

The Hokkim's callous instruction was a part of the usual Uzbek reaction of quickly clearing away any mess in order to return to the image of perfect harmony in Karimov's Uzbek paradise. The aircraft wreck had been simply bulldozed away within a very few hours of the crash and new turf and paving put down immediately over the scars on the ground. Pilot error was blamed; there was never any attempt at proper investigation.

Steve helped Jan to look at corpse after corpse to try to identify by dental record those for which we were responsible. I had commended Steve to the FCO for his courage and perseverance in these dreadful circumstances – the charnel-house smell had been overwhelming – and he had been awarded a bonus for his efforts.

I now called Steve to my office. I asked him if he had heard the various rumours about Richard Conroy's death. He had. I then asked him if there was anything about the corpses that might give credence to it.

He said there were two things that he did not understand. When he lifted the charred head of the first corpse, the brain had plopped out of the back of the skull, hitting his trousers and then landing on the floor. He had to pick it up and scoop it back into the skull. A human brain is a very slippery thing to hold, he said, like trying to pick up a handful of scrambled egg.

Then the next corpse had done the same, and he made a strange discovery. The base and back of each skull had been cut away. A large rectangular chunk of every skull was missing, cut out by something like a circular saw. We both pondered but could think of no reason why this would have been done during an autopsy. I had seen many autopsy photos in Tashkent but had never come across this procedure. And here the cause of death was very straightforward – what could they hope to learn from cutting out the backs of the skulls? And why had the backs of the skulls not been replaced – indeed where were they? Presumably the procedure had been carried out after the corpses had been moved to the makeshift morgue, or they would have had to be moved with their brains spilling out.

Steve and I pondered this for a while. Only one idea seemed to make any sense.

'Do you think,' I asked, 'that the backs of all the skulls could have been removed to hide the fact that one of the skulls had its back missing?'

We pondered. To put it at its weakest, this curious operation made it impossible to disprove my visitor's assertion of a shot through the back of the head. But with the mysterious absence of the back of the skull, you couldn't simply discount it.

'There's one other thing, which Daniel first pointed out to me,' added Steve. 'There was one more body than the Uzbeks said there was, or than the passenger and crew lists showed.'

'Are you sure? It wasn't just a case of jumble of body parts?'

'No, I'm quite certain. There was one head more than there should have been.'

In real life, not everything gets neatly resolved, and I got no further with this. The extra person could, of course, most likely have been just an extra passenger let on by a friend on the crew without paying. But the mystery of the skulls remains open. Richard was such a nice man that I would somehow prefer it if his death had had purpose.

* * *

One thing was plain on my return: nothing had caused the United States to waver one iota in its support of Karimov. John Herbst had left and been replaced by a new Ambassador, Jon Purnell. A likeable and easy-going man, the creased and homely Purnell came over as less of an ideologue than Herbst. Unlike Herbst, who gave the impression of actually believing the US propaganda about their ally Karimov, I don't think Purnell ever did. But it was still his job to argue it. I first met him at another IMF lunch. He declared that he had every confidence in Uzbek economic policy for the simple reason that there were 17 US civil service advisers embedded in key positions in Uzbek economic ministries. I intervened to say that left us with two possibilities – either they were being ignored or they were giving crap advice. Purnell looked shocked, but there was general merriment and an air of 'Craig is back. Now things will be less boring again.'

Donald Rumsfeld arrived in February 2004 and held talks with President Karimov on making the US base permanent and on support for Israel at the UN. The Americans had hit on the happy idea that it was a strong propaganda coup for a 'Muslim' country like Uzbekistan to support Sharon's partition plans – as Karimov duly did. After his meetings, Rumsfeld gave a press conference in Tashkent and praised Karimov in these terms:

> I am delighted to be back in Uzbekistan. I've just had a long and very interesting and helpful discussion with the President . . . Uzbekistan is a key member of the coalition's global War on Terror. And I brought the president the good wishes of President Bush and our appreciation for their stalwart support in the War on Terror . . . Our relationship is strong and has been growing stronger.[70]

I was able to use Rumsfeld's visit to achieve one thing. In my absence, Mrs Mukahadirova, the 63-year-old woman who had taken the photos of the boiled body of her son Avazov and got them to the British embassy had been tried for doing this and sentenced to six years' hard labour for 'Dishonouring the good name of Uzbekistan'. She would not have survived this sentence.

I arrived back to find everyone tut-tutting but, as usual, no one doing anything effective. The UK now held the local EU Presidency, and I organised EU action to approach the Uzbek Foreign Minister.

I also made plain both to the Uzbeks and to the Americans that I would kick up a major fuss during Rumsfeld's visit, including at his press conference. The pressure worked and, two days before Rumsfeld arrived, her sentence was commuted to a fine. Daniel, who had done much good work on this, came to tell me in delight, and I authorised the embassy to pay the fine for her. These small victories were very dear to us.

The German Ambassador told me that the Open Society Institute (OSI), formerly known as the Soros Foundation, was being closed down by the Uzbek authorities. This was a definite sign that the Uzbek government was moving decisively away from the path towards democracy.

George Soros had made billions of dollars out of currency speculation in the volatile markets of the late 1980s and poured a significant proportion of this into promoting democracy and economic development in the former communist bloc from which he came. In Uzbekistan, the Soros Foundation did excellent work in education, including curriculum development and provision of textbooks and other materials. They also worked on gender issues and in supporting the formation of local community groups to try to build up civil society. Following the November 2003 'Rose Revolution' that brought democracy to Georgia, the deposed Georgian President Eduard Shevardnadze had flown immediately to Tashkent, and cautioned Karimov against the influence of international NGOs. Karimov therefore moved to act against them. A new registration process was introduced, which the Soros Foundation was deemed to have failed.[71]

I called at the Soros offices to see how I could assist and found the whole complex now empty of the staff and clients who used to give it vibrant life from early morning to late evening. For their own protection, the staff had been told not to come in any more, and in consequence nothing had been tidied away. Papers were out on desks, a large photocopier stood open with a map flopping out over the side. I recall one wastepaper basket had several bits of scrunched-up paper inside, with others lying close by where shots had missed.

I worked my way through to the Director's area, and there sat Elizabeth and Tom, Americans from the Moscow office who were here to wind things up. They looked depressed but seemed glad to see me, and I asked if I could help at all. As we drank green tea, I suggested the possibility that the British embassy or British Council might take over some of the Soros programmes, including perhaps employing the local staff who ran them, with Soros providing the funding in London. They were enthusiastic.

Their immediate problem was what to do with the paperwork. They were concerned that the secret police might move in at any moment to confiscate everything. They were destroying a lot and seeking to send some stuff out by courier to New York. But papers about their human rights work caused them a real problem. There was much information there that the SNB could use against people, including lists of names of those who had obtained human rights training and of people within the authorities who had been helpful. If they tried to send this material, it could be seized at the airport by the authorities. They did not want to destroy it, because it would be invaluable if they were ever able to start their work again. I suggested that for now they send it to my embassy, where the Uzbek authorities could not seize it, and I would seek permission to send it back in the diplomatic bag. We agreed this, and that afternoon a vanload of documents arrived at the embassy and were locked in a garage within the secure compound.

The Uzbek Director of the Open Society Institute in Tashkent, Alisher Ilkhamov, had been at a conference in London and would not be coming back. OSI had been warned that a warrant was out for his arrest for treason – which carried the death penalty. This related to an OSI publication he had edited entitled *An Ethnic Atlas of Uzbekistan*. This was a work exploring the major ethnic groups in the country and their cultural traditions, with lots of jolly photographs. This had infuriated the government, which was increasingly stressing its Uzbek nationalist ideology. The definition of treason had recently been extended to include almost any opposition activity, including stirring up ethnic tension. For this harmless publication, Alisher was marked down to be the first victim. Fortunately, he was out of harm's way, and the OSI had determined to employ him outside Uzbekistan.

A couple of days later, Anthony Richter, OSI Director for the Middle East and North Africa, called at my office. A small, rather theatrical man with a beard and spectacles, he scurried in, accepted an offer of tea, sat down and started talking about the weather. As he did so, he passed me a note which read: 'Alisher's family are in the car park'.

I assured him that my office was not bugged and that the

bulletproof glass made it pretty soundproof but drew the heavy brocaded curtains. I looked across the great concrete blast wall that protected the rear of the embassy. It was a cold, grey February day, and the blocks of crumbling Soviet flats opposite looked more forlorn than ever. The thick laminated layers of super-dense glass and plastic that formed the windows of my office would foil even the most powerful directional mike but would not be enough to guard against a laser mike; a simple curtain would. Richter relaxed a bit but still kept looking around as though he expected the SNB to come crawling out from under the desk or behind an armchair.

Now that the OSI had decided to employ Alisher as an analyst in their London office, the question was how to get his family out to join him. The danger otherwise was that action would be taken against his family to force him to come back and face the treason charge.

I could not think of a clearer and more genuine case for offering political asylum. I had already informed London about both the OSI closure and the potential treason charge against Alisher. I therefore sent an urgent telegram to the FCO, suggesting that we issue visas to the family in Tashkent and get them on the plane that evening to London, where they could claim asylum on arrival. I suggested that I could arrange for my own solicitor to be on hand to help with this. I requested an answer within two hours.

Just on the deadline, I received a phone call from UK Visas to say that under no circumstances was I to issue visas to the family. If they needed asylum, they should go somewhere else. I then received an email from my line management to say that I was 'completely out of order' to suggest offering asylum to the family in the UK. I should ensure they were removed immediately from the grounds of the embassy and did not again set foot on embassy property. It seemed to me very sad that the UK, which once had a proud tradition of sheltering refugees from oppression, was now such a stonehearted country. A more genuine case of political asylum it would be hard to imagine.

In Tashkent, we decided that it would be wise, as a first move, to get the family to Moscow, for which they didn't need a visa. Given the warming political atmosphere between Putin and Karimov, and increasing cooperation between Uzbek and Russian security services, this was not completely safe, but it was a start. I offered to drive the family across the border into Kazakhstan in my flag car, but in the event they left by air, escorted through the airport by the US embassy. But the sheer meanness of the UK official reaction leaves a lasting impression on me still and increased my escalating disillusion.

* * *

I had decided to adopt a more clean-living style to reduce London's scope for criticism of me; in consequence, I was taking care to get to work at 9 a.m. On Monday, 29 March 2004, I was up early, feeling in fine fettle, gave Nadira a lingering kiss goodbye and set off from the Residence in the flag car around 8.30 a.m.

We immediately ran into traffic jams. Something was plainly up – policemen were blocking the traffic everywhere, apparently at random, and the little knots of green-uniformed policemen who generally hung around on every pavement, idly extracting bribes from passers-by, were all swarming like a disturbed hive.

The traffic on my route got stopped every day at 9.30 while Karimov passed; a sanitised corridor some four blocks wide was put in place every time he moved. This took an awful lot of manpower, but with 40,000 uniformed policemen in Tashkent, plus the same number of plain-clothes security personnel, and slightly less Ministry of the Interior troops, this was not a problem. But Karimov seldom varied his timing, and this was not the calm, practised morning routine.

Mansur worked his way to the embassy along a series of loops and back roads. When we arrived, the staff were gathered in a gaggle in Steve's office. Dmitri explained that there had been a series of bombs in the city. As usual, there was a complete media blackout of any bad news, but the telephone wires were buzzing, and one youth radio station had reported a bomb in Chorzu bazaar before the station was taken off the air.

Giles Whittell of _The Times_ had arrived to interview me, accompanied by a photographer he had hired locally. I told him I was going out to see what was happening and invited him to join me. He jumped at the chance – this was the nearest thing to a scoop a journalist was likely to get in Uzbekistan. We piled into the Land-Rover and headed for Chorzu bazaar.

We didn't get very far before we were stopped by a police checkpoint. Mansur tried another way, met another block, and then another way, another block. Sometimes we managed to get through a checkpoint; Mansur was very good at bluffing, and while the Union

Jack on the front and the diplomatic plate usually cut no ice with the police, in the pervasive air of chaos on this day we were having a little more luck. I told Mansur to tell the police that we were responding to a request from President Karimov for Scotland Yard to help with the investigation, a happy invention which may have had some effect. But every time we made a little progress there was a further layer of road blocks. We worked our way around, like we were going through a puzzle maze. But at last, and rather to my amazement, we found ourselves in the heart of Chorzu, at the site of the bomb blast.

The location was just outside the bazaar, in an enclosed triangular space between buildings, with something of the air of a courtyard. The buildings were of Russian colonial date. Two looked institutional, three stories high with large windows divided into small panes of glass. The third side looked like a squat warehouse building, perhaps disused, with plain windows heavily darkened by dust and cobwebs. The yard was cobbled, with a small railed area to one side containing a leafless tree surrounded by bare dirt; spring had not yet come to Tashkent.

The base of this triangular yard was perhaps 30 metres wide with at most 50 metres from the base to the apex. So even at the centre, you could never be much more than 15 metres from a windowed wall. Yet, I remarked, not a window was broken. Nor was there any other sign of an explosion. The tree was not damaged; there was no blood on the ground. I checked with the police, who confirmed it was indeed the site of the explosion. I found a policeman overladen with gold braid on his hat and shoulders. Adopting a conversational tone, I asked him if it was a large explosion. He just shrugged.

It was by now about 10 a.m. It was very hard to make any sense out of it all. Giles had found a stallholder who told him that there had been other bombs and that many policemen had been killed. I decided that the quickest way to discover what was happening would be to go and ask Zokirjon. Giles agreed to come, too. I was a bit nervous about this, but I decided I could trust Giles not to expose my best source. This decision was based on my experience that, contrary to popular belief, British journalists are decent people with perhaps the strongest ethical code of conduct of any profession, a code within which the great majority of them work every day in spite of constant temptation to break it.[72] So I decided I could trust Giles – but would Zokirjon take the same view? Anyway, we set off towards the town of Syr Darya.

There were police everywhere, with numerous checkpoints on

every road and drivers, passengers and luggage all being turfed out and checked again and again. Although not subject to search, we were continually delayed. As we came close to the President's residence at Durmen, security was particularly heavy. It seemed to take an age to get through all this. When finally we made it to Zokirjon's house, his housekeeper Giulia received us and insisted on making lemon tea, which was very welcome. Zokirjon was not in, she explained, but we were welcome to wait until he came back. As she said this, she motioned to us to remove our shoes, which she deftly collected and handed to a waiting man, who quickly moved to squat on the doorstep and start polishing them.

She would contact Zokirjon and tell him we were here. In the meantime, we could, if we wished, go somewhere cool to lie down. Perhaps we would stay for lunch? I caught her eye with what I hoped was a significant grimace conveying 'Do not offer them any girls.' Just at that moment, the details of hospitality at Zokirjon's house were not something I wanted plastered all over *The Times*. She gave me a secretive smile, which somehow conveyed without words that I shouldn't worry, she had thought of that already.

'We can't stop, Giulia,' I explained. 'It's a busy day. I was just hoping Zokirjon could tell me something about what's happening in town today.'

'Oh, the bombs.' She said it as though it were an everyday problem, hardly worth mentioning. 'Would you like to speak to Zokirjon on his mobile? He is at SNB headquarters.'

She picked up a phone, dialled the number, got a response, and then handed it to me. Zokirjon's voice came through, loud and cheery as ever.

'Hello, my friend. Why you didn't call to say you coming? I would prepare everything for you. Who are your friends?'

How did he know? Giulia hadn't told him.

'Journalists from England. But don't worry, they're OK. I trust them,' I said, put on the defensive.

'If you trust, I trust.'

'Giulia tells me you are at the SNB. What's going on?'

'A little trouble. When they have a problem, they call me in sometimes to help.'

'How big a problem?'

'Three, maybe four bombs. New style. Palestinian fashion. Is new style for us. They use girls.'

'Many dead?'

'Not so many. Maybe six, maybe thirteen. We will recognise it later.'

I relayed this to Giles. We wondered what 'Palestinian fashion' meant and both concluded that he meant suicide bombs, which at this time were at a peak in Israel.

One of Zokirjon's men indicated to us that there had been a further bomb – this time a car bomb – outside the President's Durmen residence. On the way back, we tried to get through to verify this but could not get past the final checkpoint at the tractor factory. However, we had a clear view of the road running past the residence, and there was no sign of the kind of damage you might expect from a car bomb.

At Giles's request, we stopped at this point to pose with the Land-Rover and the flag, while the photographer took some shots for Giles's article. The photographer had said little all day and had become more and more nervous; he was now frankly terrified that he would get into trouble through his association with us (and that was, of course, a very real possibility). As we headed back to the embassy, he started expressing his concerns volubly to Giles. It was past noon by the time I returned to my office, and Giles and the photographer left me to go and do some interviews with dissidents.

Back in the embassy, I sent a telegram to London reporting what I had seen so far and what Zokirjon had told me. I also said that in the absence of any direct threat to the embassy, I did not intend that we should close. After speaking with Carl, I agreed the temporary closure of the visa section in order to radically reduce public access to the building.

The embassy was full of rumours about what had been happening. The Chorzu bomb had allegedly gone off when the police were mustering in the square for a change of shift; it was said to be a woman suicide bomber and many police had been killed. Separately, a number of police had been killed in shooting incidents. A very large bomb had gone off near Bokhara. A car bomb had gone off at the Durmen residence, and a separate female suicide bomber had detonated a device outside Dietski Mir – the Children's World shop.

These were the main elements in a fairly consistent picture of what was happening, emerging from contacts across the city, from the international news agencies and from other embassies. But there was still no mention of it on Uzbek radio and television, and consequently the rumour mill was working overtime. The fact that you heard something from several places did not necessarily give corroboration – they could all just be repeating the same source. The absence of a free media not only prevents accurate reporting of information, it causes the wildest rumours to fly. At this stage, I remained sceptical, largely because of the absence of any physical evidence of explosions.

The Children's World shop was very close to the embassy, so I got in the car again to go there. This suicide bomb had allegedly gone off around 9.30 a.m. – either just before or just after we had passed the spot in the morning on the way to Chorzu bazaar.

At this site, and indeed on the way to it, there was a curious absence of policemen. We could park right outside the shop, and I got out and looked around. Again, no hole or crater or burn marks from the explosion. No blood. But the plexi-glass back of a bus stop was being refitted, and one of the large display windows of Children's World had evidently just been replaced – unlike the other windows it had no signs transferred on and there were puttied fingerprints around the edges. But none of the adjoining windows appeared damaged.

I called on a British engineer who had an office in the same building. There had been an explosion, he confirmed, a small one. Judging by the blood smeared on the road, there had been fatalities, or at least serious injury. But within minutes the police and fire department had arrived and simply sluiced everything down. Broken glass had been brushed up and glaziers appeared as though by magic. I asked whether there had been any attempt at all at forensic investigation.

'Not that I saw. Buggers just washed it all away and tidied it all up.'

That evening, I attended a couple of diplomatic functions, first at one of the Arab embassies and then at the German residence, where I arrived seriously late. Embassies had been exchanging information on what had happened. A consensus was developing that there had been one suicide bombing at Chorzu, at the site I had visited, which had hit a police muster parading for a change of shift. Six policemen had been killed. The second suicide bombing at Children's World had occurred when a female suicide bomber had been challenged by police; she had run, been shot at in the street and then detonated, presumably prematurely. At the Durmen residence, a car bomb had detonated after the car had been fired on at a police checkpoint. In Bokhara, there had been a large explosion the evening before when police had raided a bomb-making factory. Finally, police had been shot at two checkpoints, and there was some sort of protracted shootout in process near the Durmen residence. Most estimated about 20 dead in all.

There was a German parliamentary delegation at their ambassador's residence, and he was on tenterhooks in case I infected them with any anti-Karimov sentiments. Like the US, the Germans had an airbase in Uzbekistan, the German one being at Termez. At least the US diplomats had, by and large, the good grace to signal occasionally that they found canoodling with Karimov distasteful. The Germans seemed positively to relish it.[73] On this evening, the German Ambassador materialised at my elbow every time I spoke to one of his MPs. As it was late and had been a tiring day, I wasn't about to enter into controversy anyway. I found his attentions amusing rather than annoying. But I did make clear that I was sceptical about the official version of events.

I was worried about the lack of blast damage.[74] Enough of a bang to kill six people is going to leave some kind of damage on the ground and certainly break windows that are 15 metres away (and made of poor-quality glass). A car bomb worthy of the name will definitely leave a crater. I knew there had been at least one explosion, but from the damage it seemed more likely to be something like a hand grenade rather than a suicide bomb – people blowing themselves up generally go out with a bang, not a whimper.

Furthermore, there was no history of bombing by Uzbek dissidents. The 1999 bombs in Tashkent had had a very different signature. They had been very large, very professional and very murderous, killing scores of people and doing a lot of damage to buildings. They had been tightly timed to go off in quick succession.

No serious analyst believed that these had really been the work of the Uzbek opposition or the IMU. It was generally believed they were the work of someone in Karimov regime. But if it were the same person again, they must have lost the use of professionals in the security services, because these bombs did not compare in professionalism to those of 1999.

This history wasn't the only thing that gave me pause. There had never been a suicide bomber in Central Asia. Why were they turning up now? And I got, from my own contacts, three more bits of information about the Chorzu bomb that changed the picture. The police normally did not muster in that yard. They usually mustered inside the fenced-off courtyard of the district police station. Only on that fatal morning had they received an order to muster in the nearby public yard instead. Second, a close friend's flat was in Chorzu, and she had counted thirty bodies laid out in plastic sheets, not six – yet there was no evidence of enough of a blast to kill even six. Third, and perhaps most significantly, the evening before in Chorzu bazaar the police had beaten a stallholder to death for not having the correct tax papers. This kind of brutality had become standard in the crackdown on the private trading sector, but a beating to death in public was unusual and a near riot by stallholders had ensued.

So we were left with several conundrums. If there had been a planned operation involving suicide bombers across Tashkent and in Bokhara, why had Chorzu bazaar been the unlikely first target? Why not the Procurator's office or the Ministry of the Interior? (It was a curious fact that, with Tashkent now swarming with police, there was no extra security at either of these two places and a suicide bomber could penetrate right to the lobby without challenge. It was, as I noted to London, as though the authorities knew where would and wouldn't be a target.) How did the choice of Chorzu bazaar police as first target relate to those police killing a stallholder there some 12 hours before? Why were those police told to muster outside and not in their usual protected courtyard? How had so many died but no windows been broken? Why was there no forensic investigation? I knew there had been none at Children's World, and I had arrived at Chorzu less than three hours after the alleged explosion and found everything pristine there, too.

Almost immediately, London and Washington received very definite intelligence evidence that plainly indicated this was not the work of al-Qaeda. This was very inconvenient for the Americans, who desperately wanted it to be al-Qaeda. The timing could not have been more apposite – a fact that is worth bearing in mind. Two weeks later, Colin Powell was due to certify to Congress that Uzbekistan was making progress on human rights and democracy, a certification necessary for certain aid payments. Plainly, Uzbekistan was in fact making no progress at all, and an attack by al-Qaeda just at this time would divert attention from this. But here was very concrete evidence from intelligence that neither al-Qaeda, nor the IMU, had any part in the planning.[75]

It had, of course, no effect on Washington, who were now fully steamed up to attack this 'al-Qaeda' outrage and to pledge full support for their ally, Karimov. Colin Powell steamed into action. As Giles Whittell reported in *The Times* on 1 April 2004:

> Yesterday Colin Powell, the US Secretary of State, hinted broadly that American assistance would be forthcoming, particularly since the regime in Tashkent is under attack from Islamic militants linked to al-Qaeda. The US has thousands of troops based at the Khanabad airbase in southern Uzbekistan, which is used as a staging post for operations in neighbouring Afghanistan. Yesterday a State Department spokesman said that General Powell had telephoned Sadyk Safayev, the Uzbek foreign minister, and offered American help in containing the insurgency.

In fact, the US government knew this was nothing to do with al-Qaeda. But was there actually an insurgency, or was the whole thing cooked up by the Uzbeks? If so, how much did the US really know from their close relationship with the Uzbek security services? It is instructive to read Graham Greene's great novel *The Quiet American* and acquaint yourself with the historical truth behind it.

The Uzbek Procurator General called a series of press conferences, to which the diplomatic corps were summoned along with journalists, where he gave a briefing on 'facts'. No questions were allowed. At the first, he said the evidence was that these attacks were carried out by al-Qaeda and Hizb-ut-Tehrir. At the second press conference, he produced an alleged homemade suicide belt and said that the bombers had each detonated explosives equivalent to two kilos of TNT.

Having seen the sites of the explosion, I was certain that this last statement was totally untrue – the force of the explosions had been less than a tenth of that at most, something more akin to throwing a hand grenade. It could have been just bullets. It was also explained that 11 people had died near Bokhara, where police blew up an alleged bomb factory. After attending two of these so-called conferences, I declined to attend a third. I felt the serried ranks of ambassadors were being used to give, for the benefit of the international journalists present, a spurious weight and credence to the rubbish the Procurator General was spouting.

So what really happened in this 'insurgency'? Well, the definite facts are as follows. On the evening of 28 March, police attacked a home in a village outside Bokhara. There was a large explosion and 11 people were killed. The Uzbek authorities claim homemade bombs exploded. Local people claim the authorities shelled the house.

The same evening, police beat to death, before a crowd in the marketplace, a stallholder at Chorzu bazaar after he refused to go to the police station to have his papers checked. He was a middle-aged man with a young family, with no particularly strong religious or political affiliation. During the hours of darkness, two policemen were shot and killed in Tashkent in separate checkpoint incidents. The next morning, around first light, the police of Chorzu district were ordered to muster for change of shift, not in their usual compound but in the triangular courtyard. Six policemen were allegedly killed by an explosion at that muster along with one female, allegedly a suicide bomber. There was, however, no blast damage to windows, ground or vegetation. A reliable eyewitness I interviewed personally saw many more bodies taken away. Giles Whittell told me the hospital authorities were under strict orders not to give out any casualty figures.

About 9.30 a.m., according to a witness interviewed by the BBC World Service, a young woman was seen to dash out from the pavement beside the Children's World store, running between two buses. She was shot by two policemen with automatic weapons. She sank to her knees and then there was an explosion. Eyewitnesses could not say if she activated a suicide bomb, was carrying a bomb detonated perhaps by the bullets, or was hit by a grenade or similar device.

Around the same time, a small car – a Tico – failed to stop at a police checkpoint on the road going past the President's residence, at the adjacent tractor factory. The car was fired on with automatic weapons and burst into flames. The Procurator claimed this was a car bomb. Again, I could find almost no evidence of blast damage.

In the course of the next 48 hours, police raided a number of premises, chiefly in the Durmen area. Allegedly, these were sieges, but I found eyewitnesses to two of the raids who said shots were fired only by the police. At least 13 people were shot dead by police in these raids.

About a week after these events, I was able to interview the parents of one of the alleged suicide bombers in my office. They had an interesting tale to tell.

They had two daughters, their only children. The younger was called Dildora; I am afraid I have forgotten the name of the other. The elder was a brilliant linguist; she spoke seven languages and had entered university. She was also a notably religious Muslim; she had asked her father if she could wear the Muslim hijab. He had refused because it was banned at university. Both girls were in their late teens. They liked pop music and were interested in boys, although neither had a steady boyfriend.

They showed me a picture of the girls, happy on holiday with their parents. They wore jeans and make-up; one had sunglasses perched on her hair; they had uncomplicated smiles and looked relaxed; they and their parents were standing with linked arms. They looked modern. It was a happy family photo.

Then one day in December, over three months previously, the girls had vanished. They just walked out the door one afternoon and never came back. They took nothing with them that you wouldn't take if you just nipped out to the shop. They did not say goodbye or leave a note.

Both parents were in floods of tears, and I gently coaxed further detail from them. There had been no argument; nothing had changed recently in their pattern of behaviour; there were no boyfriends. I asked if they had given any impression of sharing a secret. The mother said on two occasions in the previous week the elder girl had received phone calls. They had been quite long, but the girl listened a lot and said very little. Afterwards, the girl had not volunteered who had called and what about. The mother had not asked, not wanting to seem to pry – she had, she said, been a teenager too, and as she gazed at her husband her rigid mask of misery dissolved for a second but re-formed almost instantly. The phone call was perhaps nothing, but now she wondered . . .

Her voice trailed off. She was in an agony of self-reproach with which I could empathise – should she have said something? Could she have stopped it? Could she have saved her daughter's life? I reminded her that the calls could well have been completely innocent and unconnected to the disappearance. She gave me a half-smile, grateful for my effort.

The parents had been frantic when the girls hadn't come home that evening. The next morning, they had reported it to the police. The police told them to come back if the girls hadn't returned in three days. They had called every relative, every friend, every classmate.

No one had seen them. No one had noticed anything wrong.

After three days, they returned to the police. They were escorted from the police station to the headquarters of the secret police – the SNB. There they had given again the full details and a great deal of information about the girls' habits and acquaintances. They were questioned intensely about their religious views. They had told the SNB about the two suspect phone calls, giving the approximate date and time. One desperate week later, they had returned to the SNB for an update; they had been told the calls had been traced and were not significant. The SNB would not tell them who had made the calls. At the end of the interview, the SNB officer told them they should best consider their daughters dead. A few days later, two men in leather jackets who said they were SNB but did not show any ID arrived at the home and removed most of the girls' possessions.

About six weeks after the girls had vanished, they received a phone call from the elder. She had said they were OK and 'in the north'. She then quickly hung up. The bewildered parents conjectured she meant either the north of Tashkent or Russia. They immediately reported the call, giving precise details of the time, to both police and SNB. When they urged them to trace the call, they were met with blank indifference.

About two weeks later, they received a phone call late one evening from an unknown man; he asked if they wished to see their daughters. They were instructed to leave their home immediately and proceed to a location in Tashkent, where they should get into a white Daewoo Nexia.

They phoned a close relative and asked them to immediately phone both the police and SNB with the details of the rendezvous. Then, dawdling as much as they dared, they proceeded to the appointed spot, where they found a white Nexia parked. Two burly ethnic Uzbeks in leather jackets were seated in the front. They paid no attention to the couple's gestures to them through the windscreen. Uncertainly, the husband opened the back door. Still no reaction. They slid into the back seats, and the car set off without a word being spoken.

The car headed north, threading its way through a maze of streets in old Tashkent before eventually emerging onto the main road to Bilraz. To their amazement, it stopped at the roadside in Durmen, right beside the long wall of the President's compound. There, the front passenger got out and said his first word to them: 'Come!'

They got out and stood beside him on the sandy verge. He lit a cigarette, put it in his mouth and clapped his leather-gloved hands together to keep warm on this frosty January night. They squinted into the headlights of oncoming vehicles; plainly, their taciturn guide was expecting a car to arrive from the north-east, coming into Tashkent.

After about fifteen minutes, a convoy of 'five or six' vehicles passed them slowly, then drew up on the roadside some thirty metres behind them. I interrupted to ask what kind of vehicles. Saloons, not four-wheel drive, and mostly white, but it was dark and there was only orange sodium lighting.

They hurried towards the convoy, the mother stumbling and hurting her ankle. Their guide swore and barged ahead of them. The rear nearside door of a car in the middle of the convoy swung open. It was a white Lada Volga. They hastened to it, casting hurried glances into each car as they passed, looking for their daughters. The cars they passed each held three or four men similar to their own escorts. When they reached the open door, sitting in the back, dimly illuminated by the feeble interior light, was their oldest daughter.

She was resting back against the seat and on the far side from the kerb. She looked happy to see her parents but made no move to the empty seat nearer them as they stooped to thrust their heads and shoulders inside the car. The mother moved to enter the vehicle but was roughly hauled back by their escort.

The daughter motioned to them not to try to come closer, but her smile appeared bright. She spoke to them briefly, assured them that both she and her sister were well and 'being looked after', and told them not to worry. She then waved and leant over towards them – not to hug them, but to pull the door closed. The car hooted its horn, and the whole convoy headed off, including the vehicle which had brought them. A little further up the road, still within sight, it turned off to the right. The next day, the father visited the scene and decided this turning was just a way to get back onto the main road, heading whence they came.

They were left standing in the dark and cold. Relief that their daughters were alive mingled with despair at this brief meeting. In Tashkent, as in the rest of the former Soviet Union, almost any vehicle will act as a taxi, and they quickly flagged one down. The driver grinned at them. 'You're asking for trouble, standing outside the President's residence.'

On returning home, they confirmed that their relative had contacted both the police and SNB as requested, and then they called them. Neither the police nor the SNB had done anything about following them, or not that they were prepared to admit to.

That was the last time they saw either of their daughters alive. Things fell into a settled routine after that. The hurt had been slightly dulled by the knowledge that the girls were alive. Until the morning of the Tashkent bombings.

That morning, the SNB came to their house at 2.30 a.m. They were taken down to SNB headquarters, where they were locked in a cell. They were not told why. At 11.30 a.m., an SNB officer entered and told them that their daughters were dead; they had been terrorists and suicide bombers. The parents had then been allowed to return home.

Two days later, the body of Dildora was returned to them. Despite the fact that the authorities said she had been responsible for the bomb at Children's World, her body showed, they insisted, no signs of injury other than a burnt hand and a small burn mark on her stomach. I asked how small, and the father said about the diameter of a walnut. There was no puncture wound anywhere on the body: nothing, her father said, that looked remotely like a cause of death. Her face was blue, but he anticipated my next question and said he could see no strangulation marks on the throat. They had been told their second daughter was also dead, but no detail had been given and no body returned.

Having told their story, they sat looking at me expectantly. I was once again uncomfortably aware that I had gained an inflated reputation in Tashkent as a righter of wrongs, and I felt inadequate. What I could do was listen, sympathise and assure them that there was a world opinion which cared about the truth, whatever the disregard of the authorities in Uzbekistan for that commodity. They thanked me and left.

So much didn't add up here. The Children's World bomb had gone off about 9.30 a.m. The SNB had apparently been unable to trace the girls for the preceding three months but knew seven hours in advance that this was going to happen and took the parents in. And the evidence was clear that the dead woman at Children's World had suffered bullet wounds and an explosion, yet if the parents were to be believed, the body showed no such trauma. The burnt hand and round burn mark were much more typical of torture cases. And the blue face? As previously mentioned, a favourite method of torture, used frequently all across Uzbekistan by the security services, was to place a gas mask on a victim's head and block up the filters. This had the advantage of suffocating them without leaving telltale marks.

Even harder to understand was the late-night rendezvous. It was inconceivable that a convoy of vehicles had been able to pull up outside the President's residence without being challenged – and what terrorist group would run such a completely unnecessary risk?

To make matters more complex, I spoke the same day with Monica Whitlock of the BBC. She had been shown photographs by the authorities said to be of Dildora's body, and it had been well and truly blown up. She had also seen photographs of the aftermath of one of the suicide bombings featuring a severed head in a tree. I wondered if the blown-up body had been the other sister and speculated that a photo of an exploded body doesn't necessarily say much about who exploded it, and a photo of a head in a tree not much about who put it there. She cautioned me about doubting things just because the government of Uzbekistan said them. I said that experience tended to point me that way.

I have skipped ahead from the date of the 'insurgency' to complete the picture of why I was so dubious of the US–Uzbek version of a concerted al-Qaeda attack. But from day one I had been sufficiently sceptical to question in detail the official version, both in diplomatic telegrams and in secret reports on intelligence channels sent to the Joint Terrorism Analysis Centre (JTAC). In my reports, I made it absolutely explicit that I was taking issue with the United States government's line that this was IMU and al-Qaeda activity. I made it plain that I believed the US security services were ignoring or wilfully misinterpreting the intelligence data. Rather to my amazement, JTAC agreed with me, and in two official analyses of the situation, drawing on all available sources, said that claims of involvement by IMU, al-Qaeda or Hizb-ut-Tehrir could not be substantiated.

What do I now believe? Well, with all knowledge subsequently gathered, I think this was most probably an Uzbek government operation, possibly in agent provocateur mode. It is most likely that some form of attacks were carried out by young people who believed they were fighting for Islam when in fact they were being kept, armed and targeted by the SNB. It is possible that the SNB themselves carried out some of the attacks and then left a woman's body conveniently behind. They could certainly have arranged for the police to muster outside, and I can't think of any other organisation that could park a convoy outside the presidential compound. Did they take Dildora's parents in seven hours in advance and keep them locked up in case the girls made a break for home or a phone call? Perhaps the missing one had already escaped? This is speculation. It is also worth noting that the only government figures killed were highly disposable junior policemen – why was no more important political target attacked?

One person who appeared put out by my refusal to believe the official version was Simon Butt. Six months later, while writing a staff appraisal of me as he left his job (to become Deputy High Commissioner in Islamabad), he wrote: 'His first reaction to the terrorist bombings in Tashkent in March was to suggest the Government of Uzbekistan itself was responsible.'

Plainly I am a deeply disreputable character.

CHAPTER 20

Once More Unto the Breach

Following the Tashkent disturbances, there was, as might be expected, a security crackdown. Thousands of actual or suspected dissidents were arrested in a huge sweep by the security services, and extra-judicial killings continued. One lady who was released came to tell me of the torture she had suffered while chained to a radiator in the basement of the SNB headquarters in Tashkent. She said that there were over four hundred women held in the basement, in eight small rooms and the corridor. There was nowhere to sit or lie on the floor that was not sticky with blood and urine.

It was at this time that I first got to know my neighbour, an aged professor who lived opposite the gates of the Residence. He was blind and crippled, and I was shocked to learn that both these conditions had resulted from beatings sustained in five years spent as one of Karimov's political prisoners. He had been a senior official of the now-banned Erk opposition party. His daughter had taken over that role, and she was for some time among the women held in the SNB basement. One of her sons had now been arrested and the other was on the run. Shortly after her release, she was assaulted by thugs on the lane where we lived. While she was pinned down, paint was poured into her mouth and her legs were broken with an iron bar. I gave the guards instruction that they were to admit any of the family to the Residence at any hour of the day or night and told the family to fight their way over to my gate if attacked in their home. The professor had a posse of great-grandchildren who played table tennis on an old trestle table in their front garden.

A peculiar phenomenon soon became apparent in Tashkent. The police were arresting the wealthy. Anyone wearing Western clothes or driving a Western car was being stopped on the streets and, unless a senior government employee or their family, taken in and held. It became apparent there were two strands to this. First, people were simply being shaken down for cash. Five thousand dollars was typically required as a bribe for release. To give an idea, that is substantially more than the cost of a Tashkent apartment. The police were cashing in big time. Second, it also fitted with the general crackdown on any kind of independent private sector.

Our reception was filling up with people waiting to see me about such cases when suddenly I had a desperate brief phone call from Nadira. She had been arrested and taken to Jubilerski police station. Concern for her safety had precipitated us into the decision that she should abandon her apartment and move into the Residence permanently. She had been arrested as she went to pick up her belongings.

I told Carl what was happening and then dashed to the police station with Dmitri and Mansur. As we pulled up outside, Nadira came rushing out and waved at me, then fell heavily down the station steps, injuring herself. She was bundled back inside by three leather-jacketed policemen. I had not seen it, but her legs had been kicked from under her when she had made a run for the door on seeing the car. When I entered, she was sitting crying on a rough bench in the outer office of the station.

She was hysterical with fear, and it took me some five minutes to calm her down. Eventually, she gasped out that they were trying to get her to sign a confession to being a prostitute and to trying to overthrow the government. That may sound a laughable combination, but this was no joke.

Dmitri was explaining who I was to a policeman behind a desk. Two others were standing in front of it. One repeatedly hit a large lump of wood off a concrete pillar, scattering long shards of wood in all directions. The other had drawn his pistol and kept pointing it around, including at Nadira and at me, making firing noises with his tongue. Dmitri was struggling with the Uzbek police who, as usual, plainly had no idea what an ambassador was. But they seemed unimpressed. It should be recalled that they had for several days been given carte blanche to do what they wanted to the wealthier section of the population. Nadira, in her jeans and fashionable jacket, wearing the watch I had given her, must have looked an easy touch.

I called Dmitri over and whispered to him, 'This doesn't look good. Go outside and call Zokirjon. Tell him where we are and what is happening.'

'But why?'

'Just do it.'

Nadira pointed to the policeman with the pistol: 'He said he would rape me.'

The policeman looked at her furiously, stepped forward and screamed something at her in Uzbek. Nadira cowered, petrified.

'What did he say?' I asked.

Nadira just shook her head, crying.

'What did he say?' I repeated. 'I can't help you if you don't tell me.'

From behind me came a female voice speaking in English.

'He said that now he is going to kill her.'

I looked round. A tall elderly Russian lady stood by the wall, clutching her handbag tightly. She smiled at me encouragingly. She was Nadira's landlady, who had been meeting her to take back the keys of the flat and had extremely courageously come along to try to help when the police had pounced. She had an evil opposite number: on a bench sat a hunched old woman in a headscarf, kneading the bench with arthritic hands. Every street, every block of flats had its secret police informant, and this crone fulfilled the function in Nadira's block. She had already signed a statement to say that Nadira brought home men at all hours of the night and she had seen some of them carrying suspicious packages.

The young policeman was waving the gun round again. I walked up to him, inside his gun arm, until our faces were touching. Mine was working with fury.

'You are not going to kill anyone, you fucking little cunt!' I spat in Russian. His eyes opened wide in surprise. 'Now sit the fuck down and keep your stupid mouth shut.'

Mansur came in and stood beside me. I walked to the desk and spoke to the senior policeman.

'Arrest that man,' I shouted, pointing to the now seated policeman. 'He just threatened to kill that girl. There are witnesses. Arrest him immediately.'

But he wasn't about to be bullied.

'But really, it is none of your business.'

He turned to the third policeman, who had discarded his bit of wood. They spoke in Uzbek, and the policeman advanced towards Nadira. Mansur and I physically blocked him, and Dmitri came back in and started speaking to the senior policeman in placating tones.

Just then the station phone rang, a white old-fashioned one with a dial. The policeman seemed inclined to ignore it. I rasped at him to answer it; something in my voice convinced him, and he did.

It was not Zokirjon but someone very senior in the police force that Zokirjon had contacted. It worked more instantly than I had dared to hope. The policeman straightened and adopted a respectful tone on the phone, and the whole room fell quiet. Then he put down the phone, apologised for the misunderstanding and started berating the old woman informant for false information. He said we were free to go. I asked for, and got, the witness statement against Nadira, which I tore up in small pieces before handing them back to him. There was nothing to stop them making another, but it seemed a wise end to tie. We had to carry Nadira back to the car, and we gave the landlady a lift home. She declared that she had finally made up her mind to leave Tashkent and go back to Russia. Nadira was on crutches for three weeks, but her mood recovered much quicker than her legs.

Now that my relationship with Nadira was becoming regular, I met her parents more often. They had in fact moved to Tashkent for professional reasons. Nadira and I joined them for lunch one day, and I was given a bowl of soup containing the breastbone of the lamb: the bridegroom's portion. After lunch, her father and I sat and discussed life over a bottle of vodka; he was a wry and interesting companion. In Uzbekistan, they have a dowry system where you pay for your bride. Eventually, with a bright twinkle in his eye, her father turned the conversation to this subject: 'Craig, you know our local customs regarding marriage?'

'Yes, of course. I am happy to make an appropriate present for Nadira.'

'You know, you should pay more if a girl is beautiful.'

'Yes, I should jolly well think so.'

'And Nadira is beautiful, is she not?'

'Yes, very beautiful.'

'And you know, you should pay more if a girl is educated.'

343

'I can see that.'

'And Nadira has a university degree.'

'Right.'

'You know, you should pay more if a girl speaks foreign languages.'

'Really?'

'And Nadira speaks five. Uzbek, Persian, Russian, Turkish and English.'

'Hang on, Uzbek doesn't count.'

'OK, she speaks four. Still, that's expensive. And she is the girlfriend of the British Ambassador. That's valuable.'

'But I'm the British Ambassador.'

'Yes, but think how much another man would pay for the former girlfriend of the British Ambassador . . .'

We opened another bottle of vodka and dissolved into giggles.

* * *

Parliamentary elections were due in December 2004. The Uzbek government were instituting a new bicameral parliament with a second, upper house. This was a sham, as only President Karimov's supporters could stand for election, but nevertheless the EU had wasted millions of euros of aid funding on consultants who had helped draw up rules of procedure for Karimov's new puppet body.

The Uzbek opposition had historically wasted more energy attacking one another than on opposing Karimov. Nevertheless, after some excellent groundwork by a young man named Greg from the International Republican Institute, they had finally agreed to come together to consider forming a united opposition front. To this end, those of the party leaderships who remained within the country had agreed to hold a joint conference in the town of Kokhand, to adopt a common platform with the aim of fighting the December elections together.

I was deeply sceptical that they would be allowed to participate in the elections.[76] But I thought the idea of uniting the opposition was highly desirable. I was invited to attend the conference and set off one bright Saturday morning for the Ferghana Valley with Farhod driving and an old dissident poet named Mabit as my interpreter.

We had not long left Tashkent when Farhod pointed out that we were being followed by a Daewoo containing four leather-jacketed men. We stopped for tea at a chaikhana in the town of Angren and the Daewoo stopped too, the men getting out and sitting at a table close to us. When we left, they again followed.

When we reached the control points at the tunnel into the Ferghana Valley, we were stopped for longer than usual. As we approached Kokhand, it was evident there were far more police checkpoints than usual. Several times they tried to stop us, and twice they told us that Kokhand was closed and tried to divert us down side roads. I ordered Farhod, who was very nervous indeed, just to keep on and ignore them, eventually instructing him not to stop at all at checkpoints, which resulted in several policemen diving into hedges to get out of the way. Farhod was sweating and his hands were visibly shaking on the wheel. All the time, that Daewoo was behind us. Otherwise the roads were empty except for police vehicles.

Finally, we arrived at the main checkpoint before Kokhand itself. At this point the road was dual carriageway. One lane was blocked by red-and-white concrete-filled oil drums. Across the other was a trestle table. In front were two policemen pointing their automatic weapons straight at us. At the table sat a fat policeman, his cap and uniform smothered in gold braid. Farhod stopped the car and looked at me inquiringly.

'Go and tell them it's the British Ambassador and I *am* coming through,' I said.

I wasn't confident Farhod could deliver this with conviction. He got out and spoke to the decorative policeman, returning to get the car documents from the glove compartment. A great deal of conversation ensued, with documents being perused and details of the documents read over police radios. After 15 minutes of this, I ran out of patience. I got out of the vehicle, walked over and snatched the documents from the table. I picked up the police radio and threw it into the cotton fields. I ordered Farhod to get back in the car and drive through the road block, then I grabbed the front of the table and tipped it up, spilling the papers and pens into the fat policeman's lap. I had not realised it was on trestles, so the whole table top fell down smartly onto his lap; judging by his face, this hurt. The policemen behind me were panicking and waving their automatics in the air. Farhod gingerly edged the car past the collapsed policeman and his table, and we drove on into the town. Little old Mabit the poet was bouncing up and down on the front seat, hooting out of the window at the police, tears of laughter streaming down his old cheeks. He turned to me: 'I have,' he wheezed, 'lived my life under Stalin, Brezhnev, Andropov, Karimov. I have waited so long to see someone do that!'

He roared again with helpless laughter. Just then, the Daewoo which had been following us for so long leaped out of a side street and drove, at speed, straight at the side of our car. It must have gone round a side way while we were stuck arguing at the checkpoint. Farhod spun the wheel and we slewed sideways, while still travelling on the same plane down the street. The Daewoo sped by, missing us by inches, and landed in the ditch as Farhod spun the wheel again and corrected us. He braked and halted, panting heavily, before moving off again and driving determinedly on.

We reached the venue for the meeting, which proved to be the large vine-covered courtyard of a private house. About 60 people sat on chairs facing a top table, on which sat the leading representatives of the parties. Represented were Erk, Birlik, the Free Farmers, the Peasants and Entrepreneurs' Party, and numerous NGO and human rights groups. Together they were establishing a new force in Uzbek politics, the Democratic Forum. A row of journalists, including one from the BBC, sat at the back. Everyone appeared to be waiting for something to happen, and I was somewhat disconcerted when the chairman of the meeting, Ismail Dadjanov, told me it was me they were waiting for.

Ismail was a vigorous-looking man with large spectacles; he had a bluff and hearty manner and a natural air of authority. His hands were red and clawed. He was a vice-chairman of the Birlik party, and some years previously a government mob had burnt down his house with his wife and children inside. He had lost the use of his hands in his desperate but vain attempts to save them.[77]

I had come to observe the meeting and had not expected to be the main event – I had not even prepared a speech. But I stood when invited and addressed them, with Mabit interpreting into Uzbek. I said how much I admired their courage and bravery in working for freedom. I denounced Uzbekistan's state-dominated economic system and the lack of economic freedoms, the internal and external visa systems and the conscription of labour. I spoke of the need for freedom and democracy, and of my belief in the potential of the country and of the Uzbek people. It went down tremendously well, and I received a great ovation. After this, everyone signed a document founding the Democratic Forum, committing their organisations to work together until freedom and democracy were established.

Afterwards, I puzzled over the fact that this meeting had been allowed to go ahead. Many people who had tried to attend had been turned away and particularly few delegates from outside the valley had got through, but the meeting had not been completely banned. I think part of the answer was that the government had good surveillance of the meeting and liked to have the opposition under easy observation. After the conclusion of the meeting, we had the obligatory meal and much friendly talk. Several of those I met that day were to die in the Andijan massacre one year later.

* * *

Back at the embassy, things were running well now. I had a good team, with Carl and Steve giving the management side the overhaul that was so badly needed and relations between British and Uzbek staff rapidly improving. I was enjoying the opportunity to prove to London that, given decent staff, I could run a well-organised embassy. Everyone was very good about accepting Nadira, and Nick Ridout and his very pleasant wife Cathy were the first to invite us, as a couple, to a formal dinner party. This was kind of them and the evening went well until after the meal when Nadira put on her Walkman. Plainly, it was going to take some time for things to settle down.

Despite my efforts to avoid trouble, relationships with the Eastern Department were still poor, and once again a visit by Simon Butt was going to highlight these strains. This time I did not offer to put him up in the Residence. He called at my office at the start of his visit and rather took me aback by saying that I was not giving the Uzbeks enough credit for their reforms. I looked at him blankly and asked what reforms he meant. He said that he was continually receiving letters from the Uzbek embassy in London outlining the steps being taken in economic and political reform; these seemed to him to be laudable. I was only reporting the negative.

I asked him for an example of a reform, and he said the Uzbeks had abolished two of the four counts liable for the death penalty. I explained that this was true. The death penalty had been abolished for genocide and for armed aggression against another state. But these counts had never been used. The other two counts, murder and attempting to overthrow the state or government, were frequently used and had not been abolished. Indeed, at the same time as the first two counts were abolished, the definition of attempting to overthrow the government had been widened so that almost any opposition activity could now result in the death penalty. This was a move backwards, not forwards.

After Simon left for a meeting, I called Daniel in and asked if he knew anything about these letters from the Uzbek embassy in London. Daniel said that he had been receiving them regularly, but they were such obvious propaganda that he had done nothing with them. I asked Daniel to find them and bring them to me, and he was right. Most of the claims on economic or political improvement were straightforward lies. I was astonished that London were paying any attention to this.

Simon Butt had a meeting that afternoon with Foreign Minister Safayev, and I received a phone call from Mr Yusupov at the ministry to say that Safayev wanted to see Simon alone, without me. That was most irregular, so I sent a quick telegram back to London, requesting advice. Angela called me at lunch to say that a reply had come. We were to tell the Uzbeks that I was the Ambassador, and Safayev could see Simon with me or not at all. The Uzbeks quickly backed down and agreed to see me, too.

In the car, Simon again said that it was vital that we congratulate the Uzbeks on their reforms. I explained that these reforms were simply non-existent. Simon referred again to the letters from the Uzbek embassy, and I said these claims were simply lies. Simon seemed horrified by this suggestion.

'Are you saying to me that these official letters from the embassy of Uzbekistan, from the Ambassador himself, contain false information?'

'Yes, that's precisely what I am saying.'

'But this is official government to government communication.'

'I don't care. It's simply not true. If you don't trust me, ask Daniel.'

'But how can you encourage reform without welcoming it when it happens?'

'Why aren't you listening to me? It's not happening.'

Simon was not to be diverted from his line. On meeting Safayev, he immediately congratulated him on the reforms undertaken by the government of Uzbekistan and said how much he appreciated his close relationship with the Uzbek embassy in London and the very useful information that they sent him. Safayev thanked him and then turned towards me.

'I am afraid, Mr Butt,' he said, 'that we have to make an official complaint against the British Ambassador. He attended an illegal political gathering in Kokhand. There he made a speech where he accused President Karimov of having 100,000 political prisoners and of committing genocide.'

'I said no such thing,' I interposed, truthfully. 'I am happy to tell you what I did say.'

'We know you said such things,' said Safayev. 'We have a tape of the meeting.'

'Really, how?' I asked. 'I should like to hear it.'

'I assure you, Foreign Minister,' said Simon, looking at me, 'we take these accusations most seriously, most seriously.'

In the car on the way back, Simon said to me, 'I shall have to report this, of course.'

'Report what you like,' I said. 'I didn't say those things. I essentially said the same as my Freedom House speech.'

'Do you have a text?'

'No, I wasn't expecting to speak at all.'

'That is very unwise. I never speak without a text.'

'I can believe it.'

'It means you can't prove your version of events.'

'Except I have 60 witnesses. If you believe your mate Safayev, ask him for the tape. Look, I said nothing startling. The BBC were there and other international broadcasters. Don't you think they would have reported it if I said Karimov had 100,000 political prisoners and was committing genocide?'

The Americans were also going into overdrive in their attempts to improve Karimov's image, and Freedom House was leading on this. Sikeena's replacement was a former minister from the Balkans, and they had a whole new agenda. The emphasis was on working with the Uzbek authorities. They brought out a Canadian pathologist to investigate, jointly with the Uzbek authorities, the case of an alleged torture victim. They held a major press conference to announce that he had died of strangulation with his belt and there were no other marks of violence. This was portrayed as vindicating the Uzbek authorities. In a second case, they announced that from photos of an alleged torture victim, the scars were healed and so could not have been the cause of death. It should be noted that these two cases were selected for investigation by the Uzbek authorities, but their findings were used by Freedom House and the US embassy to argue that Amnesty International and HRW were scaremongering and there was little torture in Uzbek jails.

* * *

There were two major highlights to our holding the local EU Presidency. We hosted a visit by Chris Patten, External Affairs Commissioner, who was commendably robust with the Uzbek authorities and who took on board the unanimous view of the EU ambassadors that the EU's aid programmes in the country were hopelessly misdirected.

On 1 May 2004, the EU expanded to admit several Eastern European states. This meant a lot to me personally, as I had thrown myself into working heart and soul for EU enlargement in Poland from 1994, when it seemed a distant dream, to 1998. On the day itself, I held a party for all EU nationals in Uzbekistan, old and new, at the Residence. This was a great success.

There was an amusing side to this EU expansion. Many more of the 'new' EU member states had embassies in Uzbekistan than the 'old' member states. Our new ambassadors included representatives from Poland, the Czech Republic, Slovakia, Slovenia, Latvia, Lithuania and Hungary. Uzbekistan had been a useful place for these countries to dump some of their old, communist-style, non-English-speaking diplomats. As a result, many of the new EU ambassadors didn't speak English or French, and I found myself conducting EU meetings at which we had to keep switching into Russian as our only common language. Even more amazingly, we were sometimes holding NATO meetings in Russian.

In May, I had to return to the UK for a six-month check-up on my heart and lungs. While there, I asked to call on Jack Straw but was instead given an appointment with Bill Rammell, the FCO minister who had taken over responsibility for Uzbekistan. This was the only meeting or conversation I was to have with any FCO minister during my period as Ambassador to Uzbekistan. This is a sad reflection on the fact that in the New Labour government, ministers' diaries were driven entirely by spin and the news agenda. If a crisis happened and a country hit the news, it would get ministerial attention. The idea of quiet, unacknowledged work to prevent a crisis had no attraction for them. 'Where's the headline?' was always the key question.

I was determined to persuade Rammell that we were making a fundamental mistake in backing the Americans and Karimov. Rammell's heart is very much in the right place, but plainly he was a prisoner of his FCO briefing, which he held in front of him and read to me. Simon Butt sat opposite me, next to Rammell's secretary, as Rammell read out: 'We believe it is essential that you encourage reform by giving the Uzbeks full credit for reforms carried out.'

He then recited a list of reforms, including the abolition of the death penalty counts. I explained patiently that this was all simple propaganda and untrue. Rammell frowned, returned to his brief and said again that I must give the Uzbeks credit for steps forward. I replied that, should I see any, I would.

As we left, I said goodbye to Simon on the staircase outside Rammell's office. Simon said that he wanted to see me back in his office about Safayev's comments on my speech in Kokhand. I replied that I had to rush, but the comments were obviously nonsense.

'But I don't know that, Craig. You don't have any proof.'

'Do me a favour. I don't need proof. Where's Safayev's proof? I told you before, the media were there.'

'It really is difficult for me to know who to believe.'

I was boiling with rage as I left. It seemed to me the general level of credence given to the Uzbek government was ludicrous, and to credit these completely daft allegations about what I had said . . .

Anyway, I had to run on to an appointment just across Westminster Bridge in St Thomas's Hospital.

I had to have an ultrasound scan of my heart. The doctor undertaking the scan was chatty: 'You live in Uzbekistan, eh? Isn't that where the Ambassador was accused of being naughty?'

But as the scan progressed, he grew noticeably tense. At the end of the procedure, I was quite worried by his manner.

'Everything OK?' I asked cheerily.

'The consultant will be able to explain when he sees you,' he said, hurrying quickly away. I had to arrange to fly back on another occasion for an appointment with the consultant.

Before returning to Tashkent, I called on Jon Benjamin in HRPD. He said he had been surprised not to see me at the big meeting that had discussed my concerns over intelligence obtained by torture. There had been quite a heated debate, and while he had tried to argue the human rights case, in the current climate there had been no chance of reason prevailing. He wished I had been there. I said I wished I had too, but no one had told me about it. He said he was surprised, as the Eastern Department had been there.

* * *

I flew back to Tashkent for what was to be the last time. The story of Abu Ghraib had broken, exposing the US torture and mistreatment of prisoners there. In response, Jack Straw had made a public speech denouncing torture, which I considered in the circumstances to be monstrously hypocritical. Equally so was a circular to diplomatic staff from Sir Michael Jay, issued while I was away and which I discovered on my return to the embassy. Jay's circular stated that we were unequivocally against torture and should report any concerns we had about torture by our allies.

I was faced with a dilemma. I had been determined to keep my head down and do my job without further clashes with the FCO. But I could not abide such bare-faced hypocrisy. After thinking it over, I decided to send another telegram, to distribute it more widely and classify it less highly than my previous telegrams on torture and intelligence. On 22 July 2004, I sent the culminant telegram of my career. It began:

> We receive intelligence obtained under torture from the Uzbek intelligence services, via the US. We should stop. It is bad information anyway. Tortured dupes are forced to sign up to confessions showing what the Uzbek government wants the US and UK to believe, that they and we are fighting the same war against terror.

I referred to the recent London interdepartmental meeting which had considered the question and decided to continue to receive the material. I argued that this was morally, legally and practically wrong; that it exposed as hypocritical our post-Abu Ghraib pronouncements and fatally undermined our moral standing.

I set out the history of my correspondence and meetings with London on the subject and referred to Michael Jay's circular on reporting torture and Jack Straw's speech on Abu Ghraib. Addressing Jack Straw directly, I said we were using double standards, obtaining bad intelligence, increasing hatred in the Muslim world and 'selling our souls for dross'. It became the phrase I am most known for.[78]

I received a most tendentious reply, stating that there had been no such meeting 'last week'. I had not said it was in the last week but 'recently'. This was typical of the tricky way the FCO nowadays responded to MPs and members of the public, but now they were applying the non-answer technique to their own Ambassador! The reply also referred me to a letter to Liberal Democrat MP Menzies Campbell. When this arrived by fax, I saw it did not address any of my key points. Plainly, the FCO were not prepared to put in writing what I had been told back at my meeting with Kydd, Wood and Duffield.

CHAPTER 21

The Last Battle

I had been under the strictest instruction not to speak to the media in Tashkent and was therefore surprised when the News Department informed me that they had given permission to Nick Paton Walsh of *The Guardian* to do a feature article in May, along with a short documentary piece for Channel Four News. Nick came with his wife Amy and a director named Fiona. I let them follow me around, with complete access, for three days. The result was a four-page *Guardian* feature entitled 'The envoy who said too much'.[79] Here I spoke in public for the first time about my feelings of shock and betrayal when the false allegations had been brought against me.

A week later, I was due to go on annual leave. I felt very pleased indeed that we had managed to get the embassy working together well after the traumatic events of the previous year. That summer, the Eastern Department was due to have a complete change of all the relevant staff. I felt that we could achieve something worthwhile in the final two years of my posting and that it would not be impossible to unite the international community to bring pressure for change in Uzbekistan.

My health was the only major cloud on the horizon. I tired easily and was still waiting for the follow-up appointment in London about whatever had concerned the doctor in my heart scan.

Nadira had come with me to London when I had come back to see the doctors in May, and she was coming back with me on holiday now. She was really excited and loved London. The sense of freedom, the cultural mix, these are all things we take too readily for granted. The first time she had seen a policeman, she had automatically moved to get out of his way, and the relief that you do not have to do that in London was a real joy to her. The fear in which people live in Tashkent is perhaps most fully appreciated when you see the joy of those released from it.

Just before I left Tashkent, I received an email from David Warren, the new Head of Personnel at the FCO. He instructed me to report to the FCO immediately on arrival.

'Bloody hell, here we go again,' I thought.

I replied saying that I was pretty tired out and had a lot of medical appointments. Could I not come later in the leave when I was rested? There was a curt response to this: no, I must report immediately.

Bryan Harris had kindly lent us his Docklands apartment again for the summer. I left this on the morning of 29 July and went in by tube to the FCO, where I met David Warren, flanked by Howard Drake. I think it is fair to say that, from his initial appointment as my executioner, Howard had become ever more sympathetic to me as he saw what was unfolding, and we greeted each other in friendly fashion.

David Warren got straight to the point. He said that the breakdown in relationships between London and me was unsustainable and that it was open to ministers to remove me as Ambassador. I did not disagree but said that I hoped that with the change of personalities at the London end, things might get better. I believed I had been treated very badly by the FCO. It would help if my concerns were taken seriously – for example, the FCO had simply not addressed the points I raised in my recent telegram on torture and intelligence.

Warren countered that, in effect, the perceived breakdown was my fault. The FCO was not happy about comments I had made to *The Guardian*. I replied that I was suspicious of the News Department's motives in setting up this interview, given the journalist's concentration on nightclubs and girlfriends. Warren then said, in effect, that the problems were my fault, and he warned me that the FCO did have the option to remove me from Tashkent and that was what would happen if the situation did not improve. This would not mean the end of my diplomatic career, as had been reported in the press; instead, I would be deployed elsewhere. I pointed out that while I did not want to get into the position of a stand-off, it was unlikely that I would wish to continue in the service of the FCO if I was removed from my post in this manner. Warren said that this was certainly not what he wanted, as I was 'a talented officer with a good record'.

After this meeting, I called round to the Eastern Department, where I met the new Head of Department, Simon Smith, and the new Deputy Head, Andrew Page. Page seemed genuinely interested and struck me as one of the people in the FCO who really care about trying to improve things in the world.

Next stop was St Thomas's Hospital. There, a young female registrar looked at me far too gravely for my liking. She had the results of the scan and said that the upper right valve of my heart was substantially enlarged and the pressures in the heart chambers far too high. She was concerned it might be pulmonary hypertension and was arranging an urgent appointment at the national centre at Hammersmith Hospital to check this out.

I didn't worry about this too much, and Nadira and I had great fun doing tourist stuff. We went to Hampton Court and the *Cutty Sark*, and to the theatre. We went to Scotland with Uncle Tommy and stayed on Islay, visiting the distilleries that produce those wonderful peat-flavoured malts.

On my return for my first appointment at the Hammersmith Hospital, I came back to earth with a bump. They carried out a number of tests, and again everyone spoke in hushed tones, wearing worried frowns. Then a nice lady came to my bed and asked if I had a bathroom on the ground floor and someone to nurse me. They gave me leaflets. I couldn't read past the second line: 'The mean survival period from diagnosis for patients with pulmonary hypertension is six months to three years.'

Bloody hell. I was going to die, pretty fast.

I was anxious to get back to Tashkent and work. I foresaw a repeat of the unpleasant wrangle over medical clearance of the previous summer. In fact, both Diana Nelson and Dr Thornton in the FCO Health Department could not have been more helpful. They were concerned well beyond the call of duty. I had misjudged Vyv Thornton, who was outstanding and was to give me advice that saved my life.

I also had my five-yearly direct vetting interview. Direct vetting, which used to be called positive vetting, is the security clearance system. A vetting officer had been assigned to my case and had for some weeks been taking statements from people who had worked with me or knew me. This was the fifth time I had been vetted in my career, and the same conclusion was reached as before – I was unorthodox but loyal and dedicated. The retired senior policeman who vetted me told me sympathetically that he had been set up with a false allegation early in his Metropolitan Police career. In my interview, he was strictly and carefully neutral, but that opening comment established his sympathy. I was very relieved; I had feared that the FCO would try to manipulate the vetting process to get rid of me.

They did. A couple of weeks after the interview, the policeman had called me in to see his report, which was fine. To my astonishment, I received a phone call from him a week later. He had, he said, been asked again to look at his conclusions. Could I answer a few more questions?

I should not reveal his name, but he was an honest and professional man and, without saying anything out of place, he made plain to me by his tone that he was furious at the pressure being put on him to find against me. At the end of the new process, he said that his conclusions remained unchanged.

In the meantime, Dr Thornton had ascertained that, for a period, there was nothing to stop me continuing to work. I would tire but not show many other symptoms, and then be liable to go out like a light. He put it to me that, when the heart attack came, I would have a greater chance of survival in London than in Tashkent. He said he would certify me fit to return to Tashkent but personally recommended I stay in London. I said that I was not going to give satisfaction to those who had worked so hard to ruin my reputation and get me out of Tashkent. I had many faults, but cowardice was not one of them. Vyv Thornton signed off the medical clearance forms. Diana Nelson told me that Dickie Stagg wanted to see me before I left, at four o'clock that afternoon.

I went round to the Eastern Department to tell them I was returning to Tashkent. They were in an internal meeting, and I opened Simon Smith's office door and poked my head round it to say goodbye. He looked annoyed at the interruption.

'Hi everyone,' I said breezily. 'I just wanted to tell you I am on my way back. I got medical clearance and I'll fly tomorrow.'

Andrew Page grinned and looked genuinely pleased. Simon Smith gave me a look that appeared to me to be undisguisedly hostile, mouth clenched, eyes steely behind his spectacles. My interpretation of that look was that I would not be going back. I closed the door and lent against it, wondering what could be happening. Presumably I would find out when I saw Dickie Stagg that afternoon. Sweat rolled down my neck, and my heart was fluttering wildly. As I walked down the stairs, my vision turned orange. My legs felt heavy and my left arm seemed stuck out from my body. I stumbled along the wall, feeling my way into the ambassadors' waiting room. There I flopped down on a couch and fell asleep, or passed out. About an hour later, I came to and walked gingerly out. The fresh air of St James's Park revived me.

I called on Dickie Stagg at the appointed hour. He sat accompanied by the inevitable Howard Drake. There was, he told me, a problem with my direct vetting status. I was not to return to Tashkent until it was resolved. I was incredulous.

'But there's no problem with my vetting,' I said. 'I have seen the report.'

Dickie Stagg looked genuinely puzzled. He turned to Howard, who offered no help.

'Anyway, that will be resolved in due course,' he said. 'Until then, you are not to return to Tashkent.'

I was not prepared to accept that as the end of the interview. I asked if I might be able to see the vetting report again, accompanied by my trade union representative. Dickie Stagg agreed, and I went and found Paul Whiteman in the First Division Association offices. Paul was genuinely angry that the FCO were mucking me around, yet again. He arranged to go with me early the next week to see the report.

The day before we went, I received an email from a journalist called Stefan Wagstyl of the *Financial Times*. He introduced himself and said that a telegram had come into his possession, allegedly written by me. It was my July blast against the receipt of intelligence obtained by torture.

The next morning, Paul Whiteman and I looked at my positive vetting report in the basement of the Old Admiralty Building. I had wondered whether the FCO had in fact forced changes, but it was exactly as I had last seen it. Paul commented that there was nothing there to prevent my return to Tashkent and plainly something else was going on.

It was. That same day, the *Financial Times* had run an article about my telegram with a few quotes from it. That evening, David Warren phoned me and said that I had been formally removed as Ambassador to Tashkent. The Uzbek government had already been informed. I replied that I was sure that they were delighted.

It was the final insult to me from the FCO – they told the Uzbeks I was sacked before they told me. I was furious.

I contacted the BBC and the next morning appeared on the *Today* programme, a radio news programme that is a national institution. As far as it is possible in five minutes, I gave a summary of the events related in this book. The result was a media storm. Unlike the year before, I no longer had any compunction about speaking to the media directly.

On 15 October 2004, I was formally suspended from duty. David Warren's letter read:

> The comments you made in this morning's *Today* programme, and others that have been attributed to you in the media following your withdrawal from Tashkent, were potentially damaging to the FCO's standing and reputation. This may constitute gross misconduct.

I was again subject to disciplinary investigation, including an allegation that it was I who leaked the telegram to the *Financial Times*. That leak had finally enabled the FCO to defeat me after a year of solid effort. A sceptic about the War on Terror, who opposed torture and the support of dictatorships, was finally done for.

I now had big problems, of which not the least was financial. As Ambassador, my monthly 'take-home' pay packet was about £6,800. Over half of that was in tax-free allowances. The actual salary was moderate. Back on my salary, I was down to £3,200 net. I had a large mortgage and about £60,000 of personal loan and credit-card debt. On £6,800 net, that was quite manageable. On £3,200, it wasn't, especially as I was both giving a large monthly sum to Fiona and paying the mortgage on the Gravesend house. Debt and mortgage repayments and the money to the family exceeded my total income. Very quickly, the money ran out and the credit cards got cancelled. Bryan had loaned us his flat, but the medical and other complications meant that we had already been there twice as long as expected. In a surprisingly quick time, we were reduced to buying stale bread cheap from the local garage and eating it toasted. The FCO were clearly moving quickly to sack me, so the situation was desperate.

The other problem was Nadira. Three months earlier, she had come to the UK on holiday. She had not expected to leave Uzbekistan for ever but had now featured extensively in newspaper reports about me and could not go back without being slammed into jail at best. Nor had she signed up for what was becoming a life of squalid poverty. Furthermore, her visitor's visa was running out. She did not want to claim asylum, because in such cases the Uzbek government has a reputation for taking reprisals against the family.

I signed Nadira up for an English language course in London, paying out almost the last available cash for the large fees. She could now apply for a student visa, but the regulations forbade her from doing so from within the country. She could not safely return to Uzbekistan, so UK Visas agreed she could apply in Dublin. We could not afford a hotel, so I got very cheap Ryanair tickets, flying out at 6 a.m. and returning late the same night.

It was a cold raw November day in Dublin; driving sleet chafed the hands. We arrived at the British embassy and joined the visa queue which stood outside, fully exposed to the elements. We queued for almost three hours and were the last to be admitted. Those behind us, who had also queued for hours, did not get in and had to return the next day. We hadn't eaten, and I felt faint standing there in the driving rain. There were no toilet facilities available. Stuck outside an embassy like that, I felt deeply my fall from grace.

Worse was to come inside. The entry clearance officer refused to issue the visa. Everything was in order, and the college was approved by the Home Office, but he refused to accept the receipt for the fees from the college as evidence of her enrolment on the course, even though it had Nadira's name, the name of the course and 'fees paid in full' all printed on it. He said that he needed a letter headed 'Confirmation of Acceptance on Course'. This was sheer unhelpful bloody-mindedness on the part of this surly truculent man. I realised again how self-satisfied and unhelpful is the organisation in which I had spent my working life. I also realised that people like to kick the fallen.

We trudged back into Dublin, soaked through, cold and miserable. I had just enough money to buy a loaf of soda bread from a baker's. It was warm, nutty and delicious. We huddled together for warmth in a doorway, and Nadira looked up at me with a loving and trusting look.

'Don't worry, darling, you'll sort it out,' she said.

I wasn't so sure I could.

I reached a real low when we returned to London and very seriously considered suicide. I was not depressed and ill as I had been the year before; it just seemed to me the best intellectual solution. Soon the banks, credit-card companies and building society would foreclose, and Fiona would lose the house. But I had over half a million pounds of life insurance. That seemed the obvious way to meet my responsibilities to Fiona, the children and, not least, Nadira.

It was now Dr Thornton who saved my life. He told me that he believed it was right that suicide used to be a crime. Nowadays people dismissed that as ludicrous, but there was a real point. There was nothing more selfish and destructive than suicide. It left those behind with irredeemable feelings of guilt. Nothing could be more devastating for a child than the suicide of a parent. It was the ultimate desertion. He had seen families and people destroyed by suicide. I was convinced.

In the end, Nadira had to fly to Kiev to get her student visa. Uncle Tommy lent us a few hundred pounds to do this. Journalists were beating a track to my door by now, and I happily accepted their offers of lunch, insisting they invite Nadira, too. I don't think they realised we wouldn't eat otherwise. Bryan's posh flat gave out an entirely false impression of affluence.

It was at this stage that freelance journalist Bob Graham investigated the case of the visa application that had been raised against me and determined that I really didn't have any connection with these people. He also pointed out to me the allegations made against James Cameron, first secretary at our embassy in Bucharest. Cameron had been involved in blowing the whistle on a visa scam there. This had led a government minister, Beverley Hughes, to resign after she falsely denied knowledge of the scandal.

As a result of blowing the whistle, Cameron had been accused of granting visas in return for sex. He had also been accused of having a flat in town which he used for entertaining women. As Bob Graham pointed out, these were identical to allegations the FCO threw at me in similar circumstances. The *Sunday Times* had reported that:

> A senior Foreign Office diplomat and friend of Cameron's said staff at the embassy in Bucharest are furious about his treatment. 'James is being set up with what appear to be completely unsubstantiated charges,' the diplomat said.

'These charges have been trumped up as a way of getting him back to London.'[80]

All of which sounds very familiar.

From other journalists at this time, particularly Stephen Gray and Frederic Laurin, I learnt the first details of the CIA's extraordinary rendition programme. This is now well understood. The CIA were flying terrorist suspects, many of them completely innocent, around the world to destinations where they could be tortured. They used apparently civilian aircraft, including Premier Executive, the company I had come across in Uzbekistan. Journalists had tracked their flight records, and Uzbekistan was a frequent destination for what have become infamous as 'torture flights'.

I now believe that in protesting about intelligence obtained by torture in Uzbekistan I had hit an even more sensitive point than I had realised. I had stumbled unwittingly across the extraordinary rendition programme, and my objections were therefore threatening the legal and political basis of a major CIA strategy in the War on Terror. That would explain the ferocity of the attacks aimed at removing me and destroying my reputation as a respected and able diplomat.

I had also been hitting at the foundations of the UK–US intelligence sharing agreement. This was put in place by Churchill and Roosevelt, and under it the Central Intelligence Agency (CIA) and MI6 exchange everything, as do the US National Security Agency (NSA) and UK General Communications Headquarters (GCHQ). As the US have four times the volume of intelligence that we do, our intelligence services view this agreement as of the highest importance and are particularly anxious that there should be no derogation from the principle that everything should always be shared. On the other hand, important players in the US intelligence community argue that it is an unequal bargain and they shouldn't give everything to the UK.

Therefore, if the CIA gets information from torture, we have to accept it in order to maintain the integrity of the agreement and the principle that everything is always shared. By arguing that we should not accept the Uzbek torture intelligence from the CIA, in the eyes of our security services I was attacking the great principle of this agreement, their most important asset.

On the personal side, things looked up. I had finally had enough, and Paul Whiteman was able to negotiate a leaving payment of £320,000 from the FCO, which was great news for Christmas. This was treated as income, so a huge cut went to the taxman, but I could pay the mortgage and debts, offer a divorce settlement to Fiona that went some way to recognising her tremendous contribution to my career, and feed Nadira and myself.

But I wasn't going to slink away. Instead, I went to Blackburn to fight Jack Straw in his own constituency in the May 2005 general election. It took most of the remaining cash. I rented a house and office, and bought a Green Goddess fire engine to campaign in. Hundreds of volunteers came, and we pushed out over 150,000 leaflets about the illegal war in Iraq and the lies that had been spread about Weapons of Mass Destruction. We also campaigned against torture and against the increasingly draconian 'anti-terror' legislation that constituted an onslaught on civil liberties in this country. It was a doomed gesture in Blackburn, but I received a lot of national publicity which was helpful in the overall context of a campaign in which New Labour had their majority slashed.

Blackburn itself was a shock to me. I had lived in happily multicultural Gravesend for a long time. But Gravesend was integrated, with the races all successfully mixed up. Blackburn has de facto apartheid. There are whole estates and districts that are entirely Asian or entirely white. The same is true in the state schools. In three months in Blackburn, I never once saw a mixed-race group of people simply socialising together. This situation has been actively encouraged by the housing and education policy of the permanently Labour Blackburn Borough Council, which sees the Muslims as a reliable block vote which they have no wish to see diffused through integration.

Levels of educational achievement in Blackburn schools are appallingly low. Blackburn with Darwen is about 140,000 people and does not have a single bookshop, unless you count WHSmith. Sheringham, with a population of 6,000, buys three times more non-tabloid newspapers than Blackburn. Blackburn also suffers from all the petty corruption that goes with permanent one-party rule in local government. This is worsened by the massive influxes of public money that have gone into the town in housing grants, urban regeneration schemes and EU regional funding. These flows, amounting to over a billion pounds in the lifetime of this New Labour government, are quietly manipulated by the local authority to Labour Party advantage.

Elections are not a level playing field either. A number of local institutions, including the college and cathedral, held candidates' debates, and I was excluded from all of them lest I get to challenge Jack Straw directly on torture and intelligence. Even BBC Radio 5 held a live candidates' debate from Blackburn and would not allow me to participate.

In British electoral law, the local authority, not an independent body, conducts the election. Under New Labour, dealing with a New Labour local authority, sadly it can no longer be taken on trust that the local authority will conduct the election impartially.

The local authority has, by law, to make available free to candidates public rooms in community centres, theatres, libraries or schools. They have also, by law, to maintain a list of such venues for inspection by candidates at 'any reasonable hour'. When I asked to see the list, I was told there wasn't one. I pointed out it was a legal duty, and the Returning Officer's staff simply laughed at me. I telephoned the Electoral Commission, who said it was the job of the Returning Officer; I should complain to him. I pointed out that it was the Returning Officer I was complaining about. The Electoral Commission said it was none of their business. We were repeatedly refused meeting rooms throughout the campaign, while Jack Straw appeared able to use schools and community centres at will.

What happened next truly shocks me still. Ever since 1832, 'treating' at elections has been an offence. That means you can't give food or drink to voters to influence their vote. Everyone involved in politics knows this basic law. It is not out of date; it has been repeated in every amended electoral law since, most recently in the Representation of the People Act 2000.

Jack Straw held a 'Muslims for Labour' rally at Jan's Conference Centre, Blackburn, at the peak of the campaign. There was a large 'Vote for Jack Straw' banner over the stage and Jack Straw was the main speaker. Over a hundred Blackburn 'community leaders' were invited. To my utter astonishment, these electors were all served a substantial, seated curry lunch that lasted about an hour.

There could not be a more blatant breach of the law. This is not just a regulation but a serious criminal law carrying a maximum penalty of two years' imprisonment. I don't know who arranged the catering, but under English law it is an important principle that the candidate is assumed to be responsible for, and in control of, his campaign. We reported it to the police. Blackburn police presented a dossier to the Crown Prosecution Service. The Crown Prosecution

Service decided that it was a 'trivial' potential breach of the law and not worth prosecuting.

There are several things wrong here. There could not be a plainer breach of this law, which had been reaffirmed by Parliament just five years previously. It is not for the Crown Prosecution Service to deem a law to be trivial. Parliament evidently doesn't think so. The second, more obvious, point is that if it had been me, rather than Jack Straw, who had offered a campaign meal to a hundred Blackburn electors, I don't believe it would have been found 'trivial'. I would have gone to jail – and rightly so.

But even this pales compared to the abuse of the postal ballot. Just a month before the election, a Blackburn New Labour councillor, Muhammed Hussain, was jailed for three and a half years for postal ballot fraud in the previous council elections. Now, among the Muslim community, some of the New Labour 'community leaders' were raking in postal ballots, taking them to collection points in community centres. In this Blackburn election, over 12,000 postal ballots were cast. That represented 29 per cent of all votes cast. Compare that to a national average of 13 per cent. Blackburn had the highest incidence of postal voting in the country.

I would have lost heavily anyway – I received just 2,085 votes. But the campaign was for me a real eye-opener to what goes on in a typical New Labour rotten borough and to the fact that our democracy is not much to boast about. If I had been observing Blackburn as I had professionally observed foreign elections, I am not sure I would have judged it free and fair.

A week after the election, on 13 May 2005, Uzbekistan finally hit the front pages across the globe when Karimov's troops opened fire with heavy weapons on a crowd of 20,000 democracy demonstrators in Andijan, killing over 600. Not all died immediately. The wounded were surrounded and left lying all night in Cholpan Square with no water or medical treatment. The next morning, troops moved through the crowd, shooting survivors in the head at point-blank range.

The unprincipled liaison between the West and Uzbekistan had already been under great strain. Karimov's increasingly closed economy was threatened by Western investors, who had more and more been driven out. In November 2004, the major oil and gas development contract, the prize which the US had been seeking since George W. Bush as Governor of Texas met Safayev on behalf of Enron in June 1997, was finally awarded to Gazprom, the Russian state company.

This deal was reportedly negotiated between Gulnara Karimova and Alisher Usmanov, the Uzbek-born Russian oligarch. Gulnara allegedly received a large cash payment – $88 million, according to my sources – on completion of the Gazprom deal, with further payments to come as gas is exported.

This web is closely associated with Karimov's succession strategy: the cash and Russian support is building up Gulnara's power base. This is the background to the diplomatic revolution of the last six months, with Karimov abandoning the US and turning back to the embrace of Mother Russia.

It is worth recalling that the Karimov regime had been aggressively anti-Russian, in terms of both propaganda and practical measures of linguistic discrimination. Approximately two million ethnic Russians have fled Uzbekistan since independence in 1991; about 400,000 are left.

This reorientation towards Russia went along with fierce anti-enterprise measures designed to stifle any entrepreneurial activity not under direct control of the Karimov family. This explained the physical closures of borders and bazaars, the crackdown on cash transactions and the channelling of all commercial activity through the state banks.

Relationships with the US had therefore been getting increasingly rocky, as Karimov turned more and more to Russia, and to some extent China. After Andijan, Karimov served the US with six months' notice to quit their prized military base at Karshi Khanabad. The US–Uzbek alliance over, it suddenly became open season on Karimov. The US and UK governments discovered that – Shock! Horror! – this guy Karimov had been an awful dictator! British ministers were at pains to claim that they had been in agreement with me about this all along. I started getting invites to seminars in Washington.

* * *

Western policy in Central Asia is now in disarray. Afghanistan is touted as the great victory, but the fact is that Afghanistan now produces more opium than ever before. Life is so good for the drug lords that, rather than smuggle opium, they are adding value and producing the heroin themselves, able quite openly to move great tankers of required chemicals into the country for industrial-scale production. Because Afghanistan produces more drugs than ever before, the heroin price in London is at an all-time low in real terms. Ruined lives in Europe are the lasting product of our policy in Afghanistan.

The General Dostum–Karimov regime axis remains central to this drug traffic. Dostum is Deputy Defence Minister and Head of the Armed Forces in Afghanistan and still America's leading hard man in the region. With Karimov also their protégé, the drug link was tolerated for reasons of high policy. Karimov probably calculates that the US still need Dostum, so he will continue to face no interference in this lucrative enterprise. Meanwhile, ordinary people in Uzbekistan plunge further into despair. This story has no ending.

Nor is there any end to the use of torture as a weapon to further the Bush–Blair agenda and stoke the fires of Islamophobia with false intelligence. In October 2005, the British government, in a historic case before the House of Lords, argued for the right to use intelligence obtained under torture. They argued for a threefold use of this intelligence: to guide security operations, to detain without trial, and as evidence in court of law. This is the first time in over 200 years a British government has sought to legalise the use of torture evidence. On 8 December 2005, the Law Lords ruled resoundingly against the government. They made plain that evidence in British courts must not be tainted by torture, and neither could detainees be held on the basis of information obtained by torture. However Charles Clarke, then Home Secretary, argued that the government had won the right to use torture material. He stated that the Law Lords 'held it was perfectly lawful for such information to be relied on operationally and also by the Home Secretary in making executive decisions'. Thus 'the exclusion of evidence obtained by torture . . . will not change, weaken or detract from our ability to fight terrorism'.[81] Thus the British government is quite shameless in its desire to obtain and to use the fruits of torture, and remains a great customer for the products of the torture chambers of dictators like Karimov worldwide. The raw material – people to be tortured – is sometimes local and sometimes delivered by the CIA through the extraordinary rendition programme.

In a sickening example of propaganda doublespeak, the article in which Clarke argued his case was headed: 'I welcome the ban on evidence gained through torture', despite the fact that lawyers acting on his behalf had fought the ban tooth and nail through every stage of the British judicial system. The collapse of the ability of mainstream media really to hold politicians to account is very worrying.

As for me, I had the best possible news on the personal front. I was getting better! The right side of my heart was shrinking, the pressures in the chambers of my heart were normalising. The lungs were rewiring themselves. The pressure the heart had been under as it struggled to force air through my clogged lungs had opened a hole, but this was closed up for me by the Royal Brompton Hospital.

So here I am, reborn, reprieved and ready for battle. I will never forget those who still suffer needlessly in Uzbekistan, in Iraq and in so many other places on this spinning globe. I am not an especially good man, but I tried to stay true to basic values of human decency. If you cross the path of tyranny, or incipient tyranny, I believe there is a duty to fight it, be it in Tashkent, Washington or London.

Some of the symptoms of tyranny are the use of torture, imprisonment without proper trial, government figures being above the law and censorship of books. The thing with tyranny is that, if you don't try to fight it when it starts, it very quickly gets too strong for you.

If you achieve a voice that will be heard, you should use it to speak up for the voiceless and oppressed. If you possess any power or authority, you must strive to use it to help and to empower the powerless. Sadly, public life in the West has come to be dominated by those driven by arrogance and by corporate greed and personal acquisitiveness. We must strive to return some integrity to public life.

As I hope this memoir has made clear, I am not a hero but a very fallible man. Yet when I learnt of men, women and children being tortured, I had no doubt that the only and overriding duty of any representative of the British people must be to stop it. Government must have some principles of conduct, and not torturing people is a fundamental one. For me, that came before my personal career.

How have we come to this, that integrity in public life is now so rare that some consider me a hero just for exhibiting the most basic human decency?

Notes

1 Salih had managed to get 15 per cent of the vote against Karimov despite no media coverage other than vitriolic attacks on him, and in the face of every form of voter intimidation, electoral fraud and vote-rigging imaginable.

2 A British ambassador gets to travel first class the first time he arrives at his new post and the last time he leaves it. The reason for this is that there may be formal state greetings and farewells on these occasions. On other business trips, he travels business class, and economy class on most leave journeys. Uzbek Air flies four times a week to London; two of these flights use a 747, which has a first class. I had chosen my departure date specifically to make sure that we could fly first class. It was not something I expected to do often with my family, so I was determined that we should take advantage.

3 If this sounds palatial, that is because it was indeed a palace – and not just any old palace. It was the home of the Kerensky family, birthplace of Alexander Fyodorovich Kerensky, who led Russia from February to October 1917, in that brief dawn of hope when Russia might have entered mainstream European history and economic development. It was he who proclaimed Russia a Republic in September 1917. I used to hold conversations with Uzbek dissidents in my office and wonder what other whispered words those bricks had heard. The Kerenskys were a Russian colonial family: lawyers, railway engineers and administrators.

Their little palace was pretty but obviously on nothing near the scale of the mighty mansions of St Petersburg, so Kerensky's coming to power in St Petersburg certainly showed that Russia was in the grip of truly revolutionary change before the Bolsheviks took a hand.

4 In December 2005, the Uzbek government announced it was going to remove the barriers protecting the embassy 'for beautification', as a part of the diplomatic row following the Andijan massacre.

5 I am giving away no secrets, as the embassy has since been internally rebuilt and reconfigured.

6 Stalin had deported trainloads of Koreans from the Russian borders of Manchuria in the 1920s, dumping them in the Kara Kum desert and leaving them to die. Somehow they struggled to oases at Nukus and Bokhara, and ultimately their community grew and added a new element to the region's already spectacular ethnic diversity.

7 The square is dominated by a huge golden globe. It encapsulates the vainglory of the regime because only Uzbekistan is marked on it. Uzbekistan starts around Dublin and ends around Beijing. Only a government with a serious humour deficit could erect such a monument. At night, the globe and its massive Uzbekistan are picked out in numerous sparkling lights and it rotates. It is incredibly tacky.

8 In fact, far from combating the narcotics trade, the Karimov regime is up to its neck in it. The destruction of the Taliban largely ended any threat from the IMU; only Karimov's persecution of Muslims now fuels the very small Islamic militant threat. There is no Islamic extremism in the Tajik government, and remaining Russian forces in the region are an important force for stability. The Uzbek economy produces very little because of mad centrist economic policies, and bans on Chinese goods were aimed to protect not domestic production but import monopolies by the Karimov family and senior regime cronies. Karimov's claim to be a reliable ally of the West was totally bogus; it was a short-term manoeuvre.

9 A few months later, his sister was to visit; she was the most tremendous personage and invitations started arriving to dinners with Countess X. I put X because she had at least eight titles and surnames, which I can't possibly remember. Like her brother, she was in her early 60s, but she partied like a student,

wore designer clothes and tons of jewellery, and seemed to have fitted in Tashkent between endless parties with the glitterati at fashionable resorts. Her brother was shy and retiring by comparison and never used a title or more than two surnames. I grew to like him immensely.

10 The FCO described this to me as essential to the security of Western hydrocarbon supplies. I viewed it as essential to keeping oil prices down and ensuring the world's very limited hydrocarbon supplies were guzzled as soon as possible, largely by the US, with disastrous results in terms of carbon dioxide emissions and global warming. So you will gather I was a bit sceptical about all of this.

11 Some details of this conversation have been censored by the British government.

12 It lay a year in the future, but Sharipov, as a result of the critical articles John quoted, was framed and convicted on charges of under-age sex, while his defence lawyer, Surat Ikramov, was kidnapped outside the courtroom, bound and gagged. He was then driven into the countryside, murderously beaten, and left for dead in a ditch, but survived. By that time, the members of the security forces convicted of murdering the detainee in Ferghana had been released.

13 For more of this telegram, go to http://www.craigmurray.co.uk/ documents/IMF.pdf or http://www.blairwatch.co.uk/murray/ IMF.pdf

14 For the full text of this telegram, go to http://www.craigmurray. co.uk/documents/declaration.pdf or http://www.blairwatch. co.uk/murray/Hillnegotiation.pdf

15 By contrast, we maintain massive embassies in all Western European capitals, staffed by many senior diplomats. Yet nowadays, if we want to discuss fish with Denmark or transport with France, it is no longer done by getting the embassy fish man to speak to the Danish Foreign Ministry fish man. Our London ministry of fish people will speak direct to the Copenhagen ministry of fish people, who they probably meet twice a month anyway in Brussels. Two ministers from EU countries who want to talk bilaterally on any subject will do it direct, not through their ambassador. Yet there has been no significant reduction in the staffing of our EU bilateral embassies. Quite the opposite.

At the same time, we are told that Africa is a priority and that the aid budget and political effort being spent on the continent is increasing. Has this been accompanied by an increase in senior diplomatic jobs based in Africa? No, again quite the opposite. Senior posts have been cut in Africa over a decade and transferred to Western Europe and the United States.

The reason is that a self-serving FCO oligarchy quite likes to live in Copenhagen or Berlin, but the vast majority of top mandarins would not be seen dead in Kampala, or indeed Tashkent. Only one of the FCO's current 15 directors has served in Africa, and that was in Pretoria. They have 87 Western Europe- or US-based tours between them.

To justify this predilection for serving in posts with access to Cannes or Aspen, there have been a number of 'resource allocation' exercises, on one of which I was working at the time. This exercise had on a page a matrix of facets of an embassy's work – political, commercial, narcotics, immigration, terrorism, defence and others. Each embassy was given a score out of five for how important it was on each particular subject. The scores were determined centrally by the Board. And, hey presto! It was discovered that our allocation of resources around the world was pretty well perfect.

To achieve this result required some farcical scoring. On narcotics, for instance, Tashkent scored 2 out of 5 and Copenhagen 5 out of 5. Now, I am not saying customs cooperation with Denmark is not useful, but Uzbekistan is a massive transit route for heroin from neighbouring Afghanistan. Berlin scored as highly as Lagos on immigration. In short, it was decided that all the resources, and the vast majority of top jobs, had to be in really nice places to live. So that was a useful exercise.

16 The cutting of the tunnels gives a good example of the way that Karimov built his personality cult through the highly controlled media. The story was run on state media that a German company had offered to build the tunnels for no payment, provided they could keep the excavated spoil. Karimov had refused the offer and declared that the Uzbeks would build the tunnels themselves. When the tunnels were dug, they excavated a huge quantity of gold and precious stones, which were used to benefit the nation.

This example of Karimov's wisdom and foresight is, of course, complete fabrication from start to finish. It says something not only about the Uzbek media but also about the level of education of the general population that this story is still widely believed.

17 In Uzbekistan bread itself is treated as holy and must be respected. It certainly must never be thrown or dropped, and you must not swear or argue in the presence of bread.

18 Carpet-making had died out in Uzbekistan in the Soviet period. The Uzbeks had a carpet tradition, although not as strong as is sometimes presumed. Bokhara carpets are the most famous oriental rugs and Bokhara was the market where they were sold, but most Bokhara carpets were Afghan or Turkmen in origin.

19 It is generally agreed that his robust interest in local women went beyond their emancipation. You can take your choice about who to believe over his death. The official line is that he was stoned by a crowd of reactionary mullahs. Unofficial versions are that he was killed by the family of one of his lovers, or in one of Stalin's early purges.

20 I was to visit several other breweries and wineries in Uzbekistan and always found the same thing: brewing and wine making is regarded solely as a science, not an art.

21 What he had told me very much squared with the briefing Chris Hirst had given me. Chris had told of a recent incident where the police had taken a dissident from his bed wearing only his underpants. When searched at the police station, he was discovered to have 12 bullets and a stash of Hizb-ut-Tehrir leaflets on his person – presumably the police claimed he had hidden them in his underwear.

22 'Excuse me, Ambassador,' asked the interpreter, 'is the sledge important, or can I just interpret it as hammer?'
    'Try fucking big hammer,' I suggested.

23 And indeed did so with the imported wool until June 2003. The textiles produced were exported. This was organised by the general manager in Tashkent. The factory never saw the revenue from these exports.

24 A year later, the British government cancelled this project, on the decision of ministers, on the grounds that there was no conflict in the Ferghana Valley to resolve, so it was an inappropriate use of Conflict Resolution Funds. Cancelling this Andijan project further exacerbated economic distress and social tension, and contributed to the events that led up to the Andijan massacre in May 2005.

25 In Lublin, Poland, in the mid-1990s, I had viewed a Daewoo

'assembly' line where they simply uncrated the cars and fixed the wheels back on.

26 Full text available at http://www.craigmurray.co.uk/documents/ Hillnegotiation.pdf or http://www.blairwatch.co.uk/murray/ Hillnegotiation.pdf

27 To Westerners, Tartars are an almost legendary people. When I served in Poland, I was very interested in the raids of the great Tartar hordes. In Krakow, every day a bugler still sounds the alarm from the City Church, cutting it off abruptly to mark the moment an arrow from a Tartar composite horn bow sliced into his predecessor's throat.

I had always imagined the Tartars to be an oriental people, rather Mongol in appearance, but in fact they are not at all. Their eyes have only the slightest trace of slant, many are blond, and to a stranger they are not easy to distinguish from Russians.

28 *Financial Times*, 14 January 2003.

29 *The Spectator*, 26 May 2005.

30 It has got worse since: as of 2005 every educational institution must teach 'National Education' for one day a week. This consists of Karimov's works mixed with a very tendentious version of history and Uzbek folk singing.

31 One striking example was a brick factory in Tashkent built by a British company with an EBRD loan. The project depended on a pre-contract committing the Uzbek government to purchase the bricks for many years. Once construction was complete, the Uzbek government immediately reneged on this contract. In consequence, the company went bust. The Uzbek government then confiscated the land and buildings, while the EBRD spinelessly sold the plant and equipment – brand new – to the Uzbek government at about a third of cost.

32 Detail on the intelligence has been censored at this point by the British government.

33 At this point the pass is only some 15 metres wide, so it is certainly possible. The historic fact does not seem to be disputed. But it makes little sense. The hills to either side are easily passable, even for an army. The main Tashkent–Samarkand road itself no longer runs through Jizzak or the gates but some few miles south-west. This does not involve any major feat of engineering, and even if no road were there, there would have been nothing to stop an army taking that route. In fact, except in deep winter,

you can walk pretty easily over the hills just a few hundred metres either side of the famous iron gates. It would only make sense if they were gates in some kind of series of fortifications running along the hilltops, but I have never seen this suggested. I was later able to spend a day searching, and I could find no physical or topographical evidence of such a system.

34 Even though Karimov is himself ethnically Tajik.

35 Uzbekistan has plenty of gas but prefers to sell it to Russia, in contracts which chiefly benefit companies owned by the President's daughter, rather than use it for the benefit of its own people.

36 Société Générale had agreed a loan but then made stipulations about political risk insurance that Oxus had found impossible to fulfil.

37 The very existence of this town is a miracle of Soviet engineering. There was no oasis here – it was in the middle of hundreds of miles of featureless desert. It is one of the most remarkable places I have been to, with a modern town starting into full swing at the clearly defined town boundary and absolutely nothing beyond. The water comes in great pipes hundreds of miles across the desert.

38 It is also worth asking why the EBRD, which is supposed to promote private enterprise in former communist Europe, was lending money to Newmont, the world's largest mining company. The EBRD is supposed to bring 'additionality' and fund projects that wouldn't otherwise happen, not sub massive corporations entering extremely low-cost, high-return operations.

39 *The Point of Departure*, Simon & Schuster 2003.

40 This should not be romanticised – there is an element of benevolent paternalism, but it is much more to do with a network of cosy, corrupt relationships with dictators. These relationships are eased by diamonds, gold or oil.

41 The African reaction to this visit mirrored Pooh-Bah: 'Another insult and, I fear, a light one.'

42 For the full text of this telegram see http://www.craigmurray.co.uk/documents/Iraq.pdf or http://www.blairwatch.co.uk/murray/Iraq.pdf

43 A Timurid cadet, Babur, claiming descent from Timur, fled into exile and conquered India, founding the Mughal dynasty. Mughal is simply a corruption of Mongol. Babur took with him the architecture, cuisine, science and poetry of his native land.

The architectural skill and ambitious design of Samarkand
combined with the delicate finery of Indian art to give us the Taj
Mahal.

44 I also had the chance to chat at dinner with old Mrs Kalashnikova,
another Tashkent resident. She told me her husband had been
chief engineer in a Singer sewing machine factory, and it was
the sewing machine action that gave him the inspiration for his
firing mechanism.

45 This is the programme from the opening Tashkent concert, held
on 5 May 2003 in the Railway Palace, Tashkent:

National Symphony Orchestra of Uzbekistan
Conducted by Professor Vladimir Neimer

1. *Jerusalem* – Edward Parry
2. *Overture, Iolanthe* – Arthur Sullivan
3. *Those Magnificent Men in Their Flying Machines* –
Ron Goodwin
4. *Overture, Patience* – Arthur Sullivan
5. *Fantasia on Greensleeves* – R Vaughan Williams
6. *Fantasy on British Sea Songs* – Henry Wood

Interval

1. *Overture, Yeomen of the Guard* – Arthur Sullivan
2. *Prelude, My Fair Lady* – Frederik Loewe
3. *Overture, Pirates of Penzance* – Arthur Sullivan
4. *Dambusters March* – Eric Coates
5. *Pomp & Circumstance March No. 1* – Edward Elgar
6. *633 Squadron* – Ron Goodwin

46 The Queen's actual birthday is 21 April, but you may hold
celebrations within seven days either side of this date.

47 Some academics have queried my description of the Uzbek state
as totalitarian. I rest my case.

48 It was this evening which inspired me and Robin Morton, the
Battlefield Band's producer, to arrange a joint tour of the UK for
these same Uzbek and Scottish musicians that was to be such a
spectacular success in 2005.

49 Kristina is now the US Ambassador's social secretary.

50 I suppose the blame must rest with the Soviets, who destroyed

existing societal obligations, relationships and mechanisms, and replaced them with the *kolkhoz.*

51 Richard Conroy had told me that a UNDP study had established that the rural poor had sold off their household possessions to eat and suffered a radical decline in living standards. I wondered who on earth a lady like this could find who would have money to buy her goods.

52 I don't suppose it did much good, but when you encounter totalitarianism you have to keep chipping away at it. Lech Walesa once told me that it is the first crack in the marble that counts.

53 As part of its border closure programme, the Uzbek government was clearing the population of a high mountain village on the border with Tajikistan. This was allegedly for the villagers' own safety. They had been loaded into a bus at gunpoint. The bus had then allegedly fallen off the winding mountain road, killing everyone on board. Many believe the villagers, who were ethnic Tajiks, had in fact been shot. I don't think any independent observer ever got to the site, which was closed off by the military, so I simply don't know what happened.

54 Afghanistan is, of course, the great success of the War on Terror. Dostum is the Deputy Minister of Defence of the democratic Afghan government and therefore a good guy. Karimov and Dostum were the lynchpins of US policy in Central Asia, so nothing is done about the heroin trafficking. As a result of the great Allied success, Afghanistan now produces more opium and heroin than ever before. Now that's not something much stressed in the Murdoch media.

55 My email and Linda's reply are at http://www.craigmurray. co.uk/documents/Duffield.pdf or http://www.blairwatch. co.uk/murray/Duffield.pdf>

56 Full text at http://www.craigmurray.co.uk/documents/Drake. pdf or http://www.blairwatch.co.uk/murray/Drake.pdf

57 *The Spectator*, 21 May 2005.

58 *The Guardian*, 18 October 2003.

59 You can see the full minute at http://www.craigmurray.co.uk/ documents/Reynolds.pdf or http://www.blairwatch.co.uk/ murray/Reynolds.pdf>

60 As a very perceptive journalist, Sanchia Berg of the *Today* programme, put it to me at the time, Fiona had 'bagsied' the embassy.

61 *The Guardian*, 18 October 2003.

62 *Mail on Sunday*, 19 October 2003.

63 On separate occasions I had been brought back for my shoulder, for a stomach ulcer, for typhoid and for damage to my penis occasioned by diving on a beer bottle top when fielding in the covers in a cricket match at Tafawa Balewa Square in Lagos. As a result of the treatment for the last I could now convert to Judaism or Islam without further pain.

64 *The Guardian*, 28 October 2003.

65 Strongly recommended. Not the greatest psychological life, but wonderful on the Scottish clan, religious and political background and, above all, a masterly exposition by someone with practical experience of guerrilla war.

66 It might perhaps now be appropriate to add a new mural to personify current British foreign policy – perhaps *Britannia Mentrix*, Britannia the Liar, handing over to her fellow damsels a dossier entitled 'Weapons of Mass Destruction', while they cast scandalised glances towards a moustachioed maiden in a corner representing Iraq.

67 They have since merged.

68 Here, two members of the British staff were named. Unfortunately, I have been forced to censor the names under threat of legal action from the British government to protect staff confidentiality.

69 I should be plain that I think Mr Hassett was unknowingly used and that I have no reason to believe there was anything wrong with Miss Safarova's visa application.

70 Donald Rumsfeld, press conference Intercontinental Hotel, Tashkent, 24 February 2004.

71 For those organisations which did register, including Human Rights Watch, new limitations were placed on their activities, including that the Ministry of the Interior had to be notified in advance about all meetings, they had to be open to the Uzbek intelligence services and all financial transactions had to go through Uzbek state banks.

72 It was also based on my having read *Extreme Continental*, Giles Whittell's excellent book on Central Asia.

73 Their aid agency was particularly appalling in this regard, and of all the Western ministers who visited Tashkent, the most frequent and the most obsequious to Karimov was Joschka Fischer, the trendy Green German Foreign Minister.

In November 2005, when the EU finally brought in sanctions against the Karimov regime, Germany immediately broke them by allowing Interior Minister Almatov into Germany. The next month, Uzbekistan instituted an overflight ban on all NATO members – except Germany.

74 I had some knowledge of explosives from training courses. God knows why they teach us this stuff, but I had enjoyed several days mucking about with things that go bang at an establishment known simply as 'the fort'.

75 Detail of the intelligence censored by the British government.

76 I was right in this, and in the event no opposition parties were allowed to register and take part.

77 In May 2005, Ismail fled the country following the Andijan massacre and now lives in exile in the Ukraine.

78 The full text of this telegram is at http://www.craigmurray. co.uk/documents/telegram.pdf or http://www.blairwatch. co.uk/murray/telegram.pdf

79 *The Guardian*, 15 July 2004.

80 *Sunday Times*, 13 June 2004.

81 Charles Clarke writing in *The Guardian*, 13 December 2005.

Select Bibliography

Allworth, Edward, *The Modern Uzbeks* (Hoover Institution Press, Stanford, 1990)

Aslan, Reza, *No God but God: The Origins, Evolution and Future of Islam* (William Heinemann, London, 2005)

Bailey, F.M., *Mission to Tashkent* (Jonathan Cape, London, 1946)

Bremner, R., Bird, J. and Fortune, J., *You Are Here* (Weidenfeld & Nicolson, London, 2004)

Buchan, John, *Greenmantle* (Penguin, London, 1997)

Burnaby, Frederick, *A Ride to Khiva* (Century, London, 1983)

Burnes, Alexander, *Travels into Bokhara 1831–3: A Journey from India to Cabool Tartary and Persia and a Voyage on the Indus* (Asian Educational Services, New Delhi, 1992)

Byron, Robert, *The Road to Oxiana* (Penguin Books, London, 1992)

Chomsky, Noam, *9/11* (Seven Stories Press, New York, 2001)

Dalrymple, William, *In Xanadu: A Quest* (Flamingo, London, 1990)

Dickie, John, *Inside the Foreign Office* (Chapmans, London, 1992)

Fieldhouse, D.K., *The Theory of Capitalist Imperialism* (Longman, London, 1980)

Forbes, Rosita, *Forbidden Road: Kabul to Samarkand* (The Long Riders' Guild Press – nfi)

Frye, Richard, *Bukhara: The Medieval Achievement* (Mazda Publishers, Costa Mesa, 1996)

Gill, Alison (ed.), *Uzbekistan: Creating Enemies of the State* (Human Rights Watch, New York, 2004)

Grey, C., *European Adventurers of Northern India 1785 to 1849* (Asian Educational Services, New Delhi, 1993)

Griffiths, Clare (ed.), *St Petersburg* (APA Publications, London, 2002)

Harris, John, *So Now Who Do We Vote For?* (Faber and Faber, London, 2005)

Hobson, J.A., *Imperialism: A Study* (James Nisbet, London, 1902)

Hopkirk, Kathleen, *Central Asia: A Traveller's Companion* (John Murray, London, 1993)

Hopkirk, Peter, *The Great Game: On Secret Service in High Asia* (Oxford University Press 2001)

On Secret Service East of Constantinople (John Murray, London, 1994)

Setting the East Ablaze: On Secret Service in Bolshevik Asia (Oxford University Press 1986)

Foreign Devils on the Silk Road: The Search for the Lost Treasures of Central Asia (Oxford University Press, 1984)

Kleveman, Lutz, *The New Great Game: Blood and Oil in Central Asia* (Atlantic Books, London 2003)

Knight, E.F., *Where Three Empires Meet: A Narrative of Recent Travel in Kashmir, Western Tibet, Gilgit, and the Adjoining Countries* (Asian Educational Services, New Delhi, 1993)

Lubin, Nancy, *Calming the Ferghana Valley: Development and Dialogue in the Heart of Central Asia* (Century Foundation Press, New York, 1999)

MacDonald Fraser, George, *Flashman in the Great Game* (William Collins, London, 1980)

Maclean, Fitzroy, *Eastern Approaches* (Penguin Books, London, 1991)

Macleod, Calum and Mayhew, Bradley, *Uzbekistan: The Golden Road to Samarkand* (Passport Books, Chicago, 1997)

Mardrus, J.C., *The Thousand Nights and One Night*, trans. Powys Mathers (Routledge, London, 1986)

Markham, Clements (trans.), *Narrative of the Embassy of Ruy Gonzalez de Clavijo to the Court of Timour at Samarcand AD 1403–6* (Asian Educational Services, New Delhi, 2001)

Marozzi, Justin, *Tamerlane: Sword of Islam, Conqueror of the World* (HarperCollins, London, 2004)

Marshall, Robert, *Storm From the East: From Genghis Khan to Khubilai Khan* (BBC Books, London, 1993)

Marvin, Charles, *Reconnoitring Central Asia: Pioneering Adventures in the Region Lying Between Russia and India* (Asian Educational Services, New Delhi, 1996)

Mayer, Karl and Brysac, Shareen, *Tournament of Shadows: The Great Game and the Race for Empire in Central Asia* (Counterpoint Press, London, 1999)

Mayhew, Bradley, Plunkett, Richard and Richmond, Simon, *Central Asia* (Lonely Planet, Hawthorn, 2000)

Melvin, Neil, *Uzbekistan: Transition to Authoritarianism on the Silk Road* (Harwood Academic Publishers, Amsterdam, 2000)

Moorcroft, William and Trebeck, George, *Travels in the Himalayan Provinces of Hindustan and the Punjab, Ladakh and Kashmir Peshawar, Kabul, Kunduz and Bokhara from 1819 to 1825* (Asian Educational Services, New Delhi, 1989)

O'Rourke, P.J., *Eat the Rich: A Treatise on Economics* (Picador, London, 1998)

Okigbo, Pius, *Essays in the Public Philosophy of Development* (Concorde Press, Lagos, 1984)

Rashid, Ahmed, *Taliban: Militant Islam, Oil and Fundamentalism in Central Asia* (I.B. Tauris, London, 2000)
Jihad: The Rise of Militant Islam in Central Asia (Yale University Press, New York, 2002)

Roy, Olivier, *The New Central Asia: The Creation of Nations* (I.B. Tauris, London, 2000)

Rumer, Boris (ed.), *Central Asia: A Gathering Storm?* (M.E. Sharpe, Armonk, 2002)

Soans, Robin, *Talking to Terrorists* (Oberon Books, London, 2005)

Soucek, Svat, *A History of Inner Asia* (Cambridge University Press, 2001)

Stein, Aurel, *On Alexander's Track to the Indus* (Asian Educational Services, New Delhi, 1996)

Taylor, Bayard, *Central Asia: Travels in Cashmere, Little Thibet and Central Asia* (Asian Educational Services, New Delhi, 1997)

Thackston, Wheeler (trans.), *The Baburnama: Memoirs of Babur, Prince and Emperor* (The Modern Library, New York, 2002)

Thubron, Colin, *The Lost Heart of Asia* (Penguin Books, London, 2004)

Whittell, Giles, *Extreme Continental: Blowing Hot and Cold Through Central Asia* (Indigo, London, 1996)

Wood, Frances, *The Silk Road* (Folio Society, London, 2002)

Select Bibliography

Wynn, Antony, *Persia in the Great Game: Sir Percy Sykes, Explorer, Consul, Soldier, Spy* (John Murray, London, 2004)

Younghusband, Francis, *The Heart of A Continent: A Narrative of Travels in Manchuria, Across the Gobi Desert, Through the Himalayas, the Pamirs and Chitral* (Asian Educational Services, New Delhi, 1993)

....

....

Index